# INDIA AND CHINA AT ODDS IN THE ASIAN CENTURY

VAPPALA BALACHANDRAN

# India and China at Odds in the Asian Century

## A Diplomatic and Strategic History

HURST & COMPANY, LONDON

First published in the United Kingdom in 2025 by
C. Hurst & Co. (Publishers) Ltd.,
New Wing, Somerset House, Strand, London, WC2R 1LA
© Vappala Balachandran, 2025

Printed in Scotland by Bell & Bain Ltd, Glasgow
The right of Vappala Balachandran to beidentified as the author of
this publication is asserted by him in accordance with the Copyright,
Designs and Patents Act, 1988.

A Cataloguing-in-Publication data record for this book
is available from the British Library.

ISBN: 9781805260622

www.hurstpublishers.com

*The opinions expressed in this book are personal and do not represent those
of the Government of India*

# CONTENTS

The term 'Asian century' was first coined by the US Senate Foreign Relations Committee in 1985 when discussing the Asian economic leap forward. From 1988, diplomats and the media also started using the term, further to the successful Deng Xiaoping–Rajiv Gandhi summit held that December in Beijing, for which Vappala Balachandran, under Prime Minister Gandhi's express directions, led a small team of officials for more than a year of discreet 'off-line' talks with key Chinese counterparts—separate from the official diplomatic engagement.

The Chinese–Indian thaw, which lasted until 1998, prompted highly optimistic visions of a 'China–India Century of Cooperation' enabling both powers to compete with the US and EU in terms of trade and military capacity. None of this happened, and instead the China–India relationship is highly rancorous, punctuated by trade spats and border skirmishing between the People's Liberation Army and the Indian Army. New Delhi has gravitated towards the US in the hope of checkmating an assertive Beijing's pursuit of global military and trade dominance. This book offers a comprehensive analysis of India and China's comparative strategic capabilities, sharing many insights drawn from the author's first-hand engagement with and research into the questions discussed.

Vappala Balachandran is a columnist, former special secretary for the Indian Cabinet Secretariat, and author of four books on Indian security, strategy and intelligence. In 1995 he organised the first discreet talks between Prime Minister P.V. Narasimha Rao and the chief 'rebel' Naga group, paving the way for a ceasefire. In 1987 he led a two member Indian team to suggest measures to revamp the security set up of an Indian Ocean country, on the specific request of its president, as it had faced two-armed coup attempts inspired from abroad. In 1993 and 1994 he headed the Indian interagency intelligence groups for annual dialogue with US agencies on terrorism.

# MISE-EN-SCÈNE

After the successful 1988 Rajiv Gandhi–Deng Xiaoping summit in Beijing, many observers believed that it would set in motion an "Asian Century" jointly led by India and China in the twenty-first century.[1] This expectation arose from Deng's words: "Why can't we share our experiences, our successes, and failures? There is much we can achieve together."[2]

In 2000 Stephen Cohen asked American policy makers to note that "India is not just another South Asian state but a player in the larger Asian sphere." This was after the second Indian nuclear tests in 1998.[3] In 2005 Dr Arvind Virmani, who was India's Chief Economic Adviser (2007–09) envisaged a "tripolar" world in the twenty-first century with the US, China and India in the lead.[4]

It did not happen that way. China and India did not cooperate on collective sharing of power, exercising regional influence or conducting trade as predicted. China progressed unilaterally while India faltered after its 1998 nuclear tests. India did not take advantage of its relative edge over China in the 1970s–80s. At that time Indian public and private sectors were far ahead in areas like electronics and computers, a momentum which had been started in 1963 by the late F.C. Kohli with encouragement from the legendary J.R.D. Tata.[5]

India's electronic prowess was showcased in the 1982 Asian Games in New Delhi when the sports were telecast in colour, "a massive statement of India's advancement in broadcast technology."[6]

KELTRON, a Kerala state government electronic enterprise led by K.P.P Nambiar, had played a lead role in this. F.C. Kohli would recall later that Nambiar, who had returned to India from his key position at Texas Instruments (USA) on Prime Minister Jawaharlal Nehru's call to engineers, had led India's electronic revolution.[7]

Indian agricultural economist Ashok Gulati had said that China's per capita income in 1978 was even lower than India's, but today it is almost five times higher.[8] Even Deng Xiaoping had told Rajiv Gandhi in 1988 that China had no superpower ambitions and would only become a middle-level power by the middle of the twenty-first century.[9]

In 2012 the US National Intelligence Council's "Global Trends 2030: Alternative Worlds"[10] assessment predicted that "China alone would probably have the largest economy, surpassing that of the United States a few years before 2030." It said that the economies of Europe, Japan, and Russia were likely to continue their decline. In a "tectonic shift," the global economy would be linked to China, India, and Brazil and regional players like Colombia, Indonesia, Nigeria, South Africa, and Turkey, that would become important.

"Global Trends 2040: A More Contested World" confirmed this trend and added that China would expect "deference from neighbours on trade, resource exploitation, and territorial disputes" and use "its infrastructure and technology-led development programs to tie countries closer and ensure elites align with its interests." This was published in 2021 after the pandemic started. It said that India, while facing "serious governance, societal, environmental, and defence challenges" would find difficulties concerning how much it can invest in "the military and diplomatic capabilities needed for a more assertive global foreign policy." In that process India may struggle to balance its aim of "strategic autonomy from Western powers with the need to embed itself more deeply into multilateral security architectures to counter a rising China."[11]

In 2014 many believed that the new "Nationalist" government elected that year with overwhelming majority on a "national strength" platform would enable India to take over Asian leadership with its "muscular" security and diplomatic policy. Even "dissident" former minister Arun Shourie, who was part of the earlier National Democratic Alliance (NDA) ministry under Atal Bihari Vajpayee had believed in 2014 that a "Gujarat Model" under Narendra Modi would be better than the "inactivity" in the last two years under the Dr Manmohan Singh government.[12]

In 2019 Subramanian Swamy, economist and Bharatiya Janta Party (BJP) member of parliament told a TiEcon meet that India could overtake China "in the next three to four years if it can get its act together in the next six months." He felt that Chinese model of economic growth had become obsolete.[13] This school of thought received a "booster shot" with the International Monetary Fund's (IMF) prediction early in 2021 that India's growth at 12.5 per cent would "surpass" China's in that year.[14]

These highly optimistic projections provoked a certain amount of braggadocio in India. The late General Bipin Rawat, Chief of Defence Staff, assured the nation on 12 November 2021 that China would be paid "in the same coin" if it attempted another "Galwan" incident.[15] On 15 June 2020 the Indian and Chinese armies had clashed in Galwan (Ladakh), the most serious incident in forty-five years. Rawat had said in 2017 that India was ready for a "two and a half front war."[16]

In this setting, the theme of this book is to cogitate upon the "Asian Century" and India's place in it along with China. It will first narrate the exultation in 1988 generated after the Gandhi–Deng Summit. It will then move to Sino–Indian relations from pre-historic times to the present day in two chapters. I shall argue that Mao's neighbourhood relations doctrine was an adaptation of the "Tributary System," exemplified by his remarks on 6 October 1962 on how a Tang emperor had sent his army for the "first War" on India in 648 CE to defeat a usurper whose predecessor was recognised by China. In later years Mao used to compare himself with Qin Shi Huang (Chin Shih-Huang), the first emperor of "Terracotta Soldiers" fame who unified China in 221 BCE.[17]

Similarly, Xi Jinping's "Belt and Road" (OBOR) is also based on the "Tributary" system of the Ming days, so lucidly explained by Harvard historian Prof. J.K. Fairbank and S.Y. Têng in 1941 as the "Chinese cultural superiority over the barbarians."[18] A key

China watcher in India has quoted Jiang Shigong, an influential intellectual, saying that a vital asset in Xi Jinping's favour is China's turn to nationalism with the slogan "The Great Rejuvenation of the Chinese Nation" which might be "the fourth phase of the evolution of the Chinese Communist Party."[19]

China's action in selecting Qi Fabao, a People's Liberation Army (PLA) regiment commander involved in the 15 June 2020 Galwan Valley clash with India, for the Winter Olympics relay in Beijing on 2 February 2022 was interpreted as a tit-for-tat for India's "Patriotism" theme in its Republic Day parade on 26 January 2022. Some Western observers believe that the probability of India and China, both "nationalistic" states, clashing in future cannot be ruled out.[20]

How will India meet this challenge? That is where the philosophy of the Rashtriya Swayamsevak Sangh (RSS) comes in, much like Mao's thoughts guiding Xi Jinping's thinking. In chapter 3, I detail the ideological orientations of the RSS, the fulcrum of the present government's thinking on "New India." This analysis will take us to the RSS ideas from "Vedic India" to *Akhand Bharat* (Undivided India), the latter to be achieved by undoing the 1947 Partition.

However, the means projected by RSS are hazy and polemical. It is hazy because there is no definite idea on the boundaries of their conception on what constitutes *Bharat*. Would it include parts of "Gandhara" and Central Asia as shown in some sixth-century BCE maps? It is polemical because the proposed Indian, Pakistani, and Bangladeshi federation "through peaceful means" might in fact endanger India's own security as it could afford more opportunity to China to influence them as it has already done with Pakistan. For example, on 29 May 2022 the United Nations Security Council (UNSC) Taliban Sanctions Committee released their report that Jaish-e-Mohammed (JeM) and Lashkar-e-Taiba (LeT) had established camps in Afghanistan–Pakistan border areas in strength.[21]

I shall then compare the concept of "New India" with the original "Idea of India" as propounded through the Jain-Buddhist era, the periods of Adi Shankara, Vivekananda and Gandhi and investigate whether the RSS's thinking would be in line with these thoughts and acceptable to most of India. This is because even in 2019 Modi could get only 45 per cent of the national vote despite garnering a disproportionate number of seats in the parliament which was possible only through our "First Past the Post" electoral system.

Also, this does not really represent India's national psyche which is presently disturbed by large-scale complaints of anti-minority violence resulting in bitter internal and international opprobrium. This leads some to wonder whether the BJP is only interested in winning domestic elections using religion rather than surging forward to catch up with China to take its rightful place in an "Asian Century," as this would require an overwhelming domestic concord embracing all sections of domestic public opinion.

For this I shall analyse whether the present government can sail through such rancorous domestic discord and yet compete with and excel China diplomatically, militarily, financially, and commercially. This is particularly relevant since the BJP's narrative in 2014 was that they would rule India for the next forty years, replacing the Indian National Congress, which was in power for 48 years since 1947.

The 2024 elections indicated a marked decline in Modi's support base, compelling him to get support from two political parties who do not share his religious leanings, to gain a majority in the parliament. In that case, would Modi's India tone down its "muscular" rhetoric to accommodate China as was done by the earlier regimes between 1988 and 2014 by keeping the border issues on the back burner?

This is relevant because there is a thinking in Washington, DC that Modi has failed to wholeheartedly condemn Russia for starting the savage Ukraine War partly because of the China factor and his "comfort level" with Chinese bellicosity. Former US Ambassador to India Kenneth Juster had said on 2 March 2022 that India had instructed US officials to neither mention Chinese aggression in any joint statement nor raise it in a strong manner otherwise.[22] How would that strategy compare with Prime Minister Modi's tweet on 13 May 2013, when he was Gujarat Chief Minister, criticising Prime Minister Manmohan Singh on the "withdrawal of Indian forces from our own territory"?[23]

If so, would India continue to tolerate a sniping and intruding China and yet have vibrant trade relations with it as in FY 2023–24, when its bilateral trade had surged to a record US$ 118.4 billion, despite its avowed policy of "Atmanirbhar" (self-reliance) via reducing dependence on Chinese imports due to the "bilateral chill"?[24]

Since the Modi government's revocation of Article 370 of the Constitution (which gave special status to Jammu and Kashmir) on 5 August 2019, and its publication of its new Ladakh maps, China had been accusing India of unilaterally violating the Line of Actual Control (LAC) position. How would China react on the ground to Indian External Affairs Minister S. Jaishankar's sharp criticism on 13 February 2022 that the deterioration of the LAC situation had arisen "due to China's disregard of written agreements in 2020"?[25]

Or would India actively participate in American dominated trade and military alliances to keep China at bay, which other Asian nations like Vietnam and Philippines seem to be reluctant to do?

How would China react to practical implications of the May 2022 Quad Summit in Tokyo, and the Indo-Pacific Partnership for Maritime Domain Awareness (IPMDA) programme which is directed against Chinese activities in that region?[26]

Finally, how would Beijing react to the comments by Tomohiko Taniguchi, former Japanese PM Shinzo Abe's "special adviser" that "without India and Modi, Quad could not fly"?[27] These are the questions to be considered in this book.

# INTRODUCTION

> You are young. You are the future. We are receding into
> history... It lies in your hands to shape the destiny of the
> new world order. Use it wisely.
>
> —Deng Xiaoping to Rajiv Gandhi, 21 December 1988

On 21 December 1988 an epoch-making drama was unfolding in
Beijing's ornate Great Hall of the People. It was watched by millions
all over the world on TV as an eighty-four-year-old "Paramount"
Chinese leader was meeting a young visiting prime minister. The
normally reclusive host was China's ultimate decision maker. None
knew how the meeting would turn out.

The visitor's grandfather was the first prime minister of a
non-Communist country to establish their embassy in China in
1950. When he visited China in October 1954, he was given an
unprecedented public welcome reception at the Chung Shan Park,
Beijing. During his visit he had met Chairman Mao Zedong. Both
countries had then proclaimed the "*Panch Sheel*" (5 principles of
peaceful co-existence) doctrine.[1]

However, their bilateral relationship deteriorated by the mid-
1960s. In 1962 they fought a border war. Thus, the visit of the
young Prime Minister in 1988 came after years of frosty relations
despite both countries having re-established ambassadorial
relations in 1976.

That was the historic meeting between China's Paramount
Leader Deng Xiaoping and Indian Prime Minister Rajiv Gandhi,

7

who was visiting China at the invitation of his counterpart Li Peng. Some journalists who accompanied Rajiv Gandhi to Beijing had said that he deserved the "credit for taking the gamble of flying blind to Beijing" as there was no guarantee through diplomatic channels that such a meeting with Deng would even take place. Till he arrived in Beijing there was no official confirmation of that meeting, nor any indication how it would go, if it materialised.

On the other hand, the Indian PM was originally dissuaded from making this visit. Journalist Dilip Bobb of *India Today*, who was in the PM's entourage, wrote in 1989: "Before the visit, a section of the foreign office and some China-watchers had criticised the timing of the visit."[2]

That was not how my organization covering foreign intelligence had felt. As one who had played a key but totally unobtrusive role for over one and half years in preparing the secret background tie-ups for the 1988 visit, I could now reveal that we were assured through a reliable third country "back channel" that the meeting would take place and that the visit "would be successful." Still, we were also edgy.

The drama was worth recounting. Veteran journalist, the late Bhabani Sen Gupta had written in his biography of Rajiv Gandhi:

> When they converged on one another, Deng clasped the Prime Minister's proffered hands for three minutes. Addressing Rajiv Gandhi as "my young friend," Deng fired the first salvos of a new uncharted friendship. "Let us forget the past," he said, still clasping the visitor's hands, and went on to say, "You are young. You are the future. We are receding into history. There is a new generation of leaders now and global desire to live in peace and end conflict and tension. It lies in your hands to shape the destiny of the new world order. Use it wisely." Deng added, "We have both made mistakes and we can learn from each other. Why can't we share our experiences, our successes, and failures? There is much we can achieve together. We can achieve nothing by being antagonists."[3]

Even Chinese leaders were surprised that Deng, who usually never spent more than thirty minutes with any foreign leader, had chosen to prolong the talks for ninety minutes with Rajiv Gandhi.

Indian diplomats felt that Deng's warmth and friendliness "was a sure sign that he was making a special effort."

Diplomatic circles and global media started using the expression "Asian Century" frequently after this meeting. However, this was not coined either by Rajiv Gandhi or Deng. The US Senate Foreign Relations Committee had used it in 1985 while referring to the Asian regional leaders who were claiming that the coming economic leap would propel them into an "Asian century."[4]

The Chinese–Indian bonhomie in 1988 had resulted in highly optimistic assessments in India on the possibility of a "China–India Century" when both were expected to overtake the USA and EU in economic and military strength. Some others conceived a "Tripolar World" consisting of China–India–USA axis ruling the twenty-first century.

An example worth quoting was the thesis in 2005 by Dr Arvind Virmani, then Director of the Indian Council for Research on International Economic Relations (ICRIER), which was an extension of his earlier paper which had projected trends till 2035. Virmani was the Chief Economic Adviser to the Government of India during 2007–09. He said that the present unipolar world would transform itself into a bipolar world by the first quarter of the twenty-first century and later into a tripolar one by 2050.[5]

Deng, however, had played it low. Dilip Bobb had said that Deng "scoffed" at predictions then by leading political scientists that the next century would be of the Asia–Pacific region: "By the middle of the next century, China will be a middle-level power only, he told Rajiv."[6] He appeared modest. Later events proved otherwise.[7]

Deng's 1988 version was confirmed by Dr Chengxin Pan of the Deakin University while writing in the Australian *Griffith Asia Quarterly*.[8] He quotes Deng: "[i]n recent years people have been saying that the next century will be the century of Asia and the Pacific, as if that were sure to be the case. I disagree with this view."[9]

Why did Deng feel that way? Bobb felt that Deng would not have confided his belief that China would eventually become a middle-level power if he was not absolutely convinced that a Sino–Indian rapprochement was inevitable as a step for bilateral peace.

"Equally, the fact that Rajiv was a scion of the Nehru family may have influenced his attitude." Hence Deng told Rajiv: "The old alliances are changing, and we must change with them. Unless we encourage that change and work together, we will both be left out in the cold. We must employ pragmatism and not rhetoric."[10]

Chengxin Pan concurs: "Obviously Deng did not lay claim to the authorship of this notion. Explaining his objection to it, Deng reasoned that 'No genuine Asia-Pacific century or Asian century can come until China, India and other neighbouring countries are developed', which seemed to him unlikely any time soon."[11]

Bobb, who felt the mood then in Beijing, said that in Deng's calculation a Sino–Indian rapprochement would give a major boost to bilateral trade and economic cooperation. That was because at that time India was far ahead in areas like electronics and computers, a momentum which had been started in 1963 by the late F.C. Kohli with the encouragement of the legendary J.R.D. Tata.[12] It was expected that China could help India in fields like agricultural production and biotechnology. The agreements on cooperation in science and technology would also benefit both countries in no minor measure.

Chengxin Pan updates us till 2013: "A quarter of a century later, however, with China emerging as the world's second largest economy and India the third largest (on a purchasing power parity basis), the Asian Century seems to have well and truly arrived."

\* \* \*

On 29 March 2006, I gave the valedictory address to a three-day seminar on "Indo–China Relations: An agenda for Asian Century" organized by the Mumbai-based think-tank Vidya Prasarak Mandal's Centre for International Studies. This was followed by a one-day dialogue between Stimson Center experts and local academics arranged by me on 8 September 2008, at the Nehru Centre, Mumbai. I was then working as a consultant to the Stimson Center on their "Regional Voices" project. This was over a Stimson Center paper "Towards 2025: Emerging trends and changes in the global order."

Both these events were based on a US National Intelligence Council (NIC) paper "Mapping the Global Future: Report of the National Intelligence Council's 2020 Project" released in December 2004. Former Princeton University Professor Ambassador Robert L. Hutchings who was then NIC Chairman had said that the report was the result of discussions held with more than a thousand regional non-governmental experts in five continents for over one year. The conclusions were "a range of possibilities and potential discontinuities" rather than "predictions" on the world of 2020.

The NIC paper assessed that the end of the Cold War had shifted the "tectonic plates" of international alignments resulting in "emerging powers in Asia, retrenchment in Eurasia, a roiling Middle East, and transatlantic divisions." Apart from problems created by these shifts, other issues which would come to the fore were "new challenges to governance, and a more pervasive sense of insecurity, including terrorism." The paper started with an optimistic note that the possibility of fewer chances of great power conflict due to greater prosperity would result in a favourable environment for coping with the new challenges which otherwise would be "daunting." Also, the role of United States would be "an important variable" in shaping and deciding the path which states and non-state actors "choose to follow."[13]

Additional points in the NIC assessment were that Asia, led by China and India would come into its own in the twenty-first century, just as the 1990s were called the "American Century." The paper stopped short of calling it as an "Asian Century." By 2020 China's gross national product (GNP) would have exceeded individual Western economic powers except America. India's GNP would have overtaken or be on the threshold of overtaking European economies. At the same time, their standard of living might not approach the Western levels to enable them to become "important" economic powers due to the sheer size of their population of 1.4 billion and 1.3 billion respectively. Yet the key uncertainty would be how China and India would exercise their growing power and whether they would relate cooperatively or competitively with other powers in the international system.

* * *

In 2024 India has drifted far away from Deng's calculations. Since 2016 Prime Minister Narendra Modi had aligned India too close with the US government's foreign policy on China in confronting its "expansionist" activities in Southeast Asia. Secretary of State Mike Pompeo, who arrived in New Delhi on 27 October 2020 for Indo–US 2+2 strategic dialogue before the November 2020 US presidential elections, urged India to do more to confront China. Indian External Affairs Minister S. Jaishankar responded that "In the area of defence we are challenged by reckless aggression on our northern borders."[14] On 2 December he said that India would not accept "less than bottom line in talks in talks with China."[15]

This is the background of this book which will analyse how a domestically stable but externally weak India would be entering the 2020s to compete with China. It will also examine India's policy trajectory to achieve its ambitious march towards the superpower league and how it would relate to post-Trump America under President Joe Biden when democracy and human rights are reappearing as the cornerstones of US foreign policy, even after the commencement of the Russian war on Ukraine.

# Part I

# INDIA AND CHINA, ANCIENT AND MODERN

# 1

# A LONG HISTORY OF CONNECTIONS

Behind the tributary system as it became institutionalized in the Ming and Ch'ing periods lay the age-old tradition of Chinese cultural superiority over the barbarians.

– Prof. J.K. Fairbank & Prof. S.Y. Teng of Harvard University (1941)

## In the beginning: cultural and religious exchanges

Ancient India's contacts with primeval China started during the Kushan Empire (30–375 CE),[1] according to British historian Michael Edwards. Originally, Kushans were known as the nomadic Yueh-chi tribe. In 174 BCE they were driven out of their original homelands in Kansu (Kan-suh or Ganzu). They then occupied Bactria, Gandhara, Punjab, Sind, and northern Gujarat.

According to French historian Alain Daniélou, the Kushan Empire was the "centre point" of major civilizations at that time.[2] H.G. Wells confirms that Yueh-chi-Kushan chief Kanishka who added Kashgar, Yarkand and Kotan to north India must have brought India into close relations with China and Tibet as a promoter of Buddhism.[3] A direct road from Gandhara to China during Kushan rule was under their control for more than a century. Yet, historians say that Kushans always considered their home as Central Asia while Indians considered them as "foreign occupiers."[4]

However H.G. Wells said that Buddhism had already reached China earlier during the rule of Asoka the Great (268–32 BCE): "From the Volga to Japan his name is still honoured. China, Tibet and even in India, though it has left his doctrine, preserve the tradition of his greatness." He mentions Pandit Kasyapa as "the apostle of China." This was during the era of Emperor Ming-Ti of the Han dynasty in 64 CE. He was followed by other great teachers.[5]

Legend goes that Emperor Ming dreamt of a golden deity of Buddha which was being brought by white horses to China. He then sent a delegation to India. They returned in 67 CE with monks Kasyapa Matanga (Zhu Yemoteng) and Dharmaratna (Zhu Falan) with white horses carrying Buddhist texts and images. Emperor Ming established the white horse temple in Luovang in Henan, which was the Han capital.

Buddhism had to struggle with Confucianism, which was deeply entrenched in Han China, and had to depend upon the patronage of successive rulers. At the same time Taoism, which was a blend of local heritage, beliefs and what H.G. Wells calls "magic and occult" practices, found a parallel with the brand of Buddhism imported to China that was evolved through a mixture of Mahayana and Shaolin beliefs. Wells says: "The two religions after an opening struggle spread side by side and underwent similar changes, so that nowadays their outward practice is similar."[6]

In later years land boundaries within and outside India changed, as did China's. The Han dynasty fell in 220 and China splintered into northern and southern dynasties. In 440 northern China came under the control of the Xianbei tribe which came to be known as the Northern Wei Dynasty. The southern areas came under the Shu and Wu dynasties till 581. Emperor Wu of Liang (502–49) was a devout Buddhist.[7] During this period Confucianism was superseded by Buddhism and Taoism.

Fights between these three kingdoms resulted in the Wei becoming the most powerful kingdom and the founding of the Jin dynasty (265–304) to take on the "barbarians." However, from

305 to 581 they lost much of the territories to the Tartars from the north. Between 581 and 618 the Sui dynasty re-unified the country, eventually leading to the Tang dynasty between 618 and 907.[8] Buddhist influence reached its peak during the Tang dynasty.

R.C. Majumdar mentions the contribution by Buddhist monks from Kuchi (identified as Kucha in north-western Uygur from Xinjiang) from the fourth century CE especially by Kumarajiva (344–413 CE), who became "Rajaguru." He was originally from present-day Kashmir and had translated Sanskrit Buddhist texts into Chinese. He passed away in Xian, China.

It was a war which made Kumarajiva shift to China. In 383 CE hostilities broke out between Kuchi and China. A Chinese general took Kumarajiva to Kansu (Gansu) in northwest China where he stayed for fifteen years with its ruler. In 401 CE the Chinese emperor invited him to the capital where he stayed till 412. Here he translated more than 100 Sanskrit texts to Chinese interpreting Mahayana philosophy to the Chinese. It is said that his translations are still in use in Chinese Buddhism.[9] His statue adorns the Kizil rock-cut caves of "Thousand Buddhas" in Xinjiang.

Kumarajiva was followed by several Buddhist Indian scholars from Kashmir during the fourth, fifth and sixth centuries. The king of Kashgar (Xinjiang Uygur province) had invited 3,000 Buddhist monks for an assembly where Buddhayasa, a Kashmiri Brahmin scholar, excelled in debates. He stayed in Kashgar for ten years and later worked with Kumarajiva in China. Buddhayasa returned to Kashmir after Kumarajiva's death.

Another Kashmiri Buddhist scholar named Gunawarman went to Sri Lanka (Ceylon) to preach Buddhism and then to Java. In 424 CE he was invited by the Chinese emperor to visit China at the request of Chinese monks in Nanking. He reached Nanking in 431 in a vessel owned by a Hindu merchant identified as Nandin. The emperor received him and made him stay in a monastery known as Jeetavanavihara, where he translated eleven Sanskrit texts into Chinese. He passed away within a year.[10]

Gunawarman was followed by several other monks from other parts of India such as Madhyadesa (central India), Benares, Ujjayini, Bengal and Assam. Three more monks (Buddhabhadra,

Vimokshasena and Jinagupta) went from northwestern India (present-day Pakistan and Afghanistan), but were originally from Kapilavastu (southwestern Nepal).

Interestingly, one of these three became the ruler of Uddiyana in Swat Valley (present-day Khyber Pakhtunkhwa province of Pakistan) and another settled down in Bamiyan (near Kabul). Later they went to Ch'ang-ngan (China) in 559 CE where a monastery was built for them by the emperor. In 572 they were forced to leave China due to some political troubles.

Majumdar says that "no name is better known in India than Paramartha," who was born in Ujjayini but had settled down in Pataliputra. A Chinese mission sent by emperor Wu approached the king of Magadha, who was perhaps Vishnu Gupta, the last imperial Gupta ruler, with a request to send a renowned Buddhist scholar. Paramartha, who was selected by the king, reached China in 546 CE with several Buddhist texts. He stayed in China till his death in 569 CE and translated seventy Buddhist texts.[11]

However, the Indian monk who "obtained the greatest celebrity in China" was Bodhidharma, probably the third son of a Pallava king of Kanchi, who became a "semi-mythical figure" as many miracles were attributed to him. He was received by emperor Wu in the second quarter of the sixth century CE. He is credited with the introduction of the "contemplative form of Mahayana" in China. According to another report he is also reported to be the founder of Zen Buddhism.[12]

Vinitaruchi, a Brahmin from south India who reached China in 582 CE, was another scholar who translated two works into Chinese. He is reported to have moved later to Tonkin (north Vietnam) where he founded the Dhyana School.

Cultural contacts between India and China during the fourth, fifth and sixth centuries resulted in Chinese monks undertaking visits to India. Another reason was a book on India written by Chinese scholar Tao-ngan (second half of the fourth century) which became popular. The first to visit was a group of five monks led by Fa-hien who entered India through Kashmir in 399 CE. He stayed in India for nearly five years and left a detailed account. He returned to China only in 414 after visiting Ceylon.[13]

Deep interest in India was shown by different Chinese rulers of all regions, including the Song (420–79), Tsi (479–502) and Leang (502–57) dynasties of southern China, who sent different delegations. Similarly in 518 Emperor Yang of the Sui dynasty sent a mission to India (605–17), while the Empress Dowager of the Great Wei dynasty sent a delegation under Sung-Yun to collect 170 sacred texts from India in 518.[14]

However the most productive exchanges, according to R.C. Majumdar, were during the Tang period (618–907). This was one of the most glorious chapters in Chinese history when the whole of China came under one political authority extending to Central Asia. Thousands of Indian missionaries and merchants "thronged" China's principal cities, while Chinese monks and royal emissaries came to India in the seventh century in greater numbers than during any other period.

Nalanda University's reputation was at its peak and Hiuen Tsang played a great role in Indo–Chinese relations. He reached India in 630 and stayed for the next fourteen years, travelling all over India. He left India in 644 after being honoured by emperors Harshavardhana and Bhaskaravarman.[15] Hiuen Tsang reached China in 649 and was greatly honoured by the emperor.

R.C. Majumdar says that cultural contacts were intense during the Gupta period through Indian missionaries in China. He says that India's global cultural influence resulted in carving out an imaginary area known as "Greater India" comprising Tibet, Korea, Japan and even the Philippines in the east and over the vast region in the north that lay along the overland route from China to India through Central Asia.[16]

The late Vasant Vasudev Paranjpe, China expert and former ambassador, had said that China, which was insular even two thousand years ago, had preferred Buddhism "because it filled a vacuum in Chinese life and had something in it for each section of the population—from the plebeian to the poet to the prince."

Paranjpe, who was perhaps the longest-serving Indian diplomatic officer in China (1951–58) had a Chinese name "Bai Chunhui" since his student days in China from July 1947. He served under three initial Indian ambassadors (Sardar K.M. Panikkar,

N. Raghavan and R.K. Nehru) and had interpreted for Prime Minister Jawaharlal Nehru during his talks with Mao Zedong and Zhou Enlai.[17] He said in his reminiscences specially written for the Indira Gandhi National Centre for The Arts that Chinese imperial rulers, not all of them from well-respected origins, had found that they could use Buddhist monks to bestow "on them divine blessings and anoint them as 'sons of heaven'." This was useful to divert the minds of ordinary Chinese from their oppressive rule to "otherworldly concerns and channelise rebellious thoughts into non-violent ways."[18] He continued:

> To the common Chinese, idol worship (of Buddha) perhaps offered an easy way to enlist divine aid to fulfil their dreams and desires and to end their worries and problems through the inexpensive means of burning an incense! The ingenious doctrine of karma offered a plausible and satisfying explanation for the disparities of wealth in the world: the Jataka stories narrating the exploits of Buddha with some music thrown in, the story of the flying monkey (*Hanuman*) and the siddhis (magical powers of sages) all provided colourful entertainment diverting the plebeian mind from the boredom and hardships of daily life.
>
> But Buddhism would also seem to have done some real service to the people by bringing to China Ayurveda (Indian system of medicine) which bases its diagnosis on *Nadi-Pariksha* (examination of pulse) and *Tridhatu* (Three primary elements in the body viz. phlegm, bile and wind). These two also became the basic principles of Chinese medicines, Indian monks also carried Indian medicinal herbs to China as evidenced by texts of the Chinese *Tripitakas* and the Chinese work called "*Bencao Gangmu*" (or Herbal Pharmacopeia).
>
> Since Buddhistic metaphysical thought came close to Taoist thought, it easily fused with it to create the school of "Qingtan" during the post-Han period from the third century onwards.

Yet, the process of assimilation of Buddhism into China was not very easy. Paranjpe says that apart from Confucian opposition, scholar Han Yu during the late Tang dynasty (eighth–ninth centuries CE) had asked the emperor to "turn these monks into men and burn their books" as they were "unproductive" members of the society.

Similarly, Dr Hu Shih, former ambassador to US (1938–42), who was a visible face during the 4 May movement after the 1919 Paris Peace Talks, had said that "Buddhism brought to China not only eighteen heavens but thirty-three hells."[19]

## Tributary system

During this era attempts were made by Chinese record keepers to write that India or its different kingdoms were Chinese tributary states. Harsha's close relationship with Hiuen Tsang made him send an Indian envoy to the Chinese emperor in 641 CE. The Chinese emperor mistook this as an act of Harsha's submission to his temporal authority and, as was the Chinese custom, he sent his envoy Liang-hoai-King with a royal patent to Harsha to submit to his authority!

A totally surprised Harsha (identified by Chinese records as Siladitya), "received the imperial decree with bended knees and placed it on his head" as was the then the Indian form of courtesy. Some historians have interpreted this as Harsha's desire to get help from China. Majumdar disagrees:

> Such a conclusion is absolutely unwarranted. It has been invariably the practice of Chinese chroniclers to represent customary presents given by an envoy as the tribute paid by a vassal state, and no wonder that ordinary marks of courtesy and politeness, which Harsha showed to the ambassador, were represented as an act of submission.[20]

Noted writer Will Durant concurs with this interpretation. In his eleven-volume *The Story of Civilisation* (1935) he says of the Chinese emperors: "In theory he ruled by divine right; he was the 'son of heaven' and represented the Supreme Being on earth. By virtue of his godlike powers, he ruled the seasons and commanded men to coordinate their lives with the divine order of the universe."[21]

Towards the end of 643 CE a second Chinese delegation came to India under Li-y-piao and Wang-hiuen-tse. They brought with them a Brahmin envoy sent to the Chinese emperor by Siladitya with Chinese emperor's reply. Wang-hiuen-tse returned to China and was again sent back to India after Chinese emperor heard Hiuen Tsang on his return in 645. By that time Harsha had passed away.

Disorder reigned after Harsha's death which led to the breakup of his empire. A Chinese account said, with the usual self-glorification, that a usurper, who was Harsha's minister identified by them as "A-la-na-shuen" (Arjuna or Arunasva), attacked Wang-hiuen-tse's delegation, which made Wang rush to Tibet to seek help from its ruler Sron-btsan-sgam-po who gave him 1,200 troops. From Amsuvarman, King of Nepal he received 7,000 horsemen as escort.

With these, Wang-hiuen-tse returned, attacked Cha-puo-ho-lo, the capital of Arjuna, defeating the usurper, taking 12,000 prisoners and 30,000 domesticated animals. "The whole of India trembled, and 580 walled towns offered their submission." The Chinese account said that Kumara Bhaskaravarman, King of Eastern India sent large quantities of provisions and equipment to the Chinese envoy. After this triumphal battle Wang returned to China with Arjuna as his prisoner, who remained in China till his death. He was given posthumous honours and his statue was placed on the avenue leading to the tomb of Chinese emperor T'ai-tsong.[22]

On 6 October 1962 Mao Zedong would quote this incident at a high-level meeting before the Sino–Indian war to justify why India needed to be severely punished for not accepting that he was facing a "new China" which had stood up and would not be "bullied" or "humiliated."[23]

Yasovarman, ruler of Kanauj (700–40 CE) sought Chinese help against the Arabs and Tibetans who were making inroads into India. Chinese records mention that Yi-sha-fu-mo, king of Central India, had sent his minister, a Buddhist monk Buddhasena (identified by the Chinese as Pu-ta-Sin), to the court of China in 731. Similarly the king of Kashmir, identified as Lalitaditya, had also sent his envoy to China in 736, conveying that he was Yasovarman's ally. It is not clear what the Chinese did, but historical records reveal that the Arabs who made a foray into Kanauj after conquering Sindh could not succeed.[24]

Earlier to this, Chandrapida, King of Kashmir sent an envoy to China in 713 asking for help against an Arab invader identified as Muhammad-ibn-Qasim who died later. According to Chinese chronicles, the emperor was reported to have granted the title of "King" to Chandrapida in 720.

The Pallava dynasty ruled a large portion of southern India for nearly 600 years (275–897 CE). During the reign of Narasimhavarman II (695–722), the great "Shore Temple" of Mahabalipuram (Mamallapuram), a UNESCO world heritage site, was built. There is another version that it was built during the time of Narasimhavarman I (630–68).[25] Narasimhavarman II sent a diplomatic delegation to China.

Interestingly, the 11–12 October 2019 summit meeting between Indian Prime Minister Narendra Modi and Chinese President Xi Jinping was held at the venue of the Shore Temple. As a retrospective the correspondent who covered the visit said:

> The emissaries of the Pallava king sought the permission of Emperor Xuangzong to fight back Arab and Tibetan intrusions in South Asia. And "pleased with the Indian king's offer to form a coalition against the Arabs and Tibetans, the Chinese emperor bestowed the title of 'huaide jun' (the Army that Cherishes Virtue) to Narayansimha II's troops."[26]

It was not only the Pallavas (275–897) and Cholas (907–1215) who maintained close trade links with China. Different rulers in what is now Kerala state also forged trade links with China. By the time Islam arrived on south India's west coast in the ninth century, Muslims had already started trading with China using maritime routes. "Kollam" (Quilon), an ancient port in Kerala, according to the records of the T'ang dynasty (618–913) was used as their chief settlement.[27]

"Mahlai" of the Chinese records of the Tang dynasty could be identified with Kollam. Arab traveller Suleiman who visited Kerala in 851 CE had reported on the flourishing trade that existed between Kollam and China. According to Suleiman, Kollam port was so wide and deep that it enabled the Chinese ship to enter the port without any difficulty. Chinese ships going to the Persian Gulf also stopped for a while at Kollam port.

Benjamin of Tudela, a Spanish Jew from Spain, wrote about the "trustworthy nature" of the trading community in Kollam when he travelled between 1159 and 1173. Venetian traveller Marco Polo, who reached Kerala during the last decade of the thirteenth century, and Ibn Batuta, the African Arab traveller who came to Kerala in the first half of the fourteenth century, had also concurred.[28]

Another account said that trade relations between Kerala and China continued during the Tang (618–907), Song (960–1229), Yuan (1229–1388) and early Ming (1368–1644) periods using Kollam. However, in later years especially in the fifteenth century the Chinese started preferring Calicut port over Kollam. This was recorded by Ma Huan, scribe of the famous Chinese admiral Zheng He (1371–1433) during his visit to Calicut in 1406.[29]

An interesting aspect of the Chinese overseas contacts was their desire to establish diplomatic legations in countries with which they had cultural or commercial contacts and to award titles to the rulers seeking such diplomatic recognition. R.C. Majumdar mentions instances in India during the Tang period. Thus, the Chinese emperor awarded the title of the King of "Pu-lu" (Bolor) to four different individuals between 717 and 741.[30] It is not clear whether Bolor is referring to Balti or "Little Tibet."[31]

China maintained its diplomatic relations with Kapisa (Kushan?), Uddiyana (Kosambi?), Gandhara (Parashawar?) , Magadha (eastern India) and Kashmir after their first political contacts from 641 CE. By 692 delegations were also received from Mo-Lo-pa-mo (identified as one Malavarman) in eastern India, Sha-lo-yi-to (identified as Siladitya III of Valabhi—Gujarat?) from western India and Che-lu-ki-pa-lo (identified as Chalukya Vallabha) from southern India.[32]

The rulers of China and Kollam exchanged embassies and there was a flourishing Chinese settlement at Kollam during the medieval period. Chinese annals said that some envoys from king of Quilon landed at Zayton port (Quanzhou) in China in 1282 CE.[33]

## Ming tributary system

In 1406 the port of Calicut had a taste of the Ming tributary system with the arrival of the legendary and "fearsome" Chinese admiral Zheng He. One description said:

> The fleet of Chinese junks stretching miles across the horizon, their white sails taut against the monsoon winds, was approaching Calicut. From the leading rowboat which came ashore later, stepped a towering seven-footer Mongol Muslim, none other than the fearsome warrior admiral Zheng He! The animated crowd was silenced. The imperial Chinaman had arrived.[34]

The independent state of Zamorin (Samoothiri in Malayalam)[35] was included in the "Tributary" system, a mechanism by which regions outside the Chinese empire were given a place in the "all embracing Sinocentric cosmos." An imperial patent of appointment was given to the ruler recognising his status as a tributary while establishing foreign policy with him.

In a 2006 working paper, Giovanni Andornino argues that the Chinese Tributary system was established to achieve the following objectives:

> Especially during the Ming and Qing dynasties, China's interaction with weaker political units of the East Asian world was geared toward a form of power which aimed at maintaining systemic stability as a function of the Empire's survival. In this context tribute performed a threefold role in keeping internal and external threats under check: it enhanced the ideological legitimacy of the emperor's rule of "All Under Heaven," it strengthened his military credibility by guaranteeing the flow of military resources, and it offered the state an economic channel thorough which to pursue appeasement policies. The versatility of the system permitted China to adjust its foreign relations within several, diverse theatres of action.[36]

It calls it "Gramscian super-national hegemony as a form of power including 'a combination of coercion and consent'."

In 1941 J.K. Fairbank, noted American scholar on China, published a long essay with S. Y. Teng on the Ch'ing tributary system which showed Bengal, Calicut, Cannanore, Cochin, Coimbatore (Coyampadi), Jaunpur, Kashmir, Quilon and Tibet among several names among "tributaries" indexed from six editions of collected statutes.[37]

The pattern described above continued during the Delhi Sultanate and Mughal era. Muhammad bin Tughluq (1290–1351), who was the Sultan of Delhi between 1325 and 1351, sent Berber Maghrebi scholar Ibn Batutah (Battuta) as his ambassador to China in 1341 or 1342. Batutah who had arrived in India in 1333 was originally appointed as the Chief Qazi (judge) of Delhi.[38] Tughluq wanted Batutah to go as his envoy along with a Chinese (Yuan dynasty—originally Mongol) delegation that had arrived in Tughluq's court.

However, Batutah did not reach China till 1345. The University of California at Berkeley hosts a rich online resource on "The Travels of Battuta."[39] As an intrepid traveller, he chose a circuitous route with "200 Hindu slaves, singers, and dancers, 15 pages (boy servants), 100 horses, and great amounts of cloth, dishes, and swords." Another ship "carried Ibn Battuta's luggage, servants, and slave-girls—one of whom was carrying his child. The captain of that ship had set sail for China without him or the goods that he was to present to the Emperor of China."

He sailed via Gujarat, Calicut, the Maldives (which had just become an Islamic nation from a Buddhist country, where he stayed for nine months), Sri Lanka (Ceylon), Chittagong (present-day Bangladesh), Assam, Aceh (northern Sumatra), Malacca, Vietnam and finally Quanzhou in Fujian.

Incidentally, on his way back Batutah did not return to Delhi but sailed to Mecca when he reached Calicut. The Berkeley site continues:

> The winter monsoons carried Ibn Battuta's sailing junk south from China. He returned to Samudra, on the island of Sumatra, where he stayed again with the sultan, this time for a few weeks. He continued on to Quilon, India and then up to Calicut. There he thought about returning to Muhammad Tughluq, his former

employer in Delhi, and throwing himself on his mercy. But fear kept him from doing that.

Also, by then Muhammad Tughluq had gone away from Delhi to wage battles against rebels in the north. He would die of some illness in 1351, a couple of years after Ibn Batutah passed through India on his way home. By then the Delhi Sultanate had weakened and reduced to a small northern state while the south was a patchwork of small Muslim and Hindu kingdoms battling with each other.

Indian princely states maintained vibrant trade relations with China. Hence it was not a surprise that in 1374 Bukka Raya I, emperor of the expansive Vijayanagar kingdom which had controlled the south and part of the east of India, had chosen to send a delegation to China. However, the advent of the European powers into India for commercial purposes from 1500 changed this pattern. The Portuguese were the first to arrive in 1503, then the Dutch in 1602, the English in 1609 and the French from 1668. They started interfering with the trade patterns of the native princes through bribery, deceit, and military threats. As a result, the Arabs and Chinese lost out.

## How the British ended the tributary system

Bengal was the most important trading post for the English in Mughal India. In 1634 Mughal Emperor Jahangir allowed the British East India Company to set up a small trading post in Bengal at a time when that province was already exporting cotton, raw silk, sugar, salt, jute and opium to several foreign countries including China. When the Mughal rule waned by 1707 the Nawab of Bengal became independent with rich resources.

In 1757 the British victory over Siraj-ud-Daulah, Nawab of Bengal, and his French allies at the Battle of Plassey changed the whole character of political arrangements in India with the British gaining the upper hand not only politically but also economically and commercially by diverting all exports to Britain leading to the decay of trade and industry in Bengal and the rest of India.

## The humiliation of China

Colonial Britain gained substantively through the opium trade from India. In 1773 the East India Company assumed a monopoly over all the opium produced in Bengal, after achieving a record export of 2,000 chests of opium to China in 1767. To counter this Chinese emperor Kia King banned the import of opium in 1799.[40] A BBC report on 5 September 2019 quoted a study by Prof. Rolf Bauer, at the University of Vienna, that nearly 2,500 clerks working in 100 offices of the Opium Agency of the East India Company monitored poppy farmers, enforced contracts and quality with police-like powers.[41]

This caused great resentment in China against British India, which intensified through the First Opium War (1839–42) between the British and Qing dynasty in which 5,000 Indian soldiers participated. This led to the imposition of the "Treaty Port System" in which five important Chinese ports at Shanghai, Canton (Guangzhou), Ningpo (Ningbo), Foochow (Fuzhou) and Amoy (Xiamen) were opened for trade.

The Second Opium War (1856–60), in which the British, French and the United States participated against the Qing dynasty, resulted in national humiliation in China as they were forced to accept a "Treaty Ports Agreement" forcibly opening another eleven ports. Gradually several more ports were opened. Thousands of square miles of Chinese territory were forced to be leased to the foreigners for nearly 100 years. Later it was the turn of Japanese to invade Qing China in 1894.

A long report in the *New Indian Express* gives details of the Indian soldiers' participation in the British colonial wars and the use of Sikh policemen by the British in China which created considerable resentment.[42] The process started after the British granted Jamsetjee Jeejeebhoy, David Sassoon & Co. and Jardine Matheson & Co. a virtual monopoly of opium distribution in China after the First Opium War. By 1860 opium shops had outnumbered other shops patronised by the Chinese. The British encouraged this as opium sales had provided 14 per cent of the revenue of Government of India during 1889–94.

In 1890 the British raised the Hong Kong Regiment with 1,000 troops recruited from the Jhelum district in Punjab. Besides "Gun Lascars," a new Indian para-military force, was raised in Hongkong. In 1899 Qing forces were defeated by these forces. Sikh policemen were deployed in Honk Kong, Shanghai, Tientsin, Shamian and Hankou. Their deployment in Zhenjiang in 1889 resulted in violent protests and had to be withdrawn. After the failure of Boxer Rebellion in 1900 against foreigners, China feared that their country would be partitioned by foreign forces which included Indian troops.

How the 1919 Paris Peace Conference confirmed this "humiliation"

No book describes this "humiliation" better than *Paris 1919: Six Months that Changed the World* by Oxford historian Margaret MacMillan. It recounts how the Big Four (Britain, France, Italy, and the United States) carved up the post-War world to suit their interests. They also left several grave problems unattended to which are responsible for many disputes even today.

The 1919 Paris Conference, which started on 18 January 1919, was supposed to represent different people aspiring for "self-determination", but this principle was not necessarily followed in choosing delegations. The leaders chose only "acceptable faces." For example, China which sent a sixty-member delegation had as its leader Lu Zhengxiang, a Chinese diplomat, and a Roman Catholic monk. It did not include Chinese "nationalists" or "leftists." The Indian delegation ignored nationalist elements. It was led by the Secretary of State to India Edwin Montagu and two members, Lord Satyendra Sinha and the Maharajah of Bikaner, who were chosen for their "loyalty." MacMillan says: "In spite of the urgings of various Indian groups, the Indian government had not appointed any of the new Indian nationalist leaders."[43]

China was then a "helpless, hopeless and inert mass," as contemptuously described by British Foreign Secretary Lord Curzon who attended the conference. The weak Qing dynasty had allowed foreigners to occupy their lands, described as "Concessions," enforcing their own rules: "The Russians in the

North, the British in the Yangtze valley, the French in the South, the Germans in the Shantung peninsula and the Japanese here, there and everywhere."

Shantung, the cradle of Chinese civilization being the birthplace of Confucius, had been seized in 1897 by imperial Germany which forced Peking to lease it for ninety-nine years. In 1914, during the First World War, an Anglo-Japanese force captured Tsintao port in Shantung. Since then, Shantung became the emotional rallying point for the Chinese students and intellectuals in China and in Europe who wanted to throw out foreigners.

However, Japan adamantly continued as an occupying power in China, bribing war-lords, politicians, and military officials. They argued at the Paris Conference that Shantung was merely a matter between Germany and Japan with no role for China. Britain, France, and Italy were disinterested although the then ruling Beiyang government of China had extended massive assistance to them for the war. They sent 100,000 labourers to relieve the Allied army to fight the Germans.

China had pinned hopes on US President Woodrow Wilson as the arbiter in the Paris Conference. He was convinced of their case. However, he also shared the worry that Japan would walk out of the Conference as Italy did on 21 April over quarrels over lands of the Austro-Hungarian empire including the Adriatic port Fiume. Also, Wilson wanted Japanese cooperation on his proposal for the League of Nations, for which he had obsessively campaigned. Japan, by then the fifth "Great Power," had put across a counter proposal on a "Racial Equality" clause for the League of Nations Charter which had raised hackles among the Western-dominated international system with its hallmark of colonial rule over non-whites.

Thus, Wilson gave priority to the trade-off with Japan for dropping the "Racial Equality" clause by granting them Shantung, which the Chinese had described as "a dagger pointed at the heart of China." The Chinese were crushed when the decision was announced on 30 April.

That announcement ignited a storm which erupted as Chinese nationalistic protests. Till then even Chinese liberals had supported

Western culture, education, and values. Deeply disappointed, they gravitated towards the template of the 1917 Russian Revolution. After a stormy meeting on Rue Danton in Paris, Chinese students held massive demonstrations at Tiananmen Square and other places on 4 May, which became a turning point in its history.

That was the day China "awakened" as an anti-imperialistic, cultural, and political movement. The movement split into the "Nationalist" way (Kuomintang) and "Communist" path when Chen Duxiu and Li Dazhao founded the Chinese Communist Party in 1921. Mao Zedong was one of the founder members. Both cooperated during 1924–27 (First United Front) when the Soviet Union was guiding both streams (Nationalists and Communists) and between 1937 and 1945 (Second United Front) to resist the Japanese invasion.[44] Later China witnessed a bloody civil war (1946–49) after which Chiang Kai-shek retreated to Formosa (Taiwan) and Mao Zedong announced a Communist Republic on 1 October 1949.

Berlin-based Indian journalist A.C.N. Nambiar in the 1920s had written that the local "Hindustan Association" used to organise lectures of Indian freedom fighters like Sarojini Naidu, Zakir Hussain and Sardar K.M. Panikkar on the nationalist urge in India, which were attended by Kuomintang Party delegates who felt that "the success of national movement in China would also result in emancipation of India."[45]

Ironically Wilson's efforts on a trade-off with Japan on Shantung did not benefit him politically. He was not able to convince his own country on the League of Nations despite travelling 8,000 miles across America in twenty-two days and suffering a serious health crisis. The Senate refused to ratify it on 19 November 1919. America never joined the League of Nations. Japan invaded China in 1937. World War II started in 1939.

*Efforts by Jawaharlal Nehru to mend India's relations with China*

The Indian National Congress, on Jawaharlal Nehru's initiative, tried to assuage this humiliation. In 1938 American Communist and journalist Agnes Smedley and Communist general Zhue De requested Nehru to urgently send some physicians to China which had suffered greatly by the Japanese invasion in 1938.[46] According to Agnes Smedley:

> Jawaharlal Nehru was primarily responsible for the Medical Mission to China. When he formed the first China Medical Committee of the Indian National Congress, hundreds of men and women doctors and nurses registered as volunteers for China. The Congress had enough money to finance, equip, and supply only five men in its initial group. It had already initiated "China days" and called for the boycott of Japanese goods throughout India.[47]

Nehru appealed to Subhas Chandra Bose, then Congress President, who made a public call to send a medical mission to China. Bose, despite being a friend of Japan in later days, had written an article in *Modern Review* that Japan should not have attacked China. Bose collected funds and an ambulance.

Dr Madan Atal from Allahabad (now Prayagraj), a close relative of Nehru, led the delegation with four other doctors and support staff in September 1938. They were the first overseas medical mission to arrive in war-ravaged China. Dwakanath Kotnis from Maharashtra was prominent among them as he stayed longer than others. Kotnis, who had just graduated from G.S. Medical College, Bombay, and was preparing for postgraduate studies, volunteered for the mission. They first reached Hankou in Wuhan from where they proceeded to Yan'an (Yenan), which was Mao's base.

Although others returned after some time, Kotnis, who was the youngest, stayed on for almost five years, working in mobile clinics and participating in the operations of the Eighth Route Army, the reorganised Red Army,[48] led by Mao Zedong, which earned him very high praise. His selfless service in Bethune International Peace Hospital, Shijiazhuang endeared him to the common Chinese people. Kotnis married a Chinese nurse Guo Qinglan in 1939 who was working in Bethune hospital. He passed away in China in 1942 due to medical complications.

In later years Kotnis would become a symbol of Indo-China friendship. His statue was erected in the Martyr's Memorial Park in Shijiazhuang city. A Hindi film *Dr. Kotnis ki Amar Kahani* (The Immortal Story of Dr Kotnis) was made in 1946 by veteran film director V. Shantaram. All visiting Chinese dignitaries from Premier Zhou En-lai (1950) to President Xi Jinping (2014) had recognised and honoured his relatives in Solapur (Maharashtra) during their visits to India. In 2017 the Chinese government presented the University of Mumbai a copy of the restored handwritten letter which Mao had written to his relatives in 1950 after the death of Dr Kotnis.[49]

*Closer relations with China and Nehru's visit in August–September 1939*

Special mention should be made of the contribution made by Tan Yun-Shan, also called "Chinese Mahatma," to Sino–Indian relations from 1928 after he joined Rabindranath Tagore's Visva Bharati as professor of China studies. He established the "*Cheena Bhavana*" (China House) or China Studies Centre in 1937. He passed away in Bodh Gaya in 1983.[50]

In 1929 Nehru, representing the Indian National Congress at the Brussels Anti-Colonial Congress, had met the Kuomintang-dominated Chinese delegation. A Sino–Indian declaration of solidarity, drafted by Nehru, was passed at the Congress.[51] According to a report, the Indian National Congress agreed to mount a propaganda offensive against the British use of Indian troops in China to suppress the liberation movement.[52] Following this a China–India Association was established in Nanjing on the initiative of Dai Jitao, a theoretician of the Kuomintang. Dai also visited Shantiniketan to meet Rabindranath Tagore.

In 1938 Nehru visited London and addressed a rally of 5,000 at Trafalgar Square organised by the India League led by V.K. Krishna Menon highlighting the conflicts in China, Abyssinia and Spain.[53] He also addressed the China Association in London expressing his anguish over the developments in China.

In May–July 1939 Nehru and Mao exchanged letters after the latter thanked him for the medical mission. Nehru said that he hoped to meet with Mao and the Eighth Route Army adding that the

Congress had long been following Mao's career with admiration. Some in India were puzzled at his acclamatory references on Communism. It was said that even his daughter Indira Gandhi, who was in London at that time, had voiced her concern at his decision to go to the Communist areas.[54] His visit to China came on 21 August.

Eminent historian Ramachandra Guha offers an explanation in his essay "Jawaharlal Nehru and China: A Study in Failure" written for the Harvard–Yenching Institute in 2011:

> As for Nehru, other than India and England, the country that interested him most was China. His first major book, *Glimpses of World History*, published in 1935, has as many as 134 index references to China. These refer to, among other things, different dynasties (the Tang, Han, Ch'in, etc), corruption, communism, civil war, agriculture, and banditry. Already, the pairing of China and India was strongly imprinted in Nehru's framework. Thus, China is referred to as "the other great country of Asia," and as "India's old-time friend." There was a manifest sympathy with its troubles at the hands of foreigners. The British were savaged for forcing both humiliating treaties and opium down the throats of the Chinese, this being an illustration of the "growing arrogance and interference by the western Powers."[55]

In China, Nehru visited Kunming, Chongqing and Chengdu. He also met Chiang Kai-Shek and his wife Soon Mei-ling and Foreign Minister Wang Chonghui as well as important nationalist leaders such as General Chen Cheng, Chen Lifu and Zhu Jiahua. He wanted to visit Yan'an to see the medical mission. He also felt that he would not be able to understand China fully unless he met Mao and his colleagues.

However, he was not able to travel to the north-west to meet with Mao and other Communist leaders as he was summoned back to India after the outbreak of the war in Europe. Yet he did have meetings with top Communist leaders Ye Jianying, Qin Bangxian and Wang Ming who were in Chongqing on the basis of the agreement reached during 1937 on the formation of an anti-Japanese "United Front."[56]

# A LONG HISTORY OF CONNECTIONS

*Chiang Kai-shek's visit to India (1942)*

During the Second World War, after Singapore fell to the Japanese in 1942, Chinese ruler Chiang Kai-shek paid an urgent visit to India to ensure that the Congress party struggle against the British in India did not hamper US troop movements towards China through India. He wanted to seek their cooperation. On 7 December 1941 the Allied powers, at their Arcadia Conference, had chosen Chiang as the Supreme Commander of Allied forces in China Theatre.

Chiang had believed that the US entry into World War II would check imperial Japan's expansion into China and the Far East. He was happy that, on 20 April 1942, US bombers had targeted Japanese naval yards and cities like Osaka, Yokohama, Kobe, and Nagoya.

However, he was horrified at the terrible Japanese retaliation on China. Japan sent 53 divisions to Chinese Chekiang province killing more than 250,000 civilians, pillaging all villages and ploughing up every Chinese airfield within 20,000 square miles as punishment for supporting the US bombing. That led him and American military strategists to think of India as a land, air, and road supply route to the Eastern Front. It brought Chiang to India in February 1942 to persuade Gandhi, Jinnah and Nehru to agree to this arrangement.[57]

President F.D. Roosevelt had felt that Chiang would not be effective unless China's internal situation was stabilised with the Chinese Communist Party's (CCP) help. For that he stationed General Joe Stilwell as his personal envoy and Chiang's Chief of Staff in 1942. President Harry Truman also wanted Chiang to incorporate the CCP and the "Democratic League" in his Nationalist Government. He then sent General George C. Marshall, the symbol of US victory in the Second World War, as his envoy.

Truman said in his policy statement that US wanted the Chinese National Government to "rehabilitate the country, improve the agrarian and industrial economy and establish a military organisation capable of discharging China's national and international responsibilities."

Hardly anybody in India knew that our country had played a leading role in the American Office of Strategic Services (OSS) activities during that era. In April 2019, my wife bought a delightful book by Donovan Webster (no relation of Bill Donovan, the founder of OSS) from a second hand bookshop in Saratoga (California) which gave astonishing details.

These operations were carried out not only in Europe but also in Asia. DET 101 (Detachment 101) was raised in mid-1942 to resist the Japanese in Burma. The Kachins were supported by an airdrop of twenty-five British-trained OSS operatives in mid-1942. The original members of Detachment 101 were recruited, trained, and dispatched to Burma in May 1942. The first leader of Detachment 101 was Major Carl Eiffler, described as a "smart, ferocious and physically imposing man of about forty". He was a US Customs agent on the Mexican border and an army reservist.[58]

As a result, a huge training centre was developed in Ramgarh, in the present-day Jharkhand province, which trained Chinese and Americans. Some 30,000 Chinese and 17,000 Americans were trained there for the Eastern Front by December 1942. Eiffler used part of them, as well as Naga tribesmen, in the Kachin resistance. They had a good run in harassing the Japanese till the end of 1943. This pattern of covert warfare became the "*pièce de résistance*" for future operations either by "Kachin V Force" or by the 5307th Composite Unit (called Galahad) by General Joe "Vinegar" Stilwell, then Chief of US Command in the Eastern theatre.[59]

However, the British administration was wary of agreeing to these arrangements as it would have meant seeking cooperation from Congress leaders and allowing political concessions to them as they were fiercely struggling for independence. Barbara W. Tuchman, biographer of General Joe Stilwell, says that Stilwell had to take up the matter with US Secretary of War Henry L. Stimson, who asked him to meet British Prime Minister Winston Churchill who was in Washington, DC at that time to complain about "Wavell's defeatism and the lethargy of the India Command."[60] Wavell was then British Commander-in-Chief and later Viceroy from June 1943.

Through such British intransigence Chiang faced difficulties in arranging a meeting with Gandhi as he wanted to go all the way to Sevagram, Wardha. The meeting however took place in Calcutta on 18 February. The two leaders, however, did not agree on their assessments. Gandhiji later wrote to Sardar Vallabhbhai Patel: "I would not say that I learnt anything, and there was nothing that we could teach him."[61]

Nonetheless his meeting with Nehru on 10 February was productive. Nehru appreciated the importance of China in terms of friendship and cooperation between both countries although he was firm that Chiang should not expect any "radical change in the Congress's policy towards Great Britain." Chiang also met other leaders like Congress President Maulana Azad and Muslim League leader M.A. Jinnah. He conveyed his impressions to Prime Minister Winston Churchill and US President F.D. Roosevelt.

### Trend setter: the 1947 Asian Relations Conference (March–April 1947)

Nehru, as the head of the "interim government" in India, had conceived the idea of holding an Asian countries' conference in 1946, according to Phillips Talbot, former US ambassador, who in 1947 was a leading journalist of *The New Republic*:

> It was conceived early in 1946 by Nehru, whose nine terms of political imprisonment have never dimmed his sense of history. After the recent war's sharp impact on the East, he looked around him and saw what he regarded as the final quivers of the Colonial Age. It was time, he argued, for Asians to get together and prepare for the new day at hand.[62]

Talbot felt that throughout the conference the emphasis was on the India–China colonial belt region. People from 30 countries participated. The conference was unique in many respects:

> They had come from the four corners of the continent. Tibetans had walked 21 days over the windy plateau and mountain passes south of Lhasa before they reached the speedier automobiles, trains, and planes of India.

Gandhi addressed the Conference on 2 April 1947. Talbot reported that he had come from the "riot torn Bihar." According to the text released by Gandhi's official site, he addressed the closing session, attended by 20,000 visitors, delegates, and observers:

> The West is today pinning for wisdom. It is despairing of a multiplication of the atom bombs, because the atom bombs mean utter destruction, not merely of the West, but of the whole world, as if the prophecy of the Bible is going to be fulfilled and there is to be a perfect deluge. It is up to you to tell the world of its wickedness and sin—that is the heritage your teachers and my teachers have taught Asia.[63]

Talbot summarised the trend of the Conference: Asia seeks independence from Western imperialism. However, it believes that political freedom without economic independence would be meaningless. Foreign interests should not control the countries' agriculture and industry. Yet Asia could not stand alone. Foreign assistance should be sought without reintroducing imperialism in a new form. Most of Asia is industrially primitive, except perhaps India. Health, sanitation, housing, and education remain at deplorable levels. To make up for such fundamental deficiencies in agriculture, industry, and human living, individual initiative is not enough. Each nation must decide for itself how far the state will intervene. The United Nations should be supported for maintaining peace and to prevent "atomic jitters."

The conference decided to set up a permanent Asian Relations Organization. However, no constitution was drafted, and it was agreed that it would be unofficial and should operate through national units of the same character. The main purpose would be to facilitate contacts between Asian nations at cultural, economic, and possibly political levels.

Talbot said that Chinese diplomat George Yeh "who have their own ideas about leadership of Asia, invited the conference to hold its next general session in China in 1949." That was not to be. The Chinese civil war was going on from December 1946 when their National Assembly, brought together by General George Marshall, Truman's envoy, failed in getting participation by Communists and Leftists. By December 1947 Communists had taken over major Kuomintang areas and Chiang left for Formosa on 10 December

1949, after Mao proclaimed a new Communist government on 1 October.[64] George Yeh, who migrated to Taiwan when the Kuomintang government fell, became their first foreign minister.

India, which had successfully organised the first Asian conference, would later translate its broad conclusions as the idea of "non-alignment" as a cornerstone of its foreign policy. It would also take initiative to form the Colombo Powers Group in 1954, holding the Bandung Asian–African Conference in 1955 and the First Non-Aligned Summit in Belgrade in 1961. That was the high point in India's global diplomacy under the leadership of Jawaharlal Nehru.[65]

# 2

# DIPLOMACY AND DIVERGENCE

> Mao came with Chen Yun and spent nearly four hours at
> the Embassy chatting away and watching the film *Jhanak*
> *Jhanak payal Baje* which had been specially flown from
> India for the occasion.
>
> — Ambassador "Bai Chunhui" Vasant Vasudev Paranjpe,
> Nehru's interpreter in 1954

In Japan "*sakura*" means cherry blossom, or the beginning of
Spring, a time of renewal and optimism. A Chinese travel guide
claims that China has similarly spectacular cherry blossom parks
in ten locations including the "Tortoise Head Garden" in Wuxi,
most famous for its giant Buddha statue, which attracts thousands
of visitors.[1]

The Japanese meaning of *sakura* is more relevant to relate to
Sino–Indian relations from 1947 to 1962:

> Tied to the Buddhist themes of mortality, mindfulness and living
> in the present, Japanese cherry blossoms are a timeless metaphor
> for human existence. Blooming season is powerful, glorious, and
> intoxicating, but tragically short-lived—a visual reminder that
> our lives, too, are fleeting.[2]

Like the Japanese *sakura*, independent India's diplomatic
relationship with China blossomed soon after the Communists

captured power in 1949, only to wither away from 1955 due to mutual suspicion leading to a final crash in 1962.

An eyewitness account of the apogee in Sino–Indian relationship in 1954 was given by Paranjpe:

> My most unforgettable memory of Mao was when he bade goodbye to Pandit Nehru. We were in Zhongnanhai at Mao's place. It was late in the evening, and the moon had come out. Mao escorted Nehru all the way to his car. While shaking Nehru's hand, he suddenly came out with two lines from the Chinese classical poet, Qu Yuan. Quoting him Mao said: "There is no greater sorrow than the sorrow of departing alive. There is no greater joy than the joy of first meeting."[3]

Nehru wrote to Burmese Prime Minister U Nu on 14 November 1954 about his visit:

> I received an extraordinarily cordial welcome everywhere in China. This was not only an official welcome but a popular welcome also in which millions joined. I was greatly impressed by it. It was clear to me that this welcome represented something more than political exigency. It was almost an emotional upheaval representing the basic urges of the people for friendship with India.[4]

From this "spring" in 1954, mutual relations nose-dived to their nadir on 6 October 1962 when Mao mockingly described Nehru's personal attitude during the meeting of China's Central Military Commission (CMC) chaired by Lin Bao:

> We fought a war with old Chiang. We fought a war with Japan, and with America. With none of these we fear. And in each case we won. Now the Indians want to fight a war with us. Naturally, we don't have fear. We cannot give ground, once we give ground it would be tantamount to letting them seize a big piece of land equivalent to Fujian province ... Since Nehru sticks his head out and insists on us fighting him, for us not to fight with him would not be friendly enough. Courtesy emphasizes reciprocity.[5]

## Nehru's internationalism

Even before independence, Nehru's thinking on foreign policy was based on a post-colonial Asian resurgence led by a free India and a free China. Nehru did not have any special preference for Communists in China as is alleged by his critics. Like US Presidents F.D. Roosevelt and Harry Truman he believed that the picture of the emerging China was not complete without Communists.

Nehru was equally at ease with the Kuomintang which represented their government since 1925. Kuomintang China had carried on relationship with the Indian National Congress during 1937–42.[6] This process had started after Nehru met them in Brussels during the Anti-Colonial Congress in February 1927. Nehru was elected as one of the vice-presidents of the Congress. A Sino–Indian declaration of solidarity was passed at the Congress on his initiative.[7]

Chiang Kai-Shek had visited India (5–21 February 1942) which coincided with the fall of Singapore on 15 February 1942. Chiang thought that he could make use of this and put some sense into the thinking of British colonial mind to give more freedom to India. Nehru had taken the lead in Chiang's talks with Congress leaders as he had already met him in China in 1939. Details of this visit were given in the previous chapter.

US State Department archives mention that Chiang had communicated directly to President Roosevelt and to the American Ambassador in China his views on India at that moment of a "critical political and military situation in India" and the need to impress upon Britain to solve the political problem. He sent another urgent confidential message to President Roosevelt urging him to advise Britain and India to seek a reasonable and satisfactory solution. Prime Minister Winston Churchill, however, replied that the British Government did not agree with Chiang's assessment of the situation. In fact, he requested the US President to persuade Chiang to cease activities on India and that Roosevelt should not permit pressure to be put on the British Government.[8]

## Apogee of India's diplomacy under Nehru

It would not be wrong to say that New Delhi was the pivot of international diplomacy in those days, whether it was resistance against colonialism or the conclusion of the Korean armistice between China and the United States in 1952, India's role as chair of the International Commission for Supervision and Control (ICSC) on Indochina or the successful release of four American airmen held captive by Communist China in 1955 when US efforts through the United Nations had failed. In addition, US President J.F. Kennedy had considered the posting of an American ambassador to New Delhi as very important not only for consulting Nehru on key international issues but also because an Indian diplomat was always the chair of the ICSC on Indochina. He therefore personally selected his advisor Professor J.K. Galbraith for the job in 1961.

In 1949 Nehru had led international resistance against the Dutch on Indonesia's behalf by organising the fifteen-nation conference including Australia which concluded that the Dutch military action launched on 18 December 1948 on Indonesia was against the UN Charter and against UN resolutions. The conference demanded that all Dutch troops were withdrawn, and an interim government should be formed by 15 March 1949.[9]

Along with diplomatic action Nehru also undertook covert action by secretly airlifting Indonesian resistance leader Sukarno and another colleague from a remote hideout in Indonesia in 1948 and flying them to India, outraging the Dutch colonialists. The dare-devil pilot who did this was Biju Patnaik, a former Royal Indian Airforce pilot who later became the Chief Minister of Orissa.[10]

A wrong impression was created in India and abroad that Nehru was "soft" on Communist China. True, India was among the first countries to recognize the government of the People's Republic of China in 1950. It was only a pragmatic decision knowing well how the Kuomintang had collapsed. Also, he was clear that India could not afford participating in any hostilities to the liking of the Western Bloc, more particularly the US–UK initiated "Cold War" against Communism.

This was evident from Nehru's discussions in New Delhi with two-time US Ambassador to India Chester Bowles. Bowles, who had worked closely with the Roosevelt and Truman administrations, was selected by President Harry Truman in 1951 as ambassador to India, then the most important Asian country after the collapse of

Kuomintang China. He held two terms, during 1951–53 and from 1963 to 1969 when he worked with four prime ministers: Nehru, Gulzarilal Nanda, Lal Bahadur Shastri and Indira Gandhi.

Nine months before his arrival in New Delhi the National Security Council, the highest policy-making body in US, had outlined US policy towards South Asia. It reflected the Truman administration's fears in Asia following "the loss of China" and Communist invasions of South Korea and Tibet as well as tensions in Indochina. It called for marshalling "South Asia's political and resource potential on the side of United States" (to fight Communism).[11]

Ambassador Howard B. Schaffer, who had written Bowles' biography, quotes the US administration's paranoia of Communism during that era. President Truman told Bowles when he called on him for a final briefing after his Senate confirmation: "The first thing you've got to do is to find out if Nehru is a Communist. He sat right on that chair, and he talked just like a Communist." Truman was referring to his discussions when Nehru visited United States in 1949.

*Politico* had described this visit: "Nehru's session with Truman proved to be a flop; the president declined to offer U.S. economic aid to a nation that recently emerged from British colonial rule and had proclaimed itself neutral in the developing Cold War with the Soviet Union."[12]

Bowles discussed the situation in Asia with Nehru soon after he assumed charge in October 1951. All these were conveyed to Washington, DC through confidential diplomatic telegrams. Nehru's prediction on the eventual split between the Soviet Union and China and that Western countries should find a way to bring China into the mainstream came to be realised by America only in 1972 when US President Richard Nixon made his epoch-making visit to Beijing.

Nehru started his discussions with Bowles on the post-colonial economic realities facing India which wanted to pursue an independent and democratic path. Nehru emphasised that India's emphasis on economic development ruled out a major arms build-up because of a resources crunch and hence "it would have to find a basis for compromise with China in the Himalayan areas." In making this assessment Nehru was also guided by the spectacular Chinese victory in the Korean War over US-led forces, the most powerful army in the world, which was evident in the same month.

Bowles also reported that Nehru had taken special precautions to bolster India's position not through military strength but by "negotiating new security treaties with the small Himalayan states that lay between India and its possibly ambitious northern neighbour." This is because Nehru was aware of the historical fact that "strong central governments in China had often sought to extend their power into adjoining regions." Bowles was referring to the 1949 treaty of "friendship' with Bhutan, the "Indo–Nepal Treaty of Peace and Friendship" and a similar treaty with Sikkim in 1950 over a special relationship with India.[13]

Additionally, Nehru wanted the United States to understand "democratic India's inability to force its people to make the sacrifices the People's Republic could demand of its population." He wanted US economic assistance to "fill the gap between the two countries' capacity to mobilise resources." Bowles cited the statement of Paul Gray Hoffman, first administrator of the Economic Cooperation Administration under the Marshall Plan, saying that "India stood in 1952 where China had in 1945" and "if the United States were to fail in India as it had in China, the results could even more disastrous to its global interests."

On China, Nehru's strategic predictions were that "it was potentially aggressive and expansionist" even though it lacked resources "to take on more than it was already doing." He felt that the Soviets would try to use China to enter into more adventures in other parts of Asia although it "had been hurt in Korea." Nehru felt that the best hope was to attempt to divide Russia and China. If this was not possible, the West should convince China that "it did not need to depend entirely on Russia." Hence the best interests of India, the US and the entire world were to keep the door open to China.

During the next meeting in February 1952, Nehru told Bowles that eventually China might show to the Soviets that "she was not going to be a pliant partner." In July 1952 he told him that Sino–

Soviet association "could not last for more than a few years." He added that there may be more chance of "China running Russia twenty years from today than Russia running China."[14] Compare this with what Kevin Rudd, one of the best China watchers, had said on 25 February 2022 in the *Australian Financial Review* that Putin had "signed on Xi's global agenda" at the Putin–Xi summit of 4 February 2022.[15]

All these would reveal Nehru's sagacity on foreign policy matters, his far sightedness on the future China–Soviet relationship and its impact on the democratic world at a time when the West was blind to realities in the emerging post-colonial countries.

Nehru's consistent policy in accommodating China and bringing it into the global mainstream should be viewed against this paradigm which he unveiled to Chester Bowles. Even before V.K. Krishna Menon came onto the scene, India's ambassador in Peking "Sardar" K.M. Panikkar had been the unofficial intermediary between Zhou Enlai, India and the US. Panikkar had warned the West that China would enter the Korean War if UN forces crossed the thirty-eighth parallel in Korea. India had also opposed efforts to condemn China for its "aggression" when even the US administration knew that it was General MacArthur who had "widened" the war without the President's authorisation.[16]

India's action in sponsoring Communist China to be a permanent member of the UN Security Council in 1950 in place of Kuomintang China rankles several commentators even now. Some Indian commentators had also felt that India should have accepted the US offer to take Kuomintang China's place.

The Woodrow Wilson International Center's March 2015 case study "Not at the Cost of China: New evidence regarding US proposals to Nehru for joining the United Nations Security council" perhaps highlights Nehru's compulsions:

> Nehru's rejection of the US offer underlined the consistency of his conviction that the PRC's legitimate interests must be acknowledged in order to reduce international tensions. Integrating the PRC into the international community by conceding its right to the Chinese seat at the Security Council was in fact a central pillar of Nehru's foreign policy. Nehru's

skepticism about accepting this offer, and thereby disrupting the dynamics of the UN, revealed the reverence he had for the international organization, despite its flaws.[17]

## Indian diplomacy during and after the Korean War

In Korea, the US military leadership was completely flummoxed when Communist forces were seen not merely reinforcing the defeated North Koreans but were, in fact, "taking over the war." Also, instead of 17,000 Chinese troops as General MacArthur's intelligence had projected, as many as 180,000 PLA soldiers entered North Korea, stealthily moving by night when American aerial reconnaissance could not detect them.[18]

The Korean War started on 25 June 1950 when North Korean troops invaded South Korea. The UN Security Council condemned this invasion and formed a twenty-one-nation UN force to help the besieged South Korea. US elements made up 90 per cent of this formation. India did not join the UN force but sent a medical mission comprising the 60th Parachute Field Ambulance.

By September, the UN and South Korean forces were on the verge of defeat. Then they decided to do a risky amphibious assault in the Battle of Incheon (10–19 September) by invading North Korea. They were progressing towards Yalu River bordering China.

However, the entry of Chinese "Peoples' Volunteer Army" (PVA) on 19 October changed the tide. Chinese forces pushed out the UN and South Korean forces. They were in South Korea by late December. The South Korean capital was captured four times. The war was disastrous for the UN forces and the USA leading to the dismissal of General MacArthur by US President Harry Truman in April 1951.

President Dwight D. Eisenhower who was elected in 1952 tried to end the ruinous war and had to seek help from "neutral nations" (Czechoslovakia, Poland, Sweden, Switzerland, and India). The armistice agreement signed in July 1953 ended the Korean War. Members of the "Neutral" nations chose India to head the Neutral Nations Repatriation Commission (NNRC) to supervise the exchange of Prisoners of War (POW).

Lieutenant General K.S. Thimmaya as Chairman of the Commission—assisted by Major General S.S.P. Thorat who headed an Indian Brigade Group, designated as Custodian Forces–India (CFI), comprising 5230 personnel—won great praise from all parties. The 60th Indian Field Ambulance was merged with the CFI which took charge of over 25,000 POWs and assisted in their repatriation. Some of the POWs who refused to be repatriated were assisted in migration to neutral nations of their choice.[19] The NNRC was dissolved in 1954.

However, China did not release all POWs. A report in *New York Times* (18 June 1955) said that fifty-one American soldiers were still held by China. This was after V.K. Krishna Menon had met President Eisenhower in June 1955. It said: "Mr. Krishna Menon obviously has been working on the matter and some claim is made that it was his diplomacy, rather than Mr. Hammarskjöld's (UN Secretary General), that resulted in the release of the four officers."[20]

Senior Congress leader and Member of Parliament Jairam Ramesh has given encyclopaedic details on how this happened in his massive tome on the life of V.K. Krishna Menon, who was helping Nehru in these delicate missions. Especially on American pilots, Menon would meet US President Eisenhower twice in three months and US Secretary of State John Foster Dulles, his bitter critic, six times![21]

Krishna Menon's first meeting with the US President was on 15 March 1955. Nine days later he met the Secretary of State, the first of several meetings with him. Since the US did not want to talk directly with the Chinese, Menon undertook that responsibility. After the Bandung Conference (18–24 April 1955), Zhou Enlai invited Menon to visit China. His visit took place from 12 May 1955.

Menon had six rounds of talks with Zhou Enlai on the release of US pilots as well as on the problems created by Communist shelling of Chinese offshore islands Quemoy and Matsu "which had alarmed the US." He also met Chairman Mao. Ramesh says that Mao had written to Menon sixteen years earlier thanking him for organising medical relief for the "beleaguered Chinese Army."

Menon returned to India on 26 May. He stopped over in Hong Kong on his return trip to India but kept mum when queried by the media on his successful efforts to release American pilots. "He became animated only when asked about Chairman Mao's health, which was then the subject of much speculation, and responded by saying that 'he thought Mao appeared in far better health that he (Menon) himself'."[22] On 27 May Nehru conveyed to US president Eisenhower about Menon's successful visit to China and their decision to release the four airmen. "Eisenhower thanked Nehru a day later and 'expressed willingness to have Menon to come to Washington for informal and private talks'."

The transcripts of Menon's six meetings with Zhou Enlai for eighteen hours ran into a "hundred and fifty pages." Apart from the subject of US airmen, the dialogue focussed on normalisation of Sino–US relations. Zhou suggested that in the first stage, contacts between China and the US could take place in Moscow, New Delhi, and London through their respective representatives there. However, he insisted that Menon would have to be a "go-between" because he understood "the situation of different parties."

Secretary of State Dulles wrote to Nehru on 29 May 1955 appreciating Menon's efforts "to put the relations between Communist China and the USA on a basis which will be free from the threat of the use of force." He also indicated that he would be most happy to meet Menon again.

On 30 May 1955 Krishna Menon announced at a press conference in New Delhi the imminent release of the four pilots. Ramesh said that the Chinese government officially corroborated what Menon had said. The pilots were released in Hongkong the next day. Menon went to Washington, DC on 14 June 1955 and met Dulles and Eisenhower. The president asked him whether he would "mind having your picture taken with us?" This photo is published in Ramesh's book.[23]

### Why then did Sino–Indian relations deteriorate?

Many theories have been suggested on why Sino-Indian relations suddenly deteriorated from the mid-50s. The oldest thesis, widely accepted from the 1960s, was because of differences over Tibet. However, in the first decade of the twenty-first century certain new documents emerged giving different reasons.

## Roots of differences go back to the "Panchsheel" treaty (1954) and Bandung Conference (1955)[24]

According to the Indian Ministry of External Affairs it was Premier Zhou En-Lai who suggested the Five Principles of Peaceful Co-existence for the first time while opening the bilateral talks between China and India on the relations between the two countries over the "Tibet region of China":[25] Mutual respect for each other's territorial integrity and sovereignty; mutual non-aggression; mutual non-interference; equality and mutual benefit; and peaceful co-existence.[26]

Ambassador N. Raghavan, leader of the Indian delegation welcomed the Five Principles saying that although India had not formulated these principles as the Chinese side had done, she had been following them as the basis of her foreign policy since she attained Independence. He suggested, at the concluding session of the talks, that the principles should be incorporated in the preamble of the agreement on Trade and Intercourse between India and the Tibet region. That was how the "Panchsheel" appeared in a document on international relations for the first time on 29 April 1954.

However Rosie Tan Segil in a Salem State University dissertation in 2015 has argued that certain practical realities were ignored while signing the "Agreement on Trade and Intercourse between the Tibet Region of China and India" on 29 April 1954 in Beijing between Indian ambassador Raghavan and Chinese Deputy Foreign Minister Chang Han-fu.

These principles were reiterated during Zhou's visit to India on 28 June 1954, which caused considerable euphoria when "Hindi-Chini-Bhai-Bhai" (India and China are brothers) slogans reverberated. In their joint statement Nehru and Zhou felt that "Panchsheel" provided "an alternative ideology dedicated to peace and development of all as the basis for international interaction, whether bilateral or multilateral." Segil argues that this treaty, through which India had relinquished its extraterritorial rights over Tibet, could not bring in peace on its borders as "it did not address the physical and geographic delineation of their shared 2,500 miles of contiguous borders from the west to the east end of the Indo–Tibetan borders."

True, "*Panchsheel*" became a "watermark in international cooperation" and was "hailed as one of the major foreign policy achievements for India." The Third World countries were the first to endorse *Panchsheel*. However, it failed to address the specific China–India border problem due to conflicting perceptions on their borderlands and territorial integrity. Also, "Nehru's inclination to support Asian fraternity came into direct conflict with the national prerequisites of security and boundary setting designed to uphold India's vital national interests."[27]

The second reason why conflicts arose, according to Segil, was during the 1955 Bandung Conference, which was again hailed as the pinnacle of Sino–Indian relations. However, under that façade, deep fault lines had appeared among the five Colombo Powers, who were the prime movers of the Conference, on their core interests:

> For India, Bandung was a forum to promote Panchsheel as an alternative to military blocs of the Cold War. Kotelawala of Ceylon was concerned about the big Indian population inside of his country and the threat of subverting its sovereignty. An anti-communist, he would rattle the committee by raising the controversial issue of defining communism as the new form of colonialism in Bandung. Sympathizing with the PRC, Burma, India, and Indonesia wanted to encourage China's independence from the Soviet Union and end her isolation. Indonesia hoped to gather support for its claims over West Irian (West Papua) against the Dutch. Pakistan, a staunch US ally, was prepped up to counter any communist gain in the conference; was ready to voice out her security concern over India, the fate of the Palestine state, and generally of the Arab world.

According to this paper Nehru himself, who was disillusioned with the poor prospects of Asian solidarity with "*Panchsheel*" as a binding glue, gravitated more towards "non-alignment" which was the theme in the 1961 Belgrade Conference. In that process he differed with China over the convening of a Second Bandung Conference. Segil quotes the transcripts of a conversation between Syrian Foreign Minister and Chinese ambassador on the subject: "India was not enthusiastic over the prospect of a Second Bandung Conference, because the Chinese Communists were pressing for such a conference." The memo continued, "The prime minister [Nehru] compared this situation to the fist Bandung at that time the Arab states had wished to utilize it in their dispute with Israel. He added he made himself unpopular at the time of the first conference with his insistence that local issues be left aside."[28]

I would however argue that the eagerness with which Nehru had first embraced "*Panchsheel*" by glossing over the China–India differences over the boundary lines was to allow enough time to achieve his priority on India's economic development as he had explained to Chester Bowles in October 1951. He knew that he would tie his government into knots had he initially agreed to delineation of the vast and contentious boundary lines as he was well aware of the expansionist nature of the new regime in China.

On the contrary, "*Panchsheel*" offered China a flexible and convenient excuse to stick to their own interpretations and pressurise other countries when occasions demanded, as a CIA assessment in 1969 made at the height of Sino–Soviet border clashes had indicated: "The Chinese have successfully exploited this artificial territorial issue for six years and clearly intend to keep it alive for use in future polemics."[29]

The Sino–Soviet border dispute began in the 1670s/1680s with the Cossacks–Manchu (Qing dynasty) wars over a Cossack settlement in Nerchinsk on Amur River basin. Gradually Russians expanded settlements on the Amur River and islands and created an enclave on Bear Island, which Russians called "Great Ussuri" while Chinese name is "Heixiazi." During the Boxer rebellion (1899–1901) the Russians killed thousands of Chinese on the Amur's banks. Almost 64 villages were wiped out.

It did not change even with the Communist takeover of China in 1949. Instead, things deteriorated when Nikita Khrushchev set in motion his "De-Stalinization" programme which was criticized by Mao. Bilateral relations nose-dived when Mao condemned Khrushchev's "adventurism" in the 1962 Cuban Missile crisis.

Nehru knew this trend in Mao's thinking and his plans to regain China's lost territories. His caution against China was vindicated by developments on the Sino–Soviet front after his death.

In 1967 clashes began when the Soviets intercepted and turned back a Chinese vessel passing through Amur to the Ussuri River. They blockaded the Amur–Ussuri confluence, preventing civilian use. They rejected the Chinese claim on Bear Island. The Chinese initially started with passive resistance which earned international publicity. A serious armed clash occurred on 2 March 1969, on "Zhenbao" island ("Damanskii" in Russian). The Chinese captured the island killing fifty-nine Soviet soldiers and suffering the loss of twenty-nine PLA troops.

The CIA paper had said that the Soviets were wrong in assessing that Mao would agree to negotiate by "Selective military punishment" whereas he was "willing to accept more punishment ... and was prepared to live with a tense border situation indefinitely."

The Soviets were alarmed. Efforts by Brezhnev to condemn China through the Warsaw Pact on 17 March failed due to Nicolae Ceausescu's (Romania) objection. On 21 March Prime Minister Alexie Kosygin tried to telephone Mao but was not connected. Beijing made Moscow wait for six months before starting negotiations. It did not even allow Kosygin to overfly their territory to return home after the funeral of Ho Chi Minh in September 1969. He had to divert his flight to Calcutta. However, he flew to Beijing from Calcutta after receiving news from Beijing through an Indian channel that Mao was prepared to talk.

Gradually the Soviets started accepting the Chinese position of basing the border negotiations on the 1860 Treaty of Peking and that the Thalweg principle should be accepted. In 1976 they lifted the Bear Island blockade. In July 1986 Mikhail Gorbachev made his historic speech at Vladivostok that "Amur frontier should not be a frontier but a means of uniting Chinese and Soviet people." He also said that the official border could pass along the mainstream, thus repealing the 1861 Kazakeevich line. However, during negotiations, he indicated that claims on Bear Island were "non-negotiable."

Nehru's caution against armed confrontation with the Chinese in Tibet in 1950 was because of this. This is often forgotten by his critics.

## Mao's suspicion of an American–Soviet–Indian arc developing against China

Nikita Khrushchev visited Beijing on 2 October 1959 to meet Mao. Their talks were "heated." Khrushchev, after differing with him on Taiwan, turned to India and Tibet: "If you let me, I will tell you what a guest should not say—the events in Tibet are your fault....We believe that the events in Tibet are the fault of the Communist Party of China, not Nehru's fault."[30] Mao considered this as another instance of an anti-China "arc" developing through an America–India–Soviet Union axis.

Sino–Soviet relations were further strained when China refused to endorse the principle of "Peaceful Coexistence" enunciated by Khrushchev on behalf of the Soviet Communist Party during the Bucharest Communist Parties' conference in June 1960. Only the Albanian delegation supported China. That was the first sign of a Sino–Soviet split. China's Deputy Premier Li Fuchun countered in the *Peking Review* of 23 August that "Modern revisionists [i.e., Soviet leaders] since 1958 have launched movements in an effort to isolate us, but they will only isolate themselves." After this Khrushchev started withdrawing thousands of Soviet technicians from China.[31]

It is for this reason that Zhou Enlai had denounced Khrushchev for inciting Nehru to "attack" China during his talks with US President Nixon on 23 February 1972. He told Nixon:

> Actually that event was instigated by Khrushchev...In looking at 1962, the events actually began in 1959.... In June of that year, before he went to Camp David, he tore up the nuclear agreements between China and Soviet Union. And after that there were clashes between Chinese and Indian troops in the Western part

of Sinkiang, the Ak-sai Chin area.... But the Tass agency said that China had committed aggression against India.[32]

Kissinger made no attempt to correct Zhou that he was chronologically wrong regarding the Ladakh incident. Khrushchev visited the US for thirteen days from 15 to 27 September 1959 as President Dwight Eisenhower's guest. It also included their talks at Camp David. The Chinese aggression in Ladakh took place on 21 October 1959 in which they killed ten CRPF men. No one in India had imagined the intensity of Chinese anger until these declassified records were published in 2002.

Introducing an e-dossier prepared for the Wilson Center, Austin Jersild explains the significance of this tearing up of nuclear co-operation between China and Soviet Union as mentioned by Zhou:[33] Originally China had willingly cooperated with Soviet Union on strategic cooperation for joint defence against "imperialist powers" including the development of nuclear technology, establishing long-wave radio receiving stations along the China coast, sharing uranium, and allowing Soviet experts to set up their defence industries. In return China wanted Moscow to modify their newly declared "reformist foreign policy" of peaceful coexistence with the Western bloc, as well as disarmament and arms control negotiations with USA and UK after Stalin's death. Mao sincerely believed that America must be punished for supporting the Kuomintang during the civil war and for supporting Taiwan. He believed that both the Soviet Union and China did not have to fear Western nuclear bombs as a "nuclear exchange was survivable for the socialist bloc" as "a significant loss of population does not necessarily mean the destruction of the nation."

This was the basis of the deep ideological differences between the Soviet Union and China leading to the Soviet abrogation of about six nuclear agreements with China on 20 June 1959. China defiantly continued its research and development and detonated their own atom bomb in Lop Nor in Xinjiang in October 1964.[34]

*Intelligence activities against China and Mao: India caught in the middle*

Originally Mao had accepted in principle Soviet intelligence officials training his intelligence staff. At that time, he was not the undisputed Chinese Communist leader. In the beginning the Comintern was not too sure whether the Chinese "Bolsheviks" (future Communists) would capture power in a vast country like China. Hence, they adopted a two-pronged policy of supporting Sun Yat-sen (Kuomintang) through their Dutch communist representative Henk Sneevliet whose pseudonym was "Maring."

Lenin's idea was to unite "leftist" oriented nationalists (Kuomintang and Chinese "Bolsheviks") in China and eventually turn the huge country Communist. Thus the "Cheka" (later GPU, KGB) started directing "Bolsheviks" while the Red Army's intelligence service GRU began training Kuomintang. While the Cheka started stationing its "residents," GRU used their military attachés for the same purpose. This the Communists willingly accepted.

However, Mao was furious when he learnt that Stalin had asked his spy chief Lavrentiy Beria to secretly spy on him during the Chinese Civil War. Hence, he was happy that Khrushchev had removed Beria and executed him in 1953.[35] To his disappointment, he felt that Khrushchev also continued spying on China and the relationship soured.

India was caught in the middle with the Tibet imbroglio. At a time when China felt that an Indian–Soviet–American axis was slowly developing with India's help, Beijing found that the CIA had started a covert programme to help Tibetan rebels by supplying 250 tons of munitions and equipment between 1957 and 1961.[36]

*Jean Pasqualini's case*

Further evidence of this axis, according to Mao, was Jean Pasqualini's case. No China watcher in India has till now connected this with Mao's anger against India. Pasqualini, a Corsican Chinese journalist, son of a Corsican father and Chinese mother, became famous for publishing a book, *Prisoner of Mao*, in 1973 as a first-person account of the horrors of the Chinese penal system. However, he was also a self-confessed spy. He was imprisoned between 1957 and 1964 as a British spy. He was released only after General Charles de Gaulle established diplomatic relations with the PRC in 1964, as demanded by China. He had worked as a translator for the United States military and the British Embassy before the Communist Party came to power in 1949. *The New York Times*, writing his obituary in 1997, said that his interrogation, "during which he was forced to write a 700-page confession, lasted 15 months was so intense that it left him begging to be sent to a labor camp."[37]

French writer Roger Faligot, in his book *Les services secrets chinois* has mentioned that Pasqualini had told him that his spying activities had "Indian connections." The Chinese services had charged him for working for the French foreign intelligence service. Pasqualini told Faligot that he was actually working for MI-6 but had never met his "handlers" Edward Youde and later John Fretwell.

However, both these officers were not known to be connected with intelligence services. Sir Youde was later the British ambassador to China in 1974 and the highly popular governor of Hong Kong from 1982 who signed the 1984 declaration on the British leaving Hong Kong in 1997. Sir John Fretwell went on to become the British ambassador to France.

Pasqualini told Faligot: "I never had any direct contact with them. I used to bring my information to the Indian High Commission in Beijing, which was collaborating with the British. It was more discreet."[38]

A clue to this could be found in Christopher Andrew's authorized history of MI-5 *The Defence of the Realm: The Authorized History of MI-5*. He had said that Guy Liddel, Deputy Director of MI-5 had obtained an unwritten agreement from all colonies like India that were getting independence that they would allow the stationing of a security liaison from MI-5 in their capitals to work closely with their intelligence agencies. It is not clear whether this arrangement extended to overseas missions.[39]

Did Pasqualini's confession in 1957 of using the Indian embassy as the "drop box" for British intelligence directly contribute to intensifying the Mao regime's paranoid feelings against Jawaharlal Nehru, augmented by his close friendship with Khrushchev and resulting in such hatred?

## Not understanding Chinese negotiating techniques

The book *The Chinese at the Negotiating Table*, published in 1994 by the US National Defense University, gives details of Chinese mental orientations and strategy. It was written by Dr Alfred D. Wilhelm Jr. who was Vice-President of the Atlantic Council. The preface is by Ambassador Alexis Johnson who, as US Ambassador to Czechoslovakia (1953–58), had negotiated with Mao's Communists at Geneva and Warsaw before diplomatic relations were started in 1979 after President Nixon's 1972 visit to Beijing.[40]

The fundamental premise under which Mao's China defined its relationship with others was that China, "after 100 years of suffering and humiliation due to Western imperialism," would not allow any "relationship that might appear to subordinate China's interests—political, ideological, economic, cultural or military— to any big power or bloc of powers." Mao expected other countries to conform to China's norms and values as even during the declining years of the Qing dynasty (1644–1912) they did not make many institutional changes.

China would uphold the principle of "equality and mutual benefit" adding that the "door swings inward more than outward." Based on this principle, the PRC did not classify America as a "friend" even in 1984, five years after normalization of relations, even when the Soviet Union was perceived as the principal threat.

The PRC's relationship with the Soviet Union deteriorated when the Soviet Union made unilateral compromises with the USA, violating Marxist-Leninist principles. China suffered as "surrogate" of Moscow during the Korean War whereas Soviet support was non-existent during the 1958 Taiwan Straits Crisis and during the 1962 Sino–Indian War.

In the Chinese lexicon different words are used to describe relationships with countries for negotiations: "*Tanpan*" suggests that both parties, even if hostile, are committed to see that the situation does not get worse. "*Huitan*" is used for normalization talks, and connotes trust with no hostility. "*Huishang*" is used between friendly countries. "*Xieshang*" connotes a greater level of trust and is used for "consulting."

This formula explains why the PRC specifically preferred Pakistan as the vehicle for secret talks to facilitate Kissinger's secret visit in July 1971 to pave the way for President Richard Nixon's path-breaking visit to Beijing in 1972. Kissinger had tried two other channels—through China's "friend" Romanian President Nicolae Ceausescu, and through the Chinese ambassador in Paris who was a "Long March" veteran.

In 1971 and 1972 China considered India as the Soviet Union's surrogate as the transcripts of the Zhou–Enlai–Kissinger and Zhou–Enlai–Nixon talks would indicate. Zhou particularly condemned Nehru for claiming "their" Aksai-Chin plateau from 1956 onwards under Nikita Khrushchev's instigation. In 1972 Zhou included Mrs Indira Gandhi among China's adversaries for threatening Pakistan. It was only in 1988 that India's status was upgraded for "*Huitan*"-level talks after the successful Rajiv Gandhi visit. This status was lost in 1998 when Prime Minister Vajpayee's ill-advised letter to President Bill Clinton blaming China for India's nuclear tests was leaked and published by *The New York Times* on 13 May 1998.

The point is, did Indian negotiators ever study Wilhelm's valuable book before undertaking negotiations with China, especially since India's senior border negotiating teams were mostly headed by police officers and not by career diplomats? Did we understand their minds?

*Tibet*

The common theory is that Sino–Indian differences had started over Tibet, after the PRC occupied Tibet on 6–7 October 1950. India had then sent a strong protest note to the Chinese foreign office on 26 October 1950:

In the context of world events, invasion by Chinese troops of Tibet cannot but be regarded as deplorable and in the considered judgment of the Government of India, not in the interest of China or peace.

After 1947, India had been treating Tibet as an independent country. Tibet was invited by New Delhi to send an independent delegation for the Asian Relations Conference in March–April 1947. Hence a note was also sent to the Tibetan government simultaneously on October 26:

> The Government of India would be glad to have an assurance that it is the intention of the Tibetan government to continue relations on the existing basis until new arrangements are reached that either party may wish to take up. This is the procedure adopted by all other countries with which India has inherited treaty relations from His Majesty's Government.[41]

Tibet's independent status was recognised even when the nationalist government of China invited Nepal and Tibet to join China after the fall of the Manchus in 1911. Both refused. American correspondent Edgar Snow, who was very close to Mao and feted as a "Friend of China," had quoted him in his classic 1937 book *Red Star Over China* telling him during the Long March that "some day they would have to pay their 'foreign debt' to Tibet for the provisions and shelter we received from them."[42]

After the invasion, China forced Tibet to sign the seventeen-point 23 May 1951 agreement under duress, by which Tibet was forced to accept the status as a "region of China under Chinese suzerainty and absolute control." Along with that China started what was called a "cartographic aggression" on India, publishing some maps of the PRC incorporating nearly 50,000 square miles of Indian territory in the present Arunachal Pradesh, then Northeast Frontier Agency, and in Ladakh.

It was indeed surprising that this happened during the Sino–Indian "bonhomie" which marked the 1954 visit of Nehru. In fact, Nehru discussed the subject of these maps with Premier Zhou Enlai during this visit. The latter assured him that the maps were of no significance as they were merely a "reproduction" of the old Kuomintang maps. Subsequent developments on the ground belied this assurance.

Chinese troops continued to intrude into Indian territory not only in the eastern and middle sectors of the border but also, more heavily, into the western sector. This was after the full military occupation of the whole of Tibet. In 1957–58 they constructed a highway connecting Tibet to Sinkiang across the Aksai Chin region of north-eastern Ladakh in the Indian state of Jammu and Kashmir. They consolidated their hold further by occupying the fort of Khurnak in Ladakh in July 1958.

Till 2006 no credible explanation was forthcoming why this happened especially when India was chaperoning China to the international arena, according to the script revealed by Nehru to Ambassador Chester Bowles in 1951. Most of the assessments by scholars on China were based on the writings of Neville Maxwell and Allen Whiting echoing the Chinese version that China wanted to "punish" an "expansionist" India for collusion with America in "undermining Chinese control of Tibet."

There is no need to dwell on Neville Maxwell's theory as it is well known in India. The way Zhou Enlai had used it extensively to base his complaints against India's so-called "aggression" in his talks with President Richard Nixon on 23 February 1972 during his secret visit to Beijing, would show Maxwell's role as a propagandist for the PRC.[43] These papers were declassified only in 2003.

Similarly, a 1977 review of Whiting's book *The Chinese Calculus of Deterrence: India & Indochina* (1975) had said:

> To be sure, it makes a bit too much use of content analysis, tends to take Peking's propaganda statements at face value…and relies unduly on the excessively anti-Indian account of Neville Maxwell…[44]

In 2006 Stanford University published the volume *New Directions in the Study of China's Foreign Policy*, with a chapter "China's Decision for War with India in 1962" by well-known China specialist John W. Garver containing a composite analysis of Indian and Chinese documents on the subject. Garver is Professor Emeritus in the Sam Nunn School of International Affairs at the Georgia Institute of Technology. This paper offers fresh insights into the Chinese reasons for going to war when the bilateral relationship was mostly friendly during the first half of 1950s.

Garver says that Chinese documents published since the 1990s "allow us to go inside the Chinese decision-making process in a way that was not possible in 1962." He says that despite the PRC occupying Tibet and notwithstanding India's strong protests on 26 October 1950 at the takeover, India's overt actions towards China were conciliatory and not hostile.

Even in October 1950 India refused to sponsor a Tibetan appeal to the United Nations. When El Salvador sponsored that appeal "India played a key role in squashing it." Many governments, including the US, Britain and Middle East governments followed India's initiative. In 1954 India formally recognised China's "ownership" of Tibet. Yet Chinese suspicions were not assuaged.

According to the history published by the PLA, Nehru's objective was the creation of a "great Indian empire" by filling the vacuum left by the British in 1947. Incidentally this was the same language used by Zhou on 23 February 1972 during his talks with Nixon: "Yes, he was thinking of a great Indian empire: Malaysia, Ceylon etc. It would probably also include our Tibet."

Zhou's interpretation was based on a deliberate misreading of Nehru's *Discovery of India* in which Nehru had described ancient India's cultural relations with Central Asia and the "Far East." Another reason was Professor Xu Yan's theory that Nehru wanted Tibet to be a "buffer-zone" like the British imperialists. Xu Yan was described as "one of China's foremost military historians" by Garver who also quotes Wang Hongwei of the Chinese Academy of Social Science who argued that Nehru was deeply influenced by the British policy objective of keeping Tibet under "India's sphere of influence."

After the Lhasa's uprising on 10 March 1959, which attributed to India's help to the CIA's covert operations in the Kham region, the Chinese "central cadres" met in Shanghai on 25 March when Mao quoted "*guo xing bu yi*—to do evil deeds frequently brings ruin to the evil doer" and told them that China would not condemn India openly, but would "settle accounts later."[45]

The Chinese reaction came gradually. On 19 April Mao personally ordered Xinhua to attack Indian expansionists when the Tibetan exodus began. On 25 April he told the Polit Bureau Standing Committee that criticism against Nehru "should be sharp, don't fear to irritate him" as he had miscalculated the situation, believing that "China would have had to seek India's help to suppress the rebellion in Tibet."

*Renmin Ribao* (People's Daily) carried it on 6 May 1959. Zhou followed this line and told an assembly of socialist countries that Nehru represented the Indian "upper class" who opposed reforms in Tibet. They had inherited the British policy on Tibet and sympathised with the serf-owners.

As already noted, Mao was irritated with Nikita Khrushchev's defence of Nehru during his talks on 2 October 1959 in Beijing. Mao rejected it saying, "The Hindus acted in Tibet as if it belonged to them." This line was indoctrinated into the PLA's strategic philosophy against India.

General Lei Yingfu, head of the "warfighting department," interpreted the Indian counterattack to cut off the Chinese on the Thagla Ridge as an example of this ambition. This was on 16 October 1962, two days before the Polit Bureau approved the PLA's plan of "self-defence counterattack". "Lee adduced various Indian actions of 1950, 1956, and 1959 to substantiate this proposition." Garver continues:

> The fact that China's leaders saw Indian efforts as attempts "to grab Tibet" to turn Tibet into a "buffer zone," to return Tibet to its return to its pre-1949 status, to "overthrow Chinese sovereignty" or to cause Tibet to "throw off the jurisdiction of Chinese central government" does not necessarily mean that those perceptions were accurate. In fact, this core Chinese belief was wrong. This belief, which the Chinese analysts explain, underpinned China's decision for war in 1962 was, in fact inaccurate. It was a deeply pernicious Chinese misperception that contributed powerfully to the decision for war in 1962.[46]

On the other hand, Nehru's policy was, according to Garver, to uphold Tibet's autonomy under Chinese sovereignty as part of grand accommodation between both countries leading to a global partnership between India and China. He believed that this, together with the resolution of the US–China dispute in Korea through Indian mediation, the PRC's admission to the UNSC, the peace treaty with Japan and other issues, could "create a new axis in the world politics."

Nehru was "dismayed" in 1959 over Beijing breaking of "what he believed was the agreement between him and Zhou Enlai" in 1956 whereby India agreed to recognize China's sovereignty over Tibet in exchange for China granting "a significant degree of autonomy to Tibet," accommodating India's "sentimental" and "cultural" interest.

As regards the CIA's activities in Tibet, Garver quotes a study by Steven Hoffman who concluded: "It is unclear how much India government in 1958 or 1959 knew about the major CIA program" to support the Tibetan armed resistance.[47] The same view was held by Indian intelligence chief B.N. Mullik who was told by Nehru that arming the Tibetans was "suicidal and counter-productive." Nehru felt that "peaceful, non-violent resistance" was the best way. Garver also cites Tsering Shakya in his *The Dragon in Land of Snows* that Nehru and other senior leaders were not aware of the extent of CIA's involvement in Tibet, until after the 1962 war.

On the other hand, ground-level CIA operatives on Tibet operations had confirmed that India's "Home Department" knew details of these operations. This leads one to refer to a similar remark made by Christopher Andrew in his authorised history of MI-5 regarding the Intelligence Bureau's (IB) close liaison with MI-5 on watching over Indian communists. Andrew found "a loud disconnect" between Nehru's strategic policies and the priorities pursued by the IB when Nehru was getting closer to Soviet Union in 1955.[48] Did the Indian agencies fail to keep Nehru fully informed of the CIA's activities?

Garver squarely blames Mao for this misunderstanding:

The fundamental attribution error must be laid at Mao's door. It was he who first determined, at the central meeting on 23 April 1959 that "Indian expansionists" wanted to grab Tibet.

Mao completely dominated China's foreign policy decision-making process by 1959. Once Mao made that determination, China's other leaders were compelled to chime in. Indeed, even today, China's scholars are compelled to affirm Mao's erroneous judgment.[49]

Starting from this faulty assessment that India wanted to grab Tibet, the refusal of Nehru to accept a Chinese proposal "subtly and unofficially but nevertheless effectively raised by Zhou Enlai during his April 1960 visit to India that China drop its claims in the eastern sector in exchange for India dropping its claim in the Western sector" appeared to China as part of India's "expansionist" policy since the road in Aksai Chin was strategically important to China for connectivity with Tibet.

This was followed by the second wrong conclusion that "Nehru's insistence on Chinese abandonment of Aksai Chin established a link in Chinese minds between the border issue and China's ability to control Tibet." That was not Nehru's intention. He was only defending the boundary as fixed by the 1914 Shimla Conference. Nehru's "Forward Policy" offended Mao who had in 1949 declared that "China had stood up" and it would no longer be bullied by foreign powers. "The final Chinese decision to inflict a big painful defeat on Indian forces derived substantially from a sense that only such a blow would cause India to begin taking Chinese power seriously."

Garver's paper reveals China's advance planning from mid-1962. To begin with, Beijing obtained an informal assurance from the USA with whom they were holding secret ambassadorial talks in Warsaw, that Nationalist China would not attack the PRC either directly or through Laos. Wang Bingnan, the Chinese ambassador who was holding the Warsaw talks, had written about it in his memoirs (*Zong Mei Huitan Jiunian Huigu*, "Recollections of nine years of talks Sino–American talks", 1985) in which he had mentioned that this assurance from his counterpart in Warsaw "had a big role" in China's decision-making process.

A wrong impression by Chinese foreign minister General Chen Yi, who was asked by Zhou Enlai to meet V.K. Krishna Menon during the Geneva Conference on Laos in 1962 also made the Chinese leadership feel that India was itching for a war. During the meeting on 23 July, Menon had apparently told Chen Yi "in an arrogant tone of voice" that there was no "dispute" as the location of the boundaries was clearly displayed on Indian maps and that the Chinese forces should withdraw. Chen then proposed a joint communique on future talks, which Menon refused. When Chen reported this to Zhou Enlai the latter commented: "It seems Nehru wants a war with us."

From then on, every move against India was personally approved by Mao. The final decision to "inflict a big, painful defeat on Indian forces" was taken from an assessment that "only such a blow would cause India to begin taking Chinese power seriously." Unlike America in Korea, India had failed to recognise the PLA's prowess. On the contrary Nehru was under the impression that "PLA would turn tail rather than fight."

It was at this stage that Mao, an ardent student of Chinese history, quoted archival history in support of severely punishing India during a high-level meeting on 6 October 1962. He said that China had fought "one and half" wars with India. The first war with India was in 648 CE when a "Tang dynasty emperor dispatched troops to assist a legal claimant to a throne to a subcontinental kingdom after the other claimant had killed 30 members of a Tang diplomatic mission." A Tang reinforcement force defeated the usurper, who was brought to Chang'an, the Tang capital, "where he lived out his life."

This was in or around 645 CE when Harsha's minister "A-la-na-shuen" (Arjuna or Arunasva) attacked a delegation led by Wang-hiuen-tse. Arjuna was taken to China as a prisoner where he died. Chinese accounts had then said that 12,000 prisoners and 30,000 domesticated animals were taken. "The whole India trembled, and 580 walled towns offered their submission."

The "half war" which Mao was referring was in 1348 when Timurlane captured Delhi. This, according to him, was a "half war" since Timurlane and his army were Mongols from Mongolia, then part of China, "making this attack half Chinese"![50]

Garver concludes that the "underlying" reason for China to undertake a war with India was to punish its leaders who "did not appreciate that the People's Republic of China was a 'new China' that had 'stood up' and, unlike pre-1949 'old China', could no longer be 'bullied' and 'humiliated' by foreign powers."[51]

The PLA official history on the war says that its objective of "*ba xibu bianjiang diqu xunsu wending xialai*" (quickly ensuring peaceful stable borders in the west) was achieved. From then on Indian leaders abandoned military means to achieve their objective and started looking "much more soberly and respectfully at Chinese power."

Garver needs to be complimented for exposing the "echo-chamber" decision-making processes embedded in the Chinese system during the Mao era, which will be a pointer for the country under Xi Jinping. In his book *China's Quest: The History of the Foreign Relations of the People's Republic of China* (2016) he reminds us how Mao's pre-eminence in the CCP elite was such that once he delivered a judgment, seldom was it doubted. Xi Jinping follows Mao's tradition of "assertive nationalism" in making China great again. That is the danger to India.[52]

*Role of the Indian Opposition in Parliament in 1962*

On the other hand, Nehru was subjected to savage attacks provoking India's most respected diplomat the late K.P.S Menon to remark, as quoted by Rup Narayan Das: "The entire attitude adopted by Parliament during the crises was unhelpful. Brave talks that not an inch of Indian Territory should be surrendered and so on, left the Government with no room for manoeuvring."[53]

On 4 December 1961 the late A.B. Vajpayee, then Jan Sangh leader, alleged that Nehru was suppressing information and "would even surrender Ladakh to China if similar kind of appeasement continued." P.K. Deo of the Ganatantra Parishad suggested an innovative way of dealing with the crisis by suggesting the transfer of border issue from diplomats to military leadership. Even during the war Parliament's attitude did not help war efforts. On 20 November 1962 veteran Praja Socialist Party leader

H.V. Kamath demanded that a Parliamentary Committee should supervise military operations on a daily basis as the government was incapable. Fortunately, Nehru rejected this suggestion.

On the other hand, the Opposition's obdurate stance inflamed Chinese belligerence. The 1954 Treaty of Trade and Commerce was allowed lapse in 1962. China closed their posts in Calcutta and Kalimpong in May 1962. In return India closed their agencies in Gyantse, Yatung and Gartok in June. This had a direct bearing on border tensions. By July massive military movement started on all sectors. On 8 September 1962 the Chinese crossed the McMahon line and attacked. After humiliating India, they declared a unilateral cease-fire in November and withdrew 20 kms from the LAC of 7 November 1962.

## China–India relations after 1962

Efforts initiated by Rajiv Gandhi to restore normalcy to the relationship have been narrated in the Introduction. This period after 1988 could be described as the second *sakura* season in Indo–Chinese relations till 1998 when a letter from Prime Minister Atal Bihari Vajpayee to US President Bill Clinton on 11 May 1998 justifying nuclear tests by India on the same day was leaked and published in *The New York Times* on 13 May , causing deep anger in Beijing.[54]

After Rajiv Gandhi's successful visit in 1988, six rounds of border talks were held by the Joint Working Group between 1988 and 1993. Premier Li Peng visited India in December 1991. Consulates were reopened in Mumbai and Shanghai in 1992. President R. Venkataraman visited China in May 1992 followed by Defence Minister Sharad Pawar's visit, the first by an Indian defence minister in July 1992.

In 1993 the "Agreement on the Maintenance of Peace and Tranquillity along the Line of Actual Control in the India–China Border Areas" was signed. It stipulated that pending the final settlement of the boundary, each side would respect the Line of Actual Control. In case one side crossed the line, they would pull back on being cautioned by the other. Differing views on alignment would be resolved by joint efforts. From then on Sino–Indian relations were formal and cautious though not "friendly."

### Pokharan II tests and Vajpayee's letter to President Clinton

However, the relationship sharply deteriorated after Indian nuclear tests in 1998. Initially the Chinese response on 12 May, as published by *Xinhua* to the first test, was a kind of "pro-forma" protest saying that it was detrimental to Asian peace. However, it was harsher after Vajpayee's letter was published.

In his letter Vajpayee had blamed "an overt nuclear weapon state on our borders, a state which committed armed aggression against India in 1962":

> Although our relations with that country have improved in the last decade or so, an atmosphere of distrust persists mainly due to the unresolved border problem. To add to the distrust that country has materially helped another neighbour of ours to become a covert nuclear weapons state. At the hands of this bitter neighbour we have suffered three aggressions in the last 50 years.

Chinese reaction to India's second test on 13 May was severe. It expressed "shock" and condemned the tests. After Vajpayee's letter was published, it went ballistic, not mainly through official statements but through diplomatic action and through academic writers like Ye Zhengjia who alleged that India was trying to escape Western sanctions on nuclear tests by playing the China threat card. The PLA also took to publishing academic articles through well respected forums like Stanford University's Center for International Security and Cooperation.[55]

Vajpayee's letter continued as a festering wound in Chinese minds for a long time. Professor Sun Shihai, Deputy Director of the Institute of Asia-Pacific studies under the Chinese Academy of Social Sciences, told a news channel on 19 November 2006 that the Vajpayee letter "did the damage." He was speaking prior to Chinese President Hu Jintao's state visit to India from 20 November 2006, the first such visit in ten years when the relationship continued to be lukewarm despite signing ten agreements. There was no assurance from the visitor to a request made by the Congress-led Manmohan Singh government of Chinese support for the Indo–US civilian nuclear agreement at the Nuclear Suppliers Group (NSG).[56]

On the other hand, China took various steps to contain the damage caused by Vajpayee's letter.[57] Most of these were not highlighted by the Indian media. Like the Modi government since 2014, the BJP government under Vajpayee had signalled a new thrust in foreign policy to take a bolder stance towards China and Tibet. This was evident from the party's manifesto and the public pronouncements of Defence Minister George Fernandes on Tibet and China's military ties with Pakistan. The two nuclear tests conducted by the government were a forerunner of this policy. China viewed open protests by Tibetan activists during the April 1998 visit of PLA Chief of Staff General Fu Quanyou as another indication of this shift. Earlier, the police would always prevent such demonstrations.

Also, China felt that Vajpayee's letter was an indication of India's overt attempts to go closer to the US in order to persuade America to isolate China on the grounds that it was a "covert proliferator" of nuclear weapons, which was a threat to India's security. It also demonstrated Indian attempts to obtain US concurrence on an Indian formula binding China on what should be its neighbourhood policy. This, despite China saying openly that India should not be concerned about its policy towards India's neighbouring countries as it was not directed against India.

From then on China's diplomacy for nearly a year was aimed at pressuring the BJP government to retract this accusation, and at obstructing India with international help, by exploiting India's nuclear explosions. Various means were used. The first was to persuade international powers especially US and UN to punish India as the "initial transgressor" rather than Pakistan, which only responded to the Indian provocation. China joined the US on 4 June 1998 to call the "Permanent 5" of the UN Security Council to pass Resolution 1172 condemning India and Pakistan for the tests, asking them to stop further production of fissile materials and weapons.

Second, when junior Indian officials visited Beijing in June for preparatory work for the eleventh round of the Sino–Indian Joint Working Group (JWG) on the border, they were given a very cold reception. Instead, they were told that India had made false accusations against China. No JWG was held in 1998.

Next was a strong statement on 9 July 1998 by the Chinese Ambassador to India Zhou Gang criticising Indian verbal assaults against China. Bilaterally, China rebuffed India's efforts in the same month to conclude a "no-first-use of nuclear weapons" agreement. Instead, it asked India to first sign the Comprehensive Nuclear Test Ban Treaty and Non-Proliferation Treaty. Along with this Chinese media started accusing India of aspirations to "regional hegemony," an epithet it had stopped using after 1988.

China felt that India's diplomatic efforts to complain against China through Vajpayee's letter on 11 May 1998 had come to naught through the "Sino–U.S. Presidential Joint Statement on South Asia" on 27 June 1998 during Clinton's visit to China, which said:

> Recent nuclear tests by India and Pakistan, and the resulting increase in tension between them, are a source of deep and lasting concern to both of us. Our shared interests in a peaceful and stable South Asia and in a strong global non-proliferation regime have been put at risk by these tests, which we have joined in condemning. We have agreed to continue to work closely together, within the P-5, the Security Council and with others, to prevent an accelerating nuclear and missile arms race in South Asia, strengthen international non-proliferation efforts, and promote reconciliation and the peaceful resolution of differences between India and Pakistan.
>
> Close coordination between China and the United States is essential to building strong international support behind the goals to which we are committed in response to nuclear testing by India and Pakistan. We will stay closely in touch on this issue, and will work with other members of the P-5 and the Security Council, with other Asian and Pacific countries, and with the broader international community to forestall further instability in South Asia, achieve a peaceful and mutually acceptable resolution of differences between India and Pakistan, and strengthen the global non-proliferation regime.[58]

For China this was the final vindication of its diplomacy in South Asia and an ultimate US rebuff to Prime Minister Vajpayee.

Looking back, one wonders what type of "deterrence" was achieved through the Pokharan II with five underground tests and Vajpayee's letter to President Clinton? In September 2021 noted defence writer Pravin Sawhney had argued that the Chinese incursions in Ladakh from May–June 2020 onwards under the Modi government which resulted in the deaths of twenty Indian soldiers on 15/16 June proved that India's nuclear weapons had failed to deter China which had occupied 100 square kilometres of Indian land. He was contradicting former National Security Adviser Shivashankar Menon's assertion that Indian nuclear weapons "have served their desired purpose."[59]

Vajpayee's letter had other consequences for Sino–Indian relations. After the 1988 *bonhomie* China had moved away from its pro-Pakistan policy on Kashmir in the 1990s.[60] After the letter China started shifting its previous stance on India's core disputes like Kashmir and Arunachal Pradesh. Initially China had laid claim only to the Tawang area of Arunachal Pradesh (which China calls South Tibet) where the sixth Dalai Lama was said to have been born. Since the 2000s China has been claiming the entirety of Arunachal Pradesh. A week before President Hu Jintao arrived in India on 20 November 2006, the Chinese ambassador Sun Yuxi claimed that the whole of Arunachal Pradesh was Chinese territory.[61]

*NDA government under Narendra Modi:*

Prime Minister Narendra Modi had met Chinese President Xi Jinping eighteen times between 2014 and 2020 at various locations. Their first meeting was in Ahmedabad when Xi paid a state visit on 18 September 2014, four months after Modi assumed charge as PM with a landslide majority, leading a new Rightist coalition.[62] Two informal "summits" were held in Wuhan (April 2018) and Mahabalipuram (October 2019).[63] Each meeting was described in official memoranda as cordial and productive with proper diplomatic semantics. Yet border situations and skirmishes continued to take place, each side blaming the other.

In September 2014 a military standoff took place in Demchok, Ladakh for three weeks when Chinese civilians, backed by the PLA, objected to the road building by India. The situation was eased when both armies withdrew according to the 1993 agreement. Since then, Chinese forces have transgressed into Indian territory 400 times in 2015, 250 times in 2016, 400 times in 2017, 300 times in 2018 and nearly 500 times in 2019.[64]

In 2019, the year when Modi and Xi met at Bishkek and Mahabalipuram, there was a 75 per cent surge in Chinese transgressions in Ladakh—497 as against 284 transgressions in 2018.[65] However, in the Galwan clash, the first major incident in forty-five years, the Chinese forces killed twenty Indian soldiers including a colonel, totally in breach of the 1993 agreement.[66]

What then was the provocation? Did India fail to understand the latent Chinese hostility? Was it connected with the Modi government's overtures to form a Quad alliance against China, teaming up with the USA and Japan?

Vijay Gokhale, India's Foreign Secretary till January 2020, feels that Modi's "assertive foreign policy," his "neighbourhood first" policy of reinforcing India's authority in South Asia, his focus on building an India-led maritime defence chain in the Indian Ocean and India's opposition to the China–Pakistan Economic Corridor might have made Beijing consider India as a rival. He also feels China would have assessed India's strategic objective in Indo-Pacific as being to "thwart China."[67]

This theory is quite acceptable. A well-known China expert, the late Professor Franz Schurmann of University of California, with whom I was in contact since the 1990s would always emphasize Mao's "Contradiction" theory, that "antagonistic contradictions" could only be resolved only by violence, but "non-antagonistic" ones could be solved by peaceful means.[68]

Alfred Wilhelm in *The Chinese at the Negotiating Table* supports this quoting American experience from 1953.[69] A 1970 CIA secret study had clearly said that China would initiate recurrent border violence when bilateral political relations sour.[70] These two papers should have been compulsory reading material for India's diplomats and intelligence officials.

Along with this we should also consider certain other factors indicating the Modi government's inadequate understanding of how the present China thinks. I am yet to trace any senior BJP political leader or government official who understands how the Chinese systems of negotiations and decision-making work and the extent to which layers of history, tradition, ideology, prejudices, dogma, and paranoia—the hallmark of the Maoist era—still control their decision making.

In simple words, China started playing harder border games with the Modi government in response to their too close alignment with Donald Trump America's orientations. India had indicated its willingness to allow US enterprises to be located in India after Trump's suggestion to withdraw from China. Senior Minister Nitin Gadkari had even suggested on 27 April 2020 that "India should look to convert world's hatred for China as economic opportunity."[71]

Another example may be quoted. On 15 January 2022 Indian dailies reported that India was signing a US$ 375 million "Brahmos" supersonic cruise missile deal with the Philippines. One paper added: "This first ever contract to export the 290-km range Brahmos missiles which India has developed jointly with Russia, will pave the way for more such deals with the Philippines as well as other ASEAN countries like Indonesia and Vietnam."[72]

This very speculative article goes against the policy of the Philippines of not siding with big powers as articulated by President Rodrigo Duterte on 21 May 2021. *Nikkei Asia* had said: "Duterte, who is set to finish his single six-year term next year, has nurtured closer ties with China under an 'independent' foreign policy to cut reliance on his country's traditional ally, the U.S."[73]

A similar policy statement was made by Vietnamese Prime Minister Pham Minh Chinh on 21 August 2021 even while they were hosting US Vice President Kamala Harris.[74] The same, more or less is the case with Indonesia whose support of the US policy of isolating China is "tepid" as China had recently become the biggest investor in new highways, power plants and a high-speed rail line.[75]

Unlike China, India has a free press. The government is not responsible for such comments in Indian media. ASEAN might buy defence equipment from India for their own defence requirements. However, for the supplying nation to indicate the purpose and who would be the target is a bit far-fetched. Such comments even in Indian media often create an impression of India's eagerness to be in the vanguard of the US policy of isolating China.

Next to be considered is the Indian preventive mechanism: The Galwan incident on 16 June 2020, in which twenty Indian soldiers were killed, was the worst incident since the 1962 Chinese aggression. It appeared to be a strategic assessment failure by the NDA government wherein prior indications were not analysed to set in motion a preventive architecture. And that too despite having an External Affairs Minister who had previously served as India's ambassador to China, when the analysis of how Beijing would react in hostile situations was either not fully understood or perhaps underplayed.

Perhaps India's first mistake was a thinking in some political quarters that China would not react adversely when the government unilaterally revoked the special status of Jammu and Kashmir on 5 August 2019 via the abrogation of Article 370 of the Constitution. Additionally on 2 November 2019, India released new maps showing the union territories of Jammu and Kashmir.

Quite rightly the new map did not take into consideration the disputed part of Aksai Chin. It showed it, according to India's traditional stance, as part of Ladakh, leading to a protest by China's Foreign Ministry spokesperson: "The Indian Government officially announced the establishment of so-called Jammu and Kashmir and Ladakh Union territories which included some of China's territory into its administrative jurisdiction." They claimed that this violated border accords signed by India.[76] None can object to the Government of India printing new maps: It was a sovereign decision. What was however lacking was an intelligence assessment of how the Chinese would react.

Had the China watchers in India's intelligence agencies been alert, they would have flagged this on the same lines as Jawaharlal Nehru's reaction to the new border maps published after 1951 which India, despite the *bonhomie* at that time, had called "cartographic aggression." In 1954 Nehru had taken this up with

Zhou Enlai who assured him that the maps were of no significance as they were merely a "reproduction" of the old Kuomintang maps.

Chinese documents prior to their decision to wage war on India, released in the 1990s, should have alerted India's China watchers that Beijing would show displeasure through aggressive border movements. They had also perhaps not studied a 1970 top secret assessment done by the CIA on the Chinese reaction to the then mighty Soviet Union on similar border problems. The study had revealed the Chinese habit of exacerbating border tensions when bilateral relations worsen. "Mao's land claim was indeed part of the bitter political feud, and Mao's main goal was to extract a political surrender, rather than small territorial concessions, as the price for a final settlement."[77]

Also, that this new Kashmir–Ladakh map was strongly objected to by the higher levels in the Chinese leadership was not known publicly in India. This only became known on 12 June 2020 when a national daily released a report by the China Institutes of Contemporary International Relations (CICIR) linking the then current LOC tension to the new map. According to the daily, this article, for the first time, criticised the new map which "posed a challenge to the sovereignty of Pakistan and China." The report was distributed by the Chinese Embassy, Islamabad. It said that the new map "forced China into the Kashmir dispute, stimulated China and Pakistan to take counter actions on the Kashmir issue and dramatically increased the difficulty in resolving the border issue between China and India."

The report revealed that the Chinese Foreign Minister had voiced "his strong opposition" to India's External Affairs Minister, S. Jaishankar, during his visit in 2019 following the abrogation of Article 370. "The week before the August visit, Home Minister Amit Shah had spoken in Parliament about taking back Pakistan Occupied Kashmir (POK) and Aksai Chin. The most important remark to be noted in the CICIR report is that India's 'double confidence' behind the change of maps is due to its 2019 election victory and that United States and some other Western countries 'puffed India up from an ideological point of view' to hedge 'against China'."

Foreign Minister Jaishankar, with his vast experience of Chinese leadership, should have anticipated a Chinese reaction on the ground at a time of their choosing. Did he alert the Defence Ministry for better border vigilance? Instead, we went on aggressively posturing in tandem with America. On 6 February 2020 the Lok Sabha was informed that the government had conveyed its concerns to the Chinese on the "so-called illegal 'China-Pakistan Economic Corridor' (CPEC) which passed through parts of the Union Territories of Jammu and Kashmir, and Ladakh, which are under illegal occupation of Pakistan." It had also asked them to cease such activities.

At the same time, India also ignored the fact that the Chinese had held India's intelligence agencies responsible for frustrating CPEC. On 3 June 2019, *Open Democracy*, a UK-based political website, published a piece "India and America collude to disrupt China-Pakistan Economic Corridor."[78] It contained sensational allegations that the US was out to unsettle Pakistan's Balochistan, the heart of CPEC, with India's help. It alleged that India's Research and Analysis Wing (R&AW), via its proxies, had "propagated" numerous murders of Chinese engineers in Balochistan. The Baloch Liberation Army (BLA), supported by India, had attacked the Chinese consulate in Karachi in November 2018.

Also, India openly did certain things which the Chinese felt were deliberately done to irritate them. The first incident was on 24 May 2020 when two prominent BJP parliamentarians attended the "virtual swearing in ceremony," along with US Secretary of State Mike Pompeo, of the second term of Taiwan's President Tsai Ing-wen. China lodged a formal protest describing their attendance as an effort to undermine China's national integrity.

The second was on 2 June 2020 when President Donald Trump invited Prime Minister Narendra Modi for the G-7 Summit where the China border "stand-off" was also discussed. Soon thereafter, Russia suggested that the G-7 would be meaningless without China's presence. China also ridiculed Trump's attempts "to draw a small circle" against Beijing.

The third was PM Modi's "Virtual Summit" with Australian Prime Minister Scott Morrison on 4 June 2020 to conclude a

"Comprehensive Strategic Partnership." Scott Morrison is a red rag for China due to his alignment with Trump on the origins of the Corona virus pandemic. He was helpless to overcome his own problem of Australian actor Karm Gilespie who was facing a death sentence in China on drug charges. Against such a background, the Indian media's interpretation that this phone call indicated that India and Australia would forge a common front against China seemed an unrealistic expectation.

It is certainly true that all these are India's sovereign decisions, and that China or for that matter any other country cannot question these steps. At the same time, India should have taken effective precautions on the border, knowing that China, as an unreliable border power, would show their anger at a place and time of their choosing—as experience since the 1950s has shown.

Several satellite videos had emerged after the killings on 15–16 June 2020 which were later used by India only to try to get a propaganda advantage over the PLA. These videos had indicated deliberate Chinese incursions well before the clash on 15 June. Surely India's intelligence agencies could have had access to these videos and must have reported to the relevant decision makers. Was there a delay at the policy-making levels like in the 1999 Kargil War which prevented India from occupying these posts as the army had admirably done in April 1984 at Siachen?

This lack of preparedness on India's part was evident on the ground. Immediately after the incident on 16 June, Chinese Foreign Minister Wang Yi seized the early propaganda advantage by accusing India of "violating the consensus of the two sides by illegally crossing the border twice and carrying out provocative attacks on Chinese soldiers, resulting in serious physical clashes." *Foreign Policy*, in its assessment on 27 August 2020, also blamed India for allowing China to "take advantage of India's intelligence failures."[79]

Compared to that, India's reaction, especially by the External Affairs Ministry, was feeble, confused, and delayed. The government were not even able to issue a statement to the distraught public, giving details. Even the casualty figures could not be confirmed till

10.00 p.m. on 16 June. There was not even unanimity on whether the incident was within the buffer zone or in India's territory.

Thus, China was using the same language it had used against India while justifying its 1962 incursions into India. In 1972 Zhou Enlai had accused Nehru of being a surrogate of Nikita Khrushchev during his talks with President Richard Nixon in Beijing. The same charge was now levelled against Narendra Modi—that he was President Donald Trump's supplicant. The 1962 attack was to insult Nehru while the 2020 attack was to discredit Narendra Modi.

Things had appeared to cool down since then. On 25 January 2021, India and China held their ninth Corps Commander-level talks at the Moldo meeting point. This was described as fruitful. On 20 February 2021, China officially admitted that they lost four soldiers in the Galwan clash when their Central Military Commission awarded posthumous decorations to them. India had estimated that they had lost 45 soldiers.

Still, China is not allowing India to relax. On 8 March 2021, *Global Times* warned that the Quad alliance countering China was "doomed to fail."[80] This was ahead of President Joe Biden's virtual summit on 12 March with the prime ministers of India, Japan and Australia. On 21 March, *Global Times* said that US efforts to unite Asian allies against China had not succeeded. This was after the visit of US Secretary of State Lloyd Austin to New Delhi. It is clear that India is still under watch, although it reserved its rebuke to Japan, sparing India and South Korea.[81]

That India needs to be ever watchful of the Chinese meddling activities is clear from a well-argued Carnegie (India) paper authored by Vijay Gokhale, former Foreign Secretary, who concludes:

> The most fundamental misperception between the two countries is the inability to comprehend each other's international ambitions, yielding the fear that their foreign policies are targeted against the other.[82]

## Part II

# COMPETING VISIONS OF "INDIA"

# 3

# THE RASHTRIYA SWAYAMSEVAK SANGH

Bharat is a Hindu nation and "Hindutva" is nationalism.

—M.G. Chitkara

In 1950 I was a confused and directionless teenager, not certain of my ultimate goals in life. My aims swung from "sacrificing" my life for the country in a battle or becoming a Communist. Somewhere in our epics it was suggested that I would go straight to "*swarga*" (heaven) if I died in battle. The problem was that no war was in sight and the government was not doing any recruitment for the armed forces. In any case no-one would have recruited a 13-year old. At the other end of the spectrum of available opportunities was joining the Communist party which was spreading in my state Kerala through immensely popular literature and drama on social revolution.

It was at that time my friends told me that a Tamil-speaking stranger had appeared in my town for imparting physical training to young boys. Apart from playing football no other physical exercise was locally available. The stranger had introduced himself as a "*Pracharak*"—a recruiter or missionary—of the revived Rashtriya Swayamsevak Sangh (RSS) which was outlawed after Gandhi's assassination in 1948. The ban was lifted in 1949. My father who was a fitness freak suggested that I should join that training since he considered me a weakling.

I went there to see the training "camp" more out of curiosity. The "camp" was nothing but a dry field after paddy had been harvested. The instructor, whose name I don't recall, spoke to me persuasively that I should join the training as it would improve my physical and mental health. I joined a group of a dozen boys in the camp, mostly my friends. Since it was early in the morning it did not clash with my school. Things went on smoothly for about a month.

One day we were asked to sit in a circle for a "memory game." All of us were asked to mention an Indian hero's name. After everyone suggested the names, we were asked to recall all the names from our memory in serial order as we were sitting. Most of the boys mentioned the names of Hindu epic idols or political leaders. Since I was a non-conformist, I mentioned "Akbar" when my turn came.

I was taken aback when the *Pracharak* objected to that name. I asked him why. He said that it was a Muslim name. I asked him why a Muslim name could not be mentioned. He replied that in the culture of RSS, no Muslim could be considered as an Indian hero. I contested that statement and argued that my school text books had taught me that Akbar was a great Indian hero.

He said our history books had been prepared by the British and were hence incorrect. As a voracious reader I would not give in and quoted Indian authors to prove that Akbar was a great ruler who had accepted Hindu customs and had also patronised our religion. He would not agree. In protest I walked out. That was the end of my RSS life as "*swayamsevak*"—literally, a volunteer; a cadre or member.

A few days later most of my friends also deserted the training and that was the end of our "*shakha*" (branch). Had I continued in the RSS *shakha*, I would have been senior in age to many of the present office-bearers in the "*Sangh*"—the assembly.

Our *Pracharak* came home to persuade my father to advise me to attend and thereby revive the *shakha*. Unfortunately for him, my father had held very liberal views as a widely travelled man who had also lived in Burma during the Second World War. He told him that he agreed with my view and that there was no point in me continuing in the *shakha* if they continued to hold such divisive views especially in Kerala which was proud of their inclusive society.

* * *

Seventy-three years later there is still doubt whether the RSS has accepted Indian Muslims as part of India, notwithstanding their public proclamations that all persons, irrespective of any religion, who are legally residing in India, are "Hindus." This change in their policy seems to have come in 2018.

*The Indian Express* carried a report on 17 September 2018 on the lecture delivered by the head of the RSS or *Sarsanghchalak* Mohan Bhagwat during a three-day conclave which was meant for "outsiders." This was to assure them that the RSS would not impose its ideology on anyone.[1]

Following this, noted political analyst and broadcaster Karan Thapar wrote an essay in the same paper on 21 September 2018 entitled "Has the RSS ground shifted?" He analysed Mohan Bhagwat's new pronouncements and found that they were radically different from the views of his predecessor, K.S. Sudarshan, on the Indian Constitution and Muslims.[2] Thapar had interviewed Sudarshan in August 2000 for the BBC's "Hard Talk" programme.

Sudarshan had firmly said that India's Constitution did not reflect the "Hindu ethos" as it was based on the colonial 1935 Government of India Act. He said he supported RSS leader Madhavarao Sadashivrao Golwalkar who had said in his book *A Bunch of Thoughts* that there was nothing in India's constitution which we could call "our own." Sudarshan had also said that RSS did not accept "minority rights."

Thapar said that Bhagwat's lectures upholding the Preamble of the Constitution including its commitment to secularism and socialism was a significant shift from his immediate predecessor's thinking. "To be honest, it feels like a U-turn." However, he wondered whether the country could accept this as a change in RSS policy especially when "many BJP MPs and MLAs who, routinely and repeatedly, say hateful things about Muslims and are rarely admonished and only infrequently apologise?" He said that the BJP did not field a single Muslim candidate in Uttar Pradesh (UP) in the 2017 elections when Muslims formed 19 per cent of the population. In Gujarat, Narendra Modi's home state, the party had not fielded a single Muslim candidate since 1989.

He added that Bhagwat was not averse to making incendiary statements. In 2015, when Mohammad Akhlaq[3] was lynched on suspicion of consuming and storing beef, he was reported to have said: "The Vedas order the killing of the sinner who kills a cow." Thapar was perhaps referring to the RSS mouthpiece *Panchjanya's* cover story "*Is Utpaat ke Us Paar*" (The other side of this mischief) as reported by the popular *India Today* magazine on 18 October 2015: "*Veda ka adesh hai ki gau hatya karne wale pataki ke pran le lo. Hum mein se bahuton ke liye to yah jivan-maran ka prashn hai*" (The *vedas* order the killing of the sinner who kills a cow. It is a matter of life and death for many of us).[4]

On 6 September 2021, Bhagwat said that "Islam came to India with invaders. This is history and should be told in that manner. Sane Muslim leaders should oppose unnecessary issues and stand firmly against fundamentalists and hardliners. The more we do this at the earliest, the less damage it will cause to our society." He was addressing a seminar in Pune organised by the Global Strategic Policy Foundation. He repeated that Hindus and Muslims share the same ancestry, and every Indian citizen is a "Hindu."[5]

On 5 October 2021, Bhagwat called for a policy to "balance" in terms of religion. He was speaking at a "*Vijay Dashami*" closed door meeting where Israeli Consul General Kobbi Shoshani was present. According to this report he had reiterated the 2015 resolution of the RSS Akhil Bharatiya Karyakari Mandal—the organisation's national council—about the rising population of Muslims and Christians.[6]

Also, would the RSS, as the ideological inspiration of the ruling BJP, prefer to maintain "friendly" relations with China, since it was one of the earliest to warn "against Jawaharlal Nehru's rose-tinted and utterly delusional notions of Indo-Chinese friendship" as observed by senior academic Makarand R. Paranjpe?[7]

## Origins of the RSS

The year 1876 could be considered as the beginning of the Indian freedom movement when Surendranath Banerjea, a dismissed Indian Civil Service (ICS) officer, founded the Indian Association of Calcutta. According to Banerjea, this was "the centre of an All-India movement" based on "the conception of a united India, derived from the inspiration of Mazzini."[8] In 1832 Giuseppe Mazzini established a secret society named "Young Italy" while in exile for spreading national consciousness for Italian unification. However, Banerjea's "Association" had very modest aims. It only wanted to organize educated middle-class Indians to create a favourable public opinion, primarily meant for recruiting more Indians into the administration.

The foundations of the future Indian National Congress could be directly related to this "Civil Service" agitation. In 1885 a retired ICS officer Allan Octavian Hume, who was also a botanist-ornithologist, established the Indian National Congress along with a Calcutta barrister W.C. Bonnerjea with official support from Governor-General Lord Dufferin who felt that such an organization would help in ascertaining "the real wishes of the people."[9]

Their placid activities did not result in wresting any real concessions from the British except perhaps the passing of the 1892 Indian Councils Act which increased the size of the legislative councils. Indian participation in governance was not granted. However, the period 1905 to 1916 saw a churning in the Indian political scene. What inspired the ferment was Japan's victory over Russia in 1904–05 and Lord Curzon's controversial partition of Bengal in 1905. This initially united Hindus and Muslims to go on agitational path. It also encouraged the "radical" wing of the Congress to organise more militant activities against British imperialism.

The leaders who came to the fore were Bal Gangadhar Tilak, Bipin Chandra Pal and Lala Lajpat Rai who urged the boycott of British goods. As a result, the Congress split in 1907 between so-called moderates and extremists. Some activists went underground and caused violence through bomb attacks. The British responded with repression.

Feelings of unity between Hindus and Muslims which emerged immediately after the Bengal partition started dissipating as both felt "outnumbered" by the other in their separate legislatures in East and West Bengal. In 1906 Nawab Salimulla of Dacca established a "Muslim League" which supported the Bengal partition. Historian R.C. Majumdar quotes a despatch from the Government of India to Whitehall, London dated 25 August 1911 detailing this Hindu–Muslim rift.[10] It described the bitterness caused by the partition and that it had affected Hindu–Muslim relations, which had spread to the rest of the country.

A panegyric and nationalist book from 2004 *Rashtriya Swayamsevak Sangh: National Upsurge* by M.G. Chitkara—which is also described as the "Encyclopaedia of the RSS"—could be considered as the official history of RSS.[11] Chitkara, a former judge, was associated with the RSS since 1950. He says that it was the Khilafat movement that pushed Dr Keshav Rao Baliram Hedgewar, a former Congressman, to establish the RSS in 1925 to protect Hindus' rights. The Khilafat movement had been started by two brothers Muhammad Ali and Shaukat Ali to protest the dismemberment of the Ottoman Empire by the British during 1918–22.

Historian R.C. Majumdar has said that Gandhi had conceived the idea of channeling this Muslim discontent towards building up a Hindu–Muslim joint struggle of non-violent civil disobedience against Britain as part of India's independence struggle. After initial success, it started turning violent in Malabar in 1921 and in Chauri Chaura (United Provinces, now Uttar Pradesh) in 1922. The Khilafat movement in Malabar district, Kerala—then part of the Madras Presidency—turned into the "Moplah Riots" in 1921 in which scores of Hindus were killed. In Chauri Chaura protesting mobs clashed with the police and burnt a police station, killing twenty-two policemen.

These events caused a deep rift within the Congress party with leaders like Annie Besant criticising Gandhi very bitterly. Besant said in 1922:

> Swaraj was to be attained in a year and on August 1, 1921 the first step was taken in the Malabar rebellion; the Musalmans (Moplas) of that district after three weeks of preparing weapons, rose over a definite area in revolt, believing as they had been told, that British rule had ceased and they were free; they established the Khilafat Raj, crowned a King, murdered and plundered abundantly and killed or drove away all Hindus who would not apostate. Somewhere about a lakh (100,000) of people were driven from their homes with nothing but their clothes they had on, stripped of everything...[12]

The killings of Hindu leaders like Swami Shradhanand, Lala Nanakchand, Rajpal and Nathuram Sharma happened during this period. Chitkara says that the "dissipated and disorganized" Muslim groups in the country came together after the movement started. "The Congress, obviously to please the Muslims and prompted by Mr. Gandhi joined the Khilafat movement."[13]

Italian researcher Marzia Casolari, in her paper "Hindutva's Foreign Tie-Up in the 1930s" quotes the "Maharashtrian Brahmin" origins of the RSS. She discovered this in a confidential unsigned report in the National Archives of India among the correspondence of Sardar Patel. It would appear that this note was circulated during the first ban on the RSS after Gandhi's assassination:

> Started in Nagpur some sort of Boys Scout movement. Gradually it developed into a communal militarist organization with violent tendencies... RSS has been purely Maharashtrian brahmin organisation. The non-brahmin Maharashtrians who constitute the bulk of C.P and Maharashtra have no sympathy with it.[14]

Even in the twenty-first century the upper-caste domination at the decision-making level continues in the Bharatiya Janata Party (BJP), described by Chitkara as one of the "front" organizations of the RSS along with the Vishwa Hindu Parishad (World Hindu Organisation; VHP), Bharatiya Mazdoor Sangh (Indian Workers' Union; BMS), Akhil Bharatiya Vidhyarthi Parishad (All-India Students' Union; ABVP), Bharatiya Kisan Sangh (Indian Farmers' Union; BKS) and Vidya Bharati, the educational wing of the RSS.[15]

In 2018 *The Print* studied the caste composition of the office bearers of the BJP in India and found that 69 per cent were from the "Forward" castes while only 27 per cent were from other communities. Out of 752 district presidents, 65 per cent were from upper castes, 25 per cent from "Other Backwards Castes", while less than 4 per cent were from "Scheduled castes", the lowest in the caste rung. Not even 2 per cent were from minorities like Muslims or Christians. As a result, the BJP is still called a Brahmin– Banya (Brahmin–trader) party.[16]

Chitkara's book gives a blow-by-blow account of the history of this movement and the gradual evolution of its philosophy. The *Sangh* was founded in 1925 on *Vijaya Dashami*, which is considered a very day auspicious by Hindus to begin education or start any new enterprise. It is the tenth and final day of the *Navratri* (nine nights) festival and also commemorates Goddess Durga's victory over the "Buffalo Demon" Mahishasura to protect *Dharma*. In 1925 only five "likeminded young men" assembled in Mohitewada in Nagpur to begin the *Sangh*. The name "Rashtriya Swayamsevak Sangh" was chosen only in April 1926.

The first task entrusted to the *Sangh* by Dr Hedgewar was to protect the pilgrims from "the rapacity of Muslim fakirs and Brahmin priests" during the *Ramanavami* (birthday of Lord Ram) at the historic Ram temple at Ramtek near Nagpur in 1926. "However, its dominant mission, as an ideological *akhara*, was clearly directed against Muslims, as the events of 1927 in Nagpur reveal."[17]

Earlier, the British administration used to prohibit the annual Ganapathi (Lord Ganesh) festival processions from playing music in front of mosques so as not to offend Muslim religious feelings. In 1927, for the first time, Dr Hedgewar led the procession with drums and music in front of the mosque, setting in motion a visible assertion of Hindu rights.

In those days Nagpur was the capital city of the Central Provinces & Berar State. Being in the centre of India, anything happening there attracted all-India and global attention. On 4 September 1927 a "*Mahalakshmi*" (Mother Goddess) procession was prevented by the Muslims in the Mahal area of the city. The ensuing riots went on for three days resulting in twenty-two deaths and several injuries. Troops had to be called in to quell disturbances.

These disturbances found their echo even in international media. This was against the background of the incendiary nature of Hindu–Muslim relations then prevailing all over India. Eleven such riots took place in 1923, eighteen in 1924, sixteen in 1925 and thirty-five in 1926. In 1927 by September the country had already witnessed forty riots. Muslim leaders then alleged that the RSS had prepared to incite riots by storing explosives.

The direct result of these riots was a heightened popularity of the RSS as the "defender" of Hindus. Their membership increased and the number of *shakhas* went up to 500 all over India. The number of *swayamsevaks*—only twenty-six in 1926—became 60,000 by 1939. By 1929, an elaborate hierarchy was set up by the RSS and Dr Hedgewar became the "*Sarsanghchalak*" (supreme leader).

## *Development of RSS philosophy and strategy*

There are several strands which constitute the fundamental philosophy of the RSS. The first claim is that it is carrying forward the "Hindu Renaissance" which was spearheaded by Shankara in the eighth century CE. Hindu renaissance sage Shankaracharya was able to successfully restore Hinduism in India through his remarkable ability in dialectics and by visiting all corners of India in order to persuade Buddhists to return to Hinduism. The Sangh also claims to be following Swami Vivekananda, Annie Besant, Sri Aurobindo Ghosh and Gandhi of the nineteenth and twentieth centuries. It claims to fight the Christian "unabashed Westernisation" and Muslim "communalism and fundamentalism."[18]

This narrative is difficult to accept, as I shall argue in the next chapter "The Idea of India" that the basic spiritual message of all these great masters was tolerance and inclusiveness whereas the RSS preaches exclusivity and conditional inclusivity.

Second is the RSS idea which is like the "melting pot" theory of nationalism, as opposed to the "salad bowl" concept wherein each community retains its distinct identities. As Manoj Mitta of the National Endowment for Democracy had said, the melting pot model is also against India's binding obligation under the 1966 International Covenant of Civil and Political Rights (ICCPR) to prevent its majority community from swallowing up minorities.[19]

The belief that there are no minority rights follows from the "melting pot" theory that there is no "majority" or "minority" in India as all are "equal". Any special minority rights would be considered as "appeasement" in a democracy. Muslims in India do not form a separate nationality. The RSS believes in a "Hindu Rashtra," that "Bharat is a Hindu nation and 'Hindutva' is nationalism."[20]

In March 2022 the Supreme Court asked the Indian government to give its stance on a plea by advocate Ashwini Upadhyay on the problem of Hindus becoming minorities in Lakshadweep (2.5%), Mizoram (2.75%), Nagaland (8.75%), Meghalaya (11.53%), Jammu and Kashmir (28.44%), Arunachal Pradesh (29%), Manipur (31.39%) and Punjab (38.40%) according to the 2011 census. The Ministry of Minority Affairs informed the Supreme Court that the states were competent to declare minorities under articles 29 and 30 of the constitution.[21]

It is not very clear how the RSS would accept this development since even on 19 September 2018 Bhagwat had said that the RSS did "not address or recognise Muslims as 'minorities'" as both communities were "India's children."[22] Yet on 16 October 2021, he expressed "concern about the rising share of Muslims in the country's population."[23]

The third belief is "*Akhand Bharat*" (Undivided India), the contours of which keep changing from time to time. This is discussed later.

A fourth strand of their beliefs is "*Chaturvarna.*" The RSS has been accused of advocating the continuance of Sage Manu's four "castes." Chitkara parries this controversy, saying that a "law laid on each one of your ancestors" is meant "for realisation of that great ideal of the spiritual man." He adds that "varnas were never castes, which followed their own laws."[24] He quotes Guru Golwalkar that "we neither oppose caste nor support it. We are aware that this system played an important role at a critical time in maintaining the life fabric of our society intact. If the society does not need it anymore, it will wither away..."[25]

An article in *The Caravan* interpreted Mohan Bhagwat's address on 25 October 2020 that a farmer "farms because farming is his *dharma* and to feed the society" to mean that even in modern India the "caste dharma" should be followed as we are "the sons and daughters of the same ancestor." It further said that "Prime Minister Modi went so far as to appoint a 14-person committee of scholars with a mission to establish that Hindus descended from India's first habitants." The journal quotes Dr B.R. Ambedkar's thesis in 1916 at Colombia University to contradict this theory. In his paper on "Indian Antiquary" Ambedkar had said that "according to well-known ethnologists, the population of India is a mixture of Aryans, Dravidians, Mongolians and Scythians."[26]

The RSS has also been accused of being "patriarchal" on the place of women in society. "More often than not, cultural practises, traditions, religious scriptures and mythological narratives are invoked to derogate power, potential and capacity from women."[27] In September 2015 the statement of Mahesh Sharma, then Culture Minister, about the rights of girls had drawn criticism. He had said that "Night out for girls" was not acceptable in Indian culture. He had earlier drawn flak by saying that President A.P.J. Abdul Kalam was a "nationalist" despite being a Muslim.[28]

On 16 March 2021, the newly chosen Uttarakhand Chief Minister Tirath Rawat joined other patriarchal RSS leaders in prescribing what women should wear in public. He deprecated the practice of women wearing "ripped jeans and showing their knees." He was shocked to meet a "woman who ran an NGO wearing ripped jeans." He blamed the parents for this lapse. This statement was criticised by hundreds of thousands of women.[29]

The next principle is protection of the cow. In 1952 the RSS collected signatures of 17.5 million people on the ban of cow slaughter and presented it to President Rajendra Prasad. In

December 1952 a "*Gau Hatya Nirodh Sammelan*" (anti-cow slaughter conference) was held in Delhi chaired by Guru Golwalkar.

"*Ghar vapasi*" (return home) is another principle which came to prominence in 2014 after Modi came to power. Chitkara traces its history. In 1956 Guru Golwalkar initiated a call "Converts, Come Back," later known as "*ghar vapasi*" to those Hindus who were forcibly converted to other religions. It justified this policy since the population in Kashmir had become majority Muslims as the local "Pandits" had prevented the Maharajah from taking back those Muslims who had volunteered to return to Hinduism. The Vishwa Hindu Parishad (VHP) which held a large conclave of heads of "*matts*" (monasteries), *dharmacharyas* and leading *sadhus* (holy men) representing all shades of Hinduism had unanimously resolved to take back such Hindus in 1966.[30]

After the BJP came into power in 2014 one of the initial programmes undertaken was "*ghar vapasi*" which resulted in several major law and order incidents. At the same time the RSS efforts to reconvert those Sikhs who had become Christians was criticised by the Shiromani Akali Dal, then a BJP ally, as Sikhs were not part of the Hindu pantheon. There were several reports that those who were reconverted as Hindus after "purification" rituals had returned to their religion soon thereafter and that the campaign was a mere photo opportunity. In the end it only gave a bad name to India as another intolerant country.[31]

The last traditional principle of the RSS was about possessing arms. Chitkara says that Hedgewar did not want his cadres to possess weapons other than *lathis* (long sticks). However, as I show below this principle was regularly breached.[32]

### A "Vedic" interpretation on the role of the Sangh

On 30 January 2021 India's *Sunday Guardian* carried a piece by Manmohan Vaidya, Joint General Secretary of the RSS, on his late father M.G. Vaidya who was a most revered personality and who had attended the *shakha* every day from the age of 15 to 95.[33]

M.G. Vaidya had told the audience during his last address when he was felicitated at the age of 95 on 11 March 2018:

It is not easy to understand Sangh. In order to understand Sangh, it is important to understand the Ishavaasyopanishad. In one of the shlokas of this Upanishad, the "Atmatattva" (loosely translated as the "self") has been described using paradoxical elements. The Shloka goes like this:

तदेजति तन्नैजति तद्दूरे तद्वन्तिके ।
तदन्तरस्य सर्वस्य तदु सर्वस्यास्य बाह्यत ॥

*Tadejati tannaijati taddūure tadvantike*
*Tadantarasya sarvasya tadu sarvasyāsya bāhyata.*

He also gave its English translation: "The Atmatattva moves but also does not move. It is far and it is near. It is inside all, and also outside all." His interpretation of the verse is of particular importance:

> The same description also applies to the Sangh. Sangh is political but also apolitical. Sangh is a religious organisation but is also not one. Sangh is a social organisation but is also not so. Because Sangh wants to organise society, Sangh is one with the Society. Sangh is the entire society itself.

I wonder whether other Vedic scholars would accept this interpretation as this *shloka* ("verse" or "mantra") is the fifth verse of the *Ishopanishad*, also called *Ishavasya Upanishad* or *Isopanishad*, which is dedicated to the "All Pervading Reality," that is God.

Elsewhere I have quoted Chitkara that the foundations of VHP were laid on the day of *Janmashtami* in 1964 at Swami Chinmayananda's Sandeepany Ashram in Mumbai.[34] The same Swami Chinmayananda's Sandeepany Sadhanalaya, which conducts educational courses on Hindu religious literature for Indian and foreign students, has given a different interpretation on the essence of this verse. They say that this Upanishad, which they call Ishavasya Upanishad "is part of the 'Shukla Yajur Veda'." Swami Chinmayananda had said, according to their publication, that the purpose of this Upanishad was "to see the all-pervading Truth in and through the disturbing trellis of the phenomenal world, is to realize the Truth in the outer world of Plurality. How this is harmoniously done is the very theme of the entire Ishavasya

Upanishad."[35] Verse 5 reproduced by the late M.G. Vaidya comes immediately after verse 4 which is also a riddle. It is called "The Elusive Atman" and begins "The Self is Motionless one—Yet it is swifter than the mind."

The translation of verse 5, according to the Sandeepany Sadhanalaya, is this: "That (the Atman) moves and yet It moves not; It is far away and yet It is near; It is within all of this; and yet It is also outside of all this." An Indologist friend of mine quoted a similar interpretation by Bhaktivedanta Swami Prabhupada (Founder Acharya of the International Society for Krishna Consciousness) in his book *Isopanishad*. Mantra 5 is: "The Supreme Lord walks and does not walk. He is far away but He is very near as well. He is with everything, yet He is outside of everything."[36]

The Sandeepany Sadhanalaya says that this and all other verses have to be read with verse 1 which is the "highest goal of the Vedic philosophy." It is summarised as follows: "The Lord is not remote from His creation. He pervades it. Here we have a vision of a God that is really close to us. He is all around us. We can worship Him in many ways. We can worship Him even by using the many forms we have in the world to represent Him."

This is exactly what other religions also teach. By equating the *Sangh* with "the Supreme Reality" (God), the RSS is doing a great disservice to those Indians and others who have no access to the correct interpretation of the Vedas.

### *Manmohan Vaidya and* Panchjanya*: criticism of Infosys*

*Panchjanya* and *Organiser*, published by Bharat Prakasan, are considered to be the RSS "mouthpieces". *Panchjanya*'s sharp criticism of the globally recognised Indian software company Infosys in its issue of 5 September 2021 had invoked sharp protests from the opposition parties and media at a time when the BJP government was trying to raise India's profile abroad to invite foreign investment.

In an unprecedented show of vitriol, the weekly ran a four-page cover story, alleging that Infosys is aligned with "anti-national" forces and as a result messed up the government's Income Tax portal. It even alleged that the company was aligned with "anti-national forces" such as "Naxals, Leftists and 'tukde tukde' gang," a favourite epithet used by the BJP and RSS to describe their critics, connoting their supposed desire to see India broken up into "pieces."

Quite surprisingly, not one business group nor NASSCOM came to the defence of Infosys, which is considered as a standard setter in India's software revolution. It was left to the lone voice of Mohandas Pai, Infosys's former Chief Financial Officer, to say that no company is anti-national and that it was unfair to use such words against "a company like Infosys which has made India proud for so many years and has single-handedly set standards in this country in many areas."[37]

Although the RSS, through their spokesperson Sunil Ambekar, distanced itself from the criticism on 5 September as reflecting the author's opinion,[38] Manmohan Vaidya, as RSS General Secretary termed the magazine "a herald of *Dharma Yudh*" (crusade for the right principles) on 7 September. He was speaking at the inauguration of the magazine's new office at Mayur Vihar, New Delhi.[39] During this function a senior RSS member revealed that there were nine publications started by *swayamsevaks* which were not part of the RSS.

## The RSS and its structure

The media has described the RSS is as "an unregistered voluntary paramilitary corporation" and the parent of the ruling Bharatiya Janata Party. In November 2020 "The Caravan" reported: "At present, 38 of the 53 BJP ministers in the Modi government—over 70 percent—have a Sangh background".[40] Despite being an NGO and getting funds from abroad, the media has been complaining that the accounts of the RSS and its "front organisations" were never audited. In 1990 Vishv Bandhu Gupta, a senior income tax officer who issued notices to the Vishwa Hindu Parishad (VHP) to produce accounts, was shifted reassigned.[41]

Former Shimla University Vice-Chancellor S.K. Gupta, in the foreword to Chitkara's book, says that that RSS is the largest NGO in the world. Chitkara says in chapter 15 that 37,000 *shakhas* exist in India with 2,500 full-time *pracharaks*. Each *shakha* represents the Vedic or ancient "*Gurukul*" system of education.

In addition, they have 350 *upshakhas* or sub-branches in 33 countries. They have "contacts" in 90 countries. In all 23,450 "service" projects are run by "Sangh inspired" organisations for social welfare. Among their "front organizations", the students' wing Akhil Bharatiya Vidhyarti Parishad (ABVP) has 3,700 chapters in 126 universities with a membership of 778,000. Similarly their trade union Akhil Bharatiya Mazdoor Sangh (ABMS) has 6 million members while their farmers' front Akhil Bharatiya Kisan Sangh (ABKS) has a membership of 1.5 million in 406 districts.

Other front organisations are the Vishwa Hindu Parishad (VHP)—which has been at the forefront of the "*Ram Janmabhoomi*" movement (Birthplace of God Ram)—the Bajrang Dal, Durga Vahini, Swadeshi Jagran Manch, and many others.

An article in *DNA* on 15 May 2014 by Priti Gandhi, Co-convener of the BJP's Maharashtra Communications Cell[42] put the RSS membership at 5 million across India. It estimated the number of *shakhas* as 40 to 50 thousand in India. It runs 27,000 Ekal Vidyalayas (schools) in remote tribal areas where more than 800,000 socially deprived tribal students are enrolled.

It is not clear why an organisation with 5 million memberships would need several "front organisations" like the VHP and Bajrang Dal who are known to be indulging in severe violence. The RSS chief claimed in February 2018 in Muzaffarpur that "RSS would be battle ready in two-three days" due to their commitment and discipline, whereas "a regular army takes six to seven months." He also claimed that during the 1962 Chinese invasion "it was RSS volunteers who stood till the army reached there."[43] This claim was surprising as even Chitkara does not mention anything in his adulatory book about the RSS presence on Chinese borders before the army arrived.

Chitkara chronicles how foreign *shakhas* were founded. In 1958 the late Laxmanrao Bhide, a *pracharak* was deputed to Kenya to organise a *shakha* there. From there RSS *shakhas* spread to Mauritius, Uganda, and Tanzania. In the 1970s Bhide helped to strengthen a Hindu organisation in Nepal to follow up Guru Golwalkar's visit in 1963.

One of the major projects undertaken by the RSS was through the "Vivekananda Birth Celebration Committee" under *Sar Karyavah* (General Secretary) Eknath Ranade who managed to erect a great memorial on the rock off Kanyakumari where Vivekananda had meditated for three days in 1892. Despite objections from some anti-RSS Congressmen, Prime Minister Indira Gandhi cleared the project which was opened in 1970 by President V. V. Giri.

## The Vishwa Hindu Parishad

Chitkara says that the VHP was founded in 1964 at Swami Chinmayanandji's Sandeepani Ashram in Powai, Mumbai. This should not lead us to believe that Chinmayananda had supported the VHP's divisive agenda which had developed later, resulting in tremendous national upheaval. The late Swami was my relation, and it is my duty to clarify his role here.

Swami Chinmayand Saraswati (born as Balakrishna Menon), who was a journalist, had gone to Rishikesh in 1947 to interview Swami Sivananda of the Divine Life Society. In 1949 he became a *sanyasi*—a renunciant—and studied Vedic philosophy for several years under the guidance of Swami Tapowan Maharaj of Uttarakashi, who was then known as the best Vedanta expert.

In 1951 he held his first Bhagawad Gita *satsang* or gathering, which he later started calling a "*yagnya*" or ritual sacrifice. He held this in the Ganesh temple, Pune, which made him immensely popular in that citadel of Maharashtrian Brahmins. This, despite his earlier experience of facing considerable opposition from the South Indian Brahmins, who believed that non-Brahmins could not interpret the Vedas.

At the same time, he believed in inter-faith dialogue. One of his early *yagnyas* in Bombay was inaugurated by Cardinal Valerian Gracias, then Archbishop of Bombay. This was revealed while coins made by the Government of India mint to commemorate Chinmayananda's birth centenary in 2016 were released.[44]

In 1991 the late Dr Abid Hussain, ambassador to the USA, had told me that the Swami had visited Vishakhapattanam for a *Gita Yagnya* where he was the District Collector during 1964–68. He recalled how the Swami's visit had helped him regain his local popularity which had been lost during a communal riot. The public were elated as he appeared in public with the Swamiji during that *yagnya* in Vishakhapattanam.

In his 1996 book *The Hindu Nationalist Movement and Indian Politics 1925–1990s*, Christophe Jaffrelot gives details of the unchecked activities of foreign missionaries in tribal areas, especially in Madhya Pradesh, that were causing serious concerns to India's national security apparatus. The Niyogi Commission set up by Madhya Pradesh Chief Minister Ravi Shankar Shukla reported in 1957 that the number had increased to 4877 from 4377 in 1951 and they were responsible for 4,000 religious conversions in 1952. In addition, it was estimated that they had received foreign money to the tune of Rs. 2.9 billion during 1950–54.

It was against this background that the idea of having a World Hindu Council was originated by the Swamiji in 1963. Chinmayananda had also found during his early foreign travels that overseas Indians were hardly interested in their original religion and culture. This had resonated among the RSS and others like K.M. Munshi to start an organization to spread the Hindu culture within India and abroad.

This movement, according to my information, materialised in the form of the VHP in 1964. True, Swamiji had also threatened to "convert" 500 Christians into Hinduism—but that was a "tit-for-tat" for an insulting announcement before the 1964 Eucharistic Congress in Bombay that the Pope would "convert" 250 Hindus to Christianity. This had enraged India. However, Swamiji had not supported the broadening of the VHP's activities into vigilante violence.

The VHP's first overt activity was on 7 November 1966, when a huge procession of *sadhus* (ascetics) marched to the parliament for cow protection. Chitkara alleged that Prime Minister Indira Gandhi's "musclemen" created trouble resulting in the police firing and some deaths. This was not strictly correct as the aggressive procession led by Swami Rameshwaranand, Bharatiya Jan Sangh (forerunner of the present BJP) MP from Karnal, wanted to storm Parliament. At that time Parliament did not have adequate security staff and the police were compelled to open fire.

However, this incident did manage to elevate the issue to a high political level and also divide the ruling Congress, compelling Indira Gandhi to appoint a committee led by retired Supreme Court chief justice A.K. Sarkar to determine if a nationwide ban on cow slaughter was feasible. She also included traditionalist "cow protection" leaders like RSS chief M.S. Golwalkar and the Shankaracharya of Puri in the committee besides Dr V. Kurien, the fabled creator of Amul (National Dairy Development Board) who wanted to weed out "useless cows" and whose brief was "to prevent any ban on cow slaughter."

Kurien wrote in his memoirs that Golwalkar had indirectly admitted to him about the RSS's role to force the issue on the government with definite political objectives in mind.[45] That was because the then Home Minister Gulzarilal Nanda, a trusted follower of Jawaharlal Nehru and Lal Bahadur Shastri and twice "caretaker" prime minister, was deeply sympathetic to the cause of cow protection as patron of the Bharat Sadhu Samaj.

The incident certainly helped in splitting the Cabinet as Mrs Gandhi chose to dismiss Nanda for his inept handling of the procession. However, the committee which was asked to submit its report within six months went on delaying it. Finally, Prime Minister Morarji Desai, who assumed power after Mrs Gandhi's defeat in 1977, dismissed the Sarkar Committee which had been unable to complete the work after more than 12 years.[46]

The VHP's next major "operation" along with others was the Babri Masjid demolition on 6 December 1992 which resulted in country-wide communal riots with more than 2,000 deaths. This incident managed to spread communal tension all over the country. Its indirect results included the 2002 Godhra riots when Narendra Modi was the chief minister of Gujarat ending in nearly 2,000 deaths, according to unofficial figures.

In 2018 the CIA, according to published reports, had classified the VHP and Bajrang Dal as "militant religious outfits."[47] The Bajrang

Dal is mostly responsible for vigilante violence after the Narendra Modi government assumed power from 2014 for "implementing" the cow-slaughter ban and more recently for enforcing the "Love-Jehad" laws passed by some BJP-ruled states, banning inter-faith marriages, which jurists say are unconstitutional. In 2001 even a Hindu website had warned the Bajrang Dal not to become "Hindu Jehadis" while analysing their proposal to recruit 3 million new volunteers.[48]

In 1966 the Sangh activities started in the UK. In 1970 Shri Chamanlal, a senior *pracharak* in Delhi, was asked to maintain "uninterrupted contact" with all Hindu workers settled abroad. Later Shri Dadasaheb Apte and Shri Lakshmana Rao Bhide were appointed to organise Hindus in foreign countries. In 1970 a Gopal Krishna Mandir (Krishna temple) was opened in London. In 1972 nearly 147 Hindu organisations came together to form a United Hindu Council of Kenya which became an important voice in Kenyan public life.

During the pro-Trump Capitol Hill riots on 6 January 2021, one *karyakarta* Krishna Gudipati belonging to the Vishwa Hindu Sangathan (VHS), an offshoot of the VHP, was prominently seen waving the Indian national flag.[49]

## The RSS and the Indian independence struggle

The allegation is regularly raised that the RSS did not take part in the Indian independence struggle. Chitkara refutes this and gives details of their "parallel" activities. He says that eminent national freedom fighters had appreciated the work done by them in resisting the then Muslim leadership which was inciting separatism by promoting Pakistan.

In 1928 Subhas Chandra Bose had met Hedgewar during the Congress session in Calcutta. Chitkara says that Bose appreciated their work. In 1929 Pandit Madan Mohan Malaviya, founder of Benares Hindu University, visited Nagpur and commended the work Hedgewar was doing. Malaviya was the president of the Indian National Congress four times in 1909, 1918, 1932 and 1933.

Although Hedgewar did not want the RSS to get involved in politics, he allowed the members to take part in the freedom struggle in their individual capacity. For instance, Hedgewar, along with his senior colleagues, participated in the Satyagraha movement in 1930 at Gandhi's call and courted arrest. They were sentenced to nine months rigorous imprisonment.

Chitkara claims that when the Congress adopted its "Total Independence" resolution on 31 December 1929 in its Lahore session, Hedgewar had sent a circular to all *shakhas* to hoist the national flag "on the evening of 26 January 1930 at 6pm and to organise lectures on the concept and need of independence. All RSS Shakhas observed the Independence Day following the circular."[50]

The author tries to prove that the RSS had very good relations with Gandhi who had appreciated their work. While Gandhi was breaking the British Empire's Salt Law on the Arabian Sea Coast in March–April 1930, the RSS—which was active only in "Madhya Bharat" (Central India)—decided to do a "Jungle Satyagraha" by breaking forest laws. Chitkara claims that twelve RSS volunteers who broke the law were sentenced to 9 years rigorous imprisonment.[51] He wanted to convey that the RSS had chosen their own path for the independence struggle.

Chitkara quotes two specific instances of Gandhi's appreciation of RSS in 1934 and 1938. This was despite the Congress passing a resolution in June 1934 prohibiting its members from associating with the Hindu Mahasabha, Muslim League and RSS. During December 1934 Gandhi was staying in Jamnalal Bajaj's farm in Wardha District. At that time the RSS was holding its annual winter camp in the same district on 23–25 December. They invited Gandhi to visit their camp. On 25 December Gandhiji arrived at 6 a.m. in their camp accompanied by Mahadev Desai, "Mirabehn" (Madeleine Slade) and a few others. Appaji Joshi received them. Gandhi visited their tents and kitchen where food for 1,500 camp trainees was being cooked.

At one point he asked the *swayamsevaks* their castes: One said he was a Mahar (Dalit), another a Teli (oil extractor—considered as a low caste), a third Maratha and a fourth Brahmin. Gandhi was "wonder struck" at how the RSS had "made different castes live, play and dine together." On the same day at 8.30 pm Dr Hedgewar, accompanied by Appaji Joshi and L.B. Bhopatkar from Pune, called on Gandhi. After exchanging pleasantries, Gandhi said: "Well Dr Hedgewar, I thought I was the only organiser in India; but there is another and that is Dr Hedgewar."[52]

In 1938 (the precise date is not mentioned by Chitkara) an incident occurred near the just completed Lakshminarayan Mandir (Birla Mandir) in Delhi when RSS cadres reportedly "saved" Gandhiji from a hostile mob of Hindu *pandas* (pilgrimage priests). In those days the RSS had a *karyalaya* (office) located in a few rooms in the Hindu Mahasabha Bhavan, New Delhi. Shri Vasantrao Oke, RSS provincial *pracharak* used to stay there. One day there was a night-time "*baithak*" (meeting) and volunteers stayed there overnight.

The following morning, they heard a commotion coming from the direction of the Birla Mandir. They found that thousands had collected there as Mahatma Gandhi had come to inaugurate the temple. He had brought a Harijan boy with him. "But some old-style Pandas would not permit Ganesh Dutt Goswami, the well-known Sanatani leader's appeal to the pandas to let the boy in, which made no impression on them. There were shouts and counter shouts, pushing and pulling. In the confusion Gandhiji was being pushed around." His companions could not save him. "He was gasping for breath in the buffeting of the crowd."

Then Vasantrao Oke and his followers jumped over the wall. V.P. Kohli who was also present recorded in his diary that Oke "carried the fainting Mahatma on his back, upto the stairs." Kohli and others brought the Harijan boy in. "And then everybody else came up. The Pandas had been defeated in their folly. The Mandir had been duly inaugurated to shouts of Mahatma Gandhi ki Jai".

These anecdotes do have an element of truth, but deserve some qualification.[53] While addressing the RSS rally in New Delhi on 16 September 1947, Gandhi recalled a visit to RSS camp in Wardha:

> Gandhiji said that he had visited the Rashtriya Swayamsevak Sangh camp years ago at Wardha, when the founder Shri Hedgewar was alive. The late Shri Jamnalal Bajaj had taken him to the camp and

he (Gandhiji) had been very well impressed by their discipline, complete absence of untouchability and rigorous simplicity. Since then, the Sangh had grown. Gandhiji was convinced that any organization which was inspired by the ideal of service and self-sacrifice was bound to grow in strength. But in order to be truly useful, self-sacrifice had to be combined with purity of motive and true knowledge. Sacrifice without these two had been known to prove ruinous to society.

The prayer that was recited at the beginning was in praise of Mother India, Hindu culture and Hindu religion. He claimed to be a *sanatani* Hindu. He took the root meaning of the word *sanatana*. No one knew accurately the origin of the word Hindu.[54]

However, Gandhi had elsewhere strongly condemned the RSS. An oft-quoted account from September 1947 runs:

A member of Gandhiji's party interjected that the R.S.S. people had done a fine job of work at Wah refugee camp. They had shown discipline, courage and capacity for hard work. "But don't forget," answered Gandhiji, "even so had Hitler's Nazis and the Fascists under Mussolini." He characterised that R.S.S. as "a communal body with a totalitarian outlook."[55]

Concerning his visit to the Birla Temple, Gandhi issued a press statement which was published in *Harijan* on 25 March 1939 with an explanatory note which read:

On 18th inst. Gandhiji performed the opening ceremony of the Lakshmi Narayan Temple and the Buddha Vihar built by Birla Brothers in Delhi. The Temple and the Vihar are open for worship to the whole Hindu public including the Jains and the Sikhs as also for those of other faiths who may care to visit them.

The vast concourse of people that had gathered made it difficult for Gandhiji to enter the Temple precincts and the microphone arrangements broke down. He therefore could not address the gathering and later issued to the Press what he would, under normal conditions, have spoken.

There is no corroboration from Gandhi's papers that the RSS volunteers had "saved" Gandhi.

* * *

On 10 June 2017, Amit Shah, then BJP chief, later Union Home Minister, was severely criticized by the Congress party for insulting Gandhi, father of the nation by calling him a "*bahut chatur baniya*" ("a very clever trader"—*baniya* carries derogatory overtones) and saying that the Congress Party was only "a Special Purpose Vehicle" created by Gandhi for gaining independence and that it had no ideology.[56]

It is true that Gandhi had envisaged all shades of people—Hindus, Muslims or Christians, religious or irreligious—taking part in the independence movement which he considered was the true combined national struggle against British imperialism. He always used to start his daily lectures with community singing of "*Ram Dhun*" which included all religions. "*Ram Dhun*" was also sung when Gandhiji and his followers undertook the "salt *satyagraha*" in March–April 1930 during the 241-mile "Dandi March". A shorter version is this:

रघुपति राघव राजाराम,
पतित पावन सीताराम
ईश्वर अल्लाह तेरो नाम,
सब को सन्मति दे भगवान

*raghupati rāghav rājārām,*
*patit pāvan sītārām*
*īshwar allāh tero nām*
*sab ko sanmati de bhagavān*

O Lord Rama, descendant of Raghu, Uplifter of the fallen.
You and your beloved consort Sita are to be worshipped.
All names of God refer to the same Supreme Being,
including Ishvara and the Muslim Allah.
O Lord, Please give peace and brotherhood to everyone,
as we are all your children.
We all request that this eternal wisdom of humankind prevail.[57]

This "inclusive principle" was justified by Jawaharlal Nehru who was quoted by Granville Austin: "Congress leaders had long believed that the party should speak for the country. Nehru wrote in 1939: 'The Congress has within its fold many groups, widely differing in their viewpoints and ideologies. This is natural and inevitable if the Congress is to be the mirror of the nation.'"[58]

One feels that those of the RSS or BJP who want to claim to be Gandhi's followers cannot justify their selective admiration of his beliefs and claim part of his legacy, as the common impression about them is that they believe only in exclusionary politics. In fact, right from the beginning they have alleged that the support of minorities, especially Muslims, by the Congress was "Vote Bank" politics.

On 12 March 2021, which was the seventy-fifth anniversary of India's independence, Prime Minister Narendra Modi "re-enacted" the Dandi March by flagging off a "march" at Sabarmati Ashram, Gujarat. It is not clear whether they sang the Ram Dhun especially "*Īshwar all āh tero nām*."

## *Core RSS philosophy: Resentment against Nehru and the forming of divergent national policies*

Chitkara says that one of the main reasons for the setting up of the RSS was because the Muslims were not reconciled to the prospects of Hindu–Muslim joint rule after the British left India as they feared that the Hindus would dominate them as the rulers. Instead, they aspired for a "Mughal–Muslim" rule. He also argues that Hindus had become "apologetic", had lost their self-confidence, and accepted the superiority of invaders and had become "their admirers." Thus Hedgewar set up the RSS in 1925 to reverse such thoughts and boost courage among Hindus. He exhorted them: "*Garv se kaho hum Hindu hain*" ("announce proudly that we are Hindus").

Chitkara outlines some of the key priciples of the RSS. Firstly, the boundaries of "cultural India" had extended "far beyond its geographical borders." Under so-called alien rule, the geographical boundaries of India had been contracting for centuries. "We have now got used to thinking of India without Afghanistan, without Punjab, half of Bengal and Sindh, and lately without Pakistan occupied Kashmir too."

The second belief was that the Hindus had got used to the idea of a "shrinking" and "shrunken" India. They have got used to large-scale infiltration, organized subversion, planned terrorism, systematic proselytizing, political blackmail and electoral manipulation. Hindus had become refugees in their own country.

Hedgewar was disappointed that the 1929 Lahore session of the Congress presided over by Jawaharlal Nehru had "damaged the territorial integrity of the country by incorporating the assurance to the 'so called' minorities like Muslims, Sikhs and others that 'no solution thereof in any future constitution will be acceptable to the Congress that does not give full satisfaction to the parties concerned'. This assurance was no less than granting the power of veto to the 'minorities'."[59]

Since then, resentment against Nehru and reverence towards Gandhi has been the constant feature of RSS policy. In later years, five conspicuously controversial strands of RSS policy developed which remain the constant feature of RSS activity even now. This trend became more marked when they distanced themselves from the mainstream independence movement on the ground that it was dominated by certain "unpatriotic" sections in the Congress. The first was their aversion to recognising minority rights, and the second was their antipathy towards Jawaharlal Nehru even as they were anxious to follow Gandhi. The third was the concept of "*Akhand Bharat*" (Undivided India). The fourth was their hesitation to hoist the national flag and the fifth was their mistrust of the constitution. The last two were later watered down for tactical reasons: On 26 January 2002, the national flag was hoisted at the RSS HQ in Nagpur for the first time since 1950.[60]

Chitkara outlines how the concept of "*Akhand Bharat*" arose. In 1931, Hedgewar visited Karachi to set up a *shakha*. In 1932 he again visited Karachi to attend the All-India Hindu Tarun Parishad (Hindu youth conference). He liked Karachi very much and wrote that it excelled other Indian cities like Bombay or Calcutta in beauty, cleanliness, broad roads, gardens, parks and electrical illuminations. The book echoes the RSS resentment against India's partition when this beautiful city had "disappeared from the political map of India."

A similar sentiment was expressed regarding Sri Lanka and Burma, perhaps reflecting the wishful thinking in the RSS. This comes in a summary of activities by year from 1925 till 2000. Against 1935 there is an entry: "Sri Lanka and Myanmar were separated from India."

In fact, these two countries were not "separated" from India in 1935. While it is true that Burma was a province of British India from 1824 to 1948, Ceylon, later Sri Lanka, was never part of the Imperial British India even during the colonial rule from 1796 to 1948. It was governed by a British governor directly under the British monarch.

In 1930 the Simon Commission, which also visited India for recommending constitutional reforms, had suggested the separation of Burma from India against the background of deep local resentment over uncontrolled Indian migration. As a result, the Government of Burma Act was proclaimed on 2 August 1935 which made Burma a dominion.

As regards Sri Lanka, nothing had happened in 1935 meriting its mention in the book. The Ceylon National Congress (CNC), which was formed in 1919, somewhat on the lines of the Indian National Congress (INC) did not seek independence. Gradually two streams of political activities developed there, like in the INC. Those who were called "constitutionalists" were moderates who wanted the gradual evolution of Ceylon towards self-rule. The Colombo Youth League and Jaffna Youth Congress were more radical who wanted "*Swaraj*" or self-rule as in the Indian model. This was after Jawaharlal Nehru and Sarojini Naidu visited Ceylon in 1926. It became a "Dominion" in 1948.

Does "*Akhand Bharat*" include Burma, now Myanmar? On 4 January 2016 an article in the *Indian Express* focussed on the RSS concept of "Bharat". It reproduced a map published by Suruchi Prakashan, an RSS publishing house, showing Pakistan, Afghanistan, Tibet, Sri Lanka and Myanmar as parts of "*Punya Bhoomi Bharat*" (Holy Bharat). It says that "All that's south of the Himalayas and north of the Indian Ocean is Bharat." Afghanistan is called "Upganathan", Kabul "Kubha Nagar", Peshawar "Purushpur", Multan "Moolsthan", Tibet "Trivishtap," Sri Lanka "Singhaldweep" and Myanmar "Brahmadesh", among others. It quotes the late H.V. Sheshadri, a senior RSS leader, saying that the "unnatural" division of Bharat could be set right one day when Pakistan, which has Hindu roots, and Bangladesh could be brought back as "their physical and mental happiness could result only from their union with Bharat and its cultural heritage."[61]

Significantly, this was published after the "surprise" goodwill visit to Lahore by Prime Minister Narendra Modi on 25 December 2015, to greet Pakistan PM Nawaz Sharif on his birthday. It was meant to mend relations with Pakistan. This, together with Al-Jazeera's interview on 26 December with RSS *pracharak* Ram Madhav, who was also BJP National Secretary, diverted the media focus from Modi's goodwill visit to a controversy. Madhav spoke about "*Akhand Bharat*" and his "hopes" that Pakistan and Bangladesh would unite with India "through popular goodwill."[62] Both these incidents raised the question of whether this was meant as a timely rejoinder, to remind the BJP that the RSS still controlled the ideological orientation of the present government. The same adverse optics were witnessed with RSS Chief Mohan Bhagwat's speech on 26 February 2021 at Hyderabad, leaving observers to wonder whether the RSS is unwilling to permit the Modi government to take any measure to bring about friendly neighbourly relations.

Like Modi's 2015 visit to Lahore, the date of 26 February 2021 was very important for India–Pakistan relations. That was when the Indian and Pakistani militaries made a landmark decision to strictly observe the cease fire along the Line of Control (LOC), which in effect, meant stoppage of cross border firing which had brought misery to the villagers on both sides.

This had raised high hopes of peace along the border which was welcomed by senior UN officials and by the political leadership and common people in Jammu & Kashmir, who were the sufferers. The 2003 ceasefire agreement had hardly survived due to tense political relations. According to the official reply in the Indian parliament, 10,752 violations had taken place during the last three years resulting in the deaths of seventy-two Indian security personnel and seventy Indian civilians.[63]

Bhagwat had said, while launching a Sanskrit book *Sanskrit Mahakavyam Vishwabharatham*, that there was no peace in those countries which were separated from India: "Gandhar has become Afghanistan. Pakistan was also part of us. Does peace prevail there now? When we talk about Akhand Bharat, we want to reunite those countries and not suppress them." He also said that "*Akhand Bharat*" was possible alongside and through Hindu Dharma: "Once they are with us, it does not matter what they practice or what they eat. Akhand Bharat did not mean colonialism, but the people would be united through 'Sanatana Dharma', which is 'Hindu Dharma'."[64]

The question is often asked why the RSS, at the highest level, should embarrass the top leadership of Modi government by such policy pronouncements? Was it done to remind Modi that they still held the key to the final political approval of any major government decision, as they had done to former NDA leaders like L.K. Advani, former Deputy Prime Minister and the late Jaswant Singh, former Cabinet Minister for their alleged pro-Jinnah views?

## The RSS and Nehru

At least two complaints of the RSS against Jawaharlal Nehru recorded by Chitkara are factually wrong. The first is that Nehru rejected the Gandhian model of development "outright" while the constitution was being written. This and another complaint on Kashmir were widely repeated by RSS and BJP stalwarts from 2014 onwards. Chitkara argues that "Nehru took pride in saying that he was the last Englishman to rule India. He sought solutions to the essential Indian problems in the foreign models of development. The genesis of maximum Indian problems was in an Oxford educated Nehru taking over as the Prime Minister of India."[65]

Nehru had studied at Cambridge University, not at Oxford. Also, Nehru had no personal role in rejecting the "Gandhian Model of Development." This was done most democratically by different committees involved in the making of the constitution. The circumstances were clearly explained by Granville Austin, a noted constitutional authority, in his illuminating 1964 book on the making of the Indian constitution.[66]

The Congress had won overwhelming majority in the elections to the Constituent Assembly in January 1946, bagging 208 seats against 73 by the Muslim League. It was thus their responsibility to generate ideas on the new constitution. The Congress party therefore constituted a "Constitution Committee" consisting of party stalwarts like Pattabhi Sitaramayya, Purushottam Das Tandon, Acharya Narendra Dev, R.R. Diwakar, S.K. Patil and S.M. Ghose, with Jugal Kishore as convenor.

Gandhi had submitted two plans: One in January 1946 and the other in January 1948. He wanted a "party-less" constitution, using the village as the nucleus. Veteran Gandhian Shriman Narayan had drafted the "Gandhian Constitution for India" by echoing Gandhi's idea that "violence logically leads to centralisation: the essence of non-violence is decentralisation."

Gandhi's plan was for village elders to elect the village *Panchayat* or council, which would control land revenue and police. Groups of village *Panchayats* would elect District *Panchayats* through indirect elections. These elected persons would constitute the provincial *Panchayat* which would elect a president as head of provincial government. Presidents of provincial *Panchayats* would constitute the All-India *Panchayat* whose president would be the head of the national government. This government would oversee all-India matters like defence, finance, and customs.[67]

However, the Congress Party's two committees—the Constitution Committee and Working Committee—did not accept this scheme as they believed that the Congress Party, after such an overwhelming mandate from the people, could not forsake its political role, nor could a diverse country like India be so decentralised. This idea was implemented when the Constituent Assembly's Constitution Drafting Committee under Dr B.R. Ambedkar, who was a non-Congressman, prepared "The Union of States" model of Parliamentary Democracy.[68]

It is not that the Gandhian plan was not discussed by the Constituent Assembly at all. The model again came up for discussion on 10 May 1948 when Dr Rajendra Prasad, President of the Constituent Assembly, wrote to Sir B.N. Rau, a non-Congressman, to redraft the relevant clauses to reflect the Gandhian ideas. However B.N. Rau firmly told Dr Prasad that it was too late to make any such changes as the debates had gone far ahead and the Constituent Assembly had also decided that the lower houses should be directly elected. Paradoxically that was the period (1946–48) when ghastly killings were taking place even within 20 miles of Delhi.

Austin felt that a Gandhian decentralized model of administration would not have worked to face such security challenges. Also, six million refugees had come to north India after partition. The situation in August 1947 was such that the Constituent Assembly members had to obtain curfew passes to attend the session. The situation reminded everybody what Jawaharlal Nehru had said in July 1946: "The scope of the Centre, even though limited, invariably grows, because it cannot exist otherwise." Granville Austin concludes: "This violence brought home the lesson that local law enforcement and local—even provincial—government could be frail reeds in time of great distress, that the centre must have the power to preserve order and the processes of government."[69]

The second complaint against Nehru was his "intervention" on Kashmir. Chitkara says: "The first proof of Nehru's British bias came at the time of Partition. Lord Mountbatten wanted Kashmir to be handed over to Pakistan, the ulterior design which Nehru supported."[70]

Nothing could be farther from the truth. There are authentic records that Lord Mountbatten and Sardar Vallabhbhai Patel had handled Kashmir from the very beginning, preventing Gandhi and Nehru from taking any major role. Maharajah Hari Singh had wanted Kashmir to be independent, which was not allowed under the Indian Independence Act of 1947, which permitted the States to merge either with India or Pakistan.

V.P. Menon, who was Sardar Patel's closest aide, who had brought about the merger of 562 princely states into India and who personally obtained Kashmir's accession to India on 26 October 1947 stated in his book:

Lord Mountbatten knew Sir Hari Singh well, having been on the Prince of Wales' staff during His Royal Highness' tour in 1921–22. He accepted a long-standing invitation from the Maharajah to visit again and went there in the third week of June…He went so far as to tell the maharajah that, if he acceded to Pakistan, India would not take it amiss and that he had the firm assurance on this from Sardar Patel himself.[71]

Mountbatten had also given a frank account of these eventful days in his letters to British Prime Minister Clement Attlee, published in 1948 as "Report on the Last Viceroyalty: 22 March–15 August, 1947." This was included in the "Transfer of Power" series. However, its circulation was restricted under instructions from Attlee since this diary contained highly secret and sensitive material. In 2002 it was decided to publish the text duly edited by Lionel Carter, former librarian of Cambridge University under Crown copyright. Manohar Publishers in India released its Indian edition in 2003.[72]

The book reveals startling details, contrary to the public impression that Nehru and Mountbatten were close personal friends. It disproves the suggestion that Nehru wanted India to remain firmly in the British Commonwealth "with a British bias": as Mountbatten records, "Pandit Nehru also told me on this occasion that he did not consider it possible, for psychological and emotional reasons, for India to remain within the Commonwealth."[73]

Further entries detail tensions regarding the Princely States in general and Kashmir in particular. Mountbatten mentions that he frankly told Nehru that he did like his "inflammatory speech" on 19 April 1947 to the princes giving them an "ultimatum" to join the Constituent Assembly,[74] telling him that this was not authorised by the Cabinet Mission. He records being happy that Sardar Patel was chosen to head the States Department as he was afraid that Pandit Nehru, if heading that department "would not have rendered negotiations with the states easy."

Mountbatten also describes having made a trip to Kashmir with the explicit aim of discouraging both Gandhi and Nehru from going: "One of the reasons for this visit was that by going I hoped to keep Mahatma Gandhi and Pandit Nehru, both of whom wanted to go to Kashmir, from paying a visit at this time."[75] Gandhi met Mountbatten early in June, wanting to visit Kashmir instead of Nehru or "prepare the way for Pandit Nehru." Mountbatten parried him by saying that he would first go to meet the Maharaja, "who was an old acquaintance." The visit took place during 18–23 June. Mountbatten advised Hari Singh not to make the independence declaration. He conveyed Sardar Patel's message that "the States Department were prepared to give an assurance that, if Kashmir went to Pakistan, this would not be regarded as unfriendly by Government of India." But Mountbatten's mission was a failure.[76]

Mountbatten received Gandhi again on 26 June. He found him "distressed about Kashmir." He demanded that either "he or Pandit Nehru must go there at once." Rajmohan Gandhi, Patel's biographer, had said that "Gandhi prayed that Kashmir would disprove the two-nation theory" with "Abdullah's pro-Indian sentiment." A reluctant Mountbatten finally relented and asked Hari Singh to "accept a visit from Gandhi as causing less trouble… than a visit from Pandit Nehru." On 29 July he met Gandhi, Nehru and Patel together to decide who (Gandhi or Nehru) should go. Patel told him that neither should go but "bluntly added: 'If it is a choice between two evils, I consider Gandhiji's visit would be the lesser evil'."[77]

Mountbatten permitted Gandhi's visit on the condition that there should be no political speeches. He added: "It was only with the greatest of difficulty that Pandit Nehru was persuaded to acquiesce in this decision. I was privately informed that, when Sardar Patel tried to reason with him the night before our meeting, Pandit Nehru had broken down and wept, explaining that Kashmir meant more to him than anything else."[78] Gandhi visited Kashmir on 5–6 August 1947.

Had Sardar Patel followed Gandhi's advice, the whole of Kashmir would have been with India. Gandhiji's private notes[79] and his symbolic gesture of taking Begum Abdullah with him (because Abdullah was in prison) for prayer meetings revealed his sharp legal mind and political acumen. He could not write openly because of Mountbatten's ban. He records that he addressed three prayer meetings attended by thousands and was struck by the communal harmony in the state. "They had one language, one culture and so far, as he could see, they were one people." He was also able to meet the Maharajah and his family.

Gandhi said that the 1846 Amritsar Treaty was a "Sale deed" between the British and Gulab Singh, which would be "dead on 15 August." He felt that "paramountcy of Kashmiri people will begin" after 15 August 1947. He was "glad to say that the Maharajah Saheb and Maharani Saheba readily acknowledged the fact." He conveyed to Patel on 6 August that he had sent a note to Nehru who would show it to him. "I think you should do something in the matter. In my opinion the situation in Kashmir can be saved." He was suggesting to Sardar Patel how to deal with Kashmir's accession through Sheikh Abdullah.

Legally, Gandhi was totally correct. Section 7(1) (b) of the Indian Independence Act 1947 had said that all treaties and agreements between the Crown and Indian rulers would lapse on 15 August. It was Gandhi's hint to Sardar Patel to do something to intensify Kashmiri people's agitation for pressing Hari Singh to merge with India. But Patel's "passivity" (to use Raj Mohan Gandhi's expression) continued.

Patel missed another opportunity. Nehru, according to Durga Das, wrote a three-page letter on 27 September 1947 to Patel about the alarming situation developing in Kashmir: "I understand that the Pakistan strategy is to infiltrate into Kashmir now and to take some big action. I hope you will be able to take some action." He suggested using Kashmiri National Conference assets. But the invasion came on 22 October 1947. Balraj Puri had said that it was the National Conference cadres who were overwhelmingly helping the Indian army in October later that year by providing trucks and manpower resulting in their spectacular success.

Given this background, Prime Minister Narendra Modi's address to parliament on 7 February 2018 was a travesty: "If the country's first prime minister was Sardar Vallabh Bhai Patel, then this part of my Kashmir would not have been with Pakistan today." On the contrary, an undivided Kashmir would have been with us had Patel, who was in total charge of the princely states under Mountbatten, followed Gandhi's advice.

On 15 May 2014, a historically untrue claim was made by Priti Gandhi, Co-Convenor of the BJP's Communications Cell in Maharashtra, that Sardar Patel had sent a message to the chief of the RSS, M.S. Golwalker, requesting him to use his influence to prevail upon the Maharajah to accede to India. "Guruji" (respected teacher), as he was fondly called, cancelled all engagements and rushed to Srinagar from Nagpur to resolve the delicate matter. A meeting between Guruji and Maharajah Hari Singh was arranged. This "historic meeting on the issue of national honour ended successfully, after which the Maharaja sent the accession proposal to Delhi and that the Guruji directed the RSS workers in Jammu and Kashmir to shed their blood to the last drop for the integrity of the nation."[80]

This story is found in Chitkara's book too.[81] According to it, Golwalkar returned to Delhi on 19 October 1947 and reported to Patel about the Maharajah's readiness to accede to Bharat. He has quoted no reference to prove this claim.

V.P. Menon's book *The Story of the Integration of the Indian States*, which is a globally accepted historical record of that era, proves that it was Menon, under instructions from Governor General Mountbatten and Home/States Minister Sardar Patel who obtained the instrument of accession from Maharajah Hari Singh on 26 October 1947. Menon, who was then a close confidante of Patel, makes no reference to a Golwalkar visit.

Similarly, the late Balraj Puri, a great Kashmir patriot, had bitterly criticised the Kashmir Rajya Hindu Sabha, "the earliest incarnation of the Bharatiya Janata Party" for passing a resolution in May 1947 supporting Hari Singh's plan of an independent Kashmir which should not merge with a "secular" India. He says: "All those who raised pro-India voices, including me, were condemned as anti-Hindu and traitors."[82]

*Madhavarao Sadashivrao Golwalkar*

M.S. Golwalkar became the second *Sarsanghchalak* of the RSS after Dr Hedgewar passed away in 1940. He was in that position till 1973 followed by Madhukar Dattatray Deoras, popularly known as

Balasaheb who was "detained" during the Emergency. The present *Sarsanghchalak* Mohan Bhagwat is the sixth head of the organisation.

In 1939 Golwalkar published a book *We or Our Nationhood Defined* with the central message that "in this country, our 'Nation' means, and independently of the question of majority always must mean the Hindu Nation and nought else."[83] He elaborates:

> At the outset we must bear in mind that so far as "nation" is concerned, all those who fall outside the fivefold limits of that idea can have no place in national life unless they abandon their differences, adopt the religion, culture and language of the National and completely merge themselves in the National race. So long as they maintain their racial, religious and cultural differences, they cannot but be only foreigners, who may be either friendly or inimical to the nation.

Having held such rigid views on "nationalism" it is not very clear why Golwalkar had requested veteran Congress leader, freedom fighter and educationist Madhav Srihari Aney to write the book's "Foreword" knowing fully well that he would not agree with him. Perhaps it was his desire to start a debate with a known follower of Bal Gangadhar Tilak and opponent of Gandhi's alignment with the Khilafat movement. Golwalkar says:

> It is a matter of personal gratification to me that this maiden attempt of mine—an author unknown in this line—has been graced by a foreword by Loknayak M. S. Aney. Himself a great and selfless patriot, an erudite scholar and a deep thinker, his foreword has, as I had expected, materially enhanced the value of the book. He has candidly expressed where he does not agree with the author, but the reader will agree with me that it is such a learned essay that it will substantially add to his knowledge and make him think.[84]

Aney, in his brilliant foreword, totally demolished the central pivot of the RSS and Golwalkar's belief from 1925:

> I find that the author in dealing with the problems of the Mohameddans' place has not always borne in mind the distinction between the Hindu nationality and Hindu sovereign State. Hindu

Nation as a sovereign State is entirely a different entity from the Hindu nation as a cultural nationality. No modern State has denied the resident minorities of different nationalities rights of citizenship of the State if they are once naturalised either automatically or under the operation of a Statute...

There is nothing inconsistent with the sovereign position of a state in giving these culturally different minorities liberty to retain and observe their religious practices and facilities to preserve their culture, subject to condition of public morals and public policy. No person born in the country, of parents whose ancestors enjoyed rights of citizenship for centuries together can be treated as a foreigner in any modern state on the ground that he follows a religion different from that of the majority population which naturally dominates and controls it. Conversion of faith can't be a condition for naturalisation of any alien in this twentieth century. Allegiance to the State is and must be possible on naturalisation to an alien if he fulfils certain conditions regarding residence, association and similar other matters. But I have not been able to find anywhere conversion to State religion, assuming there is anything like that in modern states in its true sense, prescribed as a condition precedent to naturalisation of an alien...

I also desire to add that the strong and impassioned language used by the author towards those who do not subscribe to his theory of nationalism is also not in keeping with the dignity with which the scientific study of a complex problem like the Nationalism deserves to be pursued. It pains me to make these observations in this foreword. But I feel that I would have been both untrue and unjust to myself in not enforcing my opinion in clear and unambiguous terms on the points above.[85]

It took sixty-seven years for the RSS to disown Golwalkar's theory on nationhood, which resembled the Nazi philosophy on the German *Volk* in Hitler's *Mein Kampf*. In 2006 the RSS disowned Golwalkar's book on the ground that it was "neither representing the views of the 'grown up' Guruji nor of the RSS." The reason, according to the late M.G. Vaidya, a senior leader, was that it did not represent the views of Golwalkar as *Sarsanghchalak*. Vaidya added that the book that was central to them was *Bunch of Thoughts*, a later compilation of Golwalkar's speeches.[86]

However, in 2018 *Sarsanghchalak* Mohan Bhagwat announced that parts of *Bunch of Thoughts* were also not valid anymore as they were made in particular contexts and "cannot remain eternally valid." He quoted the RSS founder Dr Hedgewar "who said that we are free to adapt to times as they change." [87] He added that the RSS has put together Guruji's relevant thoughts in a new book, *Guruji: Vision and Mission*.

## The RSS and violence during the Partition and later

Veteran Indian Civil Service (ICS) officer Rajeshwar Dayal, who was India's ambassador to many countries, later Foreign Secretary and also UN Secretary General's Peace Representative to Lebanon (1958) and Congo (1960), had written about an incident in Lucknow during the Partition period when he was Home Secretary, Uttar Pradesh. He was the first Indian to be appointed to that post in 1946. Pandit Govind Ballabh Pant was the Chief Minister (then called Premier) of the popular government under the Government of India Act 1935.

As Home Secretary Dayal had to face the Partition turbulence. One day B.B.L. Jaitley, the Deputy Inspector General of Police of the Western Range, "a very seasoned and capable officer" came to him with evidence in two "large trunks" to report a serious conspiracy to create widespread communal disturbances throughout the western districts in the state:

> The trunks were crammed with blueprints of great accuracy and professionalism of every town and village in that area, prominently marking out the Muslim localities and habitations. There were also detailed instructions regarding access to the various locations, and other matters which amply revealed their sinister purport. [88]

Dayal took the police officers to the Chief Minister. Timely raids on the premises of the RSS "had brought the conspiracy to light." He and Jaitley wanted the immediate arrest of Golwalkar as there were sufficient grounds that "the whole plot had been concerted under the direction and supervision of the Supremo of the organisation himself." However, Pant, instead of agreeing, wanted this to be discussed in the cabinet next morning.

> It was no doubt a matter of political delicacy as the roots of RSS had gone deep into the body politic. There were also other political compulsions as RSS sympathisers, both covert and overt were to be found in the Congress party itself and even in the Cabinet... what ultimately emerged was that a letter should be issued to Shri Golwalkar on the contents and nature of the evidence.... Golwalkar, however, had been tipped off and he was nowhere to be found in the area. He was tracked down southwards but he managed to elude the couriers in pursuit. This infructuous chase continued from place to place and weeks passed.[89]

Not too long later, on 30 January 1948, Gandhi was assassinated by a "former member of the RSS, Nathuram Godse" as stated by Priti Gandhi of the BJP's Communications Cell in *DNA* in 2014.[90]

Did this incident violate Dr Hedgewar's principle on carrying arms? Chitkara had said that Hedgewar did not want the *swayamsevaks* and arms to mix. He quotes an incident in 1935 when the Collector of Nagpur pointed out the possession of arms by RSS members: "He was particularly upset when the pistol of Shri Pande, a revolutionary leader, was used without his knowledge in a dacoity in Balaghat in January 1931 when Doctorji was in jail. As soon as he came out, he ordered all revolutionary arms destroyed."[91] The RSS has given no explanation why this principle was later breached.

### Revelation in 2017 from the Delhi Police archives

On 10 February 2017 senior journalist Bharat Bhushan reproduced extracts from the Delhi Police archives which made for very disturbing reading. This was after Congress leader Rahul Gandhi was sued by the RSS for his statement in 2014 linking the RSS with Gandhi's assassination. Bhushan wrote:

> Reports available in the public domain in the Delhi Police Archives say that the RSS did threaten Gandhi and claimed that it had the means to silence him. These are the secret source reports of the

Criminal Investigation Department (CID) of the Delhi Police for the months preceding Gandhi's assassination...[92]

"On 8.12.47 about 2500 volunteers of the Sangh collected in their camp on Rohtak Road. After some drill, MS Golwalkar, the Guru of the Sangh addressed the volunteers. He explained the principles of the Sangh and said that it was the duty of every individual to be prepared for facing the coming crisis with full force. Very soon, they would be placing a complete scheme before them. The time for playing had gone...

"Referring to the Government, he said that law could not meet force. We should be prepared for guerrilla warfare on the lines of the tactics of Shivaji. The Sangh will not rest content until it had finished Pakistan. If anyone stood in our way we will have to finish him too, whether it was the Nehru Government or any other Government. The Sangh could not be won over. They should carry on their work.

"Referring to Muslims he said that no power on earth could keep them in Hindustan. They shall have to quit this country. Mahatma Gandhi wanted to keep the Muslims in India so that the Congress may profit by their votes at the time of election. But by that time not a single Muslim will be left in India. If they were made to stay here the responsibility would be Government's and the Hindu community would not be responsible. Mahatma Gandhi could not mislead them any longer. We have the means whereby such man be immediately silenced, but it is our tradition not to be inimical to Hindus. If we are compelled, we will have to that course too."

Bharat Bhushan also produced documentary evidence that *The Indian Express* on 6 February 1948 had said that the revolver that Nathuram Godse used to kill Mahatma Gandhi was presented to him by an RSS leader in Nagpur.

*The RSS and the Emergency (1975–77)*

Chitkara had given high praise to the valiant "freedom" activities of the RSS during Indira Gandhi's Emergency between 1975 and 1977. My impression in Mumbai during that phase was different. In 2015 during the fortieth anniversary of the Emergency, some people had claimed that the RSS had been at the forefront of this silent agitation against Mrs Gandhi. It was claimed that thousands of RSS workers were printing and circulating clandestine pamphlets all over the country.

Quite a few people believed this fiction in the wake of the BJP's overwhelming win in the 2014 general election. Nothing could be farther than the truth. I was in charge of the Emergency enforcement in Bombay till May 1976, and I can unhesitatingly say that the RSS took no part in this till at least the middle of 1976.

On the other hand, they were very meek and submissive, ready to cooperate with the government to avoid arrests. A senior BJP leader had called me to his home in Malabar Hill and pleaded with me not to arrest him. They were ready to cooperate with Indira Gandhi's twenty-point programme. They said they were anti-Communists like Sanjay Gandhi.

During those days I saw three letters from Balasaheb Deoras, RSS Chief, to the Prime Minister requesting her to lift the ban on the RSS and release the cadres to enable their volunteers "to participate in the planned programme of action relating to country's progress and prosperity under the PM's leadership." Copies of these letters were marked to Chief Minister S.B. Chavan who used to send them to me for my remarks. Deoras also wrote to Chavan five times to release him on parole so that he could discuss these issues. Two letters were written to Acharya Vinoba Bhave, a noted Gandhian too. The last one, which was undated, written from St. George's Hospital, Bombay was to request him to speak to Mrs. Gandhi who was visiting Pavnar Ashram to meet him.

During the Emergency a policy decision was taken at New Delhi that those who would sign an "undertaking" could be considered for release. Not a single Socialist leader signed this undertaking. On the other hand, RSS leaders were prepared to sign. The letter from Shri Deoras dated 12 July 1976 is clear on that.

Texts of these letters as placed on the table of the Maharashtra State Assembly have been reproduced by noted jurist, scholar and author A.G. Noorani in his book *The RSS: A Menace to India*.[93]

*Vigilante violence after the Modi government came to power in 2014*

Soon after the Modi government came into power, stray assaults on Christian pastors in tribal areas started. Even Delhi "bore the brunt" with attacks on five churches.[94] *The Guardian* (UK) ranked India fifteenth in the world in terms of danger to Christians, up from thirty-first four years earlier. According to this report, a church was burnt down or a cleric beaten on average ten times a week in India in the year to 31 October 2016, a threefold increase on the previous years.[95]

A report in *The Indian Express* stated that the VHP in Madhya Pradesh, a state that had been "captured" by the BJP after a large number of Congress MLAs defected in May 2020, was systematically "identifying" missionaries allegedly carrying out illegal conversions. VHP national general secretary Milind Parande announced that they had identified fifty-six missionaries allegedly indulging in illegal religious conversions.[96]

The VHP and other RSS front organisations say that the number of Christians in India is increasing, and these conversions pose a national security threat. A study in *The Print* ridicules this fear:

> The Census data shows that the Christian population in India is either static or dwindling since 1951. In the 2001 Census, Christians' share in Indian population was 2.34 per cent; in 2011, it fell to 2.30 per cent. The decadal growth of Hindus during the same period was 16.8 per cent, higher than the increase in Christian population, which was 15.5 per cent.[97]

*Cow vigilante violence against Muslims*

On 18 February 2019 *Human Rights Watch* reported that the BJP had elevated their communal rhetoric since May 2014, initiating a violent vigilante campaign against beef consumption and trade.[98] Between May 2015 and December 2018, at least forty-four people—thirty-six of them Muslims—were killed across twelve Indian states. Around the same period, nearly 280 people were injured in over 100 different incidents across twenty states. A group of Dalits who were removing the skin of a dead cow for processing the hide as leather were savagely beaten up in Gujarat in July 2016. Home Minister Rajnath Singh condemned the violence but refused to accept its origins.

On 10 April 2017, RSS Chief Mohan Bhagwat deplored violence in the name of the cow but called for a countrywide ban on cow slaughter. This came immediately after the brutal murder of Pehlu Khan in Rajasthan which was seen all over the country on TV showing *gorakshaks* (cow protectors) beating him with sticks until he collapsed. Prime Minister Narendra Modi also condemned this violence in August 2018 and January 2019. However, it did not have much effect even in BJP-ruled states.

A survey by Indian, foreign media and by NGOs had said that this type of violence, which was very rare till 2013 (one case in 2012 by the VHP and two cases in 2013), shot up to a total of eighty-two incidents between 2014 and 2020 involving forty-three deaths and 145 injuries, mostly of Muslims and Dalits.[99] These incidents have not only disturbed the communal harmony in India but also adversely affected a flourishing trade in the export of beef and leather, causing financial losses even to Hindus.

Details of this trade are as follows: India is said to have the largest livestock population in the world. The country is also the biggest producer of milk in the world and also the third largest bovine meat exporter to about seventy countries. Some 55 per cent of India's population are engaged in agriculture. They possess nearly 190 million cattle and 108 million buffaloes which supplement their income and food requirements.

With the rise in cow vigilante violence, the number of animals traded in cattle fairs has fallen. Farmers usually sell their "spent animals" or milk-dry cattle and buy new ones. Rajasthan, which organises ten cattle fairs a year, saw less footfall in such fairs after the violence started. On average, 31,000 of 56,000 heads of cattle brought to the fairs were sold during 2010–11. In 2016–17 this fell to 11,000 cattle, of which only 3,000 were sold. Since farmers cannot sell their aged cattle, they abandon them into the open, thereby swelling the number of stray cattle. As a result, the rural cattle trade collapsed, and the law and order problem worsened.

According to government data, while the export of leather and leather products grew by more than 18 per cent in 2013–14, growth fell steeply to 9 per cent in 2014–15. The growth declined by nearly 20 percentage points to −9.86 per cent in 2015–16. It grew again but at a much smaller rate of 1.4 per cent in 2017–18.[100]

An article in *The Indian Express* in June 2019 said that for decades "spent animals" would move to Bangladesh and Myanmar via the northeast of India. According to unofficial records, almost 2.5–2.8 million cattle used to cross the border every year—this illegal trade was estimated to be worth more than Rs 20,000 crore (c. $2.5 billion/£2 billion). In 2014 Home Minister Rajnath Singh announced a policy that "Bangladesh would be starved of their beef." Strict controls have thus been placed on cattle movements across the border.

At the same time no-one thought about what would happen to these cattle straying around in the country. Since nearly 10 per cent of the country's livestock of over 250 million becomes unproductive every year, this has become a huge problem. It is estimated that there are more than 10 million stray cattle in the country damaging crops. Shelters and fodder could not cater to even 10 per cent of these animals. In the Delhi–National Capital Region, more than 200 cows and bulls die every year due to lack of such resources.[101]

In December 2018 farmers in Aligarh district in Uttar Pradesh were seen driving these stray cattle into local schools disrupting studies since they were eating their crops.[102] Experts thus feel a purely economic problem could spiral out of control if viewed purely through an ideological prism.

## The RSS' role in "shepherding" the Modi government

In 2014 I was talking to a senior former BJP functionary, who was closely associated with former prime minister Atal Bihari Vajpayee and deputy prime minister L.K. Advani. He was no longer in the good books of the RSS. He had told me, well before the general elections, that then Chief Minister Narendra Modi had assured the

RSS top brass that he would usher in a "Hindu Rashtra" if their cadres supported him in the elections. It is common knowledge that tens of thousands of *swayamsevaks* had done grass root campaigning in 2014 for Narendra Modi's candidates all over India.

Yet *The Indian Express* carried a report on 18 September 2018 that Bhagwat had embarrassed the BJP, their own political front.[103] It listed five occasions when he had contradicted the BJP's political strategy, including: he praised the Congress party for its role in the freedom struggle, which Prime Minister Narendra Modi did not; he did not endorse the BJP's election slogan under Modi's leadership of "Congress Mukt Bharat" ("Congress-Free India"); and he did not believe that only Prime Minister Narendra Modi was responsible for the BJP's 2014 victory.

That surprised everybody since it was made in the background of an image spread by BJP's spinmeisters through their overarching propaganda that Modi alone was responsible for the 2014 landslide victory. As the report put it:

> Just after the BJP government came to power at the Centre following a landslide victory in 2014, Bhagwat struck a discordant note with the party's suggestion that win was solely due to Narendra Modi's personal image. Bhagwat said an individual could not have ensured the BJP's victory.

Eyebrows were raised when the BJP National President J.P. Nadda told *The Indian Express* on 22 May 2024, during the general elections, that that the party "has grown from the time it needed the RSS and is now 'saksham' (capable) and runs its own affairs." The RSS, he said, is an "ideological front" and does its own work.[104]

### *The RSS and Modi's cult of personality*

Or was Bhagwat's speech meant to publicly disapprove of the cult of personality that has developed around Narendra Modi since 2014? Compared to the senior government functionaries, the RSS leadership adopts a spartan and disciplined lifestyle.

Chitkara describes this as *"Vanaprastha"*, which in Vedic texts denotes the third or fourth stage of a Hindu life meaning "retired."

Or it could be, as described by Chitkara, where the person "becomes an intense seeker of truth and spends his time in self-reflection."[105] The speech of Mohan Bhagwat on 17 February 2020, to follow the Gandhian principles to usher in "Gandhiji's Bharat," might have been an example of this thinking.[106]

This was also my experience throughout my seventeen-year service in Maharashtra Police in different districts like Nashik, Sangli, Yeotmal and in Bombay city where I had the chance to interact with several RSS functionaries at different levels. Some of them were my personal friends. They lived spartan lives and showed no interest in flamboyant living, which their families also adopted.

One person deserves special mention. It was Ramdas Nayak, a senior RSS and BJP leader from Bandra, one of the most pleasant politicians I had ever met. He used to drop in at my Special Branch office frequently during 1973–76 to discuss the political situation. He was also a fearless anti-corruption crusader who had earned fame later as the person who had lodged a criminal complaint against the powerful Maharashtra Congress Chief Minister A.R. Antulay after obtaining sanction from the Governor, which compelled the latter to resign.[107]

It was a tragedy that the Bombay underworld led by Dawood Ibrahim had shot and killed him in 1994. Had he been alive he would have been the BJP Chief Minister of Maharashtra or even an important Central minister.

In this background it was disappointing to find some RSS *pracharaks* indulging in excessive and incredulous hyperbole while describing Narendra Modi. On 14 March 2021, the newly anointed Chief Minister Tirath Singh Rawat of Uttarakhand, who had been a *pracharak* since 1983, said that Modi would be "worshipped" in future like Lord Ram for the good work done by him for society.[108]

On 6 March 2021, Rajmohan Gandhi, eminent intellectual and grandson of Gandhi, published a scathing article in *The Indian Express* captioned "Dear Leader" on Modi's personality cult:

> He can build the world's tallest statue for Sardar Patel one day and later calmly agree that his own name should replace that of

Patel for the prestigious stadium.... He can write in the New York Times "The world bows to you, Bapu" and permit the humiliation of India's minorities for whose protection Gandhi gave his life.... For years our Prime Minister has been here, there and everywhere. He smiles down at us from huge hoardings.... Although he seems to talk to us all day and everyday, we cannot speak to him.... And we certainly cannot ask him questions. During his seven years so far as Prime Minister, he has not held a single press conference....[109]

## The RSS and the Krishna Janmabhoomi movement

After the Ram Janmabhoomi/Babri Masjid verdict in favour of the Hindus on 9 November 2019, it was thought that the RSS and its front organisations would not press for similar legal settlements in respect of some other temples where Muslim rulers had built mosques. On the day of the verdict, RSS chief Mohan Bhagwat "suggested that the Sangh was unlikely to get involved in Hindu seers' and Right-wing groups' claims over the Gyanvapi mosque in Varanasi and the Shahi Idgah in Mathura."[110]

Despite winning the 2019 state assembly elections especially in UP with a comfortable, although reduced majority, a trend was seen all over to whip up communal tensions in the country, especially in BJP-ruled states with a view to winning the 2024 general elections. A reopening of the Gyanvapi–Kashi temple and Mathura Krishna Janmabhoomi temple was interpreted as RSS–BJP attempt to polarise voters.

However, on 2 June 2022, Bhagwat surprised the country by saying that the RSS did not want to escalate the Gyanvapi matter which is before the court: "One should not raise a new issue every day. Why escalate fights? Regarding Gyanvapi, our faith has been there for generations. What we are doing is fine. But why look for a Shivling in every mosque?"[111] This was welcomed by some Muslim leaders. However, the news report added, quoting a BJP leader that neither the party nor the RSS would stop pushing for amendments to the 1991 Places of Worship (Special Provisions) Act as it reflected "the sentiments of the Hindu majority." In other words, the religious momentum could be continued till 2024 without street agitation.

Harish Khare, one of India's most senior journalists, felt that Bhagwat had "rescued" Prime Minister Narendra Modi from his "tactical silence on the whole Kashi–Mathura caboodle" which was threatening "to explode our social peace and overwhelm India's growth story."[112]

The RSS has huge organizational power and disciplined cadres to help transform India into a disciplined, tolerant, law abiding and inclusive nation to meet various challenges especially on economic and security fronts. This cannot be achieved merely by building up our military capacity, which is only one aspect of security competence. Equally important is economic strength, which cannot be achieved without an inclusive society where opportunities are available for all. This is the only way India can catch up with China in a democratic manner by 2047.

4

# THE IDEA OF INDIA

> The Ganga to me is the symbol of India's memorable past
> which has been flowing into the present and continues to
> flow towards the ocean of the future.
>
> Jawaharlal Nehru

Jawaharlal Nehru travelled to Europe in the summer of 1938 with
his daughter Indira. He had been released from Almora Jail on
3 September 1935 after undergoing his seventh imprisonment,
which had started on 12 February 1934. While in Paris he asked
his friend A.C.N. Nambiar, who was staying in Prague, to meet
him. Nambiar, a prominent journalist, had been arrested in 1933
and expelled from Berlin by the Nazi government for his alleged
anti-Nazi activities. Travelling from Prague by train, he met the
Nehrus at their hotel near the Chambre de Deputies (Parliament).

Among many other things, Nehru told Nambiar that Andre
Malraux, the famous French writer/philosopher, had met him in
Paris in a restaurant. That was their first meeting. After introducing
himself Malraux suddenly asked him: "What is the force in
Hinduism that kept Buddhism greatly out of India?" Nambiar
stated that this was the reason why Jawaharlal Nehru wrote *The
Discovery of India*.[1]

The book became a landmark volume on the "Idea of India" with its message to its own people and to the world. Albert Einstein wrote to Nehru on 18 February 1950 from Princeton: "I have read with extreme interest your marvellous book The Discovery of India. The first half of it is not easy reading for a Westerner. But it gives an understanding of the glorious intellectual and spiritual traditions of your great country...."[2]

Legendary New York Times correspondent A.M. Rosenthal who was stationed in New Delhi during 1954–58 said in his column "India's Gift—The Discovery of Each Day" in 1984:

> Jawaharlal Nehru, who was Prime Minister of India when I lived there, wrote a book I took everywhere with me in my years of travel in the country. It was called "The Discovery of India." To me, the title meant that India was a perpetual discovery, too large to be known entirely but always available for one more journey, one more discovery.[3]

Another great man who acknowledged Nehru as his inspiration was Martin Luther King, who inscribed a copy of his newly published book Stride Toward Freedom in 1958 to Nehru with these words: "In appreciation of your genuine good will, your broad humanitarian concern, and the inspiration that your great struggle for India gave to me and the 50,000 Negroes of Montgomery."[4]

Nehru confirms his meeting with Malraux in his book. He started writing it only when he was lodged in Ahmednagar Fort prison during his ninth term of imprisonment from 1942 to 1945. He recalled how "the beautiful and courageous queen Chand Bibi had defended this fort and led her forces, sword in hand against the imperial armies of Akbar before she was killed by her own men."[5] He completed writing Discovery in five months from April to September 1944. Later he was transferred to Almora Jail nearer his home in Allahabad. The book was published only in December 1945 after he was finally released from jail on 15 June 1945. Nehru was imprisoned for his freedom activities for more than nine years in nine phases, the longest ever suffered by any Indian freedom fighter.

At Ahmednagar jail he was assisted in his research by eleven of his compatriots who were with him. Fortunately, they were very proficient in major Indian languages like Hindi, Urdu, Bengali, Gujarati, Marathi, Telugu, Sindhi, and Oriya, as well as classical languages like Sanskrit, Pali, Arabic and Persian. He specifically mentioned Maulana Abul Kalam Azad, Govind Ballabh Pant, Narendra Deva and M. Asaf Ali, who were of great assistance to him.

His meeting with Malraux is mentioned in Chapter Five ("Through the Ages") under the caption "How did Hinduism absorb Buddhism in India." The expanse of Malraux's epistemological inquiry is best understood with a quotation from Nehru:

> Eight or nine years ago Malraux put me a strange question at the very beginning of our conversation. What was it, he asked me that enabled Hinduism, to push away organized Buddhism from India, without any major conflict, over a thousand years ago? How did Hinduism succeed in absorbing, as it were, a great and widespread popular religion, without the usual wars of religion which disfigure the history of so many countries? What inner vitality or strength did Hinduism possess then which enabled it to perform this remarkable feat? And did India possess this inner vitality and strength to-day? If so, then her freedom and greatness were assured.[6]

## The idea of India: its unity through mutual understanding

Nehru's extensive travels within his home district from June 1920—along with agitating *kisans* (farmers) during the agrarian upheaval in the 1920s—opened his eyes to the reality of rural India, its poverty, its deep religiosity, and essential unity.[7] These farmers were demanding justice from the "crushing exactions" of *taluqdars* (revenue officials), *zamindars* (landlords) and money lenders. They were led by one Baba Ramchandra, once an indentured Maharashtrian labourer in Fiji, who returned to India and became a peasant leader in Pratapgarh, Rae Bareli and Faizabad in Oudh (Avadh) region in the United Provinces, now Uttar Pradesh.

Ramchandra used to go from village to village, recite Tulsidas' *Ramcharitmanas* and remind the villagers that they were living in the holy land of Rama and Sita in the legendary kingdom of Ayodhya. He also taught them to organize themselves as "*sabhas*" or collectives, to boldly put across their grievances. In addition, he taught them to communicate from village to village through word of mouth. On receiving "alerts" they would stream out of their villages to the meeting place at a moment's notice with a slogan of "Sita Ram."

From 1921 onwards Nehru witnessed Gandhi's prayer meetings in the evenings which always began with a recitation of a few verses from Bhagavad Gita and how it emotionally moved the villagers. Gandhi had adopted the "Upanishad" style of teaching where the guru always started instructions with a "peace chant." It was then that Nehru started believing in the "spiritualisation of politics, using the word not in its narrow religious sense" which seemed to him a fine idea.[8]

Later Nehru travelled the length and breadth of the country, observing its mighty rivers, valleys and mountains, its forests and plains and visiting monuments like Ajanta, Ellora and Elephanta. During 1936–37 he had to visit several places from the borders of Tibet to Balochistan for electioneering by using planes, railway trains and even "an elephant, a camel, or a horse; or travel by steamer, paddle-boat, or canoe; or use a bicycle, or go on foot" as he said later.[9]

One of his most absorbing experiences was at the Kumbh Mela in his hometown where "hundreds of thousands come, as their forebears had come for thousands of years from all over India, to bathe in the Ganges." He would remember what the Chinese pilgrims and others had written thirteen hundred years ago about these festivals, even when these *melas* were ancient and lost in an unknown antiquity. "What was the tremendous faith, I wondered that had drawn our people for untold generations to this famous river of India?"

He said that innumerable pictures of this past would fill and flash in his mind when he visited each such place which had given India a cultural stability for thousands of years: like in Sarnath near Benares where he could visualize Lord Buddha preaching his first sermon or in Fatehpur Sikri where he could imagine Akbar conversing with the learned of all faiths to find answers to the destiny of man. "Thus, slowly the long panorama of India's history unfolded itself before me, with its ups and downs, its triumphs and defeats."

Nehru says that "the roots of that present lay in the past and so I made voyages of discovery into the past, ever seeking a clue in it, if any such existed, to the understanding of the present." He quotes Professor Gordon Childe, Australian culture-historical archaeologist, who had said that the Indus civilization represented a very perfect adjustment of human life to a specific environment that could only have resulted from years of patient effort. "And it has endured; it is already specifically Indian and forms the basis of modern Indian culture."

He found that the continuous thread of Indian history from the Aryan entry from the second millennium BCE onwards to the end of British Empire in 1947 was one of migration or invasion followed by efforts to impose their alien culture, which instead resulted in a cultural synthesis through assimilation with the local milieu and finally settling down as Indians. One could see this in religion, culture, arts, food, and music. Another continuous feature of this process was that this pattern peacefully endured for long periods although interspersed with violent skirmishes, thus exhibiting a large amount of tolerance towards a composite Indian culture.

Nehru was astonished that any culture or civilization should have this continuity for five or six thousand years or more and after coming into intimate contact with the Persians, Egyptians, Greeks, Chinese, Arabs, Central Asians, and Mediterranean people. Although India influenced them and was also influenced by these contacts, her cultural basis was strong enough to endure. He asked himself, what was its secret? He concludes that India was something like "an ancient palimpsest on which layer upon layer of thought and reverie had been inscribed, and yet no succeeding layer had completely hidden or erased what had been written previously."

Eminent historian R.C. Majumdar also concurs in Book 1 (*The Vedic Age*) of a mammoth 11-volume series (*The History and Culture of the Indian People*) on Indian culture and history published by Bharatiya Vidya Bhavan in 1950 under guidance of Dr K.M. Munshi:

> The modern peoples of Egypt and Mesopotamia have no bond whatsoever with the civilization that flourished there millennia ago and its memorials have no more (usually very very much less) meaning to them than to any man in any part of the world.
>
> But not so in India. The icons discovered at Mohenjo-daro are those of gods and goddesses are still worshipped in India, and Hindus from the Himalaya to Cape Comorin repeat even today the Vedic hymns which were uttered on the banks of the Indus nearly four thousand years ago. This continuity in language and literature and in social usages, is more prominent in India than even in Greece and Italy where we can trace the same continuity in history.[10]

During these travels Nehru noticed a deep feeling of "oneness" among Indians, which had held them together for ages, despite their diversity, infinite variety, and political differences. This was due to a mixture of popular philosophy, tradition, history, myth, and legend which was shared by common people whether educated, uneducated or illiterate. They could quote the old epics *Ramayana* or *Mahabharata* and other holy books which they had learnt through popular translations or in village banyan-tree meetings. Every incident together with its story and moral was etched in their minds.

He found that their conversations would be full of references to these incidents in the epics. Even illiterate villagers would quote verses from these epics during their conversation while discussing present-day affairs. He saw the moving drama of the Indian people in the present, which could often trace "the threads which bound their lives to the past, even while their eyes were turned towards the future." For Nehru, the unity of India was no longer merely an intellectual conception—it was an emotional experience which overpowered him. He felt that the essential unity was so powerful that no political division, no disaster, or catastrophe had been able to overcome it.

## Pre-Aryans and Aryans: How history affected the Indian ethos

Nehru dwelt at some length on the highly developed Indus Valley civilization, "which must have taken thousands of years to reach that stage", and was "a predominantly secular civilization"—"the religious element, though present, did not dominate the scene."[11] Sir John Marshall, authority on the Indus Valley civilization, had said that Mohenjo-daro and Harappa must have had millennia of human endeavour behind it, like Persia, Mesopotamia, and Egypt. It was also clearly the precursor of later cultural periods in India. Marshall had said that the religion of the Indus people was "so characteristically Indian as hardly to be distinguished from still living Hinduism." From then on, India witnessed a latent sense of continuity connecting modern India with that far distant period of six or seven thousand years ago especially in popular ritual, craftsmanship and even in fashions in dress.

British Historian Michael Edwards has quoted the inscription made by Darius I on his own gravestone in 486 BCE to prove that the original homeland of the Aryans must have been Persia: "*Parsa, Parahya putra, Arya, Arya cithra*" ("A Persian, son of a Persian, an Aryan of Aryan descent").[12] Aryan invasions started in the second millennium BCE. Gradually they married female "slaves" or "*Dasyus*" (Dravidians—local inhabitants) who were most probably of the Indus Valley civilization.

They absorbed the conquered population into a new system of occupational society calling them Brahmins (priests), Kshatriyas (warriors) and Vaishyas (commercial classes). Initially, Vaishyas included cultivators, traders, goldsmiths, and others. Historians say that similar social divisions had existed among Iranians and in early Greece and Rome. However, the Indo-Aryans added a fourth category called "Shudras" or serfs who were the descendants of Dasyus.

Twentieth century "Dalit" or "Neo-Buddhist" writers have described this period as the first subjugation of depressed classes by upper castes. Others have said that the basic Indian culture grew out of this synthesis by intermarriage. It had the distinct elements of both.

Yet caste (derived from the Portuguese word *casta*) was not exclusive for performing duties during the Vedic period. A warrior could become a priest and the king could perform priestly functions. Caste rigidity started increasing with the rise of Brahminism which was resisted by Buddhists and Jains in the sixth century BCE. That was also the period of the Upanishads and the Sankya School of Kapila.

## The epic period

During the Vedic period the Aryans reached only as far as Ambala. The need for more pastures made them move towards the "*madhya desa*" or middle country which was the area between the Jamuna and Ganga rivers. From then on the Ganga replaces the Indus as the sacred river in the epic literature. That was the era of the *Ramayana* and *Mahabharata*.

Both the *Ramayana* and *Mahabharata* were written during the pre-Buddhist period with additions made later. The Aryans were settling down and consolidating themselves in India. Probably this was the period when foreigners were coming to India and bringing their customs with them as seen in Draupadi's marriage with five brothers when Aryans did not have polyandry among them. The *Ramayana* story is perhaps the Aryan expansion to the South. In the *Mahabharata* there was every attempt to prove the fundamental unity of India, or "Bharatavarsha as it was called, from Bharata the legendary founder of the race." Earlier it was called "Aryavarta," the land of the Aryas which was confined to the Vindhya mountains in central India.

## The development of Hinduism

Most historians and theologists, including Nehru, say that the word "Hindu" was not mentioned in India's ancient literature.[13] It was mentioned in the Avesta and in old Persian. It is said that the Persians could not pronounce the letter "s" correctly and mispronounced it as "h". Hence the word "Sindhu" became "Hindu." The ancient Persian Cuneiform inscriptions and the Zend Avesta refer to the word "Hindu" as a geographic term rather than a religious name. When the Persian King Darius 1 extended his empire up to the borders of the Indian subcontinent in 517 BCE, some people of the Indian area became part of his empire and army. Thus, for a very long time the ancient Persians referred to these people as "Hindus." The ancient Greeks and Armenians followed the same pronunciation, and thus, gradually the name stuck.[14]

Nehru says the word had clearly derived from Sindhu, the old, as well as the present, Indian name for the Indus. From this Sindhu came the words Hindu and Hindustan as well as Indus and India. The use of the word "Hindu" in connection with a particular religion was of very late occurrence. He also says that the old inclusive term for religion in India was "*Arya dharma*." Dharma really meant something more than religion. It is from a root word which meant to "hold together"; it was an ethical concept which included the moral code, righteousness, and the whole range of man's duties and responsibilities. This was the same meaning conveyed by the late Prime Minister Atal Bihari Vajpayee to the then Gujarat Chief Minister Narendra Modi to follow "*Raj dharma*" during the 2002 Gujarat communal riots when a large number of Muslims were killed.[15]

Nehru said that "*Arya dharma*" included all faiths (Vedic and non-Vedic) that originated in India; it was used by Buddhists and Jains as well as by those who accepted the Vedas. Buddha always called his way to salvation the "Aryan path." All those who acknowledged the general authority of the Vedas could be said to belong to the Vedic dharma. Similarly, "*Sanatana dharma*," meaning the ancient religion, could be applied to any of the ancient Indian faiths, including Buddhism and Jainism. Nehru laments that the expression was "more or less monopolised" by some orthodox sections among the Hindus who claim to follow the ancient faith.

He believes that Buddhism and Jainism were certainly not Hinduism or even Vedic dharma. Yet they arose in India and were integral parts of Indian life, culture, and philosophy. A Buddhist or Jain in India is a product of Indian thought and culture, yet neither is a Hindu by faith. It is, therefore, entirely misleading to refer to Indian culture as Hindu culture. In later ages this culture was greatly influenced by the impact of Islam, and yet it remained basically and distinctively Indian. A Christian or a Muslim often adapted himself to the Indian way of life and culture, and yet remained in faith an orthodox Christian or Muslim. He had "Indianized" himself and become an Indian without changing his religion.

Nehru quotes Mahatma Gandhi on the definition of Hinduism:

> If I were asked to define the Hindu creed, I should simply say: Search after truth through nonviolent means. A man may not believe in God and still call himself a Hindu. Hinduism is a relentless pursuit after truth.... Hinduism is the religion of truth. Truth is God. Denial of God we have known. Denial of truth we have not known.

Gandhi had expressed some more thoughts on the "Idea of India." As Dr Usha Thakkar, President of Mani Bhavan Gandhi Museum, Mumbai conveyed to me in December 2020, Gandhiji said in 1921: "I do not want my house to be walled in on all sides and my windows to be stuffed. I want the cultures of all lands to be blown about my house as freely as possible. But I refuse to be blown off my feet by any."[16] In 1927 he said: "I do not expect the India of my dream to develop one religion, i.e., to be wholly Hindu, or wholly Christian or wholly Mussalman, but I want it to be wholly tolerant, with its religions working side by side with one another."[17] And in 1930 he asserted: "There never can be any conflict between the real interest of one's country and that of one's religion. Where there appears to be any, there is something wrong with one's religion, i.e., one's morals. True religion means good thought and good conduct. True patriotism also means good thought and good conduct. To set up a comparison between two synonymous things is wrong."[18]

## How Buddhism spread, yet is not considered a separate religion

Both Jainism and Buddhism were considered not in revolt against Hinduism but an attack on polytheism and Brahminism. Vardhamana Mahavira (540–468 BCE) and Siddhartha Gautama were both Kshatriyas and believed in Hindu tenets of karma and rebirth. Mahavira believed in extreme penance and that it was holy to take one's own life. Gautama was more moderate. Both preached non-violence and casteless societies; yet neither claimed that they were breaking away from Aryan tradition. That was one reason why the common people did not feel that these two were new religions.

Common people found Buddha's message attractive. Michael Edwards said that it offered a new revelation which resembled a classless religion. However, it was not a new religion at all but "the restatement of social truths in a new and dynamic form." His messages were simple which common people could understand: "Let a man overcome anger by love, let him overcome evil by good"; "Let him overcome the greedy by liberality, the liar by truth."[19]

The ruling elite also found Buddhism appealing. It received an impetus during the regime of Bimbisara ruling Magadha, South Bihar (540 BCE) who had met Gautama before his enlightenment. In fact the Magadha empire, the doyen among such contemporary kingdoms like Kosala (Oudh), was famous as one of the sixteen kingdoms known as "*Mahajanpadas*" (great foothold of the people) in ancient northern India for all the three religions: Hinduism, Jainism and Buddhism.[20] The episode of Bimbisara offering his kingdom to Gautama is an important episode in the life of the Buddha.[21] According to Hiuen Tsang, he built Rajgir in Bihar, famous for Buddhist writings. His son Ajathasastru (492–460 BCE), who imprisoned his father to take over the throne, patronised both Jainism and Buddhism. Under him Magadha became the most powerful kingdom in north India.

From 413 BCE onwards Magadha was captured from the House of Bimbisara by the Nanda dynasty, which in turn was overthrown by Chandragupta Maurya in 322 BCE. His rule till 297 BCE was described by Buddhist, Jain, Hindu, and Greek texts, since he patronised all religions, as was the trend then. His chief adviser was Kautilya, a Hindu Brahmin. Megasthenes, Greek ambassador historian and Kautilya had recorded that the state-owned slaughterhouses and gambling places were running despite the ruler's sympathy towards Buddhism. Also "wines and prostitution had each a separate government department."[22]

In 298 BCE Chandragupta Maurya either retired to become a Jain monk or died. His son Bindusara ascended the throne and after his death in 273 BCE, Ashoka the Great became the ruler. By 250 BCE he expanded his empire through violent wars to practically the whole of India including present-day Afghanistan. His empire extended from the Himalayas to Mysore and from Assam to the Hindu Kush. Anguished by the bloodshed in the wars, he was reported to have converted to Buddhism through the famous Buddhist ascetic Upagupta of Mathura. However, historians doubt whether Ashoka ever renounced Hinduism. "Ashoka was merely a Hindu monarch...for the separateness of Buddhism from the mainstream Hindu thought was, in the eyes of its contemporaries, only as sectarian as the various faces of Christianity today."[23]

Ashoka's foreign policy was based on co-existence rather than expansion, which was also the corner stone of Nehruvian foreign policy of "Peaceful Co-existence." In his edicts he hoped that "unsubdued borderers should not be afraid of me, that they should trust me, and should receive from me happiness not sorrow." This did not mean that he was a lax ruler. Along with establishing a strong Central authority he wanted to produce "peace necessary for ordered economic expansion, and an assurance of the justice and morality of the central authority."[24]

Peace during Ashoka's reign allowed the development of pure Sanskrit language into the realms of elite society, trade and commerce, something like French in eighteenth-century Europe. It also allowed Brahminism to thrive and for the development of Hindu gods like Vishnu–Krishna and Siva who replaced the Vedic gods.

Ashoka's death in 232 BCE saw the disintegration of his empire with Taxila, Kalinga and Andhra breaking away. The Mauryan dynasty ruled till 185 BCE. The last Mauryan emperor Brihadratha was killed by his army chief Pushyamitra who founded the Sunga dynasty which lasted for 100 years. Pushyamitra moved the capital from Pataliputra to Malwa. The Sungas reverted to orthodox Brahminism for statecraft. Brahmin ministers became powerful. They also "laid the foundations for destruction of Buddhist shrines, monasteries, icons and history."[25]

In a way they were the forerunners of later Muslim invaders who destroyed Hindu temples. Dr Suraj Yengde, Senior Fellow at the Shorenstein Center at the Harvard Kennedy School, holds the view that Muslim invaders attacked the Hindu temples more for their wealth and capital rather than for destroying a religion as the "Brahminists" had done: "The most famous temples in India, Pakistan and Nepal originally used to be the Buddhist places of learning and worship."[26]

By the first century BCE the landscape of India was made up of the Sungas ruling the centre and west Gangetic plain, the Andhras occupying the north of the peninsula and Malwa, and Kalinga strongly holding the east coast. South of the Andhras the peninsula was divided between the Cholas in the east, Keralas (Cheras) in the southwest and the Pandyas in the southeast.[27]

*Flow of foreigners into India after Mauryas collapsed and their integration into India*

The Mauryan break up encouraged the Greeks to cross over to India. Even during Ashoka's reign (250 BCE) Diodotas, governor of Bactria (Balk), had proclaimed himself to be independent. Later Gandhara was occupied. The flow included Iranians, Greeks, Parthians, Bactrians, Scythians, Huns, Turks (before Islam), early Christians, Jews, and Zoroastrians. They were also absorbed despite India's caste system and exclusiveness. Even the Muslims were powerfully affected by Indian custom.

Nehru says that many of the Rajput Kshatriya clans could trace their origins to the Shaka of Scythian invasions which began from about the second century BCE or from the later invasion of the White Huns. All of them accepted the faith and institutions in India and then tried to affiliate themselves to the famous heroes of the epics. It is significant that coins of the period just before and after the beginning of the Christian era showed this rapid change during two or three generations. The first ruler could have a foreign name. His son or grandson would have a Sanskrit name and be crowned according to the traditional rites meant for Kshatriyas.[28]

That did not mean adopting "Hindu" culture in the religious sense. Here Nehru differs from the eminent British civil servant-turned historian Vincent Arthur Smith (1843–1920) who had said that they were "Hinduised": "The foreigners (Muslim Turks), like their forerunners the Sakas and the Yueh-chi, universally yielded to the wonderful assimilative power of Hinduism and rapidly became Hinduised."[29] Nehru felt that they had only adopted the Hindu or Buddhist culture and not the religion. It was a melange of all that was in India.

"Menander", the greatest of the Indo-Greek kings of Punjab (155–130 BCE), who was initially the king of Bactria (Afghanistan), became King Milinda after conversion to Buddhism. His capital was Sagala, present-day Sialkot. British historian Michael Edwards says that his conversion was recorded in a celebrated dialogue "The Questions of Milinda."[30]

The Greek rulers of Punjab were defeated by the Saka-Scythian tribes of Central Asia and Iran in the second century BCE. Their rule lasted till the fourth century CE. They occupied different areas in Sindh, Punjab, Kashmir, Haryana, Uttar Pradesh, Bihar, Rajasthan, Gujarat, and Maharashtra. The Saka dynasty ruling Ujjain adopted Hindu names like Rudraman. They intermarried with the Andhras. This dynasty was defeated in 388 CE by Chandragupta II, the Gupta emperor. Another Saka dynasty ruled Nashik for a period, but they were defeated by the Andhras.

In 174 BCE a nomadic tribe named Yueh-Chi (Yuezhi) was chased away by the Huns from their homeland in western China, then known as Kansu (now Ganzu province). They moved to the south and occupied Bactria in 126 BCE. In 48 CE one of their tribes, the Kushans, wrested Gandhara from the Greeks. Later they expanded their rule to Punjab and Sindh, northern Gujarat, and parts of central India. Not much is known about their rule except about Kanishka who became their leader in 120 CE with his capital in Peshawar.

According to a story, Asvaghosha, a Brahmin priest from Ayodhya who had become a Buddhist, had converted Kanishka to Buddhism.[31] It was under his influence that Kanishka introduced a new version of Buddhism called "Mahayana" (the Great Vehicle) which incorporated Hindu, Greek, Christian, Zoroastrian, and Central Asian features, then prevailing in northwest India. The theory of incarnation of Adi Buddha was adopted from Hinduism. Buddha was elevated to a god from a preacher. Earlier there was no image to worship. The original form of Buddhism was called Hinayana (the Little Vehicle). Mahayana Buddhism spread to China and Japan through Central Asia.[32]

Kanishka, a great patron of literature and art, encouraged Gandharan art which introduced new Hellenistic features for Buddha's statues like Apollo, at times with moustache and ornaments. His court had great "jewels" like Nagarjuna, originally from south India, who was the great proponent of Mahayana Buddhism and Charaka, the great Ayurvedic physician from Kashmir.

It is amazing how local influence works to transform such deities. This writer had seen the transformation of the revered Sai Baba's temple in Shirdi, in Ahmednagar district in Maharashtra. In 1964 when I visited his temple it was a very modest place which suited the ascetic "*fakir*" (mendicant dervish) with just a simple marble statue in an open hall, shorn of all ornamental embellishments. It was then patronized by Hindus, Parsees and also by Muslims who considered him a "*pir*" (saint). In later years Hindus converted him to a Hindu god with gold crown and ornamentations with only Hindu rituals.

Kanishka, who ruled the second largest empire in India after Ashoka, died in 162 CE. After his death, the empire started withering away when the Sassanian Persians under Ardeshir I invaded and occupied northwestern India (Sindh) and Bactria.[33] Their influence over Sindh waned by 651 CE. However, in 711 CE it was occupied by Arab invaders.

*A short history of Gujarat, described as "the laboratory of Hindutva"*[34]

Modern Gujarat was *Gurjjara-rāshtra* in Sanskrit. According to James M. Campbell, who wrote the *History of Gujarat* in 1896, the Gurjjaras were a foreign tribe who came into India from the northwest and settled in many states including Punjab, Rajasthan and the Gujarat/Khandesh area of the Bombay Presidency. Like the Ahirs of Kathiawar, they were herdsmen of cattle.[35]

The area was originally occupied by Yadavas (1500–500 BCE) followed by successive hordes of "Yavanas" or Greeks, Bactrians, Parthians, Scythians (300–100 BCE) and Parsees who were pursued by Arabs in the period 600–800 CE. They were followed by Parsi and Navayat Musalman refugees from Khulagu Khan's devastation of Persia between 1250–1300 CE, proving Nehru's theory that migration into India resembled an ancient palimpsest.

This disproves the theory that Hindus were the original inhabitants of India and that the Hindu religious culture was the core Indian culture, put forward by RSS chief Mohan Bhagwat, who in 2021 also suggested that "*Akhand Bharat*" or undivided India with "Hindu dharma" would be good for Pakistan and even Afghanistan.[36]

Another important feature of this mixed culture was that most of the so called "foreign" origin Muslim rulers had adopted Indian culture and encouraged its literature. They were accepted by the common public and in some cases "*mahākāvyams*"—literally "great poems"—in Sanskrit were dedicated to them. Aparna Kapadia has so persuasively put this across in her 2010 PhD dissertation "Text, Power and Kinship in Medieval Gujarat, c. 1398-1511."[37] In Chapter 4 ("The Sultan as a Kshatriya King") she narrates the rule of Fateh Khan who became Sultan Mahmud Begada (c. 1456–1511) when panegyrics dedicated to him were written in Sanskrit. She concludes: "The relationship between the Islamic kings and their Hindu subjects has been widely recognised as a dialogic and interactive one rather than one driven by straitjacket monolithic ideas of conquest and destruction."

In 2018 eminent historian Irfan Habib cited the "Gurjjara-rāshtra" theory of Gujarat and suggested that the surname of Amit Shah, present Union Home Minister has Persian origins of "Shah".[38]

## The rise of Hinduism

The collapse of the Kushan empire freed the local chieftains from a central authority existing till the fourth century CE. The first person to consolidate an empire was Chandragupta I, a chieftain in Bihar who had married an influential Lichchhavi princess. He captured Magadha and Pataliputra. His Gupta Empire included Bihar, Bengal and possibly some parts of present-day Uttar Pradesh, including "Prayaga" (Allahabad) which is modern Prayagraj. It was during his son Samudragupta's rule (330–80 CE) that more expansions took place. Historians say that he was an orthodox Brahmin, musician, and poet. He also employed Buddhist advisers.

His son Chandragupta II (Vikramaditya) extended the Gupta empire to the Arabian sea after annexing the Saka territories of Kutch, Kathiawar, Sind, Gujarat and Konkan. He also acquired Ujjain, the Saka capital during his reign between 375–415 CE. Legends say that the "nine gems" ("*navaratnas*") including the poet Kalidasa adorned his court. Michael Edwards says that this was the apogee of the Gupta dynasty.

Skandagupta, his grandson (455–80 CE), beat back the invasion by the "White Huns" in 460 which led the renowned diplomat-historian K.M. Panikkar to remark that a major disaster was averted.[39] Others say that the Huns had already established their presence in India starting from Kanishka's period as they also belonged to the Yueh-Chi (Yuezhi) tribe. In an article for the *World History Encyclopedia* Muhammad Bin Naveed writes:

> In Litvinsky's *History of Civilizations of Central Asia*, there is mention of Chinese sources identifying them variously with either the Ch'e-shih of Turfan (now in the Uighur region of China), K'ang Chu or Kangju from southern Kazakhstan or the widespread Yueh Zhi tribes from Central China. These Yuehzhi were driven out of the Chinese territories that they occupied by another band of tribes known as the Hsiung Nu. One of these tribes of the Yueh Zhi was the White Huns or Hephthalites.[40]

This paper also mentions the lineage of the White Huns in India: Tunjina (Khingila) from 455–84, Toramana (484–515), Mihirakula (515–33), Pravarasena (537–97), Khinkhila (600–33), Yudhishthira (633–57) and Lakhana (657–70). The gradual adoption of Hindu names is significant.

This theory further indicates that they were the "Hunas" mentioned in the Puranas. Their "*mandalas*" had existed in Malwa (Madhya Pradesh) and in Rajasthan and Gujarat. Naveed suggests that they could be the ancestors of Rajputs, Gujars and Jats in India and of the Abdalis, Karluks and Khalachs in Afghanistan and Central Asia.[41]

Nehru had also said that coins discovered from time to time indicated a pattern of rapid change in one or two generations. The first ruler is identified in his foreign name. The second or third generation appears with a Sanskrit name and is crowned according to the traditional rites meant for Kshatriyas. Thus, many of our Rajput Kshatriya clans relate to the Shaka of Scythian invaders of the second century BCE or to the later invasion of the White Huns. All of them accepted the religion and customs of India.[42]

By the middle of the sixth century the Gupta empire disintegrated. The next notable ruler was Harshavardhana of the Vardhana dynasty who ruled from Kannauj (Kanyakubja) during 606–47 CE after uniting the north Indian principalities (Punjab, Bengal, Mithila, Kannauj, and Orissa). His attempts to invade beyond the Narmada River were frustrated by the Chalukya king Pulakesin II.

Chinese travellers Fa-Hsien and Hsuan-Tsang who stayed in India during the regimes of Chandragupta II and Harshavardhana (405–643 CE) left detailed commentaries on the religious, social, and administrative features of that era. From this we come to know that Jainism and Buddhism did not appeal to the masses even though the rulers were patronising Buddhism, "[t]he ascetic realism of these faiths having little appeal in contrast with the colourful deities of the Hindu Pantheon."[43]

The old Vedic gods were ignored and the trinity of Brahma (creator), Vishnu (preserver) and Siva (destroyer) were widely circulated through eighteen Sanskrit poems known as "Puranas" during the Gupta period—also of Krishna as the "Avatar" of Vishnu. Sanskrit was popularised among the noblemen and Brahmins while Prakrit was used by the lower classes. Universities like Nalanda flourished, and art was patronised as in the Ajanta frescos and Ellora carvings.

At the same time the system of the self-supporting village community emerged which had its influence on Buddhism, which was patronised only by the upper classes and kings. The villagers did not need expensive monasteries for spiritual elevation since the "New Brahmin" started rendering door-to-door services as priest, agricultural adviser, Ayurvedic doctor and astrologer. "Of the new social and economic order, the Brahmin is the prop and inspiration—Buddhism, concentrated into the luxury of its monasteries was too degenerate and flabby for the new world of the village."[44]

This is one of the main reasons why Buddhism started disappearing from India. Nehru had also said that while Shankara (Shankaracharya, 600 CE), the Hindu renaissance seer from Kerala, was said to have been responsible for putting an end to Buddhism in India as a widespread religion, it was also true that Buddhism had shrunk in India even before Shankara's time. On the other hand, some of Shankara's Brahmin opponents had called him a "disguised Buddhist." Nehru felt that Buddhism had influenced him considerably.[45]

## The development of Vedic literature

Vedic literature indicates a strong materialistic tradition. Nehru quotes Yagnavalkya, considered as the first Vedic philosopher well before Buddha and seven hundred years before Christ, as having said: "It is not our religion, still less the colour of our skin, that produces virtue; virtue must be practised. Therefore, let no one do to others what he would not have done to himself."[46] Yagnavalkya is considered as the first proponent of "*Advaita*" (non-dualism or monism). Later Shankara consolidated this thought as "*Advaita Vedanta.*"

Will Durant quotes Yagnavalkya's dialogue with King Janaka of Vedeha, father of the legendary Sita, on how rebirth could be avoided. He replied that "ascetic elimination of all personal desires through Yoga would unite himself in supreme bliss with the Soul of the world and so escape rebirth." Durant says: "We shall find this philosophy of the Upanishads—this monistic theology, this mystic and impersonal immortality—dominating Hindu thought from Buddha to Gandhi, from Yagnavalkya to Tagore."[47]

Shankara presented his *Advaita* philosophy saying that the whole hierarchy of gods were not real but were "*maya*" (illusions) and were "the secondary emanations of the one ultimate absolute being, the impersonal neuter entity known as Brahman characterised by the three attributes of being (Sat), consciousness (Chit) and bliss (Ananda). Brahman was unchanging and eternally stable, while everything else, being finally unreal, was subject to change...."[48]

Swami Ranganathananda (1908–2005), the thirteenth president of the Ramakrishna Math and Mission, succinctly explains Shankara's mission: "Unity was his aim and not uniformity—unity in diversity." The purpose of all great thinkers in India was preserving the great variety in India, creating "harmony out of all the diverse thoughts and faiths in this land, instead of reducing everything to a single uniform faith at the point of the sword, as has happened in some other countries."[49]

Nehru describes Shankara as a curious mixture of a philosopher-scholar, agnostic-mystic, poet-saint, and in addition, "a practical reformer and an able organizer." He set up, for the first time within the Brahminical fold, ten religious orders. Of these, four are very much alive today. He established four great "*maths*" (monasteries), locating them far from each other, almost at the four corners of India. By doing this he wanted to prove a "culturally united" India indicated by four great monasteries in the north, south, east, and west.

No doubt these were great pilgrimage places, but by adopting the Buddhist practice of the "*sangha*" and establishing monasteries he gave an official touch to India's cultural unity. "Previously there had been no such organizations of Sanyasins [renunciants] in Brahminism, although small groups of them existed."[50]

When the Greeks invaded India's northwest towards the end of the fourth century BCE, they found that the Indians had already developed a national culture of their own. This endured till the British era despite waves of Persian, Greek, Scythian, and Muslim invasions. It was noticed that the development of the Indo-Aryan race's life and literature remained practically unchecked and unmodified. No other branch of the Indo-European group had experienced this type of isolated evolution. Nehru says that no other country except China can trace back such uninterrupted development for more than 3,000 years in its language and literature, its religious beliefs and rites, its dramatic and social customs.

He quotes Max Muller, famous German-born philologist and Orientalist, speaking at Cambridge University in 1882: "There is, in fact, an unbroken continuity between the most modern and the most ancient phases of Hindu thought, extending over more than three thousand years." The same was recorded fifty years later by Romain Rolland, French writer and mystic: "If there is one place on the face of the earth where all the dreams of living men have found a home from the very earliest days when man began the dream of existence, it is India."

Nehru was referring to the Upanishads which were developed from 800 BCE. Swami Paramananda (1884–1940), disciple of Swami Vivekananda who founded the Boston Ramakrishna Mission in 1919, says in his book *The Upanishads*:

> The Upanishads represent the loftiest heights of Indo-Aryan thought and culture. They form the wisdom portion of the Vedas in addition to the "Karma Kanda" or "sacrificial portion". In each of the Vedas (Rig, Yajur, Sama and Atharva) a large portion is devoted to rituals and ceremonials while another portion named "Upanishad" gives the "philosophical discrimination" and "ultimate spiritual vision."

For this reason, the Upanishads are also known as "*Vedanta*", the end or goal of wisdom (*veda*: wisdom; *anta*: end). The Swami says that *upanishad* has two meanings: The first interpretation is that it is a compound Sanskrit word "*Upa-ni-shad*", meaning "sitting near or at the feet of the teacher." The other is "to shatter" or "to destroy" the fetters of ignorance. Upanishads were also called "*aranyakas*" (forest books) since this knowledge was being imparted in the forests when the teachers or gurus who would have retired to the forests during the "*vanaprastha*" stage of their lives could devote all their time to spiritual studies.

The Upanishads are also classed as "*srutis*" (what is heard). This was because the wisdom was orally heard. In the course of time "*srutis*" developed another meaning, which was what was ordained by God as opposed to "*smritis*" (recorded through memory).[51] Nehru objects to this interpretation as some latter-day Hindu scholars had claimed, that this wisdom was "ordained" by God.

Swami Paramananda too says that there was nothing racial or local in the messages of the Upanishads: the message applies to all mankind, equally to the modern world as it did to the Vedic Aryans. He sums up the message in two "*mahavakyams*" (great sayings): "*tat twam asi*" (that thou art) and "*aham brahmasmi*" (I am Brahman). He says: "This oneness of soul and God lies at the very root of all Vedic thought."[52]

The first introduction of the Upanishads to the western world was through a Persian translation in the seventeenth century. A century later a French scholar, Anquetil Duperron, made French and Latin translations. However, he published only the Latin text. Swami Paramananda says that the first English translation was made by Raja Ram Mohan Roy (1772–1833), the founder of the Brahmo Samaj, a reformist movement.

Roy was a man of many parts, at times contradictory to each other. He was a "Kuleen" (upper crust) Brahmin; yet he founded the Brahmo Samaj to fight against Brahminical excesses in Hinduism including child marriage and *sati*, whereby a widow burnt herself on her husband's pyre. He allied with the Christian church to introduce reforms in Hinduism by integrating traditional Indian culture with the west; yet he resisted their proselytism. He drew a salary from the British East India company; yet he was also a political agitator against them for exploiting India. In 1830 he travelled to England as the ambassador of the Mughal Emperor Akbar Shah II. It was also to persuade the British Parliament not to annul Governor General William Bentinck's Bengal Sati Regulation of 1929. He died in Bristol in 1833.

These translations were hailed by German philosopher Arthur Schopenhauer (1788–1860), American scholar Henry David Thoreau (1817–62) and German orientalist Max Muller

(1823–1900) as the best spiritual message which was emitted by ancient India and which was valid for all generations. However, Paramananda cautions the common man against considering these as easily understood popular scriptures. They were originally only textbooks and "like all textbooks they need interpretation." The language is extremely condensed, metaphysical, obscure and in the form of aphorisms.

Nehru adds in *The Discovery* that interest in magic and supernatural knowledge was sternly discouraged as rituals and ceremonies without enlightenment were in vain. The duties and obligations imposed by life were to be carried out with a spirit of detachment. He quotes C. Rajagopalachari:

> The spacious imagination, the majestic sweep of thought, and the almost reckless spirit of exploration with which, urged by the compelling thirst for truth, the Upanishad teachers and pupils dig into the "open Secret" of the universe, makes this most ancient of the world's holy books still the most modern and most satisfying.[53]

According to Nehru the Upanishad philosophy had led to a powerful wave of materialistic philosophy, agnosticism, and atheism: "Out of this again grew Buddhism and Jainism, and the famous Sanskrit epics, the Ramayana and the Mahabharata, wherein yet another attempt was made to bring about a synthesis between rival creeds and ways of thought." The materialist "Sankya" school founded by Kapila around the time of Upanishads rejected "*atma*" (soul). This had influenced philosophical thinking in India and abroad, for example on the Gnostic schools in Greece.[54]

Swami Paramananda says that every Upanishad begins with a "peace chant" (*shanti-patha*) to create an atmosphere of purity and serenity. "We must hold a peaceful attitude towards all living things and if it is lacking, we must strive fervently to cultivate it through suggestion by chanting or repeating some holy text." In this he finds a strange parallel with Jesus Christ who had said: "If thou bring thy gift to the altar and there rememberest that thy brother hath aught against thee; leave thy gift before the altar and go thy way; first be reconciled to thy brother and then come and offer thy gift."

*A contrarian interpretation of Vedic thought:*

In 1941 Swami Dharma Theertha, a Dalit philosopher who was born in 1893 as Shri Parameswara Menon, a high caste Hindu in Kerala State, published a book *History of Hindu Imperialism* from Lahore in pre-Independence India.[55] In 1923 he encountered the famous religious reformer Sri Narayana Guru (1855–1928) of Kerala who had preached "One Caste, One Religion, One God for mankind." Among Narayana Guru's admirers were Rabindranath Tagore and Mahatma Gandhi who visited him in his Ashram in 1922 and 1925 respectively. It was to the credit of Narayana Guru that he was highly successful in interpreting the "*Advaita*" principle of the legendary Shankara from "an elite theoretical doctrine into a relevant principle of practical applicability."[56]

The preface to Theertha's book was written by Justice A. Varadarajan, who was the first Dalit judge in the Supreme Court of India. The book was promoted by renowned constitutional expert and social reformer Dr B.R. Ambedkar and India's oldest newspaper *Amrita Bazaar Patrika*, which was founded in 1868.

In this context it is relevant to quote advocate A. Ahamed Fayiz's essay on the extent of discrimination against Dalits even in the twentieth century. Fayiz had done a case study of the high judicial appointments in India since independence by citing George H. Gadbois Jr.'s research. Gadbois, Professor Emeritus of Political Science, University of Kentucky had conducted 116 interviews with more than 66 Indian Supreme Court judges. He concluded that until 1989, Brahmins had occupied 42.9 per cent of the positions of judges and non-Brahmin high castes 49.4 per cent. "Other Backward castes" had held only 5.2 per cent while Dalit and Adivasi communities were able to hold only an abysmal percentage: 2.6 and 0 respectively.[57]

Swami Dharma Theertha's theme was the same: how religious and caste discrimination had been practiced in India from Vedic times. After the Aryan invasion, a set of terms that could all loosely be translated as "demon" was applied to the locals in India; called "dark skinned *dasyus*" or "*rakshasas*", they were systematically annihilated. Mahabali and Ravana, who were called "*asuras*", had a more civilised form of life and behaviour than the invading Aryans. Seeds of Hindu decay were sown four or five thousand years ago when ancient priests, leaders and aristocrats of society separated themselves from the homogeneous body of the people as a distinct nation of Brahmans and established a monopoly on learning, power and religious authority.

Hindu leaders of the nineteenth century used the British government and its judicial, legislative, and executive machinery to strengthen the chains of inferiority of the lower strata. They ignored the teachings of national icons like Raja Ram Mohan Roy, Dayananda Saraswati, Swami Vivekananda and Gandhi, and denied millions of Dalits, their Hindu brethren, not only access to temples, but the solace and benefits of education, sanitation, good water and air, use of tanks, wells and roads, thus stunting their growth.[58]

Historian A. Sreedhara Menon of Kerala also says that laws in the princely states of Cochin and Travancore were made in favour of Brahmins and Nairs who were the land-owning classes. At the same time, it was heavily tilted against Mappilas (Muslims), Ezhavas (Other Backward Castes/OBCs) and Dalits. While the Brahmins enjoyed immunity from the death penalty, the lower classes were freely given death sentences for killing cows and even for thefts. Slavery was rampant even in the beginning of the nineteenth century. These two states also had a system of sub castes even in higher classes like Nairs where certain classes of people in the so-called lower strata were treated as untouchables.[59]

Swami Vivekananda was very upset with the inhuman oppression of non-Brahmins by the caste Hindus even in states like Kerala, with higher education levels. In 1892 he called Kerala as a "lunatic asylum." This practice was so cruel that he decided to appoint Srimad Ramakrishnananada and Sister Nivedita (born as Irish teacher Margaret Elizabeth Noble) to lead the struggle for reforms in that state. It was therefore not surprising that Kerala state had the distinction of electing the first Communist government in the world in 1957 which was responsible for social emancipation and wholesale land reforms whereby the higher castes, who were absentee landlords were dispossessed of their lands and possession given to the tillers.

Swami Ranganathananda says in his *Science and Religion* that "religion is a matter of inner experience, a coming in touch with spiritual facts, and not a matter of belief or dogma or conformity... Strengthened by the spirit of the Upanishads, no all-powerful church, therefore rose in India to organise the faithful on the basis of dogma and creed, and claiming divine authority for its opinions and judgements."[60] This is in stark contrast to the Rashtriya Swayamsevak Sangh, which would claim the right to prescribe to Indian citizens what constitutes being a true Hindu, to the exclusion of others.

*Composite culture: A case study of Kerala and Gujarat*

Buddhism and Jainism had spread to even far-off Kerala, according to A. Sreedhara Menon, during the region of Chandra Gupta Maurya. He quotes famous Scottish scholar-historian William Logan (1841–1914) who, as the Collector of British Malabar in the old Madras presidency, had written the *Malabar Manual*, the best history of that state. Logan wrote that snake worship, which is so extensive even in the twenty-first century in that state among Hindus and even Muslims, was a result of Jainism's influence there. Logan also said that some of the Hindu temples and Muslim mosques were built in the style peculiar to the Jains. He says that even "*Bhagavati*" worship (Goddess Durga) which is so extensive in Kerala even now was drawn from the Jain pantheon.[61]

Menon says that the famous deity Sastha or Ayyappan on Sabarimala (Sabari Mountain) in south Kerala where 40 to 50 million devotees visit every year for pilgrimage from all over south India has traces of Buddhist influence. These features are strict vows of non-violence, vegetarianism, and abstinence from worldly pleasures for two months before the pilgrimage. Also, the sing-song repetition of "*Saranam Ayyappa*" by the devotees while going to the secluded temple in the forest, reminds one of the triple "*Saranam*" formula of the Buddha, the Dharma, and the Sangha.[62] Another key feature of this temple is the practice of all devotees paying obeisance first to the shrine dedicated to "Vavar Swami", a Muslim saint, believed to be Ayyappa's friend. The Vavar shrine has no deity like a mosque and pilgrims offer only black pepper as an offering.

Christianity came to Kerala in the first century CE, three centuries before it became the established religion in Rome. Legend says that the apostle St Thomas landed in Maliankara near the Muziris, the ancient harbour in 52 CE. This is near the present Kodungallur (Cranganore). Here he converted several Brahmin families. Stoic philosopher missionary Pantaenus is said to have found a "flourishing Christian community" here during the second century CE. Menon says that the traditional accounts preserved by the Jews who came to Kodungallur in 68 CE "contain a reference to the existence of a Christian Community here."[63]

In April 2024 another example of communal harmony was reported from Kerala, when a 400-year old temple of Devi (Goddess Durga) in a small village called Muthuvallur in Malappuram, a Muslim majority district, was totally renovated with generous financial help from Muslims led by Indian Union Muslim League (IUML) president Panakkad Sadikkali Shihab Thangal, the Qazi of hundreds of mosques in Kerala state.[64]

Noted Indian mythologist Devdutt Pattanaik says that there is a temple for a goddess called "Harsiddhi Mata" on a hill overlooking the Arabian Sea on the Sindh–Gujarat coast. For ages, she was considered as the protector of ships. She is also called "Vahanavati—Sikotar Mata", a name derived from "Socotra" island of Yemen, notorious for its treacherous shoreline. It also reminds one of the era of the old spice trade. Pattanaik says that the once flourishing sea trade between the west coast of India and Greece and later Roman countries had received a serious setback through the Brahminical rule of "losing caste" if any Hindu travelled abroad. Consequently, Arabs filled in the vacuum by taking over the spice trade and spreading Islam to the west coast of India and Southeast Asia.[65]

*Syncretic culture in music*

The earliest cultural fusion in music between Aryans and local inhabitants resulted in the development of many *ragas* or musical modes like Pundalika, Saveri, Takka, and Botta. Some of these *ragas* are not heard any longer except Saveri which originated from some tribes in Orissa and Andhra. Takka had its origin in Sind. Other *ragas* like Chenchu Kamboji, Bhairav and Bhairavi were all named after tribes in Andhra. Hejjajji is most probably a melody (*maqam*) from Hijaj in Arabia. Turushoka Todi and Yaman are foreign melodies.

The Central Asian tribes who migrated to India had brought instruments such as the *sarangi*, *sarod* and *shehnai*, which together with Vedic instruments like the *bana veena*, *kanda veena* and *godha* and drums like the *bhoomi dundubhi* and *vanaspati* enriched Indian music. Western culture brought in the violin and harmonium. In the nineteenth century the legendary Carnatic musician Balusvami Deekshitar adapted the violin to Carnatic music. However, there is also a theory that the violin is an adaptation of the *ravana hasta veena*, still played by villagers in northwest India. India also exported instruments during this era. The Chinese *hu ch'in* (a bowed instrument) has its origin in India. Indonesia has the *pataha* (a kind of drum), *vipanchi* (harp) and *ghanta* (bell) from India.[66]

Both Hindu and Muslim rulers patronised music in India. Gopal Nayak, one of the earliest *Dhrupad* or Hindustani classical singers was patronised by the Turco-Afghan emperor Allaudin Khilji (1296–1316). The famous Tansen, originally Tanna Misra, converted to Islam under the influence of a Muslim *fakir* Hazrat Mohammad Gouse and was patronised by the king of Rewa, Ramachandra Baghela. He later became among the "nine gems" in the court of Mughal emperor Akbar (1542–1605). This tradition has continued till today.

In 1915 Gauhar Jan, a famous singer, recorded a *hori* (semi-classical singing) of Prophet Muhammad celebrating the Hindu festival of Holi in Medina. She did not feel that she was committing blasphemy. Senior journalist Kuldeep Kumar says:

> She and her contemporaries did not think so because they were carrying forward India's syncretic traditions and the obscurantist values were completely foreign to them. Who can forget Bade Ghulam Ali Khan's rendering of the bhajan "Hari Om Tatsat

Mahamantra Hai, Japa Kar Japa Kar"? The unforgettable bhajan "Man Tarpat Haridarshan Ko Aaj" in Hindi film *Baiju Bawra* (1952) is a shining example of the secular nature of our music. It was written by Shakeel Badayuni, composed by Naushad and sung by Muhammad Rafi—all Muslims. The Oscar-winning Indian music director A.R. Rahman is also a Muslim.[67]

## *The inclusive nature of the Indian Constituent Assembly*

India's inclusive nature was evident even in the greatest political exercise in Indian history when our constitution was adopted. General Elections for the Central Legislative Assembly and Council of State were held by the Imperial government in December 1945. The Congress won 59 of the 102 elected seats. Similarly, provincial Assembly elections were held in January 1946 through direct polls. Out of a total 1,585 seats for Provincial Assemblies, the Congress, led by its president Abul Kalam Azad, won 925 seats against 425 by the Muslim League under Muhammad Ali Jinnah's leadership.

For the proposed Constituent Assembly, the Crown decided not to hold another election but to treat the Provincial Assemblies as the Electoral College who would indirectly elect the members. Thus, the July–August 1946 indirect elections to the 296 seats in our Constituent Assembly resulted in persons nominated by the Congress Party winning 208 seats against 73 by the Muslim League.

Had the Congress adopted the present BJP government's strategy of stifling discordant voices by bulldozing their brute majority in all legislative forums, they could have easily chosen their own candidates for the proposed Constituent Assembly and dominated the making of the Constitution. However, this did not happen. Care was taken to make the Assembly as inclusive as possible by adding several non-Congress candidates, including some diehard Congress opponents among the list of candidates nominated by Provincial Congress Committees.

Eminent historian and constitutional authority Granville Austin admired the great statesmanship and larger national vision shown by the Congress leadership. He had written two landmark books on the making of India's constitution. He says:

> The Assembly was the Congress and the Congress was India.... One might assume, aware of the character of monolithic political systems in other countries, that a mass-party in India would be rigid and narrow in outlook and that its powerful leadership would silence dissent and confine policy and decision making to the hands of the select few. In India the reverse was the case.[68]

He outlines how it was done. Under the restricted franchise of the 1935 Government of India Act, only 28.5 per cent of the adult population in the provinces could vote in the January provincial elections. To broaden the base of representation, the Congress deliberately decided to enlist several candidates who would take care of the interests of such excluded people. The same principle was followed by the Congress leadership led by Jawaharlal Nehru, Vallabhbhai Patel, Maulana Azad, Pandit Pant, C. Rajagopalachari, and Rajendra Prasad in selecting candidates for the Constituent Assembly.

Consequent to this, they started sending communications to the Provincial Congress Committees to include specific names among "persons of exceptional ability" and "minority communities" even if they were not official members of the Congress. In this manner the Communist Party, the Socialist Party and the Hindu Mahasabha, who would not have been able to elect any of their cadres, were able to get representation. Also, minorities like Christians (7), Anglo-Indians (3) and Parsees (3) were elected, who on their own, would not have been able to win the polls.

Included in the list were Dr B.R. Ambedkar, who had clashed with Gandhi for over 20 years, K.M. Munshi, an estranged Congressman, Socialist leaders like Rammanohar Lohia, a bitter critic of Nehru, and also some Hindu Mahasabha leaders who were totally opposed to the secular policy of the Congress. It was significant that even on 25 April 1945 Dr Ambedkar had told the Scheduled Castes Federation, of which he was the President, that "A Constituent Assembly was not needed, the 1935 Act would do."[69] He later agreed to join the Constituent Assembly when he received an invitation from Nehru on 27 April. Ambedkar felt, according to Austin, that he could serve the interests of Scheduled Castes better by being within the government, than from without.[70]

Originally, prominent Hindu Mahasabha leaders like Pandit Madan Mohan Malaviya were part of Congress. However, the Sabha started moving away from the Congress policies since 1920s under the influence of Balakrishna Shivram Moonje, Vinayak Damodar Savarkar and others who were opposed to the secular policy of the Congress. In 1925 Keshav Baliram Hedgewar founded the Rashtriya Swayamsevak Sangh (RSS) which advocated keeping away from politics. The Sabha did not support the Gandhian freedom movement nor the freedom struggle.

Austin mentions that the Congress leadership nominated Shyama Prasad Mookerjee, Narayan Bhaskar Khare and M.R. Jayakar from among the Hindu Mahasabha members for the Constituent Assembly and got them elected. Mookerjee had even officially written to the British Governor of Bengal on 26 July 1942 opposing Gandhi's Quit India Movement. However, he was invited by Nehru to join his first cabinet after Independence in August 1947. True, he resigned in April 1950 over the India–Pakistan accord known as Nehru–Liaquat Ali Khan Pact.

Narayan Bhaskar Khare, who was a long time Congressman was ousted from the Congress in 1938 by Netaji Subhas Chandra Bose, then its president, for sacking his senior Congress colleagues like Ravi Shankar Shukla and D.P. Mishra. Khare then joined the Mahasabha. However, he had to resign from the Constituent Assembly in February 1948 when he was arrested on suspicion of having been involved in the Gandhi assassination conspiracy.

Several other non-Congressmen were nominated by the Provincial Congress Committees who rendered extremely valuable service to the framing of India's constitution. Among them were eminent lawyer Alladi Krishnaswamy Iyer, former civil servant N. Gopalaswamy Iyengar who was prime minister of Kashmir during 1937–43, famed economist John Mathai, journalist Ramnath Goenka, illustrious academic Dr S. Radhakrishnan, prominent historian K.M. Panikkar and several others.

Granville Austin concludes that the success of the Constituent Assembly, which had deliberated under trying conditions created by the Partition and Communal violence, was because of two or three commendable steps by the Congress leadership: Nehru's efforts to try and reach unanimous decisions; Prasad's strategic actions of postponing debates so that a problem could be worked out privately; and Pant's tactical acts of passing over a particular article if it was not possible to reach unanimity. They all believed that a vote might result in "something not wanted by anybody": "Had the constitution come from the Constituent Assembly sanctioned by a meagre majority, opposed by many, it would have been attacked as untrustworthy of general support and unrepresentative of India's best interests."[71]

That is the essence of the traditional "Idea of India" from the Vedic times. It stands in stark contrast to the "majoritarianism" practised by the BJP government since 2014.

# PART III

# THE CONTEMPORARY RELATIONSHIP

# 5

# THE UNITED PROGRESSIVE ALLIANCE:
## 2004–2014

As Prime Minister I let my work to speak for me rather than speaking for myself.

Former Prime Minister Dr Manmohan Singh,
18 February 2022[1]

*Was the UPA a "Weimar" government?*

There is a tendency among some Indian writers to compare the Congress-led United Progressive Alliance governments (UPA: I 2004–9; II 2009–14) to the Weimar Republic (1919–33) which had paved the way for the Third Reich. It is not clear who originally coined it, but it seems to have stuck in some quarters.[2]

Perhaps the inference is because the BJP-led National Democratic Alliance (NDA) government, which succeeded UPA-II in 2014, was as radically different in its ideology and policies compared to the Congress-led UPA government as the Third Reich was from Weimar. Also, in the 2014 general elections, the NDA had won a massive majority with 282 parliamentary seats, trouncing the Congress which could get only 44.

Possibly UPA-II (2009–14) might have been called "Weimar" for an appearance of lawlessness, disorder and scams resembling the waning years of the Weimar Republic, as strikingly described by A.C.N. Nambiar in his columns in *The Hindu* from 1923. On 18 February 1933, Walther Funk, economist, journalist, and chief Nazi spokesperson, addressed foreign correspondents in Berlin on behalf of the Third Reich. This was attended by Nambiar, a Berlin-based journalist, and other international correspondents: "Gentlemen, I want you all to grasp the brutal fact that the accession of Hitler to power does not mark a mere change of government but a change of regime in Germany."[3]

Like Walther Funk, BJP President Amit Shah, who crafted his party's spectacular victory in 2014, also announced on 9 August 2014 that a new government with a new ideology had arrived: "Congress ideology should be replaced with BJP's—when history is written, the former UPA government will be known as a government of scams."[4]

At its outset in 1919, the Weimar Republic's constitution had been hailed "as the most modern democratic constitution of its day."[5] It had brought democracy to Germany with a two-chamber parliament and a popularly elected president who was given emergency powers. Some say that the emergency powers in the Indian constitution were based on the Weimar constitution.[6] The constitution had been drafted in the historic German town of Weimar, famous as the birthplace of Goethe and Schiller: Johann Wolfgang von Goethe was a German polymath, poet, and scientist; Friedrich Schiller was a playwright, poet, and philosopher whose famous poem "Ode to Joy" was used in 1824 by the legendary composer Ludwig van Beethoven in the finale of his Ninth Symphony. In later years music and poetry lovers in Europe, America and China would copy the famous Goethe–Schiller twin statue monument in Weimar in their own cities.

This graceful cultural tradition was not transferred into Germany's post-World War I administration. Its ruling Social Democrats, who were struggling to administer a war-ravaged country, were badgered from both sides by the Conservatives and Communists who were jostling for power. In 1923 the government defaulted on the 1919 Versailles Peace Treaty "Reparations", described by Germans as "a Peace of Shame", which were to the tune of US $33 billion.[7] As a result, France and Belgium occupied the Ruhr region. This massive unrest led to the "Beer Hall Putsch" by Adolph Hitler in 1923.

German Communist activities by way of street brawls with Nazis came to benefit Hitler. Nambiar had recalled an incident on 14 January 1930 when a Red Front activist had shot and killed a Nazi poet named Horst Wessel. Joseph Goebbels took advantage of this incident to write his poem "*Hort Wessel Lied*" (Hort Wessel Song) and make it a Nazi anthem which was used at his funeral to publicize Communist atrocities.[8] From then on Hitler marched to power in 1933, exploiting the weaknesses of Weimar's democracy.

Former Indian Foreign Secretary Vijay Gokhale referred to a parallel incident in his book. He claims that Indian Communists, in a similar manner, sabotaged the Indo–US nuclear deal at the behest of China, which wanted to "build domestic opposition" between 2007 and 2008.[9] The inference is that the four left parties which had supported the Congress in 2004 to form an anti-BJP front had tried to bring the UPA down with street protests, similar to how the Communist parties had sabotaged the Weimar Republic. Yet the UPA-II government managed to be formed after the 2009 elections even without the Communists' help.

*The UPA government's social reform measures and laws*

Right to Information Act 2005 (RTI)

Unlike the declining years of Weimar, the UPA government under Prime Minister Dr Manmohan Singh had many landmark successes. Many have forgotten these democratic gains in the wake of their poor performance in the 2014 and 2019 elections. The UPA introduced several measures towards transparency in bureaucracy to reduce the distance between the common public and administration. Their first success was the Right to Information Act 2005, whereby the citizens' rights were codified, enabling them to find out more about government decision making.

No government from 1947 onwards, including the regime of Jawaharlal Nehru, the most democratic prime minister in Indian history, had thought of conferring this right on the common citizen. True, Nehru had a regular habit of explaining his government's major decisions to the chief ministers through his fortnightly letters from 1947 to 1963. These letters touched upon subjects covering the problems of a newly independent country like nation building, minority protection, development, planning, land reforms, food supply, defence, and foreign affairs.

On 14 November 2018 a popular online news daily recalled three such letters Nehru wrote to the CMs as proof of his concern for the common man.[10] On 1 March 1950 he wrote about the frequent complaints about the "loyalty" of "minorities". He said: "There is a tendency among some of us to demand loyalty from the Muslims in India and to condemn tendencies amongst them which may be pro-Pakistani. Such tendencies, of course, are wrong and have to be condemned." The second letter published was from 20 September 1953 on "narrow nationalism". He said:

Communal organisations are the clearest examples of extreme narrowness of outlook, strutting about in the guise of nationalism. In the name of unity, they separate and destroy. In social terms they represent reaction of the worst type. We may condemn these communal organisations, but there are many others who are not free from this narrow influence.

On 12 June 1960 he even wrote about brooms for cleaning:

A broom or a brush with a long handle, which can be used while a person is standing, is far more effective from the point of work and far less tiring to the person using it. So far as I know, all over the world these standing brooms or brushes are used. Why then do we carry on with a primitive, out of date, method which is inefficient and psychologically all wrong? Bending down in this way to sweep is physically more tiring and, I suppose, encourages a certain subservience in mind.

In this Nehru was pinpointing the health issues of millions of street sweepers and also trying to raise their dignity of labour by giving them better implements. Through the same letter Nehru also requested the chief ministers to introduce modern ploughs for millions of our agriculturists.

In a similar manner, Prime Minister Narendra Modi had also introduced his "*Mann Ki Baat*" (Talking from the heart), a weekly radio programme from 3 October 2014 through which he would address the common people. In his first address he advised the public to buy "*khadi*" or hand-loomed clothes which would bring prosperity to millions of poor weavers. By the end of 2021 he had made more than eighty-two such addresses, covering subjects as varied as yoga, *chandrayan* (moon exploration vehicles), healthcare, natural calamities, garbage disposal and the Olympics. All these talks were well received. On an average nearly 1.6 million subscribers listen to them.[11]

However, these efforts do not address the difficulties facing a member of the public in pursuing individual or collective grievances against the bureaucracy. A department for public grievances and administrative reforms had been created as early as 1954 in the Cabinet Secretariat on the recommendations of Paul H. Appleby, the well-known American theorist of public administration. This unit was shifted to the Ministry of Home Affairs in 1964 and tossed back to the Cabinet Secretariat in 1970 under the prime minister. Presently it is an online platform.

During this era, citizens could regularly visit the government's secretariats in New Delhi and state capitals. Even now long queues of such grievance-redressal-seeking members of the public can be seen outside every government office. Till 1985 the public were freely admitted into government secretariats. However, the Coomer Narain spy episode in 1985, involving a spy ring operating in several high-level offices like the President's office, Prime Minister's secretariat, Defence and Economic ministries, compelled the government to restrict access to such visitors.

Ironically it was the failure of government in restricting movements of sensitive papers from offices to residences that had enabled the spy ring to operate and not the visits of members of the public. Yet, in the final analysis the public became the victims. Terrorism, which manifested simultaneously, also prevented easy access of the public to such government offices. In these circumstances the RTI Act afforded a very convenient mode of seeking information without having to visit a government office.

The Second Administrative Reforms Commission under the chairmanship of Shri Veerappa Moily in 2005 had commended the RTI Act as "pathbreaking" towards a "Citizen Centric Administration." It also listed fourteen major difficulties experienced by common citizens who were unable to meet the relevant officials to redress their grievances. The Commission hoped that these difficulties would be solved by pinpointed responsibilities of "Information Commissioners."[12]

However, the bureaucracy was not enthusiastic about this right of citizens to be exercised unhindered. For example, former Information Commissioner Shailesh Gandhi had written to the Chief Information Commissioner of Maharashtra Sumit Mullick on 16 March 2020, that 57,000 RTI applications had been pending in Maharashtra for the last two years: "The pending number of appeals and complaints has risen to over 57,000 and many of them are pending for over two to three years. For a law which promises to deliver information within 30 days, a wait of years before the Information Commission makes the law irrelevant."[13] Similarly, about 32,000 RTI appeals were pending with the Central Information Commission according to a parliamentary answer on 16 December 2021.[14]

It is true that there are serious roadblocks to effecting more transparency in the administration. Yet the RTI Act was a pathbreaking achievement. Despite the apparent pendency in furnishing details, a study some years ago said that it was an effective means of transparency at the grass root levels. This was because 39 per cent of applications were filed at the local bodies that directly impacted the lives of common people like panchayats, municipal departments, and other civic bodies, whereas only 29 per cent of all applications were filed at government ministries and department level offices. "People have started seeking information on Ration supplies, BPL-ration cards, human rights, distribution of school uniform, PDS, etc. Villages in rural areas have benefited the most from the RTI Act."[15]

Unique Identification project (*Aadhaar*) for transferring welfare grants to the poor

On 3 March 2006, approval was given by the Ministry of Communications and Information Technology for the project titled "Unique Identification for BPL [Below Poverty Line] Families" to be implemented by the National Informatics Centre (NIC) over a period of twelve months. This was formalised on 28 January 2009. By September 2010 the enrolment process of *Aadhaar*— translating as "foundation" or "basis"—began with its nationwide launch. In 2012 Prime Minister Manmohan Singh launched an *Aadhaar*-linked direct benefit transfer scheme.[16]

However, the UPA government, which faced several litigations in various courts over the project, could not set in motion detailed transfer scheme as it was defeated in the 2014 general election. On 1 July 2014 Nandan Nilekani, who had operationalised the scheme, met the late Arun Jaitley, then Finance Minister, to explain the scheme. On 5 July Prime Minister Narendra Modi declared that the NDA government would operationalise the project. The Aadhar Act (Targeted Delivery of Financial and other Subsidies, Benefits, and Services) was passed on 11 March 2016 and came into force on 12 July–12 September 2016. Millions of below-poverty-line Indians are now getting direct transfers of welfare benefits, apart from its use as basic identification document.

Right to Education Act 2009 (RTE)

A BBC report on 1 April 2010 said that "a landmark law" which made education a fundamental right for children had been passed by the Indian parliament. At that time an estimated 8 million children between 6 and 14 did not attend school in India. Nearly 220 million children were in this age group. Out of this about 9.2 million children either dropped out of school or never attended any educational institution. After the new law, these children were ensured elementary education by local and state governments.

A Centre for Public Policy Research (CPPR) paper had said in 2019 that it was Gopal Krishna Gokhale (1866–1916), leader of the Indian National Congress, who had first advocated in 1910 compulsory and free primary education to all children. However only Kerala state had achieved this by 2009 when the national RTE Act was passed. "By enacting the RTE law, India also joined the league of 135 countries to have primary education as Fundamental Rights in the constitutional provision under Article 21A as amended in 2002."[17]

The BBC report quoted the World Bank saying that the number of children enrolled in elementary education in India had increased by 57 million to reach 192 million between 2003 and 2009. Two thirds or more of this increase had taken place in government schools. It also said that the number of children who were out of school education declined from 25 million to 8.1 million during the same period.[18] A survey published in *Reader's Digest* ten years later revealed that India, with 35 per cent of the world's illiterates and poised to become the world's third largest economy with the largest young working population, could achieve almost 100 per cent enrolment rates in schools after this law. In 2018 it was 97.2 per cent.[19]

A welcome side effect of this new law was the improvement of school infrastructure. The report quoted the Annual Status of Education Report (ASER) to say that usable girls' toilets doubled, reaching 66.4 per cent in 2018; schools with boundary walls increased by 13.45 per cent to reach 64.4 per cent in 2018. "The percentage of schools with a kitchen shed increased from 82.1 to 91. Schools with books, other than textbooks, increased from 62.6 to 74.2 per cent over the same period, the NGO's report added."

The survey also identified serious shortcomings. Along with higher enrolment, the number of qualified teachers did not increase. In 2015 a survey revealed that "social inclusion" became a problem in private schools which had to reserve 25 per cent of seats for underprivileged children. Experiences of "social exclusion" of underprivileged children included making such children sit separately, sometimes even on the floor, causing humiliation. Sometimes their poor parents were deceived into signing papers withdrawing their children.[20]

The CPPR quoted a survey, ten years after the RTE law was enacted, that found serious shortcomings in implementation: "The practical enforcement of the RTE in letter and spirit was faced with numerous challenges across the states and UTs." It found that the 25 per cent reservation had not been implemented by more than half the thirty-six states and Union Territories (UT) by 2015. By October 2019 nearly thirty-three states/UTs had notified the Act including 25 per cent reservation.

Another survey by "Indus Action" revealed a strange shortcoming: 4.1 million students were studying in the country by October 2019 under the quota system. 68 per cent of these belonged to four states: Madhya Pradesh, Rajasthan, Karnataka, and Tamil Nadu. Other states provided no statistics, nor did they have the infrastructure to implement this programme. 43 per cent had no playgrounds and no facilities for children with disabilities. Nearly 70 per cent of schools had no library and 20 per cent of schools had no compound wall for the safety of the children.

All these show that there is a wide gap between claims and practical achievement, which is a common feature in every sector in India. This applies even to primary education. Yet it was the UPA which attempted to solve the intractable problem.[21]

### The Right to Fair Compensation and Transparency in Land Acquisition, Rehabilitation and Resettlement Act, 2012 (RFCTLARR)

In India both the national and state governments have rights to pass laws for acquiring private lands for development purposes. Such land acquisitions were enabled by the Imperial Legislative Council under an 1894 law. It was the UPA government which thought of introducing a new law replacing this old code. Till the new law was introduced in parliament in 2011, the old 1894 law with seventeen amendments by the national and state governments was the basis of land acquisition in India.

The preamble of this new law said that it was to ensure fair compensation to the owners of the affected families whose lands were acquired for development purposes and to ensure that those moved from their lands are resettled. This was because several serious problems had arisen under the old law, even as amended.

A detailed survey by *Frontline* from 2007 had found that much of the blame for the growing strength of the Maoist movement in India was because of lapses by the national and state governments in understanding the underlying issues of land. As a result, both the centre and affected states dealt with this only as a law and order problem despite several socio-economic issues emerging during the process, which was recognised by the government by forming an "Inter-Ministerial Group" (IMG) to investigate the issue.[22]

The Asian Centre for Human Rights (ACHR) was quoted by the magazine that an estimated Rs. 65 billion (US $775 million) for the National Rural Employment Guarantee Programme (NREGP) could not be spent during 2005–06. Similarly, Rs. 15 billion ($180 million) for tribal development could not be released by the Ministry of Tribal Affairs to State governments because the latter did not submit utilization certificates.

In 2006 D. Bandopadhyay, Chairman of the Planning Commission's Expert Group on "Development Issues to deal with Causes of Discontent, Unrest and Extremism", blamed successive governments for that situation since no care was taken to resettle jobless tribal people displaced from Central India due to mega projects. "There is no official figure estimating the number of displaced people due to coercive acquisition of land for development purposes."[23] Scholars' estimates vary: One, Walter Fernandes, had estimated that between 1951 and 2005 roughly 55 million were displaced. Of these only 28–30 per cent were properly resettled; in the case of tribal people, it was estimated that only 18–20 per cent of them were properly rehabilitated.

Fernandes said that the states were not interested in utilizing central funds in the Maoist belt: "The States are not interested in looking at that segment of the population, which according to them, are not part of the mainstream." Perhaps it could have been due to electoral considerations as the affected population did not occupy an important segment of the electorate. He compared the situation with the old West Bengal United Front government's experience of 1967 in controlling the Naxal menace within two and half years by re-distributing 1 million acres of land to the landless.[24]

As a result, the new law was hailed as it contained features like more transparency, requirements for social impact assessments (SIA), people's consent, compensation, resettlement and rehabilitation (R&R). It restricted government's power to take over private property for public use. It put a check on the government from indiscriminately acquiring land for vague public purposes. It also ensured greater public participation by seeking consent from 70 per cent of the people affected by land acquisition in public–private partnership projects and from 80 per cent of people in private projects. Also, through its compensation formula, landowners would get four times the market value of rural land and twice that of urban land. It made it mandatory to resettle and rehabilitate title holders and livelihood losers.

However, the NDA government which came in power in 2014 played politics and tried to dilute the effect of this new law by passing an ordinance in 2014. This was criticised by Jairam Ramesh, a Congress minister in the UPA government, who had piloted the original bill in 2011. He said that the ordinance made it "look like the 1894 law." The amendment bill was passed by the Lok Sabha in 2015 but could not succeed in the Rajya Sabha, which referred it to the Joint Committee of the Parliament. The last we heard was that the NDA government had lost interest in this bill.[25]

Meanwhile some state governments played havoc with this law. In 2018 the Delhi-based Centre for Science and Environment (CSE) filed RTI applications in twenty-eight states to find out how land acquisitions were conducted in the states and whether they had complied with the four points mentioned in the RFCTLARR Act. The results were shocking and revealed the bureaucracy's apathy: Gujarat, Madhya Pradesh, Bihar, Karnataka, West Bengal, and Uttar Pradesh did not reply to the RTI applications at all. Other sent "half baked" replies. Replies from others were disquieting as Tamil Nadu, Telangana, Gujarat, Haryana, Maharashtra, Jharkhand, and Andhra Pradesh had ignored the national act and implemented their own acts by replicating the ordinance.[26]

Some states complained that the procedure under the RFCTLARR Act was lengthy and cumbersome, involving several stages. It also reduced the power of the state. Hence many states had tweaked the law to short circuit its procedures. The notice period was reduced, and social impact assessment requirements were diluted.

Several landowners complained that they had received only two to three days' notice for public hearings instead of the three weeks mandated by the law. For the "Bullet Train Project", a pet project of Prime Minister Narendra Modi, there was a complaint lodged by Jayesh Patel, president of Gujarat Khedut Samaj, that no social impact assessment was done nor were the "*gram sabhas*" (village councils) consulted. Several states had diluted the mandatory social impact assessment by outside experts for independent pre-audit. They managed to do it with "in house" bureaucrats. This was sharply criticised by N.C. Saxena, former secretary to the Ministry of Rural Development: "Such subversion of the law is against the spirit of democracy."[27]

## Mahatma Gandhi National Rural Employment Guarantee Act (MGNREGA)

Another important piece of legislation passed during UPA–I was the National Rural Employment Guarantee Act (2005), to which "Mahatma Gandhi" was added in 2009. It is said that it was MGNREGA which brought the UPA again into power in 2009.[28] The philosophy of this act was social inclusion, poverty alleviation, gender parity, social security, and equitable growth.

This scheme was first started in Anantapur in Andhra Pradesh on 2 February 2006, to provide work for unskilled, semi-skilled rural labour or those living below the poverty line. MGNREGA is considered the largest social security scheme in the world with a grass roots approach giving more power to local bodies for guaranteeing 100–150 days of unskilled manual work to all rural households in India. Originally only 200 districts were covered, which was later extended to 648 districts.

Polemics started when Prime Minister Narendra Modi described MGNREGA as "a monument of UPA's failure" while addressing the Lok Sabha on 27 February 2015, one year after his BJP government won the elections. Yet he said that he would not discontinue it.[29]

In April 2015 MGNREGA introduced an "add-on" called "Project Livelihoods in Full Employment" by the Ministry of Rural Development for promoting self-reliance by improving the skills of labourers, in order to help them secure full rather than partial employment. Similarly, a skill development programme "Deen Dayal Upadhyaya Grameen Kaushalya Yojana", named after veteran Jan Sangh President Deen Dayal Upadhyaya, was also started for the diversification of the skills of workers between 15 and 35 years of age to enable them to get suitable placements as poverty alleviation.[30]

As a result, the Congress complained that the Modi government had taken credit for their scheme. This is not correct as the Modi government, in their official release on 2 February 2016, the eve of the tenth anniversary of MGNREGA, had described its achievements a "cause of national pride and celebration."[31] This included the UPA period too.

In fact, the NDA statement listed the scheme's achievements during the preceding decade: A total of Rs. 3,138.45 billion ($37.8 billion) had been spent on the scheme of which 71 per cent was wages to workers. Of these poor workers, 20 per cent were from scheduled castes and 17 per cent from scheduled tribes. Women constituted more than the statutory 33 per cent.

In February 2022 the Economic Survey preceding presentation of the Annual Budget said that allocation schemes under the act in FY 2021–22 had risen by 18.7 per cent on the previous year, and the allocation was being further enhanced. In the same year, over 87 million individuals and 61 million households were provided work. In the actual budget, Finance Minister Nirmala Sitharaman allocated Rs 730 billion ($8.8 billion) for 2022–23.

At the same time the inability of governments to make full payments to the workers as revealed in the Rajya Sabha by Sadhvi Niranjan Jyoti, Minister of State for Rural Development on

2 February 2022, was disconcerting. An amount of Rs. 33.6 billion ($0.4 billion) were pending payment as wages in West Bengal, Uttar Pradesh and Rajasthan. An NGO watchdog "NREGA Sangarsh Morcha" estimated that only Rs. 546.5 billion ($6.6 billion) would be available for the scheme during FY 2022–23 given all the pending liabilities, thus reducing the employment under this scheme to sixteen days per year against the mandatory 100 days.[32]

The NDA government's disinclination to specially praise this scheme was evident when Finance Minister Sitharaman did not mention the Scheme in her ninety-minute budget speech in 2022, a repeat of the year before. It was not therefore surprising that some members of parliament had complained about this omission, despite the NREGS emerging "as a safety net for the poor and migrant workers during the Covid-19 pandemic."[33]

Congress leader Rahul Gandhi told the parliament on 2 February 2022 that the UPA government "had pulled 27 crore [270 million] people out of poverty" while the Modi government had "pushed 23 crore people back into poverty" through wrongheaded policies like demonetisation and a flawed good and services tax (GST) resulting in unemployment at a fifty-year high, with 30 million young people losing their jobs in 2021 alone.[34]

## Whistle Blowers Protection Act 2014

This was a landmark piece legislation by UPA, which was being used by former Maharashtra BJP Chief Minister Devendra Fadnavis, currently Deputy Chief Minister, to defend himself from the charge that he had leaked details of a telephone surveillance programme undertaken by IPS officer Rashmi Shukla, against whom two cases were launched by Mumbai Police for surreptitiously tapping telephones of opposition leaders (the case was quashed in 2023).[35]

The background to this legislation can be traced to 2003 when an engineer named Satyendra Dubey was murdered for blowing the whistle on the then BJP government's "Golden Quadrilateral Project" of the National Highways Authority.[36] In 2005 a state-owned Indian Oil Corporation official Shanmugham Manjunath was killed when he sealed a petrol pump for fuel adulteration in the notorious Lakhmipur Kheri district in Uttar Pradesh.

In October 2021 this village, under the tight control of NDA Union Minister of State for Home Ajay Kumar Mishra, would see serious violence resulting in eight deaths caused by mowing down protestors during a farmers' agitation in which Mishra's son Ashish Mishra was the main accused.[37] In 2011 a senior police officer Devendra Dutt Mishra, who wanted to expose corruption in Bahujan Samaj Party (BSP) leader Mayawati's government, was alleged to have been forcibly admitted into a mental asylum.[38]

As a result of public pressure, the Lok Sabha passed the bill in December 2011, followed by the Rajya Sabha in February 2014. It received Presidential assent on 9 May 2014 before Narendra Modi took over as prime minister on 26 May 2014.

*The UPA's defeat: Was it due to their poor economic progress record?*

In the din of the 2014 general election (7 April–12 May) which finally saw the NDA trouncing the ten-year-old UPA government, a well-researched article by Maitreesh Ghatak, Parikshit Ghosh, and Ashok Kotwal, "Growth in the time of UPA: Myth and reality", appeared in the *Economic & Political Weekly* on 19 April. Since *EPW* does not compete with broadsheets or tabloids in publicity, the findings in this article might have been ignored by the electorate who pushed UPA to a mere 44 seats in the Parliament against 206 in 2009. The NDA under Narendra Modi scored 282 seats against 116 in 2009. They wrote: "If opinion polls are to be believed, the Congress Party is headed for a rout." It contradicted the popular view that the likely UPA rout would be due to economic factors like neglecting economic growth through populist welfare schemes.[39]

On the other hand, economic indicators had made the authors believe that the UPA had achieved higher savings and investment, increased foreign trade and capital inflows, and higher infrastructure spending together with partnership with private capital thereby resulting in faster growth.

The UPA's problems arose due to the lack of an efficient bureaucratic machinery to tackle the consequences of faster growth like emergence of unprecedented law and order problems to deal with increased conflicts over land, rent seeking and resultant corruption in the "booming" infrastructure and natural resource sectors. Also, they failed in the delivery of welfare schemes despite gaining more revenue. They also failed to educate the public on their achievements "commensurate with increased public demand and rising aspirations."

This peculiar feature of economic growth not resulting in human development was highlighted in 2008 by the United Nations Conference on Trade and Development (UNCTAD). It listed problems like nutrition, health, education, gender equality, and environmental sustainability despite rapid economic growth.[40] Although this analysis was about "Least Developed Countries", it was found to be applicable in India during the UPA government as the *EPW* article had said: "Growth can also unleash powerful aspirations as well as frustrations, and political parties who can tap into these emotions reap the benefits." Narendra Modi did exactly this: he tapped into frustrations.

The UPA failed to devise new mechanisms and institutional innovations to solve the problems of growth. For example, land acquisition had started rapidly for development projects because the economy was growing fast. Pressure started building to convert thousands of hectares of agricultural lands to high-value use— industrial, residential, or infrastructural. The new land acquisition law came too late and did not solve all the problems. It also had serious loopholes. Skilled labour and educational facilities did not keep pace with growth. Educational facilities were of poor quality.

Growth allowed them the chance of introducing welfare schemes like NREGA, which won them the 2009 elections, but they did not set up a control system "to run these schemes effectively by plugging leakages and stopping the graft. In the process, they showcased not its egalitarian pro-poor politics but its ineptitude and corruption."

At the same time the authors also found that Modi's "*vikas*" (development) philosophy had "no real content in terms of policy ideas" like how his "market fundamentalist" supporters had believed: cutting taxes and entitlements, privatising public sector undertakings, relaxing environmental regulations, labour market reforms and curbs on union power, and generally reducing the role of government. Oddly the last idea on reducing government control was abandoned by Modi in due course after winning the 2014 and 2019 elections.

## *How growth faltered through infrastructural problems*

The Maoist problem in India would make an excellent case study how this had happened. Prime Minister Manmohan Singh told the State Directors General of Police on 4 November 2004 that Maoists constituted an even greater threat to India than militancy in Jammu and Kashmir and the north east. He repeated this on 13 April 2006 while addressing the Maoist affected states. However, neither UPA-I nor UPA-II managed to set up an effective machinery to tackle this grave problem as it needed state police cooperation since police and law and order came within the purview of state control under Schedule 7 of the constitution.

In 2007 the UPA government appointed the Punchhi Commission (The Second Commission on Inter-State Relations) to examine centre–state relations in order to tackle this problem which was affecting law and order and also hindering development. It was constituted on 27 April 2007 under the chairmanship of Justice Madan Mohan Punchhi. The Commission submitted its report on 31 March 2010. The Ministry of Home Affairs, which should have given logistical support to the Commission, failed. The Chairman complained that no full-time secretary was appointed, and no residential accommodation was provided for him for the entire duration of the Commission. He had to operate from Chandigarh.[41]

Yet they gave a good report. They took note of the general reluctance of political parties to allow the centre to take over their state administration even if law and order had broken down. The states would consider such "take over" as political punishment. Hence the Commission adopted a middle road.

It recommended adopting "Localized Emergency provisions" under Articles 355 (duty of the centre to protect the state against external aggression and internal disturbance) and 356 (failure of constitutional machinery in the state), bringing a district or even part of a district under central rule. In the rest of the areas the state government would continue undisturbed. This was what had been done successfully in Telangana in 1950–51 during the "Revolt."

This was an innovative proposal in a multi-party democratic system where opposition parties are suspicious of every central move. The Commission also recommended that any such takeover should not be for longer than three months. Another recommendation was to amend the Communal Violence Bill to include a provision whereby state consent should not become a hurdle in deployment of central forces in a serious communal riot. However, such deployment should only be for a week and post-facto consent should be taken from the state. This was to prevent a Babri Masjid type of situation.

At the same time the Communal Violence (Access to Justice & Reparations) Bill introduced by the UPA government on the first day of the Winter session (6 February 2014) had to be withdrawn due to objections from the combined opposition including the BJP, Samajwadi Party, CPI(M), AIDMK and DMK as they alleged that it went against "Federal principles." The new bill was to replace an earlier version of the Communal Violence Bill withdrawn by the Government.[42]

Due to the same parliamentary gridlock, the UPA government could not introduce constitutional changes recommended by the Punchhi Commission although they remained in office for a further four years. The Modi government which took over in 2014 has totally ignored this Commission's findings.

*"Scams" and failures which brought the UPA down in 2014*

The optics of various "scams" or failures which remained as indelible images in the public attention throughout the two tenures of the UPA affected the government's credibility, leading to their rout in 2014. In many cases, a lack of imaginative machinery to maintain public dialogue also contributed to this poor image.

Chief Minister Narendra Modi who was aspiring for a national role knew the necessity of a convincing public relations exercise as he had hired the American lobbying company APCO Worldwide for the Gujarat government from 2006 to 2013.

1. Cash for votes scam, July 2008

The 2005 India–US civilian nuclear agreement should be the starting point of all the UPA-I's woes which continued during UPA-II from 2009 to 2014. On 18 July 2005 President George W. Bush and Prime Minister Manmohan Singh announced at a White House meeting the draft outline of an India–US civil nuclear deal, also called the 123 Agreement, in addition to several other areas of cooperation.[43] President Bush agreed to seek agreement from the US Congress to permit this and also lobby friends and allies to adjust international regimes to enable full civil nuclear energy cooperation and trade with India.

However, this was strongly opposed by both Communist parties who were part of the UPA alliance. It was opposed by the BJP for different reasons. While the Communists felt that this would make India subservient to America, the BJP felt that such an agreement would force India to throw open its nuclear facilities to International Atomic Energy Agency (IAEA) inspection.

On 22 July 2008 the UPA faced its first test in parliament by way of vote of confidence after the withdrawal of Communist support. Although the government finally won with 275 favourable votes and 256 against, the entire process was marred by what was called a "Cash for Votes" scam in parliament. During the debates three BJP members of parliament interrupted the proceedings by waving wads of currency notes which they alleged were paid to them to vote in favour of the government. The late Somnath Chatterjee, who was then Lok Sabha Speaker, directed the Delhi Police to investigate the matter. Simultaneously a Parliamentary Committee also enquired into it.

The Congress alleged that the whole scandal was stage-managed by the BJP to bring down the government. Suspicion was focussed on Samajwadi MP the late Amar Singh and on Sudheendra

Kulkarni, close aide to BJP leader L.K. Advani. The Parliamentary Committee reported in December 2008 that no bribes were paid in the parliament. It recommended that the police should investigate an incident that took place outside parliament involving three persons who were related to certain political parties. The police charged them with attempted bribery but on 22 November 2013 they were acquitted in court.[44]


2. The 26/11 Mumbai terror attack:

The BJP took full electoral advantage of the national resentment against the UPA regime for their lapses in handling the Mumbai terror attack on 26 November 2008. They also ridiculed the government that no strong reprisal action was taken against Pakistan that had trained and despatched ten Lashkar terrorists and invaded India. This was despite the BJP assuring the nation on 26 November that it stood with the UPA government given the "full-scale war" on India.

However, within twenty-four hours the BJP reneged on this promise. Chief Minister Narendra Modi became the face of the party's *volte-face* on the attacks. Modi visited Mumbai and addressed the press outside the Oberoi Trident Hotel, which was where two terrorists had taken 143 people as hostages and killed thirty-two. It was also true that the two terrorists were undeterred by the intervention of a posse of Naval Commandos called "Marcos" and local police until the National Security Guards (NSG) arrived at the scene eleven hours late.

Modi's press conference came just before two elections: in Delhi on 29 November and in Rajasthan on 4 December. The BJP ran advertisements in national dailies and displayed posters showing red against a black background—starkly signifying the blood-spilling in Mumbai. The advertisement read, "Brutal Terror Strikes at Will. Weak Government. Unwilling and Incapable. Fight Terror. Vote BJP."[45]

The 26/11 attack was a colossal failure of the UPA government at the centre and the Congress-led coalition government in Maharashtra. Ominous signs of the impending terror attack were coming even from 2006. The reports made available to the two-man High Level Committee (popularly known as the "Pradhan Committee" consisting of retired Governor Ram Pradhan as chairman and this author as the second member) by the Maharashtra government clearly indicated that Pakistan-based Lakshar-e-Toiba was preparing to strike Mumbai through a sea-borne attack, that they were training a team in water-borne operations and that it would most probably be a commando-style operation.

Despite these signs, the Central Government organs like the Ministry of Home Affairs and the National Security Council (NSC)—especially the NSC Secretariat which was supervising central intelligence organizations—failed to perform their statutory duty under Article 355 of the Constitution of "protecting" the state from external aggression. The state government did not set up any preventive machinery to ward off a sea-borne attack.[46]

Even with this disastrous failure on the security front, the UPA government at the centre defeated the BJP-led NDA in the April–May 2009 general election, winning 206 seats in parliament against 116 by the NDA. Even in Maharashtra the Congress-led alliance won against the Shiv Sena–BJP front in the October 2009 elections.

However, the downfall of the UPA at the centre started with a series of scams throughout their second term, culminating in their humiliating defeat, proving what the economists had predicted in April 2014: "Growth in the time of UPA: Myth and reality."

3. The 2010 Commonwealth Games:

The 2010 Commonwealth Games were held on 3–14 October 2010 in New Delhi. It was the biggest sports event held in India, much bigger than the Asian Games in 1951 and 1982. Nearly 4,300 athletes from seventy-one countries participated. Even before the Games were planned, controversies had erupted, some on the advisability of holding such games in Delhi with poor infrastructure and the wrong choice of venues leading to the eviction of thousands of slum dwellers to make way for events. The BBC said on 3 September 2010:

By staging the Commonwealth Games successfully in its capital, India wanted to announce to the world that it was an emerging superpower. But the run-up to the Games has been a huge public relations disaster. Delhi was told it would be "world-class" by 2010. But the Games start in just over a month and the city is nowhere near ready.[47]

Critics included business tycoon Azim Premji, former UPA minister Mani Shankar Iyer, and others who censured the colossal expenditure on the events when "one in three Indians lives below the poverty line and 40% of the hungry in the world live in India, when 46% of India's children and 55% of women are malnourished."[48]

On 28 July 2010 the Vigilance Commission publicly released reports on irregularities in fourteen of their projects.[49] There were also allegations of corruption. A high-level committee under the Comptroller and Auditor General of India was appointed to investigate. Agencies like the Central Bureau of Investigation, Income Tax Agency and others were entrusted with the probes. Suresh Kalmadi, a high-profile Congress leader and the Organising Committee chairman, was arrested on 20 May 2011. Several others were charged.

Even by 2020 there was no clarity on the exact stage of a number of pending cases in the court, except a bland admission by the Ministry of Youth Affairs and Sports that fifty cases were pending before various courts and in arbitration as of July.[50]


4. The S-band scam

In 1992 the Department of Space set up a private limited company named Antrix Corporation Limited for commercially exploiting space "products" of the Indian Space Research Organisation (ISRO) and for offering consultancy services and transferring technologies to other customers including foreign clients. It was meant to be the equivalent to the consumer goods division of the American National Aeronautics and Space Administration (NASA) through which it sells or transfers its technology to private industry including consumer goods as detailed in their popular magazine *Spinoff*.

It was officially stated in parliament on 24 July 2019 that a total of 239 satellites had been launched by the ISRO's commercial arm in the last three years, which brought in revenue of Rs. 62.89 billion ($700 million).

In 2005 Antrix signed a deal with a start-up company called Devas Corporation (Digitally Enhanced Video and Audio Services). It agreed to build, launch and operate two satellites and lease out 90 per cent of the satellite transponder capacity to the latter which planned to offer hybrid satellite and terrestrial communication in India. However, the UPA government cancelled the deal in 2011 due to "security reasons", which were not revealed. Some media exposures revealed that 70 MHz of S-band spectrum, usually used by security services, were also included in the deal and sold only for Rs. 10 billion ($100 million), which would have meant a loss of Rs. 2 trillion ($24 billion) for the government.[51]

Devas, founded in 2004, had some prominent individuals such as Kiran Karnik, former Chairman of NASSCOM on its board and had planned to offer broadband services in India. G. Madhavan Nair was Chairman of ISRO and Antrix when the deal was finalised. In August 2016, Nair and others were charged by the Central Bureau of Investigation (CBI) for "facilitating a wrongful gain" to Devas to the tune of Rs. 5.78 billion ($70 million).

The CBI accused Madhavan Nair of withholding crucial information from the Space Commission which had approved the deal. It said that Devas did not have the technical competence to provide delivery of videos, multimedia content and information services using S-band transponders through the various satellites and terrestrial systems in India.[52]

Despite this Nair was formally inducted to the BJP by President Amit Shah on 27 October 2018.[53] He told the media that he was not a politician, and his role was to provide help in a technical capacity to further Modi's nation-building agenda.

However successive arbitration proceedings in foreign courts filed by Devas in 2017, 2019, and 2020 went against the government.

In November 2020 the Supreme Court of India stayed the October 2020 US Federal Court ruling and asked the Delhi High Court to hear the case. Simultaneously Antrix filed a "winding up" petition against Devas under the Indian Companies Act. In September 2021 the National Company Law Administration Appellate Tribunal (NCLAT) upheld the "winding up" petition.

The government of India was hugely embarrassed in November–December 2021 when a Canadian court in Quebec ordered the seizure of Indian assets belonging to the Airport Authority of India and Air India held by the International Air Transport Association (IATA), after Devas investors filed a case against the government of India. In January 2022 the same court amended its order and ordered the seizure of only 50 per cent of Air India assets lying with IATA.

On 17 January 2022, the Supreme Court of India upheld the NCLAT verdict on an appeal by Devas, saying the seeds of the commercial relationship between Antrix and Devas "were a product of fraud perpetrated by Devas" and "the plant grew out of seeds…are all infected with the poison of fraud."[54]

Following this, Finance Minister Nirmala Sitharaman attacked the Congress Party on 18 January 2022, saying that the Antrix–Devas deal "was a fraud of the Congress, by the Congress and for the Congress." She claimed that it was only the NDA government which initiated action from 2015. She also "accused the Congress-led government of the time of handing over airwaves used by the defence to the private firm for a pittance."[55] She did not, however, say why the main actor in the "fraud" had been admitted into BJP in 2018.


5. The 2G spectrum scam

On 16 November 2010 Vinod Rai, Comptroller and Auditor General (CAG) of India, reported a loss of a staggering figure of Rs. 1.75 trillion ($21 billion) to the government exchequer in a report on the issue of licences and allocation of India's 2G spectrum.[56] America's *Time* magazine had called it the second biggest instance of abuse of executive power in history.

The alleged scam had a side story involving the then CBI chief Ranjit Sinha who was accused of meeting some of the suspects at his home. In 2014 the Supreme Court ordered: "We direct the CBI director not to interfere in the 2G-scam investigation or prosecution. He will recuse himself from the case."[57]

However, suspicions around this scam had erupted well before the CAG report which had only confirmed and quantified the loss. That was when A. Raja, Telecom Minister since 2007, announced in October 2007 that there would be no auction of spectrum, which would be allocated as recommended by the Telecom Regulatory Authority of India (TRAI). The Department of Telecommunications (DoT) received 575 applications from forty-six firms.

In January 2008 the DoT decided to issue licences on a first-come, first-served basis with a retrospective cut-off date of 25 September 2007. In May 2008 the Central Vigilance Commission started an enquiry on receipt of complaints from an NGO, Telecom Watchdog, of irregularities in allotment. In July the Delhi High Court ruled that the retrospective cut-off date for licence applications was illegal. An FIR was registered by the CBI in October against "unknown government officers and companies", and the investigation began.[58]

The CBI in their chargesheets (2 April 2011) alleged that Raja, a DMK member of the UPA government, had favoured Kalaignar TV Private Ltd, a DMK family company. Ms. Kanimozhi, a sitting member of Rajya Sabha and daughter of DMK supremo K. Karunanidhi, was also charge sheeted for receiving favours. Along with them other businessmen and government officers were charged in a scam, described by Vinod Rai's office as the "biggest scam in the history of Independent India."

Even in 2011 there was no unanimity on the accuracy of the "presumptive losses" arrived at by the CAG. Several Congress leaders lashed out at Vinod Rai for dramatizing the extent of the scam by quoting absurd figures of "presumptive losses." Prime Minister Manmohan Singh chided Rai for "commenting on policy issues."

However, it was left to the Central Board of Direct Taxes (CBDT) to expose the hollowness of Rai's logic. The CBDT told the Joint Parliamentary panel (JPC) investigating the 2G scam on 11 December 2011 that the "concept of presumptive loss" which the CAG had used "does not appear in any statutory provision of the income tax laws."[59]

This was after the CAG had told the same panel on 15 November 2011 that the idea of presumptive loss had the "statutory backing" of the Income Tax Act 1961. The CBDT denied this and explained that the provision applied only for computing profits of businesses on a presumptive basis on a fixed percentage of turnover. A JPC member had told *The Economic Times* that Rai, who was scheduled to appear again "would find it difficult to answer the Panel's questions" after the assertion by the tax authorities. "He will be defensive just as he was last time."[60]

During the CBI investigation the TRAI told the investigation that Raja, instead of causing losses to the government, had in fact earned a profit between Rs. 30–70 billion for the government.[61]

However, none of this mattered to Rai. He went from success to success. For quite some time he rode on the crest of a publicity wave as Saint George, the dragon killer. In May 2014 the Supreme Court appointed Rai to take charge of the assets of the ancient Padmanabhan Swamy temple in Thiruvananthapuram following a report filed by *amicus curiae* Gopal Subramaniam that the authorities had failed to perform the temple's administrative duties. In January 2017 the Supreme Court appointed Rai as the head of four "administrators" of the Board of Control of for Cricket in India (BCCI) after its president and office bearers were barred by the apex court from managing its administration, in the wake of severe controversies.

Rai's reversal of fortunes started later. On 13 July 2020, after a long meandering process, the Supreme Court upheld the rights of the erstwhile royal family of Travancore in the administration of the Padmanabha Swamy temple by setting aside the Kerala High Court order of 2011, which had asked the state government to take over the administration of the temple.[62]

On 3 August 2018 Amitabh Choudhary, acting BCCI secretary and former Additional Director General of Police (Jharkhand), criticised Rai for being "a complete failure" in implementing the Supreme Court-mandated reforms by the Justice Lodha Committee in the cash-rich and scandal-riven BCCI. He accused Rai of making appointments without transparency and side-lining his colleagues like him and Treasurer Aniruddh Chaudhary. Besides, he alleged, Rai was guilty of contempt of the court by always blaming the Supreme Court for "the long-time taken to pass the final order on the constitutional reform" of the BCCI.[63]

Finally, Rai's "crusade" against UPA-era corruption, as manifested in the form of the 2G spectrum scam, turned out to be a damp squib. On 21 December 2017, the special CBI/PMLA court in New Delhi acquitted all the nineteen accused persons in the 2G spectrum case including prime-accused Raja and Kanimozhi. The court held the view that the Enforcement Directorate's (ED) case of money laundering ("proceeds of crime") did not survive since the primary crimes charged by the CBI against all the accused persons were not proved. It said: "Without the existence of proceeds of crime, there cannot be any commission of an offence of money laundering."[64]

Former Congress minister Kapil Sibal said that the 2G scam verdict was a moral and legal victory for the UPA government. He asked all those, including Prime Minister Narendra Modi, to stop referring to this incident as so-called scam. Senior Congress leader and MP Manish Tewari in a tweet asked the former CAG chief Vinod Rai to apologise to the nation: "Mr Vinod Rai, former C&G must apologise to the nation for throwing presumptive sensational Corrosive numbers into public discourse. He was author of imbecile 1.76 thousand crore loss theory that I had destroyed during my cross examination of Rai in JPC. Court has affirmed JPC Report."[65]

On 29 October 2021 Rai had to apologise to Sanjay Nirupam, a Congress leader who had filed a defamation case against Rai for his remarks in 2014 that Nirupam had asked him to drop former prime minister Manmohan Singh's name from the 2G spectrum report. Rai submitted an affidavit to the Metropolitan Magistrate that he had inadvertently and erroneously mentioned Nirupam's name while he was giving an interview to the media prior to the launch of his book *Not Just an Accountant: The Diary of the Nation's Confidence.*[66]

Salman Khurshid, former minister in the UPA government, cited the above case on 2 November 2021 to allege that Rai was an "agent provocateur" and part of the "concerted and deep-rooted conspiracy" to malign, defame and bring down the Congress government during UPA-II: "To recollect, Rai had authored a CAG report that threw a sensational number of presumptive losses of Rs 1.76 Lakh crores to the exchequer in the grant of 2G spectrum licenses. The report was a figment of the imagination and a flight of fancy."

Khurshid also alleged that the Modi Government had appointed Rai as Chairman of the all-powerful Banking Recruitment Board with Union Minister of State status. Yet Rai had nothing to say about the massive Rs. 135 billion PNB Bank Fraud or on the billions lost in other bank frauds. Nor did he have any comments on the escape of fugitives like Nirav Modi, Mehul Choksi, Lalit Modi, Vijay Mallya and many others during the NDA's rule.[67]

6. The Anna Hazare anti-corruption movement (2011): How mishandling a popular movement sank the UPA

What ultimately brought down the UPA government leading to its humiliating defeat in 2014 was the inept handling of an anti-corruption movement led by veteran Gandhian Anna Hazare, who came to be the symbol of the 2011 anti-corruption movement. Had they calibrated their strategy with patience and tact, this emotive issue would not have spread all over the country like wildfire. Instead, they neglected it initially as being of no consequence, then tried to use force to suppress it, failing which they caved in to accept most of his demands. In that process the leadership appeared to be weak and directionless.

This movement also became a wellspring of future political leadership of several independent-minded persons who would struggle for a corruption-free government without aligning themselves with any opposition political parties.

The opposition BJP took full advantage of this movement to defame the UPA and eventually managed to attract some prominent persons from this group, like retired police officer Kiren Bedi and retired general V.K. Singh, former Army chief.

This anti-corruption movement saw several offshoots emerging in the country which would assume regional and leadership roles in future. One was the Aam Aadmi Party (AAP—Common Man's Party) floated by Arvind Kejriwal, a former Indian Revenue Officer. Another was the Krishak Mukti Sangram Samiti (Liberation of Agriculturists Movement) led by Assam RTI activist and peasant leader Akhil Gogoi. Yet a third was yoga guru Baba Ramdev's fast against "Black Money" in 2011, which finally led to the UPA capitulating to his demands after using brutal force against his followers. In later years Ramdev, who was once close to some top echelons in the Congress leadership, would align with the Narendra Modi regime.

Even while he was in government service, Kejriwal, along with his friends, had started an NGO named Parivartan (Change) to check corruption by making use of the Right to Information Act (RTI). In 2006 he was awarded the Ramon Magsaysay Award for Emergent Leadership, recognising his grassroot level work in Parivartan.

Anna Hazare was born in 1937 in Bhingar near Ahmednagar in Maharashtra. He spent fifteen years in the Indian Army in lower ranks. On discharge after the mandatory period of service, he returned to his drought-prone village Ralegan Siddhi and worked tirelessly to alleviate extreme poverty there. He spent his own money to restore a village temple which became the focal point of his activities. He then started a drive against alcoholism and its adverse impact on women by their alcoholic husbands, a problem which was rampant in his village.

Along with this he led the local people to do "*shramdan*" (voluntary labour) to improve the soil and water resources for the betterment of their lives. This led to dramatic results. On their own they built a watershed embankment for ground water enhancement for drinking and irrigation. A case study by the

Indian Institute of Public Administration, "Escaping Poverty: The Ralegan Siddhi Case", in September 2008 said:

> Ralegaon Siddhi qualifies as a best practice case of poverty reduction since it has not only reduced poverty, but has led to sizeable poverty reduction with the prevention of slippage or loss of gains. Such cases provide important lessons and have tremendous potential for context-based replication and scaling-up. Other criteria used in the literature of best practices include initiatives which have demonstrated tangible impacts; are socially, culturally, economically and environmentally sustainable; based on collaborative partnerships; allow full community participation and decision making and are replicable.[68]

From 1991 onwards Anna Hazare took his battle through Gandhian methods for a corruption-free government in Maharashtra. Although he was imprisoned for his long agitation, he was successful in generating public pressure in forcing a Shiv Sena minister named Babanrao Gholap to resign from the cabinet in 1999.[69] From 2000, Hazare started a campaign to compel the Maharashtra government to pass a Right to Information Act (RTI) which was done in 2002. It is said that the UPA government's RTI in 2005 was based on this legislation. He also made the government accept a "Citizens' Charter" for the first time in its history.

Another important piece of legislation he managed to get passed in Maharashtra was a transparent transfer policy for government servants every three years. He compelled the government pass an ordinance in 2003, which was later codified as the Maharashtra Government Servants Regulation of Transfers and Prevention of Delay in Discharge of Official Duties Act 2006. The "Citizens' Charter" was codified in Section 8(1) which said that every office or department should publish a Citizens Charter within six months of the commencement of the act.

In 2011 Hazare shifted his anti-corruption activities to the national scene. On 11 March 2011, he addressed a press conference in New Delhi flanked by His Eminence Cardinal Oswald Gracias and Arvind Kejriwal. He said that the UPA's bill for checking high-level corruption was drafted by a group of nine ministers who themselves were corrupt. He also personally attacked Prime Minister Manmohan Singh. Although he "had a good character," the reason why he failed to take action against corrupt ministers was "because of remote control." He wanted the proposed ombudsmen—the Lok Pal at the centre and Lok Ayuktas in the states—to be autonomous and be able to investigate any high functionary.

Hazare began an indefinite fast from Jantar Mantar on 5 April 2011 to strengthen the "Lok Pal" (Ombudsman) bill drafted by the UPA government by adding some more stringent provisions. He wanted the government to follow the "Jan Lokpal Bill" jointly drafted by former Supreme Court judge Santosh Hegde, Supreme Court lawyer Prashant Bhushan and Arvind Kejriwal.

This fast became a catalyst for attracting all the disparate elements opposed to the UPA. It facilitated the emergence of new anti-establishment leadership as a spinoff of Hazare's anti-corruption movement. It was something like the 2004 "Orange Revolution" in Ukraine. Nearly 5,000 people gathered at Jantar Mantar to support him and his cause. Sympathetic "relay" rallies were held in several cities. The public were agitated when Hazare told the audience that Manmohan Singh had conveyed to him that he had no time to meet him until 15 May to discuss his demands.

Jantar Mantar became a place for "pilgrimage" for all wanting to express their annoyance with the UPA—as well a nursery for learning new leadership techniques for some others like former army chief General V.K. Singh, who had locked horns with the UPA government on the issue of his age prior to his retirement.[70] Singh would later gravitate to the BJP.

Among those who made regular visits were social activists Medha Patkar, former IPS officer Kiren Bedi, former IAS officer Jayaprakash Narayan, spiritual leaders like Sri Sri Ravi Shankar, Swami Agnivesh, Swami Baba Ramdev, and even former cricketer Kapil Dev. The audience booed and rejected former BJP minister Uma Bharti and Indian National Lok Dal leader Om Prakash Chautala as Hazare did not want "tainted ministers" coming to him.

These optics produced dramatic results. On 7 April 2011, Union Minister Sharad Pawar resigned from the UPA's Group of Ministers panel which was formed to formulate the Lok Pal Bill "after being held up as an example by Hazare of a 'corrupt minister' who was a member of the government body considering measures to check graft."[71] However, Hazare was not much impressed with his resignation. He told his audience that he had returned his Padma Shri award in 1994 to the President to protest against Sharad Pawar who was the Chief Minister of Maharashtra.[72]

Finally, the UPA government relented, and accepted Hazare's demands on 8 April 2011. Hazare ended his fast on 9 April but gave an ultimatum that the bill should be passed by 15 August. Meanwhile, the forcible police eviction of Swami Ramdev, who was keen to carve a niche for himself by using the anti-corruption movement leadership, upset Hazare who decided to boycott the drafting panel. On 6 June 2011 the police evicted Ramdev's 50,000 followers in a midnight raid.

In July the UPA Ministers' Committee finalised the Lok Pal Bill without bringing the prime minister, judiciary or even bureaucracy under the proposed jurisdiction of the ombudsman. Hazare protested and said he would start a fast unto death. This had country-wide repercussions. The Vishwa Hindu Parishad, a front organisation of the RSS, supported the fast. Delhi Police working under the central government muddied the waters by arresting Hazare on 16 August 2011 with his followers and lodging them in Tihar Jail. Even when they were released, they adopted Gandhian methods and would not leave the jail unless the law was made stronger.

This police action served to strengthen the movement. Large crowds thronged the Ramlila Maidan to support Hazare's fast from 20 August. A country-wide "I am Anna" campaign started, with people wearing T-shirts emblazoned with the slogan. Reuters beamed this movement worldwide giving details of institutionalised corruption in India. It quoted internationally acclaimed film maker Shekhar Kapoor: "Many of those who are coming out haven't voted or were not of voting age. They realise they have to take charge to change society."[73]

Finally, the UPA government had to cave in under public pressure to pass the bill on 28 August. It also had to requisition the services of a Maharashtra bureaucrat named Umesh Sarangi, who had negotiated with Hazare successfully in the past to persuade him to give up the fast. This was considered as a glaring political failure of the UPA government.

In September 2013 Manmohan Singh's government's public image took a severe beating when Rahul Gandhi, Vice-President of the Congress party, publicly assailed an ordinance being issued by the government. This was an ordinance which was prepared to help some RJD members to continue as members of parliament who would have had to vacate their seats consequent to a Supreme Court ruling that those facing a jail sentence of at least two years jail sentence should quit.

It is true that the move to placate a few Congress allies in the UPA government was morally repugnant as it was intended to dilute a Supreme Court judgment. However, the way Rahul Gandhi expressed his opinion publicly was highly damaging to the stature of Singh. He said on 3 October: "My opinion of the ordinance is that it is complete nonsense and should be torn up and thrown away."[74]

The BJP opposition played this up and said that the Congress party and government were at loggerheads. The media echoed this and said that this open denunciation of the government by the scion of the Nehru-Gandhi family did great damage to the stature of the prime minister who was shortly to meet President Barack Obama in New York and have talks with Pakistan Prime Minister Nawaz Sharif. Rahul Gandhi expressed regret for this incident in 2019: "Everyone makes mistakes, I'm only human." However, the damage was done.[75]

Spinoffs from Hazare's movement and the UPA's sullied image

Protests spread to other cities like Mumbai, Bangalore, Chennai, Ahmedabad, Guwahati, Shillong, Aizawl and other places. Regional media spread this fast and wide all over the country. Media reported on the Krishak Mukti Sangram Samiti's (KMSS) sympathetic fast led by RTI activist Akhil Gogoi in the farthest eastern corner of the country on the bank of the picturesque Dighali Pukhuri lake in

Guwahati. Akhil Gogoi had clashed in 2015 even with the longest serving (2001–15) Assam Chief Minister Tarun Gogoi (Congress) over his suspected Maoist links. He was part of the Anna Hazare agitation.

Years later Gogoi would win the Sivasagar constituency in 2021 defeating his BJP rival from jail, where he had been since 2019 for taking part in anti-Citizenship Amendment Act (CAA) protests against the Assam BJP government, which had won the 2016 state elections. He was jailed under the dreaded Unlawful Activities (Prevention) Amendment Act (UAPA) and could not get bail even for elections. The local BJP government had put up fifty-two criminal cases against him. On 1 July 2021 Akhil Gogoi was acquitted of the charges.

Similarly, the mishandling of Baba Ramdev's movement also helped brand the UPA government as directionless. In June 2011 the Congress leadership was worried that Baba Ramdev, who had joined Hazare's movement, had independent political ambitions. They tried to persuade him to give up his proposed fast by the unprecedented action of sending four senior ministers led by Pranab Mukherjee to the airport to receive him on 1 June on his arrival from Ujjain. Even the cabinet secretary was in this group.[76] When persuasion failed, Delhi Police, as usual, created problems for the authorities by swooping on his followers at midnight at Ramlila Maidan on 4 June and dispersing them by using force. Women and children who were sleeping were not spared.

Pranab Mukherjee, who was later elected as President of India (2012–17), revealed to the media on 25 October 2017 that his visit to the airport had been a "misjudgement" and he should not have gone to receive Ramdev in 2011. The newspaper added: "The entire episode—how the government first went out of its way to talk to the yoga guru to dissuade him from holding a protest against the government, and then cracked down on him days later—contributed to the turning tide of public opinion against the UPA government."[77]

However, the biggest offshoot of the anti-corruption movement was the Aam Admi Party founded by Arvind Kejriwal in November

2012. In so doing, he caused a rift with his guru Anna Hazare who believed that his anti-corruption movement was not political. However, Kejriwal firmly believed that, without political support, no fight against graft could succeed. In the end Kejriwal proved to be right whereas the Hazare movement has now faded away.

Kejriwal had a startling success in the 2013 Delhi Assembly elections by winning twenty-eight seats against the Bhartiya Janata Party (BJP) which won thirty-one, cashing in on the UPA's unpopularity. He contested against the highly popular incumbent Congress Chief Minister Sheila Dikshit and defeated her by more than 25,000 votes. Kejriwal formed the government with outside support from the Congress and independents.

This government was short lived and fresh elections were held in 2015 when he won a landmark victory by wresting sixty-seven of the seventy seats in the Assembly. In the 2020 elections he won sixty-two seats, trouncing the BJP which won eight seats. The Congress lost all its seats.

Buoyed by these victories, the AAP extended its activities to Punjab and other states. It won four seats in the 2014 general election in Punjab. In the 2017 state assembly elections it improved its performance by winning twenty seats.

The AAP's biggest victory was in 2022 during the Punjab assembly elections. The Congress, through a series of poor decisions, indirectly helped Kejriwal. First the leadership supported a former BJP leader Navjot Singh Siddhu, who had joined Congress, and made him the state Congress chief. Siddhu started open warfare against Chief Minister Amrinder Singh who had won the 2017 elections by a good majority. As a result, Amrinder Singh resigned from the Congress on 2 November 2021 and floated his own party.

Siddhu persuaded Rahul Gandhi to choose Charanjit Singh Channi as the Chief Minister, under whom the state went to polls in February 2022 which was disastrous as he lost both seats from where he was contesting and could win only eighteen seats for the Congress. The AAP tapped the public discontent and the party's Bhagwant Mann won a record ninety-two seats in an assembly of 117.

*UPA vs. NDA image problem*

On 17 February 2022, former Prime Minister Manmohan Singh would severely castigate Prime Minister Narendra Modi for reducing global diplomacy to symbolic acts of "hugging, swings and eating biryani." He was speaking to the electorate in Punjabi on the eve of Punjab state assembly elections: "I hope leaders of the ruling party have understood by now that relations do not improve by hugging politicians or moving on swings or turning up to eat biryani without invitation."[78]

Singh was referring to Modi's practice of hugging global leaders, his sitting beside the visiting Chinese President Xi Jinping in a swing on the Sabarmati riverfront in Gujarat on 13 September 2014, and his surprise visit to Lahore on 25 December 2015 to greet Prime Minister Nawaz Sharif on his birthday. These symbolic acts of friendship did not improve India's foreign relations and India, after eight years of NDA rule, has the most adversarial relations in its history with both China and Pakistan.

In doing this Singh wanted to remind Modi of what he had said and continued to say about Singh's leadership by calling him "*Maun* [Silent] Mohan Singh."[79] He said that as Prime Minister he had let his "work speak" for him "rather than speaking for myself."

6

# THE NATIONAL DEMOCRATIC ALLIANCE:
## 2014–2024

Congress ideology should be replaced with BJP's—when
history is written, the former UPA government will be
known as a government of scams.

—Amit Shah, BJP President, 9 August 2014

In 2014 the Bhartiya Janata Party (BJP) found it easy to capitalise
on the UPA government's failure to connect with people during its
ten-year rule. The BJP aggressively exploited this failure to design
their template with innovative propaganda for image-building
during electioneering. This model was used by them year after
year till the February–March 2022 state assembly elections when
they won four of the five deeply contested states (Uttar Pradesh,
Uttarakhand, Goa, and Manipur). Only Punjab was lost by the BJP
to the Aam Admi Party.

On the eve of the Punjab assembly elections, former Prime
Minister Manmohan Singh, the most prominent Punjabi leader in
recent years and the first Sikh to be prime minister, thought that
he would easily win Punjab, where 57 per cent of the population
are Sikh. He criticised Modi's personality cult and conveyed to
the electorate in Punjabi that he had always endeavoured to let his
"work speak" for him "rather than speaking for myself" like Modi.

However, Singh and the UPA leadership ignored that, in a democracy, something more was required than mere developmental work to convince the public—and that the government's "visibility" mattered. This was totally absent during the UPA regime (2004–14).

As my analysis in an earlier chapter shows, UPA-I and II had indeed introduced several steps for the common man's benefit. However, their mistake was to engage with the public only through bureaucratic channels. Also, they did not realise that the aspirations of the electorate had changed as senior journalist Harish Khare had argued in 2015:

> Thousands across our cities felt genuinely outraged and emboldened enough to raise their voice against seemingly never-ending civic injustices. By 2014, India was a remarkably confused land and was vulnerable to grand manipulations. It was ready to embrace the idea of challenging the orthodoxy. Questioning "authority" had become a fun and acceptable proposition.[1]

In 2022 Singh could not convince his own Punjab electorate to re-elect the Congress in the state assembly elections. As a result, the Congress government there suffered a humiliating defeat, getting only eighteen seats in an assembly of 117. A rookie political party like the Aam Aadmi Party ran away with the crown by bagging ninety-two seats.

Apart from propaganda, another ingenious method of the BJP's electioneering was to adopt different strategies in different states. In the crucial Uttar Pradesh elections in February–March 2022, where the caste factor was predominant, the BJP identified twenty-two sub-castes among the "Other Backward Castes" (OBC) formation. They then started connecting with them by organising caste-specific *sammelans* (assemblies) in all seventy-five districts. This was intended to offset the reverses it had suffered to its image owing to the administrative breakdown during the "Migrant Exodus" and "Oxygen deaths" which are discussed later in this chapter.

Also, "minority bashing" against Muslims was cleverly used in 2022 during the assembly elections. Noted political academic Suhas

Palshikar described how the BJP had intentionally exacerbated deep religious divides to offset its loss of image due to administrative failures: "Once the electorate is deeply divided on religious basis and once the voters are convinced of the extraordinary powers and sincerity of The Leader, governance failures can be easily overlooked."[2]

Another well-known journalist observed that this veneration of the "leader" was originally triggered by Prime Minister Modi himself in 2017. He started the trend by invoking religion with a slogan "*Kabarastan*" (Muslim cemetery) versus "*Shamshaan*" (Hindu cremation ground) against Samajwadi Party leader Akhilesh Yadav, who was accused of preferring Muslims over Hindus. This was reinforced by Chief Minister Adityanath in 2022 to offset complaints on rampant unemployment with "16 lakhs [1.6 million] fewer people employed in the state in 2022 than they were in 2017."[3]

On 3 March 2022 *The Wire* analysed thirty-four speeches made by Adityanath and BJP leaders during electioneering. It found that objectionable slogans like "*Abajan*", "Jinnah" and "80 per cent versus 20 per cent" (meaning 80 per cent Hindus vs 20 per cent Muslims) had "become so normalised as to be taken for granted." These hate speeches also encouraged Hindu fundamentalist groups like the Bajrang Dal and Vishwa Hindu Parishad to justify violence against Muslims.[4]

Although the BJP finally won the keenly contested UP state elections, deeper examination of the results revealed the party's Teflon was melting despite Prime Minister Modi and Chief Minister Adityanath claiming that the renewed mandate was a portent for the 2024 general election. For one thing, the BJP could not match its 2017 record of winning 325 seats. In 2022 its tally went down to 273. On the other hand, the Samajwadi Party, its main opponent, had won 125 seats against 54 in 2017.

More important, the BJP's Hindutva poster boys, known for their rabid anti-minority utterances, were defeated. The most important bigwig to lose was Keshav Prasad Maurya, Deputy Chief Minister, who had incited the right-wing vigilante groups to storm a mosque in Mathura. But for the presence of the police, this would have created a serious situation. He had linked skull caps to violence. Raghvendra Singh, Chief Minister Adityanath's close aide and a Hindu Yuva Vahini leader in Purvanchal (east UP), also lost this election. During his campaign, Singh had delivered a virulent anti-Muslim speech labelling Hindus who would vote for the opposition as traitors with Muslim blood running in their veins.

Sangeet Som and Suresh Rana, who were accused of inciting the 2013 Muzaffarnagar communal riots, also lost their seats. Rana was a cabinet minister in the Yogi Adityanath government. Another key BJP leader Anand Swaroop Shukla, minister of state for parliamentary affairs in the UP government and noted for his anti-Muslim rhetoric, also lost the election.[5]

Other studies of the 2022 results revealed that the BJP might not easily win the 2024 elections if there is unity among the opposition groups. A *Times of India* study on 20 March 2022, immediately after the 2022 assembly elections in four states, found that regional parties had maintained their hold despite the BJP's success and Congress being unable to improve their tally.[6]

This will be clear if the composition of population of states in India is studied. In 2022 the BJP ruled states with a population of 538 million. Non-BJP parties held the reins of power over other states with a population of 845 million. Also, some states like Karnataka and Madhya Pradesh where they are now in power could be considered "swing" states as the BJP had captured power only by initiating defections from other parties through questionable means. The BJP's top brass was worried that Karnataka, which had become the crucible of the anti-Muslim movement in India with their *"Hijab-Halal-Aazan"* agitation (against the wearing of hijab, the practices of halal food production, and the call to prayer), had neglected governance and would slip out of the BJP's hands. This was the message given to Karnataka Chief Minister Basavaraj Bommai when he visited New Delhi on 8 April 2022.[7]

On 22 May 2022 *Times Now* TV published a tweet by BJP Rajya Sabha member Subramanian Swamy that the BJP was heading for a "India Shining fiasco" in 2024 due to their "gross" neglect of the economy and their failure to admit that China had "gobbled up" 4,000 square kilometres of Indian territory.[8] The Vajpayee NDA government had based their 2004 election propaganda on an illusory perception that "India was shining" merely on urban growth while neglecting distress in rural areas. *India Today* had called it as the "worst poll strategy" in Indian history.[9]

Another portent which is very uncomfortable for India's future is the likelihood of a re-emergence of the proverbial north–south divide. The south is also joined by the east represented by West Bengal. Pro-Hindi narratives by some BJP leaders have irritated leaders in these regions. An example is Union Home Minister Amit Shah's speech on 8 April 2022, at the thirty-seventh meeting of the Parliamentary Official Language Committee, that people of different states in India should communicate with each other only in Hindi and not in English. He claimed that 70 per cent of the Union Cabinet agenda is in Hindi.[10] This was attacked by Tamil Nadu Chief Minister M.K. Stalin, who said Hindi imperialism was causing great harm to the diversity of India.[11]

On 13 June 2022 the ruling Dravida Munnetra Kazhagam (DMK) lashed out at Tamil Nadu governor R.N. Ravi for saying that "*Sanatan Dharma*" was India's guiding spirit. Ravi is a former police officer and close to the national BJP leadership. As is well known, the RSS and BJP advocate "*Sanatan Dharma*", which is resented by the Dravidian parties as they feel that it a domination of north Indian rule over the south.[12]

Despite persistent efforts, the BJP could not make inroads into Kerala, Tamil Nadu, Telangana, Andhra Pradesh, and West Bengal. Hence, as of early 2024, they were concentrating all their energies in destabilising Maharashtra where a fragile Shiv Sena–Congress–NCP coalition was ruling, their only glue being hatred of the BJP. This, they managed to achieve by enticing some Shiv Sena members to vote against the official candidates in the June 2022 Rajya Sabha and Legislative Council elections.

The second part of the drama happened after the elections when they managed to split that party when a sizable faction led by Cabinet Minister Eknath Shinde deserted the party on 21 June and sought refuge in Surat where they were accommodated in a luxury hotel by a BJP leader close to the Gujarat Chief Minister.

From there they were whisked away and flown by a chartered aircraft to the far-off Guwahati on 22 June and accommodated under the care of Chief Minister Himanta Biswas Sarma when the state was reeling under the impact of severe rains and floods. The Congress condemned the chief minister for his "shameful indulgence" in sabotaging a rival government when millions of his people were caught in the rain emergency.[13]

## The Modi era: How it began in 2014 with a Modi campaign

Gujarat Chief Minister Narendra Modi was selected at the Goa Conclave of the BJP in June 2013 to be the party's star campaigner and the head of the twelve-member Central Election Committee. This possibility had caused unease in US media even earlier as reported by the *Christian Science Monitor* on 14 May 2013, with the headline "US, India dance awkwardly around the man who might be India's next leader."[14]

L.K. Advani, who was the senior-most BJP leader after the ailing Atal Bihari Vajpayee, initially protested and resigned. Later he agreed to join the campaign team as "mentor." Modi addressed an astounding number of 437 public rallies, visiting every state from September 2013, traversing 300,000 kilometres after he was named the BJP's prime minister candidate. In addition, he also remotely addressed his enthusiastic audience at 1,350 places through innovative "3D rallies."[15] It was truly a Modi campaign.

In doing this he also exposed himself to considerable personal risk as he was targeted by jihadi groups. On 27 October 2013, his mammoth rally at the historic Gandhi Maidan in Patna was subjected to a serious bomb attack by the outlawed Indian Mujahideen, killing five and injuring eighty-three people. On 1 November 2021 a special court convicted and sentenced nine people. Four were given death sentences, while the rest were sentenced to varying terms of imprisonment.[16]

The 2014 general election was held in nine phases from 7 April to 12 May. Although the BJP won 282 seats against the Congress, which could get only a dismal forty-four seats, the former garnered only 31 per cent of the vote, which was the lowest in India since independence by a party winning a majority of seats. However the BJP-led National Democratic Alliance (NDA) won a comfortable 336 out of 543 Lok Sabha seats. The Congress, which got only 19.3 per cent of the vote, the lowest since 1947, could not even become the official opposition party which required 55 seats.

Veteran journalist Harish Khare, who was media advisor to Prime Minister Manmohan Singh (2009–12) analysed Modi's stunning electoral results. The title of his article was "The Modi Triumph: From 1984 to 2014 and back to 1984."[17] In 1984 Rajiv Gandhi had triumphed in the Lok Sabha elections, winning 400 seats. His nearest rival the Telugu Desam Party could win only 30 seats. Other opposition parties were decimated.

Khare reminded us why he had compared Modi election with Rajiv Gandhi's triumph by referring to what he had written in *The New York Times* on 7 January 1985:

> The Congress Party's triumph is frightening because Rajiv Gandhi depicted the assault on the state as the work of separatist Sikh fundamentalists. His campaign theme of "unity in danger" deeply touched many Hindus, appealing subtly to their historical fears and mistrust of non-Hindus. Rajiv Gandhi's mandate can be summed up as a triumph of neo-Hinduism. Thousands of chauvinistic Hindus abandoned their traditional champion—right-wing parties like the Bharatiya Janata Party—to rally under his banner. And though those parties have been decimated, the right-wing constituency has in fact been strengthened and enlarged, putting the liberal, democratic fringe in mortal danger.[18]

In a similar manner, Narendra Modi reclaimed "brilliantly and imaginatively" that "right-wing constituency" in 2014, "tickling its visceral mistrust of non-Hindus." Faced with this, the Congress campaign in 2014 was lacklustre, based on a total misjudgement that Modi would not be effective outside Gujarat and would be checkmated by the Advani camp.

Further, the Congress wrongly believed that the country had become "irretrievably liberal" after ten years of UPA rule, as it had rejected a "Modi-scarred Vajpayee in 2004[19] and then an Advani-led NDA in 2009." The Congress did not realise that the electorate had changed—that they wanted a change. Khare said that Modi understood the pulse of the people: "With his sneering pugnacity, he focused the spotlight at the dynasty's feet of clay":

> Implicit in this sentiment was a cumulative, unconscious perception that the Congress, the UPA, Sonia Gandhi, Manmohan Singh and every congress minister [like Salman Khurshid and Sriprakash Jaiswal] appeared to be interested only in making Rahul Gandhi the next king. What was more, the projected king himself did not behave like a king, nor did he assure the realm he was interested in learning his kingly duties.[20]

*Modi's inauguration*

Modi's swearing-in function on 26 May 2014 was a brilliantly curated, glittering ceremony reflecting his penchant for show and grandeur associated with all his public performances. No swearing-in ceremony of any new prime minister since 1947 was held outside the forecourt of the magnificent Rashtrapati Bhavan with a large presence of the public except those of Chandra Sekhar (1990–91) and Atal Bihari Vajpayee (1998–2004). All others were simple ceremonies inside the President's House in the presence of selected invitees.

Modi added colour to the ceremony by inviting the heads of all neighbouring countries. Perhaps he wanted to send a message of his friendly neighbourhood policy which was also reflected in the BJP manifesto. Pakistan Prime Minister Nawaz Sharif, Afghanistan President Hamid Karzai, Nepal Prime Minister Sushil Koirala, Bhutan Prime Minister Tshering Tobgay, Sri Lankan President Mahinda Rajapaksa, and Maldivian President Abdulla Yameen Abdul Gayoom attended. Bangladesh was represented by Speaker Shirin Chaudhury as Prime Minister Sheikh Hasina was visiting Japan. This would be the first time that heads of states of SAARC nations were invited to attend the swearing-in ceremony of any Indian prime minister.

The public mood in India in 2014 following Modi's victory could, in a way, be compared to that of France in July 1981 when Francois Mitterrand was elected as Socialist president after twenty-three years of conservative rule. As *The New York Times* had observed at the time: "Mitterrand upended the loose assumption that only a conservative could be elected President in a Fifth Republic whose institutions were devised by de Gaulle to favour the right."[21]

It was a "swing vote" which had not existed in France for nearly 25 years. Mitterrand won re-election in 1988 for another seven years. Likewise, Modi punctured the popular feeling that only a Gandhi–Nehru party could rule India by getting re-elected in 2019.

## Initial assessment of the Modi government, 2014–22

The Modi government began its innings with a confident and pro-active note on all its manifesto promises. The media and public could discern a distinct change in governance. One of the visible changes noticed by my friend, a former World Bank official, was that the corridors of the Government Secretariat were cleared of power brokers, which he said, had not been the case earlier.

*Wada Na Todo Abhiyan* (WNTA; "Never break a promise movement"), a civil society organisation monitoring government promises and its achievements since 2004, published a report in September 2014 on the first 100 days of the Modi government. Its members are NGO workers from the marginalised sectors like the Right to Food Campaign, National Campaign for Dalit Human Rights, Bharatiya Muslim Mahila Andolan (Indian Muslim Women's Movement), and so on, who are usually quite critical of government performance in the unprivileged sectors.[22]

Their very first assessment commended the Modi government's performance after analysing twenty-four areas, including governance, inflation, functioning of parliament, black money, foreign policy, education, health, agriculture, media freedom and minorities. It complimented the government's policies on food security, a mission attempting to end financial exclusion, the announcement of schemes for women and girls and its continued focus on flagship schemes like MGNREGA.

WNTA was critical of the way the Planning Commission was wound up without consulting the states. It said: "Abandoning sixty years of accumulated knowledge and institutional wealth without deliberation or attempt at reform might prove to be a hasty act with little impact on actual improvement of governance." Prime Minister Modi had announced on Independence Day 2014 that the sixty-four-year-old Planning Commission, which was based on the Soviet Union's "command economy" or top-down model, would be replaced by a new body to do "creative thinking, public-private partnership, optimum utilisation of resources, utilisation of youth power of the nation, to promote the aspirations of state governments seeking development, to empower the state governments and to empower the federal structure."[23] In its place National Institution for Transforming India or NITI Ayog was created in 2015.

### Ghar vapsi and anti-cow slaughter vigilante violence

The first disconcerting resonance of the new rule appeared as "*ghar vapsi*" (the "return home" of converts) when the RSS, VHP, and Bajrang Dal resumed their movement with full vigour, which resulted in the Modi government facing domestic and international opprobrium for its coercive methods. In 2014 Modi had disapproved the vulgar language used by Union Minister Sadhvi Niranjan Jyoti and BJP MP Sakshi Maharaj as it would have distracted from government's focus on development.[24] Union Minister Venkaiah Naidu, later vice-president, had also criticised it as it would "damage" the BJP's prospects for the February 2015 Delhi Assembly polls. As anticipated by Venkaiah Naidu, the BJP lost heavily in the Delhi Assembly elections when the Aam Admi Party (AAP) won sixty-seven of the seventy seats.

This did not prevent BJP member of parliament Yogi Adityanath, who was later elected as chief minister of Uttar Pradesh in 2017, telling a Vishwa Hindu Parishad meeting in February 2015 that *ghar vapsi*, which was mainly directed against Christian conversions, would continue as long as "conversions" were not "banned".[25]

One of the earliest *ghar vapsi* programmes was on 10 December 2014 at Agra when 350 pavement dwellers—rag pickers and other destitute sections—were promised that they would be given ration cards and Below the Poverty Line (BPL) papers if they participated in the religious function. This was done by a Bajrang Dal activist and the Hindu Janjagriti Samiti, both outfits affiliated to the RSS.[26] There was no violence.

However, in tribal areas, especially in Chhattisgarh and Jharkhand states, Christians who had converted even twenty-five years ago were assaulted and their houses burnt. Attacks on Christians on Christmas eve in December 2014 in tribal areas for singing Christmas carols shocked the nation when they faced the intolerant face of the above hard-line elements in the NDA.

*The New York Times* released a special feature on these atrocities on 22 December 2021: "Arrests, Beatings and Secret Prayers: Inside the Persecution of Indian Christians."[27] This was after Modi had called on Pope Francis at the Vatican on 20 October and invited him to visit India. It quoted Father Emmanuel, formerly of Delhi Catholic Church who now lives in Vienna, saying that a Papal visit would not change much as the attacks had spread even to Karnataka.

One of the first instances of assault on Christians after Modi came to power was on 12 December 2014 when radical Hindus assaulted a small community of Christians in Hyderabad (Andhra Pradesh and Telangana) with sticks and clubs. They were "guilty" of singing Christmas carols in the streets of the city's tribal Singareny Colony. They were also accused of "converting" Hindus. Pastor Bhim Nayak, head pastor of Banjara Baptist Church, was seriously injured.[28] Such attacks continued even in 2021 when St Joseph School in Ganj Basoda in Madhya Pradesh was attacked by 100 VHP workers while classes were taking place. The school was accused of proselytizing.[29]

However, the Hindu vigilante violence including lynching of Muslims on suspicion of cow slaughter was more serious. Between 2014 and 2021 there were eighty-two incidents resulting in forty-three deaths. In a 2015 incident a mob beat 52-year-old Muhammed Aklaq to death in Dadri in Uttar Pradesh on mere suspicion. His elder son Mohammad Sartaj was working in the Indian Airforce as a corporal technician. The local mob fury and violence against police arrests of suspects was such that the then Airforce Chief Air Marshal Arup Raha had to shift the whole family to a secure Air Force zone.

There were many more serious incidents leading to an impression that lawlessness was prevailing all over India. In 2017 a dairy farmer named Pehlu Khan from Haryana who was transporting cattle was waylaid and mercilessly beaten to death in Alwar, Rajasthan, on mere suspicion. Although he had papers to prove his innocence, the mob did not accept it. His murder was filmed and shown all over India for days.[30] These incidents were mentioned by US State Department's annual report on "International Religious Freedom" for 2018[31] and also 2021.[32]

## Surgical strikes

The Modi government, which had criticised the UPA government's weak response to the 26/11 Mumbai terror strikes, had proclaimed "surgical strikes" as the foundation of its "muscular" security policy. During campaigning in 2014, Modi had announced that Indian forces would cross over the border into Pakistan to strike at terrorist camps if Indian territory was hit.

On 1 March 2019 he claimed that he took prompt action after Pakistan-based Jaish-e-Mohammad hit an Indian army camp in Uri on 18 September 2016, killing nineteen soldiers and injuring thirty.[33] He was speaking at a public meeting in Kanyakumari, Tamil Nadu. He blamed the UPA government for policy paralysis after the 26/11 Mumbai terror attacks when India should have hit Pakistan. Since 2016, 29 September has been observed as "Surgical Strikes Day" by the NDA government.

After the Uri attack the NDA government authorised Indian para commandos to penetrate deep into Pakistani territory in Pakistan Occupied Kashmir (POK) to hit terror camps located there. Lt General Ranbir Singh, Director General of Military Operations (DGMO) said that "Surgical Strikes" were conducted by Indian forces on 29 September 2016 to neutralise terrorists who were preparing to cross the border and strike Indian targets. He said that he had informed his counterpart in Pakistan.

However Pakistani paper *The Express Tribune* denied that any such surgical strikes had crossed into Pakistan and said that Indian Minister Rajyavardhan Singh Rathore who had earlier claimed that its army had "carried out 'surgical strikes' inside Pakistan with the support of military choppers," had later denied involvement of any aerial operations.[34]

Congress, however, questioned Modi's assertion that UPA had not carried out surgical strikes into Pakistan. On 2 May 2019 Rajiv Shukla, senior Congress spokesperson, claimed that the Indian army had conducted six such surgical strikes between 2008 and 2014 but had not publicised them as they were tactical military operations and the party did not want to take credit.

The first strike, according to him, was on 19 June 2008 in Bhattal Sector in Jammu and Kashmir's Poonch. The second was during 30 August–1 September 2011, in the Sharda sector across the Neelam River Valley in Kel. The third was on 6 January 2013, at Sawan Patra check post. The fourth was on 27–28 July 2013, at Nazapir Sector. The fifth was on 6 August 2013, at Neelam Valley and the sixth one on 14 January 2014.[35]

The above statement came soon after former prime minister Manmohan Singh rebutted Modi's claim that the UPA did not give a free hand to the armed forces to deal with cross border incursions. According to the *Hindustan Times* he told his interviewer that "our armed forces were always given a free hand to operationally respond to every threat. Multiple surgical strikes took place during our tenure too. For us, military operations were meant for strategic deterrence and giving a befitting reply to anti-India forces than to be used for vote garnering exercises."[36] The paper said that this was in response to Modi's claims during 2019 election rallies that his government had neutralised a huge Jaish terror training camp in Balakot (Khyber Pakhtunkhwa) during the air strikes on 26 February 2019, in retaliation for the 14 February terror attack in Pulwama which had killed forty members of the Central Reserve Police Force.

As a PR exercise the Pakistani government took a group of international media representatives to the site of Indian bombing on 10 April 2019. According to the BBC only a medium-size crater was seen to have been caused by the Indian bombing. Only a house was found damaged, and some trees uprooted. When the BBC questioned Indian authorities, they said: "The fact that media was taken on a conducted tour to the site only after a month and a half after the incident speaks for itself."[37]

The NDA's manifesto for the 2019 general election had highlighted "surgical strikes" and "air strikes" as their achievements along with its Swachh Bharat (Clean India) Mission, Ujjawala Yojana and Saubhagya Yojana (energy supply schemes), Demonetisation, GST, total electrification, provision of housing for 25 million families, health insurance for more than 500 million people and disbursement of loans to more than 140 million people. It had claimed that the next five years would be "the foundation laying period for India of 2047 when India would complete 100 years of freedom.... The Congress led UPA government could never have dreamt of achieving, let alone envisaging such watershed policy initiative."[38]

### Swachh Bharat Abhiyan

One of the earliest initiatives undertaken by the Modi government was the "*Swachh Bharat Abhiyan*" (SBA; Clean India Campaign) against open defecation, "professing to achieve 100% toilets for the citizens by 2019." It was inaugurated by Modi on 2 October 2014—Mahatma Gandhi's birthday. The campaign focussed on celebrities "voluntarily" sweeping the streets in protective gear. Even top bureaucrats in New Delhi took breaks from secretariat work to sweep the streets in front of cameras![39]

All governments in office since 1954 have struggled to solve this problem, without much success. The NDA's performance since 2014 was no better. In 2001 out of 138.2 million rural households, only 3.5 million had independent toilets.[40] The UPA government had its own plan—"*Nirmal Bharat Abhiyan*"—to make India public defecation free by 2022. In 2015 this was criticised by the Comptroller and Auditor General of India for the period 2009–14 due to its "bottom-up" approach, whereby Gram Panchayat or local plans were not linked to district plans. The programme suffered from unrealistic targets and poor utilisation of funds: "The targets for construction of toilets were fixed by the state governments without considering the fund availability and their capacity to execute the approved plans. This resulted in substantial amounts remaining unspent at the end of each year ranging from 40 per cent to 56 per cent of the available funds."[41]

The same, more or less was said by WNTA about the SBA: that only 8.4 per cent of the 100-day target of 5.2 million toilets had been met. "At this rate, the target for 2014–15 can be fulfilled only if the construction is paced up to at least 1 toilet every second."[42] In 2014 the Swachh Bharat Abhiyan had aimed at making India public defecation free by 2019.

A CAG physical audit on the SBA in Rajasthan in August 2020 revealed that 590 houses listed as "completed" in fifty-nine Gram Panchayats across seven districts did not have toilets although the State had declared itself as "Open Defecation Free" in 2018.[43] A UNICEF report on water, sanitation and hygiene released on 1 July 2021, said that at least 15 per cent of India's total population (22 per cent rural and 1 per cent urban) defecated in public.[44]

On the contrary, this programme had imposed a heavier burden on street cleaners as SBA did not envisage repairing underground sewage systems in urban areas but only building latrines. Commentators reminded us that that in 1858 when London started tackling the "Great Stink," the government had introduced a holistic sewerage plan of connecting toilets to improved underground sewerage system. Since this was not done in India, choked manholes and drains in Indian cities became common, adding to the health problems of street cleaners. In December 2017 the Minister of Social Justice and Empowerment told the Lok Sabha that 300 cases of deaths due to manual scavenging had taken place that year.[45]

On 22 December 2021 the Observer Research Foundation, quoting Ramdas Athawale, Minister for Social Justice and Empowerment, said that there were 43,797 manual scavengers in India. Out of these 42,500 were from the Scheduled Castes. Apart from deaths, manual scavengers were exposed to infections such as cholera, hepatitis, tuberculosis and typhoid. Studies also indicated that women in large numbers work as manual scavengers in rural areas cleaning "dry latrines" on very poor wages.[46]

The fifth edition of the National Family Health Survey (NFHS) 2019–21 covering the second phase for fourteen states and union territories was released on 24 November 2021. The results for twenty-two states and union territories covered in phase one were released in December 2020. The findings revealed that 19 per cent of households did not have access to toilets, implying some of those who had the facilities did not use them and preferred open defecation. This had disproved the government's claim that India had become an "open defecation free nation" in October 2019.[47]

### Black money and demonetisation

Unearthing "black money" was one of the important election promises made by Modi. During campaigning he had promised that he would bring back black money stashed away by Indian tax evaders in foreign banks. In fact, the opposition parties had alleged that he had even promised that he would deposit Rs. 1.5 million ($18,000) in the bank account of each Indian citizen.

Fact checking by *Yahoo News* on 24 January 2009 revealed that Modi had made a mention of this amount in November 2013 at a rally in Kanker (Chhattisgarh): "If, even once, the money hoarded by these crooks in banks abroad… even if we bring only that back, every poor Indian would get Rs 15 to Rs 20 lakh, just like that. There's so much money."[48] He did not say that he would credit this amount in individual accounts, but that impression persisted.

WNTA, in their 100 days report card, were sceptical about the methodology used by the NDA government in checking black money by appointing a Special Investigating Team (SIT) led by Justice M.B. Shah in May 2014. It said that most of this money comes back into India as "white money" through a process called "round tripping." It felt that the role of tax treaties in aiding this round tripping needed to be reviewed by the government to understand the extent of public revenue losses being accrued.

Yet, a survey done by *India Today* in 2018 on the eve of the 2019 general election found that considerable progress had been made since 2014: Rs 693.5 million ($8.4 million) were recovered under The Black Money (Undisclosed Foreign Income and Assets) and Imposition of Tax Act which was passed in 2015. Around 650 people had declared money worth Rs 410 million ($5 million) deposited in foreign banks. [49]

However, this survey found that the demonetisation of Rs. 500 and 1000 notes announced suddenly by the prime minister on 8 November 2016 did not achieve the desired results. The prime minister in his address to the nation had said that it was done to flush out black money from India's financial system and to stop the "shadow economy." In one stroke 86 per cent of the currency in circulation was made illegal. Panicky citizens started queuing up in front of banks. The *Mumbai Mirror* reported that over eighty people had died standing in queues outside ATMs. [50]

Independent observers say that demonetisation had severe adverse economic effects. The first was India's growth rate, which dropped to a four-year low of 6.5 per cent from 7.1 per cent in 2016–17. [51] Also, the Reserve Bank of India (RBI) spent Rs. 210 million in carrying out demonetisation and subsequent remonetisation. *The Guardian* (UK) said that more than 99.3 per cent of the currency notes declared void were surrendered to the banking system, indicating that hardly any "black money" was detected. [52] It quoted The Centre for Monitoring Indian Economy that 1.5 million jobs were lost due to demonetisation.

Arun Kumar, Professor at the Institute of Social Science, said in 2021 that demonetisation had adverse effects on the unorganised sector which employs 94 per cent of the workforce. It consists of the micro and small units which work with cash and not through formal banking. Most of them are economically weaker sections. While the organised sector was hit due to shortage of demand as people lost incomes, the unorganised sector just could not function without cash. He said that the Indian economy suffered a man-made economic slowdown even before the Covid-19 pandemic hit in 2020. [53]

Pronab Sen, former Chief Statistician to the Government of India, said on 12 November 2021, on the eve of the fifth anniversary of demonetisation, that no one was consulted before taking this drastic step and the RBI was not prepared: "The net result was that the remonetisation process to replace the cash took almost a year, when it should have been over within a month." Also, it had no effect on cash circulation. Sen said that in 2021 an amount of Rs. 28.5 trillion cash was "floating around, compared to Rs. 18 trillion in 2016."[54]

An incident in December 2021 in Uttar Pradesh, on the eve of the state assembly elections in February–March 2022, finally proved the total failure of demonetisation, which some had felt at that time was against the use of black money in the 2017 assembly elections. On 28 December Modi alleged that raids on a perfume merchant named Peeyush Jain at Kannauj, allegedly close to the Samajwadi Party, the main political group opposing to the ruling BJP government, had unearthed "perfume of corruption." A sum of Rs. 2.84 billion in cash was recovered during the raids. The Samajwadi Party denied the allegation and claimed that Peeyush was a BJP supporter and the tax authorities had goofed by raiding him.[55]

## 2020 migrant labour crisis

The great migrant labour crisis, in the wake of the Covid pandemic, came before the country could recover from the adverse effects of demonetisation. To quote Pronab Sen, many micro, small and medium enterprises (MSMEs), which were very badly affected due to inadequate cash flows, had to be shut down throwing migrant employees out of jobs.[56] Somehow, they could eke out a living in urban centres doing other daily wage labour. However, the sudden twenty-one-day country-wide lockdown from 14 April 2020 and suspension of rail services due to Covid brought them to sheer misery.

A Supreme Court judgment on 29 June 2021 on the plight of migrant labour in India in response to a *suo motu* writ petition filed by the Bandhua Mukti Morcha (Bonded Labour Liberation Front) had said:

> According to survey carried out by National Statistics Office (NSO) in 2017–2018, there are around 38 crores [380 million]

workers engaged in the unorganized sectors. Thus, the number of persons in the unorganized sector is more than 1/4th population of the entire country. Contributions of these labourers towards different projects, industries, make considerable additions in the economic development of the country.[57]

The Supreme Court took notice of the plea made by the litigants that central and state governments had failed to discharge their constitutional responsibilities towards this important segment of the population by way of "right to life" under Article 21 of the constitution and of food security under the National Food Security Act 2013. The court directed the central government to hold consultations with the states who had failed to do this especially through "One Nation One Ration Card."

Historian Ramachandra Guha called it the "greatest man-made tragedy" as the prime minister could have given at least a week for the thousands of migrant labourers to move to their homes. He said: "That he or his advisers did not think of the consequences of a lockdown at four hours' notice is mystifying. They bear direct responsibility for the humanitarian tragedy that has since unfolded."[58] Guha said that had the migrants moved to their home villages in mid-March, "when few had Covid," there would have been no danger of them infecting their family members. He said that with the panicky movement in trucks and private buses in April, the danger of them infecting their villages was very serious.

The migrants' exodus in April 2020 to their home states was one of the darkest chapters in Indian history, when millions of hapless labourers had to walk, cycle or hitchhike on goods trucks, often paying heavy bribes to reach their homes. *The New York Times* said, "Thousands of migrants in Delhi, including whole families, packed their pots, pans and blankets into rucksacks, some balancing children on their shoulders as they walked along interstate highways. Some planned to walk hundreds of miles." The paper reported that 45 million migrant labourers worked outside their home states.[59] The BBC said that 10 million, most of them working on construction sites in big urban areas, fled "on foot, on cycles, on supply trucks and later in trains. More than 900 of them died on their way home, including 96 who died in trains."[60]

One of the indomitable tales of courage and determination was that of the 15-year-old girl Jyoti Kumari, who carried her injured father on the seat of a bicycle all the way from Gurgaon in Haryana to Darbhanga in Bihar state, traversing 1,200 km. He was working in Gurgaon as an auto-rikshaw driver. It took ten days for her to reach her village.[61] Another heart-wrenching story was that of a 12-year-old girl who died after walking 150 km from the southern state of Telangana to Chhattisgarh state in central India. She had walked for three days when she died, 14 km from home.[62]

However, the nation was shocked when the prime minister blamed the states for allowing the migrants leave their bases. On 7 February 2022, Modi accused the AAP government in Delhi and MVA government in Maharashtra of adding to the panic in the initial days of the Covid lockdown by "pushing" the labourers out of their states. He said: "Congress gave free train tickets to migrant workers to leave Mumbai. At the same time the Delhi government went around slums in jeeps and announced on mics that whoever wants to go home, buses have been arranged to leave the city. This led to the spread of covid in Uttar Pradesh, Punjab and Uttarakhand."[63]

## The oxygen crisis during the pandemic

India started relaxing the strict lockdown in September 2020. However, Covid infections started surging in small towns and cities. This resulted in demands for industrial oxygen (for making cylinders) and medical oxygen shooting up. Hospitals and care centres started consuming 2,700 tonnes of medical oxygen every day in September, compared to 750 tonnes in April, according to data obtained from All India Industrial Gases Manufacturers Association.[64]

Yet Union Minister for Health, Harsh Vardhan, declared in March 2021 that the country was "in the endgame" of the pandemic and, under Modi's leadership, was an "example to the world in international co-operation." This was because from January onwards India had started exporting vaccines to foreign countries.

No doubt, there was a reason for this euphoria. From the average of 93,000 cases per day in September 2020 infections had steadily come down to an average of 11,000 a day with deaths below 100.

However, massive election rallies in five closely contested states (West Bengal, Kerala, Assam, Tamil Nadu, and Puducherry) in April 2021, where the BJP wanted to capture power, added to the surge of infections. Another reason, noted by foreign media, was how a gigantic cricket-loving crowd numbering 130,000 had assembled in "Narendra Modi" stadium in Ahmedabad in March to witness two cricket matches between India and England.[65]

By mid-April the second wave started raging in India, and the country was averaging more than 100,000 cases a day. On 18 April the country reported 270,000 cases and over 1,600 deaths, which were new single-day records.

Yet the Union Health Ministry did not initiate a nationwide coordinated plan to move oxygen from production centres to the hospitals. A survey by *India Today* magazine on 10 May 2021 revealed that the centre failed in building up a "war reserve" of medical oxygen, which should have started from September 2020 itself.[66]

The Health Ministry knew that India's major oxygen production facilities were located in the east of the country, from where supplies had to be transported across the nation. Problems included shortage of trucks, cryogenic containers, and also portable cylinders.

The lull in the Covid wave between the end of the first wave in October 2020 and the beginning of the second in March 2021 had made them drop their vigilance. Two examples were quoted in the survey: First, the tender process floated by the centre for 162 oxygen generation plants across the country was not implemented seriously. As a result, only thirty were operational by the time the second wave arrived.

The second example was more egregious: *India Today* reported that the Thiruvananthapuram-based public sector undertaking HLL Lifecare had floated a global tender on 14 October 2020 for the staggered supply of 100,000 metric tonnes of medical oxygen every 10 days after the first shipment of 15,000 metric tonnes, which was to start a month after the order was placed. This would have provided comfortable reserves for the country. Unfortunately, the tender was cancelled after bidders quoted more than the government was willing to pay.

In May 2021 the Ministry again started issuing tenders when Covid cases spiked. On 16 April, HLL Lifecare floated a fresh tender for 50,000 metric tonnes of medical oxygen. The order for this supply had not been placed when the magazine report was written. The report said that questions on this subject put to Union health minister Dr Harsh Vardhan and officials from the Ministry of Health and Family Welfare were yet to be answered at the time of going to press.

Strangely, the shortage of oxygen became a point of political warfare against non-BJP governments like Delhi where the AAP was in power. On 5 May 2021, Amit Malviya, in charge of BJP's IT cell tweeted: "Delhi with approx 90,000 cases is consuming 433.1 MT of oxygen per day (allocation 590 MT) and demanding 900 MT. Mumbai, with comparable case load, consumes much less (245 MT). Delhi also has the highest per capita allocation (61 MT). Can Arvind Kejriwal better manage oxygen?"[67]

However, the Supreme Court pulled up the Central Government on 5 May 2021 in partial answer to this tweet by a non-elected propagandist with a terse order to make full supply to Delhi "by 10:30 am tomorrow." The court had already ordered that 700 MT should be supplied. The failure of the government in complying with this had already attracted the Delhi High Court's "contempt" notice to the central government. Justice D.Y. Chandrachud rejected Solicitor General Tushar Mehta's submission that Delhi would be able to manage with 500 MT. He also asked the centre to study how Bombay Municipal Corporation was managing oxygen as "it has done a good job in managing oxygen supplies."[68]

The acute shortage of oxygen resulted in country-wide deaths in alarming numbers. Panic started when twenty-three patients died in the elite Gangaram Hospital in New Delhi on 23 April

2021. The hospital said that sixty more people were at risk as only two hours of oxygen was available. Many hospitals in the capital city displayed boards outside that no intensive care beds were available. Patients waited outside the hospitals in ambulances, and some died. The panic spread countrywide. Only Kerala was able to supply oxygen outside the state.

On 7 July 2021, there was a cabinet reshuffle in New Delhi when Health Minister Harsh Vardhan resigned.[69] Strangely, in July 2021, even the opposition-ruled states joined the Union Health Ministry in telling the Rajya Sabha that no deaths were reported on medical records due to shortage of oxygen! On 20 July, Minister of State for Health Bharati Pravin Pawar said that, since health was a state subject, states and territories were responsible for collecting data on Covid-19 deaths.

The statement was in the form of a written response to a question raised by Congress MP K.C. Venugopal in the Rajya Sabha. Venugopal had asked whether "it is a fact that a large number of Covid-19 patients died on roads and hospitals due to acute shortage of oxygen" in the second wave. He had also sought a response from the government on the total demand for oxygen by the states and how much had been supplied to states during the last three months.

Union Health minister Mansukh Mandaviya added that Centre was only responsible for compiling and publishing data sent by state governments: "Our job is to publish that data, and nothing else. We haven't told anyone to show fewer numbers (of deaths) or fewer positive cases. There's no reason for that. PM had said the same in meetings with chief ministers."[70]

In the din of allegations and counter-allegations, the nation lost sight of a well-researched study done by *The Wire* on 12 May 2021 which said that 223 Covid deaths were attributed to oxygen shortage. The data was culled from media reports and from a Twitter thread created by Aditi Priya, a research associate at Leveraging Evidence For Access and Development (LEAD) at Krea University, Tamil Nadu.[71]

*Covid deaths in Uttar Pradesh*

The website *Article-14*, which is a joint effort between lawyers, journalists, and academics conducting "independent research on issues necessary to safeguard democracy and the rule of law," had reported on 21 June 2021 that the number of people who died in twenty-four Uttar Pradesh (UP) districts over nine months to 31 March 2021 was, cumulatively, forty-three times higher than the total official Covid death toll reported from these districts over this period. It said: "Documents this reporter obtained for Article 14 under the Right to Information Act, 2005, revealed that during the no-pandemic period between 1 July 2019 and 31 March 2020 these 24 districts registered around 178,000 deaths. Over the same period in 2020–2021, deaths increased by 110% to 375,000, an excess of 197,000."[72]

This was quoted by other media, including foreign media, with shocking photographs to show the mass burial of hundreds of dead bodies on the banks of the river Ganges and exposed half-buried bodies. *The Times of India* published sickening photographs on 11 May[73] followed by *The Indian Express* on 12 May conveying that panic was caused when nearly 100 bodies were found floating in the Ganga.[74]

The BBC said that the "horror" came to light on 19 May 2021 when seventy-one corpses washed up on the riverbank in Bihar's Chausa village, near the border with UP.[75] It said that a day later dozens of heavily decomposed bodies were found on the riverbank in Gahmar village in Uttar Pradesh's Ghazipur district, 10 km from Chausa.

On 7 February 2022, the government through the Minister of State for Water Resources Bishweswar Tudu, informed Trinamool Congress (TMC) MP Derek O'Brien in the Rajya Sabha that the information regarding the number of Covid-related bodies estimated to have been dumped in the Ganges was not available! He added that the media had reported incidents of unclaimed or unidentified, burnt or partially burnt dead bodies that were found floating in or on the banks of the Ganges and that these were reported from certain districts in the states of Uttar Pradesh and

Bihar. Perhaps the central government wanted to convey that this was the state governments' concern.

## Farmers' protests since November 2020

On 17 September 2020, Parliament hurriedly passed two contentious agricultural bills—the Farmers' Produce Trade and Commerce (Promotion and Facilitation) Bill, and the Farmers (Empowerment and Protection) Agreement on Price Assurance and Farm Services Bill—which were criticised by the opposition and by a large majority of farmers in Punjab, Haryana and UP, as favouring big businesses and against the farmers' interests. As a result, the Shiromani Akali Dal, the NDA's ally in Punjab, left the coalition and their lone representative Harsimrat Kaur Badal, Food Processing Industries Minister, resigned from the cabinet.

After two months of protests, thousands of farmers led by the Samyukta Kisan Morcha (SKM; United Farmers Front) converged on New Delhi's borders, camping there for over a year. In the resultant agitation SKM claimed that 670 farmers had died.[76] The government was accused of callousness in disregarding farmers and branding the protestors as "Khalistanis"—or Sikh separatists—since many of them were Sikhs. The protests drew international opprobrium as the NDA government was accused of total insensitivity.[77]

On 19 November 2021 Modi made a televised address, timed to coincide with the Sikh Gurpurb celebrations, that he was repealing the farmers' laws. Observers interpreted this as an attempt to garner Sikh votes during the 2022 Punjab elections and also during the elections in UP. However, this had no impact on the Punjab elections as the BJP managed to win only two seats out of 117. The AAP won a landslide victory garnering ninety-two seats.

One fall-out of the farmers' agitation was confirming an impression that Prime Minister Modi was in the habit of taking unilateral decisions on important subjects without consulting important stakeholders: the 2016 demonetisation which was disastrous for the economy and the 25 March 2020 total Covid lockdown for sixty-eight days, described as the "world's strictest lockdown," confining 1.3 billion people to their homes, bringing misery to hundreds of thousands of migrant workers.[78] The farmers' agitation was the third. The fourth was to be the new military recruitment procedure "Agnipeeth" which will be discussed in the next chapter.

Two strands of the NDA's internal policy throughout their rule were antipathy towards Muslims—which had proved to be a successful electoral weapon to win more seats—and the continuous use of central agencies for unearthing criminal cases against political opponents.

However, what jolted the NDA government in June 2022 was the grave diplomatic quagmire they had landed in. Even the "friendly" Gulf countries were outraged by the intemperate remarks made by the BJP's official spokespersons Nupur Sharma and Naveen Jindal with their comments on the Holy Prophet and his wife. Seventeen Islamic countries and three organisations furiously protested at this outrage forcing the BJP to disown their own chosen spokespersons. The government attempted to glibly describe them as "fringe elements" which none believed.[79]

Such prompt action was never taken earlier although the statements of Nupur Sharma and Naveen Jindal were in continuation of some Hindu extremists' rants against Islam throughout the 2022 UP elections. It was also in line with such comments against Islam in the wake of Gyanvapi mosque/Kashi Vishwanath temple controversy, which was revived by sympathetic elements to prepare the ground for the 2024 elections. During this period the Modi government followed a Janus-faced policy of antipathy towards Muslims within the country and Pakistan but maintaining very friendly personal relations with the Muslim rulers of oil-rich gulf countries.

In fact, the Modi government had, throughout its rule, faced criticism that it had lost the confidence of India's neighbouring countries through needless arrogance and antipathy towards Muslims.

For example, on 7 March 2019, Indresh Kumar, a senior RSS leader told a closed gathering of supporters in Mumbai that "Pakistan will become a part of India after 2025." He was speaking at the "Forum for Awareness of National Security", a pro-RSS body in Mumbai on the subject of "Kashmir—the way ahead." According to a report, he told them that they would "soon" be able to buy houses and conduct business in Karachi, Lahore, Rawalpindi, and Sialkot. He said: "There was no Pakistan before 1947…. It will again be a part of Hindustan after 2025."[80]

Biplab Deb, former Chief Minister of the sensitive border state of Tripura, had boasted on 13 February 2021 that Amit Shah, the powerful Indian Home Minister, had told them during an interaction with state leaders in the State Guest House that "that the party was planning to expand its footprint and establish its rule in Nepal and Sri Lanka." Shah was then the president of the ruling BJP. This had caused deep resentment in both countries, and Nepal lodged a protest. The media also reported on 17 February that the Sri Lankan government was verifying the claim that Shah "had plans to establish the party in neighbouring countries after winning in most of the states in India."[81]

The constant habit of bragging by the ruling party on the innate "super-strength of a Hindu nationalist party" to win domestic elections on strong pro-Hindu orientations while demonising Muslims as terrorists has antagonized not only Indian minorities but also friendly countries like Bangladesh which had always stood by India on terrorism.

Disregarding good neighbourly relations, Home Minister Amit Shah, who dashed to Hyderabad on 29 November 2020 to campaign for a municipal election in the Muslim-dominated Hyderabad city, indulged in a diatribe against Bangladeshis and Rohingyas, calling them terrorists. He wrongly charged that Hyderabad city was a den of Bangladeshis and Rohingyas and that the Muslim leadership were supporting them.

In his zeal for promoting sectarian interests for political ends he forgot that his Prime Minister Narendra Modi might be put in an embarrassing situation in Bangladesh when he would be visiting Dhaka towards the end of March 2021 as a VIP guest to attend Bangladesh's fiftieth Independence Day celebrations.

Shah also paid a conspicuous, TV-monitored visit to the "ancient" Bhagyalakshmi temple to expand his party's religious base. Some Hindu propagandists had claimed that this temple had been edged out by the word famous "Charminar" mosque built by the Qutb Shahi dynasty in 1591 which had become the symbol of Hyderabad.

In actual fact, the "Bhagyalakshmi temple" was declared as an "unauthorised construction" by the Archaeological Survey of India (ASI) in 2012. That structure had come up much later next to "Charminar, the Centrally protected monument" which they were maintaining.

In February 2021 the ASI reiterated the above position in reply to an RTI query that the temple "came into existence after taking over Hyderabad by the Government of India."[82] The Dominion of India had taken over Hyderabad State from the Nizam in September 1948 through a "police action."

Amit Shah also ignored that 800,000 Rohingyas had fled Myanmar's Rakhine province due to the Myanmar army's atrocities in 2016. They are considered by the UN as a "stateless minority" and Bangladesh was finding it extremely difficult to maintain them. Shah also forgot that it was the Arakan Salvation Army (ASA) which was considered globally as "terrorists." In fact, Modi's visit to Myanmar in September 2017 was deeply resented by Bangladesh when Myanmar was facing global censure on its excesses concerning Rohingyas.[83]

Ironically, Shah's visit to Hyderabad resulted only in exacerbating Hindu–Muslim tensions and did not win the city for the BJP. On 11 February 2021, the positions of mayor and deputy were won by two members of the coalition opposing the BJP.

Such controversial epithets were often used by senior leaders like Shah during electioneering in states like West Bengal and Assam to sway Hindu voters. The fact that Shah, despite being the union home minister in charge of internal security, chose to ignore a huge farmers' protest which had encircled Delhi to give more priority to do canvassing in a municipal election was also adversely commented upon.

As a result, China has found it easy to forge closer relations with India's neighbours. The latest is a close defence relationship that had developed between Pakistan and Myanmar despite earlier

Pakistani criticism over the way Myanmar had ill-treated their Rohingya minorities. A team of fifteen Pakistani Air Force experts was expected to visit Mandalay in June 2022 to extend technical support to their Chinese-made JF-17 airforce planes. Pakistan is expected to be the channel for more Chinese partnership with Myanmar in defence purchases.[84]

*Using central agencies to score political victories over the opposition*

On 26 November 2016 I attended a commemoration ceremony organised by *The Indian Express* newspaper at Kala Ghoda, near Jehangir Art Gallery, Mumbai, to salute the sacrifices of policemen and members of the public who were killed by ten Pakistani terrorists who crossed the Arabian Sea to launch armed attacks on civilian targets on 26 November 2008. The Maharashtra Government had appointed me as a member of the two-man high-level committee to enquire into the police failure in adequately responding to this terrorist attack.

During this function I met a Congress General Secretary for Maharashtra who was known to me from the 1970s while I oversaw the Bombay Special Branch. He told me that the NDA government had decided to launch prosecutions against all major leaders in opposition using central agencies if they get re-elected in 2019. They would try to keep as many opposition leaders as possible in custody by launching prosecutions by state police or using central agencies in the states where the BJP was not in power. Since then, opposition parties have been alleging that central agencies like the CBI, Narcotics Control Bureau (NCB), Enforcement Directorate (ED), National Investigation Agency (NIA) and Income Tax department were let loose against opposition leaders.

Senior journalist P. Raman said that Modi had warned the Congress in a 2017 election rally: "Hold your tongue, I have your entire *janampatri*" (horoscope). Perhaps he meant that Modi knew all their previous activities.[85] He also alleged that three months later, on 15 May 2017, the CBI filed a first information report in the INX Media case involving Congress leader P. Chidambaram. Raman also listed twenty-seven cases in which central agencies had raided or made out cases against political opponents especially on the eve of elections from 2019.

In November 2020 the NDA government gave an unprecedented "retrospective" extension to the director of the Enforcement Directorate who was in the limelight for raiding opposition leaders and booking them under the draconian Prevention of Money-Laundering Act where getting bail is difficult.

The first part of the drama was played on 14 November 2020, when the president modified his order of 19 November 2018, appointing Sanjay Kumar Mishra as ED director for two years and allowing him one more year retrospectively. This was perhaps the first time that the president had made such retrospective amendment to his own orders and allowed an officer a three-year tenure.[86] This was challenged in the Supreme Court in September 2020 when the bench of Justices L. Nageswara Rao and B. R. Gavai said that "no further extension shall be granted" to Mishra beyond November 2021.

The second part of the drama was on 15 November 2021, when the government issued two ordinances extending the tenures of the CBI and ED directors from two to five years. This benefitted Sanjay Kumar Mishra, who was given one more year's extension a day before he was to retire.[87]

On 22 March 2022, Bollywood actor Shatrughan Sinha, who had been a Union minister during the Vajpayee government, accused these agencies of working in tandem to cement the NDA's "authoritarian" rule.[88] Opposition parties accused the ED, CBI and at times NIA and Income Tax department for working as the NDA's "B team" to achieve political objectives. They alleged that the intention was to smear the character of such leaders through selective leakage of investigation details, exercise pressure on opposition politicians to defect to the NDA and cause political impediments for them in the run-up to elections.

On 16 May 2022, the CBI raided ten places linked to former Congress minister P. Chidambaram and his son Karti Chidambaram for investigating an incident that had happened in 2011. Wide publicity during the raid was given that Karti had received bribes in the name of his father to expedite irregular visas for Chinese workers. P. Chidambaram was then the union home minister. However, the media also noted that the raid coincided with a Rajya Sabha election when P. Chidambaram was soon contesting for a Rajya Sabha seat.[89] If that was the purpose, it failed to achieve any result as Chidambaram was elected unopposed to the Rajya Sabha on 3 June 2022.[90]

On 26 May 2022, raids were conducted by the ED on an alleged MNREGA scam in Jharkhand. This was after a public interest litigation (PIL) was filed on 2 May in Jharkhand High Court alleging that Chief Minister Hemant Soren had "leased" some mines to himself and to his close relations. He was also accused of allotting an eleven-acre plot to his wife Kalpana Soren's firm in an industrial park in Ranchi.[91] Soren had been heading a non-BJP coalition along with the Congress since December 2019.

Against this background when Rajya Sabha candidates were announced on 30 May 2022, Soren surprised all by nominating Mahua Maji of Jharkhand Mukti Morcha although there was an expectation that he would cede this seat to the Congress after his meeting with Sonia Gandhi on 28 May. Some commentators ascribed this *volte-face* by Soren to the BJP pressure on him through the central agencies.[92]

The drive against opposition leaders was not undertaken only by the central agencies. BJP-ruled states were also excelling in this. In some cases, religious bias was also alleged. The Socialist Party (Samajwadi Party) founder-leader Azam Khan, who was an elected member of the UP state legislative assembly ten times from 1980 and at times elected to the Indian parliament since 1996, was arrested in eighty-eight criminal cases since 2020 by the Yogi Adityanath government. He was continuously in prison from 2020. Most of these criminal cases were filed after long delays. One was registered sixteen years after the incident. Twenty-two were registered thirteen years after the alleged crime took place. Finally, the Supreme Court had to intervene, and he was given bail.[93]

Another incident which was originally given a distorted colour for political gains was the suicide of Bollywood film star Sushant Singh Rajput in June 2020. Although it was a clear case of suicide which Mumbai police could have investigated, central agencies like the CBI, ED, NIA and NCB rushed to the scene to probe the alleged "conspiracy" and drug use by Bollywood personalities. Opposition leaders alleged that this sensational twist to a suicide case was to transfer its political advantage in the forthcoming polls in Bihar as Rajput hailed from Bihar.[94]

During this period efforts were allegedly made by certain groups to link Bollywood icons with drug use. The media reported that Rakesh Asthana, then officiating as NCB director general (later Commissioner of Police, New Delhi) who was allegedly close to the ruling party in New Delhi, had paid a "quiet visit" to Mumbai to review investigations.[95]

This in turn resulted in what is known as the "Aryan Khan" drug case in which the son of world-famous Bollywood icon Shah Rukh Khan was arrested by a controversial officer named Sameer Wankhede of the NCB and kept in custody for nearly four weeks. He was finally released uncharged by the NCB on 27 May 2022, as the Special Investigating Cell did not find any evidence against him.

*The Indian Express*, an independent newspaper where top BJP/RSS stalwarts also write "op-eds", wrote an editorial on 28 May that the mishandling of Sushant Singh Rajput's case had "more than a little to do with Maharashtra being an opposition ruled state and the imminence of an election in Bihar, Rajput's home state." As far as the case regarding Aryan Khan was concerned "the whole episode was to take Khan down": "The shabby episode does nothing for the reputation of Central investigating agencies. It has been apparent for some time that the government is not above wielding these agencies to fix political rivals and others who cross its path."[96]

*The Indian Express* also wrote a strong editorial on 3 June over the ED's habit of conducting selective raids for political reasons to favour the ruling party. In a piece "Enforced Directorate" it said:

> An overwhelming majority of the politicians under probe by the CBI, ED and NIA belong to the ranks of the Opposition, only rarely to the ruling party or its allies... On paper and in principle these agencies are supposed to work independently of

the government, insulated from all political agendas and motives. The reality, however, is messier, and the NDA presides over a disturbing number of deviations from the norm.[97]

More than eighty petitions challenging the constitutionality of several sections in the Prevention of Money Laundering Act 2002 relating to arrest, bail, search and seizure were pending before the Supreme Court. In fact, on 17 December 2021 the court had "slammed" the ED for "weaponizing Prevention of Money Laundering Act (PMLA) by invoking its stringent provisions even in minor cases to put people behind bars." Then Chief Justice N.V. Ramana had said: "you are diluting the Act by invoking the PMLA provisions indiscriminately."

On the same day, the Kerala High Court reminded the ED of its responsibility to investigate "persons outside India" in the fake antiquities case against the infamous dealer Monson Mavunkal and that the ED and Crime Branch should work in tandem to reveal the full picture.

This was a timely reminder to the ED that it was created not only to chase Indian politicians. I had then pointed out in a column that the ED had been established in 1956 as an enforcement unit of the Department of Economic Affairs, and to meet our international obligations under the United Nations General Assembly's special sessions of 23 February 1990 and 8–10 June 1998 calling upon member states to adopt national money laundering legislation and programmes.[98]

Under the NDA, it looked as though the ED had lowered its priority of international responsibilities almost like India's Narcotics Control Bureau, which was chasing Bollywood actors, also highlighted by me in another column.[99]

Had the ED been faithful to its international obligations, the government should not have been surprised by the 2016 "Panama" papers revealed by German newspaper *Sueddeutsche Zeitung* or the 2021 "Pandora" papers unearthed by the International Consortium of Investigative Journalists (ICIJ) in Washington, DC leading to the detection of Rs. 20,353 crores of unaccounted money from 930 "India linked entities" as revealed in parliament on 16 December.

Like a typical Bollywood comic film, the ED was seen rushing in after the thief was caught by the hero. This, despite the 2020–21 annual report of the Department of Economic Affairs (DEA) saying that this international responsibility was the ED's "primary function."

*The Wire* gave details in twelve cases pursued by the ED directed against opposition parties like the Congress, Nationalist Congress Party (NCP), Samajwadi Party (SP), Bahujan Samaj Party (BSP), DMK, YSR Congress, Jammu and Kashmir National Conference (NC) and Trinamool Congress (TMC).[100] Interestingly the paper said that cases against those who were inclined to defect or cooperate with the BJP were never pursued. Prominent among them were former Chief Minister Narayan Rane who jumped from the Shiv Sena to Congress and then to the BJP, and Y.S. Chowdary of the Telugu Desam Party. It also said:

> The most prominent examples given by opposition leaders are of Mukul Roy, who switched to the BJP from the Trinamool Congress (TMC), and Assam's Himanta Biswa Sarma, who crossed over from the Congress. Both were named in the multi-crore Saradha chit fund scam but the ED has mostly ignored them while probing these cases. Bellary's infamous Reddy Brothers and their alleged role in mining scams also appears to be similarly on the back-burner.[101]

A prominent Shiv Sena legislator Pratap Sarnaik was raided by the ED on 24 November 2020 for alleged money laundering. He was reported to be close to the top Shiv Sena leadership. On 20 June 2021, Sarnaik publicly urged Maharashtra Chief Minister Uddhav Thackeray to re-join the BJP as "having an alliance with the BJP would be beneficial for leaders like him who are facing harassment due to cases being foisted on them by central agencies."[102]

Sarnaik's warning came true when Eknath Shinde, a senior minister in the MVA coalition government, escaped to Surat on 21 June 2022 with a number of MLAs who were being pursued by the ED. The list included Sarnaik, Yamini Jadhav and Bhavana Gawli. When the defection drama was going on the ED was "grilling" another Shiv Sena MLA Anil Parab for a third day, allegedly preventing him from giving strategic advice to Chief Minister Thackeray.[103] Similarly Sanjay Raut, also close to Thackeray and who was "trying to rally Sena MLAs and workers", was repeatedly summoned by the ED, even on 29 June, although he had appeared before them earlier.[104]

The BJP's tacit hand in this horse-trading was very visible in splitting the Shiv Sena where Gujarat BJP chief C.R. Paatil was seen making all arrangements for their stay in a five-star luxury Le Meridien hotel with full police protection to prevent them from escaping. Surat BJP leader Paresh Patel then flew them to Guwahati in Assam, which was reeling from heavy rains and floods.[105]

Assam Chief Minister Himanta Biswa Sarma pretended that he did not know about the presence of Shiv Sena rebels in his state. Yet the heavy police presence at the luxury hotel belied his claim. Eminent journalist Mrinal Pande castigated Sarma ("Horse-trading Amidst Floods") or allowing his state to be misused and scarce administrative resources diverted where rains had killed almost 100 people, rendered 300,000 homeless and submerged thirty-two out of thirty-six districts.[106]

"Operation *Kamal*" (or "lotus"—the symbol of the BJP) seemed to have succeeded on 29 June when Thackeray submitted his resignation as Chief Minister when asked by the Governor to conduct a "floor test", which was approved by the Supreme court

A similar split of the National Congress Party (NCP), founded by former Union Minister Sharad Pawar, was engineered by BJP in June 2023 which resulted in Ajit Pawar, his nephew and his followers joining Eknath Shinde's "rebel" Sena, which had formed the Maharashtra ministry on 30 June 2022. On 21 March 2024, Devendra Fadnavis boasted publicly that he could split two parties, Sena and NCP, although he had been out of power for two-and-half years.[107]

*The Wire* also analysed the results of the ED's investigation by March 2020 and said that although the agency had conducted over 1,700 raids from March 2011 to January 2020 in connection with 1,569 specific investigations, it could secure convictions only in nine "paltry" cases.[108]

Another section of law constantly used by the BJP is the archaic colonial-era sedition law. When the three-judge bench of the Supreme Court was about to take up the validity of Section 124A (Sedition) of the Indian Penal Code in May 2022, the Home Ministry filed a fresh affidavit saying that it was doing a comprehensive revision through the legislative route in parliament and requested the court to defer the hearing. Surprisingly, only two days earlier it had defended the sedition law and had urged the court to dismiss the petitions. This was interpreted as an attempt to forestall the possibility of the court giving an adverse verdict. NCRB statistics had revealed that out of 548 people held under the 356 cases filed under the section in 2015–20, only twelve had been convicted.[109]

However, the Supreme Court did not agree with the ministry and directed the central and state governments to keep the section in abeyance. It defines sedition as any act or attempt "to bring into hatred or contempt, or…excite disaffection towards the government." In other words, no coercive action could be taken by either centre or state governments even in pending cases until the government undertook a "comprehensive review."

On the eve of the 2024 elections, *The Indian Express* published a sensational story on 3 April, that twenty-five opposition leaders facing corruption probes had crossed over to the BJP or split their original political parties since 2014 under pressure from Central enforcement agencies like ED, CBI and others. The paper claimed with chronological information that twenty-three of them got reprieve from cases launched against them.[110]

Prominent among them were NCP leaders like Ajit Pawar, Praful Patel, Chhagan Bhujbal who split the parent NCP, former Congress leader, now BJP chief Minister of Assam, Himanta Biswas Sarma, industrialist and Congress MP Naveen Jindal, former Congress Chief Minister of Maharashtra Ashok Chavan, former Shiv Sena leaders Pratap Sarnaik, Bhawana Gawali, and TMC leader Suvendu Adhikari, who is now the fiercest opponent to Mamata Banerjee.

*Electoral bonds*

On 15 March 2022 *Al Jazeera* published their twenty-two-month study of Facebook advertisements during ten elections in India and said that several "ghost and surrogate advertisers" had secretly funded the BJP's election campaigns to boost the governing party's visibility. They found that such advertisers either hid their identities or their connections with the BJP and paid "tens of millions of rupees" to Facebook, to promote the party and its leaders. Thus, these ghost advertisers were able to "double" the BJP's visibility along with their own advertisements, without the party having been held responsible by the Election Commission for exceeding mandatory advertisement expenditure limits.[111]

However, there was a serious dip in the BJP's electoral bond income in 2020–21 from Rs. 36.2 billion to Rs. 7.5 billion. This is the first time since 2013–14 when it introduced the controversial provision that its income fell so drastically. Electoral bonds, a bearer bond instrument through which companies can give funds to political parties, were announced in the 2017 Union Budget, and passed into law with the Finance Bill 2017. Amendments were made to the Reserve Bank of India Act 1934, Representation of Peoples Act 1951, Income Tax Act 1961 and Companies Act. Following this, the scheme was notified in January 2018. The electoral bond is interest-free. The most controversial part is that the bond holder would remain anonymous. The government claimed that it was a transparent process, but opposition parties said that it was to recycle black money and facilitate secret funding to the party in power by corporates.

*The Indian Express* had observed on 11 April 2022:

> The fact that the BJP has cornered more than 75 per cent of all such bonds issued to date gives credence to this criticism. Another key area of concern is that the government, as part of the introduction of the electoral bonds, had removed the cap on how much money a company could donate. A quick closure in these matters is necessary to ensure transparency in campaign financing, critical to the integrity of the electoral process.[112]

It was not until February 2024 that the Supreme Court struck down the scheme as "unconstitutional and manifestly arbitrary".[113]


*Prelude to the 2024 elections*

With a realisation that they might not easily win the 2024 election, the BJP started planning for it from 2022. A recurring allegation made against them was that they were fanning communal divides all over the country, which by experience, had helped them in elections as revealed in 2014 through a Yale University study. Researchers from Yale, after conducting surveys in 315 districts in India between 1962 and 2000, had concluded that the "Bharatiya Jan Sangh" (the BJP's earlier incarnation before 1977) and BJP had experienced "a 0.8 per cent point increase in their vote share following a riot in the year prior to an election."[114]

The first choreographed step, according to the BJP's opponents, was releasing a highly controversial film *Kashmir Files* on the exodus of "Pandits" from the Kashmir Valley in the early 1990s due to Kashmiri Muslim militants' excesses. The official patronage for the film was heralded by Prime Minister Modi on 16 March 2022, while addressing BJP members of parliament when he accused the opposition parties of hiding the truth behind that tragedy. He said that the film had "rattled the entire ecosystem which claims to be the torchbearer of freedom of expression but does not want the truth to be told."[115]

Soon thereafter a severe controversy broke out all over the country over its director Vivek Agnihotri, a BJP supporter, who had the habit of distorting historical details. He had done so in his earlier film *The Tashkent Files* on the death of late Prime Minister Lal Bahadur Shastri, where he had alleged conspiracy. This was objected to by the Shastri family.

Similarly, the family members of the late squadron leader Ravi Khanna, who was killed by Kashmiri militants on 25 January 1990, had obtained a court injunction from a Jammu magistrate on 12 March 2022, against Agnihotri's inaccurate depiction of Khanna's murder. They alleged that the film had insulted the martyr and the

Indian Airforce. The magistrate, while passing the injunction, said that there were serious flaws in the film which were not based on facts. Critics said that the criticisms against the film were muted in the Indian mainstream press due to government interference. It was only carried by the BBC[116] and by a little-known web paper *Transcontinental Times*.[117]

The second notable and coordinated action by the Hindutva fringe elements, unchecked by the police in BJP-ruled states, was exploiting communal tension already existing in some parts of the country. In coastal Karnataka the "Hijab row" in schools was already on the boil from January 2022. On 2 January 2022 six Muslim girls in Udupi were denied entry into the school for wearing hijabs, as it violated the school uniform regulations.

Coastal Karnataka had earlier seen religious polarisation due to "love jihad" agitations originated by Hindu extremist groups like the Bajrang Dal and Viswa Hindu Parishad against inter-religious marriages. The hijab row was resisted by a Muslim fundamentalist group called Popular Front of India (PFI). On 15 March 2022 this issue was judicially decided against the Muslim girls by the Karnataka High Court, but the agitation is still going on. The case is pending appeal in the Supreme Court.[118]

Ramnavami celebrations on 10 April in Bhopal resulted in riots after BJP leader Kapil Mishra visited the city.[119] Ten houses were burnt, and many people were hurt. Mishra was already accused of inciting the six-day anti-CAA 2020 Delhi riots by delivering a very provocative speech. On 22 February 2020 he told the media that he did not regret giving that speech and would do it again.[120]

Similar clashes and arson had erupted in Gujarat and West Bengal by combative Hindu crowds. At Jawaharlal Nehru University (JNU) violence broke out between the "left" students and pro-Hindutva students when the latter violently objected to the serving of non-vegetarian food, as was the custom on Sundays. 10 April was a Sunday.

Consumption of food is deliberately being made a cause of dispute by the BJP. Vegetarianism is being forcibly thrust on others when National Family Health Surveys have revealed that 75 per cent of Indians eat non vegetarian food. In 2021, *India Today* had quoted a 2014 government Sample Registration Baseline Survey to prove that almost 97 per cent of the people in Kerala, Telangana, Andhra Pradesh, West Bengal, Tamil Nadu, Odisha and Jharkhand eat non-vegetarian food regularly, compared to 40 per cent in Punjab, Haryana, Gujarat and Rajasthan.[121]

Another continuing feature of Hindutva politics since 2014 has been vitriolic communal attacks against Muslims by saffron-clad "god-men." During 17–19 December 2021 a "Dharma Sansad" (Religious Assembly) was held at Haridwar in Uttarakhand to discuss "The future of 'Sanatan Dharma' in Islamic India." Ordinarily it should have been an academic discussion on the Mughal period of Indian history.

However, the organisers had a different intention. Yati Narasinghanand, the priest of the Dasna Devi temple in Ghaziabad, a known Muslim baiter who organised the function, believes that Muslims would recapture India in twenty years by increasing their population. He had been advocating that Hindus should produce more children. The occasion was used by seers to seek the genocide of Muslims in India.

During the event Prabodhanand Giri, a former RSS *pracharak* turned ascetic, running the *Hindu Raksha Sena* (Hindu Protection Army) in Haridwar, asked the audience to emulate what was done in Myanmar and "cleanse" the nation (meaning ethnic cleansing of Rohingyas). Sadhvi Annapurna of the Hindu Mahasabha called for the killing of Muslims. The police registered a criminal offence only on 23 December 2021 but no arrests were made till 14 January 2022 under Supreme Court orders.

The BBC had reported that these rabid utterances were made to inflame the Hindus in Uttar Pradesh and Uttarakhand with a view to winning the assembly elections in February–March 2022.[122] The same trend has continued since then with a view to inflame the region for the 2024 elections. Yati Narasinghanand repeated this violence call on 3 April 2022 at a "*mahapanchayat*" in New Delhi. He stoked Hindu fears by sparking yet another row with his comment that "50 per cent of Hindus will convert" in twenty years if a Muslim became the prime minister of India, exhorting Hindus to take up arms to fight for their existence. Although this rally was organised without police permission, the Delhi Police took their own time in taking action. During this rally some fanatical supporters assaulted some journalists.[123]

On 8 April 2022, another "seer" was booked by Sitapur police in Uttar Pradesh for threatening Muslim girls with rape. Mahant Bajrang Muni, priest of the Badi Sangat Ashram in Uttar Pradesh's Sitapur district, had threatened mass sexual violence against Muslim women in the presence of the police on the occasion of the Hindu new year. He has been a "serial offender" in his vitriol against Muslims and was actively canvassing for BJP during the February–March elections.[124]

On 9 May 2022, the Allahabad High court passed strictures against Union Minister of State for Home Ajay Mishra Teni for his provocative utterances against agitating farmers belonging to the Samyukta Kisan Morcha which had led to a serious incident on 3 October 2021 at Tikonia, Lakhimpur Keri district. The court said that several innocent lives were lost in a "most cruel, diabolic, barbaric, gruesome and inhuman manner by his very promising son and other accused."[125] Yet the minister continued to hold his important charge till he was defeated in the 2024 elections.

Another incident which has inflamed Muslim feelings was the Court ordered "survey" of the seventeenth-century Gyanvapi Mosque next to the Kashi Viswanath temple in Varanasi in Uttar Pradesh. It is said that Mughal emperor Aurangzeb demolished a Lord Shiva temple and built a mosque in its place in 1669. It is known as "Gyanvapi" (Well of Knowledge) as Lord Shiva had dug it to "cool the Linga." Since then, as in the case of Ayodhya temple, both Hindus and Muslims have been claiming prayer rights on the premises. This case filed by some Hindu women on 18 April 2021 has come up for hearing. The petitioners had asked for year-long access to offer prayers at a Hindu shrine, what they claimed was a Maa Shringar Gauri *sthal* behind the western wall of the Gyanvapi Mosque complex.

On 26 April 2022, a civil judge permitted video survey of the premises which was objected to by a huge Muslim mob. They pointed out that under the Place of Worship (Special Provisions) Act 1991, any such survey cannot be done as the status of all places of worship was frozen as on 15 August 1947 except in Ayodhya where the dispute was old. But the court did not pay any heed.

On 16 May the startling news—with photos—was leaked that a *Shivling* had been found within the mosque premises. On hearing this the local court asked the District Magistrate to protect the spot. Muslim groups contested this saying that it was part of a water fountain (*wuzkhana*) used for ablution before prayer.[126] On 17 May *India Today* published a fact check showing that the image of a *Shivling* that circulated widely on social media was not from the Gyanvapi Masjid in Varanasi, but from the Nakhoda Masjid in Kolkata.[127]

Unfortunately, none of TV channels showed this correction. Almost every channel reproduced the sensational Hindu extremist views. However, the local court removed Advocate Commissioner Ajay Kumar Mishra for leaking information to the media through a private cameraman who was illegally taken inside, which the Muslims had objected to. The Court also extended the survey by two more days.

On 17 May the Supreme Court refused to stay the survey despite being told that any such survey was prohibited under the Place of Worship (Special Provisions) Act 1991. The Court however specifically directed the local authorities to permit unrestricted access to Muslims to pray in the mosque.

### *Ethnic conflict in Manipur 2023–24: a failure of the BJP government*

Manipur is a small state in northeast India with a population of 3.8 million. It has the "Imphal valley" (10 per cent of the geographical area with 57 per cent of the population) and the hills (90 per cent of the geographical area with 43 per cent of the population). The valley is inhabited mainly by Meiteis, mostly Hindus, while thirty-four tribal groups, categorised as Nagas and Kukis occupy the hills area. The tribal people have "Scheduled Tribe" (ST) status to gain access to welfare schemes while the Meitei have "Other Backward Class" (OBC) social position. It is generally believed that ST status people get more educational and career benefits than OBC category people.

Imphal valley's forty Assembly constituencies dominate the political establishment in the state while the hills, with only twenty seats in the Legislative Assembly, always voice complaints of neglect in not having roads and schools. The relationship between the Meiteis and hill tribes has throughout been strained due to various reasons, but especially the cross-border links of Nagas and Kukis with their kinspeople in Myanmar. Meiteis allege that "foreigners" are creating security and societal problems. Also, there is a religious dimension to this as the hill tribes are mostly Christians.

Since 2012 an organisation called Scheduled Tribe Demand Committee of Manipur (STDCM) started agitating for ST status for Meitei, which was repeatedly rejected by successive union governments. On 20 April 2023 the Manipur High Court directed the state government to consider conferring ST status to Meitei, which triggered severe unrest between Meiteis and hills people with rioting, arson, rapes and murders. Each group blames the other. Law and order broke down entirely. Till now at least 221 people have been killed and more than 60,000 displaced. Several churches were burnt down. Chief Minister Birendra Singh, a Hindu BJP leader, has been criticised for being soft on Meitei rioters and hostile toward the hills people.

The opposition allege that Prime Minister Narendra Modi did not visit Manipur even once despite continuing violence since 2023. The State is very sensitive from a security point of view as it has borders with Myanmar. Former army chief M.M. Naravane had said in July 2023 that intervention by foreign agencies in the violence could not be ruled out.[128] This is correct as in 2009 evidence by way of a CD with a confession of a Manipur Peoples' Liberation Army (PLA) cadre had surfaced that sixteen platoons of PLA had returned from China after training.[129]

The Manipuri PLA (not to be confused with the Chinese Army) is the oldest insurgent group in Manipur consisting of Meiteis, Nagas and Kukis wanting to establish a Communist revolutionary front in Indian northeast. Thus, if China wants, it could open gaping holes on India's eastern front, taking advantage of its close relationship with Myanmar's Tatmadaw, its army, and taking advantage of the breakdown of law and order in Manipur.[130]

In the 2024 elections, the Congress (as part of the "INDIA" coalition) won the Manipur Lok Sabha seat as people were highly critical of the BJP government. This is partly because of Congress leader Rahul Gandhi's highly successful "Manipur-Mumbai Nyaya Yatra–2" (public contact march for justice via bus and on foot covering 6,700 kms) from January 14 to March 20 wherein he spent the initial days in Manipur listening to Meitei and hill tribes' grievances which no BJP leader had done.[131]

## The 2024 elections

Prime Minister Modi started preparing for the elections well in advance. In August 2023 he held his first "cluster meeting" of NDA leaders including MPs from Uttar Pradesh's Kashi and Awadh region. The second cluster was meeting MPs from Telangana, Andhra Pradesh, Tamil Nadu, Karnataka, Kerala, Puducherry, Andaman and Nicobar Island, and Lakshadweep islands.

The second step was to utilise global or domestic events to boost "perception gain" against the opposition. America's Public Broadcasting Service (PBS) said on 6 September 2023 that Modi's pictures stood out from "every traffic circle" during the G20 nations' summit in New Delhi to market the leader's image and elevate his party's prospects ahead of the elections in 2024. It said that "ahead of the summit, historical monuments, airports and major landmarks are projecting this year's G20 logo—an image of a globe inside a lotus, using the colors of the Indian flag. The opposition says it is no coincidence that the lotus is also the election symbol of Modi's Bhartiya Janata Party."[132]

The next choreographed event was the glittering "Prana Pratishtha" (consecration) ceremony of the "Ram Lalla" idol (infant form of Lord Ram) in a newly built temple on 22 January 2024 on Ram Janmabhoomi, at the mythical birthplace of the god on the site where the Babri Masjid was built in the sixteenth century after demolishing the original temple. The temple construction had started in 2020 and the cost was reported to be Rs. 1.8 billion

(US$ 21.5 million), raised through fund-raising drives. CNN said that half a million people thronged the temple on the day of the inauguration.

The 2024 elections were highly personalised as "Vote for Modi", unlike the "*Achchhe Din*" (Better Times) in 2014 and "*ghus ke maarenge*" (will kill the terrorists/enemies inside their homes) in 2019. Simultaneously, nearly ten films like *Article 370* or *The Kerala Story*, giving one sided religious versions of events, were introduced into the market to sway popular feelings. BJP state governments waived taxes on *The Kerala Story* and *Kashmir Files* and the BJP's cadres organised free screenings of these films. On 5 May 2023 Modi personally lauded *The Kerala Story* saying that it was based on terrorism and criticised Congress for "shielding terrorists."[133]

All the top BJP leaders started demanding votes in the name of Modi who went on claiming that his party would get 400 seats out of 543 in the Lok Sabha (Lower House). Carpet bombing was done regularly through favourable mainstream visual and print media, about the certainty of the wholesale victory of the BJP in the elections, with Modi's photo figuring daily.

Simultaneously opposition parties started complaining that they were not given level playing field for publicity through mainstream visual and print media. They also complained against coercive steps on the eve of the 2024 general elections. The Congress Party complained on 16 February 2024 that the income tax department had frozen their bank accounts leaving no money to pay their staff's salaries.[134]

On 21 March 2024 the Enforcement Directorate (ED) arrested Delhi Chief Minister Arvind Kejriwal, leader of the Aam Admi Party, five days after the Election Commission (EC) formally announced the seven-phase election schedule on 16 March 2024, when the Model Code of Conduct came into force. This was for a 2022 case of money laundering on which he had been questioned earlier. Normally government agencies are not supposed to take such actions after the announcement of elections without the permission of EC unless the matter is serious. Kejriwal publicly complained that it had been done to stifle opposition voices during the elections.

Following this, US State Department Spokesperson Mathew Miller said the country was closely following Kejriwal's arrest and actions taken against opposition parties in India. The German foreign ministry said it hoped that Kejriwal would get a "fair and impartial trial as India is a democratic nation." India summoned senior diplomats of both the US and Germany to register its protest.[135]

On 10 May 2024 the Supreme Court made an unprecedented intervention to grant bail to Kejriwal and "pass the present order, namely, 18th Lok Sabha General Elections, which are in progress," emphasising the sanctity of participating in elections. The Court made a note of the fact that investigation had been pending since August 2022, and that Kejriwal had no criminal antecedents. The court ordered that Kejriwal should report back to the prison on 2 June 2024. [136]

Midway through campaigning Modi and his party abandoned positive mention of "economic progress" and started relying more on Islamophobic language. CNN said: "As turnout in the polls so far shows a slight dip from five years ago, the popular leader—and overwhelming favourite—has embraced negative campaigning, they say, and received little pushback from civil society or election authorities."[137]

Modi addressed 181 rallies across the country covering twenty-four states. At the end of the campaign, he undertook a highly visible tour to Kanyakumari, the southernmost tip of India to "meditate" at the "Vivekananda" rock temple even as the polling in the last phase, including in his constituency, was going on. Opposition parties appealed to the Election Commission to stop video broadcasting his travel, clad in saffron, as it would be tantamount to breaching the Model Code through visual propaganda. However, the EC ignored it. Modi claimed at the end of the meditation that he "felt a divine energy."

However, the results announced on 4 June 2024 dampened the BJP's brouhaha over winning more than 400 seats. The party could win only 240 seats on its own and had to depend upon allies in National Democratic Alliance (NDA) for to form a government, including the Janata Dal (United) under chief Minister Nitish

Kumar which won twelve seats and the Telugu Desam Party under Chandra Babu Naidu which won sixteen seats. As *The Guardian* (UK) said: "Instead of a coronation, he got a rebuke. Far from winning a landslide, his Bharatiya Janata party's seats fell from 303 to 240, leaving him reliant on political allies."[138]

The BJP lost seventy-five constituencies to the INDIA coalition where Modi held rallies. In the heartland state of Uttar Pradesh, where Modi held twenty-seven rallies and four "roadshows," BJP could win only thirteen seats. The Faizabad seat with Ayodhya, where the consecration of Ram temple had taken place in January, was lost to the Samajwadi Party, a constituent of the INDIA coalition. This was because locals complained against outsiders who had managed to corner all the benefits of the presence of the Ram temple while local shops and houses were demolished to build a new road known as Ram Path. In that process heritage temples like Janki Shukla Mandir and Dashrath Mahal, once considered to be the birthplace of Ram, were also demolished".[139]

Also, it was found that the BJP did not gain by splitting the parties or coercive action by agencies. Nine of the thirteen politicians being probed by central agencies who jumped parties lost the elections. Also, in Maharashtra, voters punished the BJP for splitting the Shiv Sena and NCP: the BJP lost fourteen seats out of twenty-three it had won in 2019. The original Shiv Sena won nine seats while the turncoat Shiv Sena managed to win only seven. The original NCP won eight seats while the turncoat NCP managed to get only one. The biggest beneficiary was the Congress which won thirteen seats. This was a clear message from the electorate that they had rejected the BJP's predatory tactics of splitting the parties and pressuring others by coercive action through central agencies.[140]

One of the remarkable features of this election was the rise of hundreds of "citizen journalists" through social media like YouTube, Instagram or X (formerly Twitter) which reached far and wide. India has 476 million "YouTubers." They were very effective in influencing anti-BJP opinion since mainstream TV channels did not allow a level playing field to the opposition parties.[141] As Samajwadi leader Akhilesh Yadav said, these social media users became the "torchbearers of the social justice movement" by carrying the news to the "marginalised communities."[142]

It may be mentioned that the BJP government had introduced a "Fact Checking Unit" under the Information Technology Rules on 6 April 2023, to detect "fake" news. The Editors Guild and a stand-up comedian Kunal Kamra challenged this notification saying that that it was a surreptitious way of censoring broadcast contents unfavourable to the government. On 21 March 2024, the Supreme Court stayed this notification.[143] The explosion of social media in India during the 2024 elections could be attributed to that.

# CONCLUSIONS

## PORTENTS OF A STORM BEFORE 2047

In the next two decades, China almost certainly will look to assert dominance in Asia and greater influence globally; while trying to avoid what it views as excessive liabilities in strategically marginal regions. In Asia, China expects deference from neighbors on trade, resource exploitation, and territorial disputes. China is likely to field military capabilities that put US and allied forces in the region at heightened risk and to press US allies and partners to restrict US basing access.

Although India benefited from growth in Asia, it could take years for it to be able to take on, much less contain, its more powerful neighbor.

—US National Intelligence Council,
"Global Trends 2040"

*New Indian Government*

On 7 June 2024 Narendra Modi was elected as the leader of the National Democratic Alliance (NDA) which could assemble 293 seats in the 543-member parliament, although the BJP by itself had secured only 240 seats. Thus, he became the second prime minister in Indian history after Jawaharlal Nehru to secure a third term. Nehru was prime minister for seventeen years from 1947 till his death on 27 May 1964. He was also *de facto* PM from 1946 till 15 August 1947 as the head of the interim government under British rule.

The NDA coalition won 42.74 per cent of the votes, while the opposition INDIA coalition secured 40.66 per cent of the ballots and 232 seats. The 72-member cabinet took oath on 6 June in the forecourt of Rashtrapati Bhavan. There was no Muslim in the cabinet to represent 14.2 per cent of the Indian population. *The Times of India* said: "A council of ministers without any Muslims may be read by some in the context of the community's near-total support for the opposition in the elections."[1]

This time too, many foreign leaders attended the swearing-in ceremony. But the hype of 2014 was remarkably absent. Those present were Bangladesh Prime Minister Sheikh Hasina, Nepal President Pushpa Kamal Dahal, Sri Lanka President Ranil Wickremesinghe, Mauritius Prime Minister Pravind Kumar Jugnauth, Bhutan Prime Minister Tshering Tobgay and Seychelles Vice-President Ahmed Afif. The opposition, except Congress President Mallikarjun Kharge, decided to boycott the function as "the PM had indulged in 'hate speech and lies' during the election campaign and besmirched the dignity of the high office of the PM."[2]

Already some "coalition blues" have started appearing: one was on the recruitment of soldiers through the "Agniveer" scheme introduced by the NDA which was highly controversial and was partly responsible for the BJP's losses in north India as, according to the opposition, it turned "soldiers into labourers" by denying them pension benefits; the other is the highly contentious "Citizenship Amendment Act" which was discriminatory against Muslims. The Janata Dal United (JDU), a present coalition partner, has been vocal about it.[3]

## *Modi's discomfiture from four different quarters*

China decided to play spoilsport on 6 June as Narendra Modi was forming the new government after the 2024 elections. The reason was Modi's reply to Lai Ching-te, Taiwan's president who joined other world leaders like US President Joe Biden, Pakistan

Prime Minister Shahbaz Shariff and Ukraine President Volodymir Zelensky to congratulate him. Lai Ching-te mentioned "the fast-growing" Taiwan–India partnership and Modi responded by endorsing "closer ties" between the two governments as well as a "mutually beneficial economic and technological partnership." China's official spokesperson Mao Ning publicly reacted that "Taiwan is an inalienable part of the territory of the People's Republic of China" and adding that "China has protested to India about this."[4] While President Xi Jinping was one of the first world leaders to congratulate Modi on his re-election in 2019, this time it was left to Chinese Premier Li Qiang to send a brief letter of congratulations on 11 June as mentioned by Xinhua.[5]

The second source of worry was the sudden spurt in terrorist violence in Jammu and Kashmir. Terrorists mounted four deadly attacks within three days, the first on 9 June when a 53-seater passenger bus carrying pilgrims going to Shiv Khori caves in Reasi was attacked, causing the driver to lose control and plummeting into a deep gorge, killing ten including small children and injuring forty-one. Pakistan-backed Lashkar Front claimed responsibility for the attack through what is called the "Resistance Front." The incident happened when the bus was returning from Shiv Khori shrine *en route* to Katra, the base camp of Mata Vaishno Devi shrine.[6] Three more attacks were reported from Doda district, one at Chattergalla and the other at Gandoh area, while on 12 June newly infiltrated terrorists fired upon security forces in Kathua. However, security forces managed to kill one terrorist.[7]

A startling new allegation came through *Eurasian Times* on 18 June 2024 that China is surreptitiously helping Pakistan-based terrorists by digging a "tunnel somewhere in Lipa Valley that joins the Kashmir border with the Karakoram Highway" which terrorists are using "to move to the border locale to dump arms, ammunition, and other war material." The paper said that Pakistan-based terrorists have conducted "no fewer than 26 cross border attacks from 2021."[8]

The third embarrassment came on 10 June when suspected Kuki militants ambushed a police convoy on the Jiribam–Imphal highway in Kangpokpi district, which was part of the advance guard sent ahead of Manipur Chief minister (CM) N. Biren Singh's planned visit to the district. Singh interpreted this as a "direct attack" on the CM as a police constable was injured. [9]

The fourth came from unexpected quarters. On 11 June RSS chief Mohan Bhagwat made certain remarks while speaking to a Karyakarta Vikas Varg—a periodic training programme for RSS workers in Nagpur—which were interpreted as being against the BJP and Modi in particular. He said that "a true *sevak*" (one who serves the people) does not have "*ahankar*" (arrogance) and works without causing any hurt to others. Referring to the bitter poll campaign, he said "decorum was not maintained." On Manipur he "reiterated the Sangh's concern over continuing violence in Manipur and asked who was going to pay attention to the problem on the ground."[10] The last statement was interpreted as a veiled criticism of Modi not visiting the state even once.

One day earlier Ratan Sharda, a lifelong RSS member, wrote in *The Organiser*, an RSS-affiliated magazine, on 10 June that the 2024 polls were a "reality check for overconfident" BJP workers, adding that their leaders were busy sharing posts on social media and "did not hit the ground." "The false ego that only BJP leaders understand 'realpolitik' and RSS cousins were village bumpkins is smirk worthy."[11] This was perhaps a retort to BJP president Nadda's statement in May that the BJP was confident of conducting its business independent of the RSS.

*Economy: 100-day action plan*

Simultaneously, a 100-day action plan was outlined on progress to correct distortions in the economy, such as the low share of manufacturing in Gross National Product (GDP), low exports, ease of doing business, low health and education allocations and energy security. Two developments in this respect were also noticed; one was industrial production slipping to a three-month low in April.[12] The other was the International Energy Agency's (IEA) estimate released on 12 June that India would become the "driver of global oil demand" due to a rise in consumption by a "massive 1.3 million barrels between 2023 and 2030." The IEA saw

CONCLUSIONS

India's refining capacity rising from 5.8 million barrels per day in 2023 to 6.8 million in 2030. [13] Would it be a boon or turn India a foreign energy-dependent economy?

## Priorities of the new government on foreign relations

On 11 June External Affairs Minister S. Jaishankar, who is often described by the media as "the face of India's assertive foreign policy", outlined the "third term priorities" on foreign relations: "our focus with regard to China will be on finding a solution to the border issues that still continue. With Pakistan we would want to find a solution to the issue of years-old cross border terrorism."[14] This was interpreted to mean dialogue and reconciliation as against shades of grandiloquence which had been seen earlier.

## Was China a factor in the 2024 elections?

I did not find any mention of China during the campaigning except by some opposition leaders accusing the Modi government of allowing China to encroach into India and the external affairs minister strongly rebutting that allegation. However, *The Print* published a report by a fellow at the Taiwan Asia Exchange Foundation and George H.W. Bush Foundation for US–China Relations on 15 May 2024 quoting the *Global Times* that had published several editorial and opinion articles attributing the deterioration in India–China relations to the Modi government's rhetoric aimed at securing votes. According to this analysis, Liu Zongyi, director of the Center for South Asia Studies at the Shanghai Institute of International Studies, had felt that the previous Congress governments did not emphasise Hindu nationalism and were also friendlier toward China. [15]

## A lesson to India: How China was/is important to United States

In 1992 Harvard scholar the late James C. Thomson Jr said this about the traditional US attitude towards China:

From the unwelcomed coolie labourers of the 19th century to the adored Mme. Chiang of the 1940s, from the evil Dr Fu Manchu of the pulp magazines and movies to the wise detective Charlie Chan, from Pearl Buck's heroic Chinese peasants to Mao Zedong as a tyrannical enslaver of millions, China remained the obsession of significant American constituencies—as our place to do good (the missionaries) as our place to find markets (the businessmen), as our place to help implant democracy (statesmen, professors, journalists).[16]

Is this the reason why America is seeking India's help in trying to "contain" or "reform" China through The Quad or Indo-Pacific Economic Framework even in the twenty-first century?

On 7 August 2021 I wrote a column "When America favoured Chinese Communists"[17] on the efforts by US Presidents Franklin D. Roosevelt and Harry Truman to unite the Chinese Communists (CCP) and Nationalists (KMT). This policy was not merely to check Imperial Japan's expansionist activities. It continued even after Japanese surrender on 2 September 1945.

In 1941 the Allied powers, at their Arcadia Conference, chose Chiang Kai-shek as the Supreme Commander of Allied forces in the China theatre. Roosevelt felt that Chiang would not be effective unless China's internal situation was stabilised with the CCP's help. For this he stationed General Joe Stilwell as his personal envoy and Chiang's Chief of Staff in 1942.

Following this line, Truman wanted Chiang to incorporate the CCP and "Democratic League" in his Nationalist Government. He then sent General George C Marshall, the symbol of US victory in the Second World War, as his envoy. Truman said in his policy statement that US wanted the Chinese National Government to "rehabilitate the country, improve the agrarian and industrial economy and establish a military organisation capable of discharging China's national and international responsibilities."

Marshall arrived in Shanghai on 20 December 1945. His first appointment, on reaching Chunking, the temporary capital of the national government, on 22 December was with CCP leader Zhou Enlai. He met Zhou and his team before he met Chiang, then Chairman of the National Government of the Republic of

China. Zhou was unrestrained in his public praise of America, saying that China should learn three things from America: spirit of independence, democratic form, and agricultural and industrial reforms. A three-member committee was constituted for unification under Marshall's Chairmanship, along with Zhou and Chang Chun (Zhang Qun), Chiang's confidante.

Chiang's "Cessation of hostilities" announcement on 10 January 1946, also granting fundamental rights, multi-party system and elections was hailed as the first step towards a democratic China. An MOU on the merger of the Communist Army with the National Army was signed on 25 February by a committee consisting of Zhou and General Chang Chih-chung (Zhang Zhizong) of the National Army with Marshall as adviser.

Three days after the signing, Marshall accompanied by Zhou and General Zhang toured northern China, especially the Communist strongholds. They met Mao and Chu teh (Zhu De). Marshall was hailed as the "Saviour of China" wherever he went. On that ebullient note Marshall left for America for five weeks on 12 March.

That was the undoing of all the hard work he did. Taiwanese historian Wei Liang Tsai says that even Mao advised him not to leave China at that juncture. The Soviet Union vacated Manchuria in April and encouraged Communists to fill the vacuum. Malinovsky, under Stalin's orders, gave all weapons captured from the Japanese to the CCP army. Clashes broke out between Communists and the Nationalist Army in Manchuria which spread all over China for the next three years till 1 October 1949 when Mao ousted Chiang to Taiwan. Perhaps history would have been different had Marshall not left China for five weeks between 12 March and 17 April 1946.

*Dr Harry Harding's book in 1992*

Sometime in June 1992, Dr Harry Harding, noted China expert and Fellow of Foreign policy studies at the Brookings Institution, invited me to the launch of his book *A Fragile Relationship: The United States and China since 1972*, which was attended by many dignitaries including the late Robert McNamara, former Secretary of Defense and then President of the World Bank.[18] The book, described as one of the "first comprehensive surveys" of US–China relationship since the 1972 visit of President Richard Nixon to China, was written soon after the 1989 Tiananmen Square incidents. The 1989 incidents had seen a drastic deterioration in bilateral relations after their dramatic elevation with the Nixon visit in 1972. This was followed by the China tour of Zbigniew Brzezinski—President Jimmy Carter's National Security Advisor—in May 1978, which saw the establishment of diplomatic relations between both countries upon which Washington, DC ended official ties with Taiwan.

Harding divides the US–China relationship after the Second World War into four phases: first, continued hostility from 1949 for twenty years; second, strategic alignment against the Soviet Union from 1969 till the early 1980s; third, American cooperation in China's modernization and reform till the 1989 Tiananmen Square incidents; and fourth, a period of suspicion over the ultimate objective of diplomatic and trade relations. The American aim during the fourth period was a sweeping restructure of China's Marxist-Leninist economic and political institutions while China hoped that US would assist in "China's socialist modernisation and reform." The Chinese expectation was, as the late James C. Thomson Jr had put it in 1992 while reviewing Harding's book: "How much can we Chinese let in from the West in order to modernize without losing our Chineseness?"[19]

In 1992 Harding envisaged five alternative scenarios for the US–China relationship: First, a revived Sino–American strategic alignment against a common enemy, which was most unlikely; second, diverse American relations with a fragmented China, which he felt was "improbable" but "conceivable"; third, a resurrection of partnership in China's reform as in the 1980s; fourth a second period of confrontation, which is "more plausible"; and fifth, "a strained relationship characterised by a complex mixture of conflict, competition, and cooperation."

Harding was almost prescient if we review his book in 2024 on the US–China relations when he describes the fifth scenario: "But despite strained relations there would also be less chance of military conflict, more intense economic interaction, and more frequent diplomatic cooperation on regional and global issues than would occur in an outright confrontation."

However, Harding did not envisage a situation in which China would be leading a China–Russian strategic partnership in the 2020s, which Jawaharlal Nehru had predicted even in July 1952 while speaking to Chester Bowles, two-time US Ambassador to India in New Delhi: "There may be more chance of China running Russia twenty years from today than of Russia running China."[20]

Harding's recommendations in 1992 are valid even today: "But China is relevant to many important issues in which the US has immediate interests including preserving peace in the Korean peninsula, balance of power in the Western Pacific, protecting international environment, managing global economy, preventing proliferation of weapons of mass destruction and building new institutions to maintain global and regional security."

He finally warns US against a policy of confrontation with China. "Treating China as a potential military adversary would require far larger deployments in the Western Pacific than the United States is envisioning in the post-Cold War period.... A hostile policy toward China would also throw broader Asia policy into disarray, for at this point the friends and allies of the United States in that region would not wish to join America in an antagonistic posture toward Peking."[21]

This prediction has been repeatedly proved during the US diplomatic engagement with countries like Vietnam, South Korea and Philippines.[22] A CNBC report dated 3 April 2024, "U.S. loses its spot to China as Southeast Asia's most favored ally, survey shows", on a poll conducted by The ASEAN Studies Centre, Singapore is also relevant here.[23]

*Harvard Business Review: What the West gets wrong about China*

This article by Rana Mitter, professor of the history and politics of modern China at Oxford University, and Elsabeth Johnson, senior lecturer at MIT's Sloan School of Management, should be compulsory reading for those who want to understand how the new China works. They say that many in the West think that political freedom would automatically follow the new economic freedoms as in the liberal democracies in the West.

The authors say that such thinking arises from a belief that democracy and economics are "two sides of the same coin"; authoritarian political systems are not "legitimate"; and the Chinese "live, work, and invest" like the people in the West. This misunderstanding arises out of ignorance that the Communist system gives great importance to "Chinese history and of Marxist-Leninist doctrine." "Until Western companies and politicians understand this and revise their views, they will continue to get China wrong."[24]

This is almost the same as what James C. Thomson Jr had said in 1992: "There is an overwhelming continuity between what the late 19th century Confucian officials were seeking and what many of the octogenarian leaders in Beijing in 1992 are still looking for: 'Chinese learning for fundamentals, Western learning for practical application'."[25]

## The Ukraine War: Did Modi fall back on Nehru's non-alignment policy?

The Russian invasion of Ukraine from 24 February 2022 and its brutal devastation of the country continues to pose serious policy uncertainties for the Modi government. Initially the Modi government was urged by the US and Europe to take a strong position against Russia.

An article in *Foreign Affairs* in May 2022, "How Long Can India Carry On" by Lisa Curtis, described India's dilemma in meeting US expectations. Curtis is an influential American strategic thinker with over twenty-one years' experience in the US government in NSC, CIA, State Department and in New Mexico Senate. She wrote: "Yet Washington's patience is not endless, and the longer Russia prosecutes its war without India changing its position, the more likely the United States will be to view India as an unreliable partner. It may not want to, but ultimately New Delhi will have to pick between Russia and the West."[26]

# CONCLUSIONS

So far India has managed to calibrate its policy without taking sides. At the same time, India was earnest in reinforcing its adherence to the American-led Quad policy to checkmate China, especially when the latter started openly siding with Russia. As of now, it appears that India will have to indefinitely pursue these two contradictory strands of foreign policy.[27]

From 2014 Modi had shown his disinclination to pursue the Nehruvian non-alignment policy. He decided to skip the seventeenth Non-Aligned Summit in Venezuela and the eighteenth in Baku, Azerbaijan. Although he addressed the on-line summit in 2020, India was effectively following a new policy as explained by its former Foreign Secretary Vijay Gokhale who told the "Raisina Dialogue" in 2019: "India has moved on from its non-aligned past. India is today an aligned state—but based on issues."[28]

Even on 17 June 2022, Modi had found time to release a Hindi book by journalist Ram Bahadur Rai blaming Nehru for the 1947 Indian partition.[29] Yet, the South Block—the Ministries of External Affairs, Defence and the Prime Minister's Office— scrambled to take refuge in the non-alignment policy to justify its reluctance to engage in wholesale condemnation of Russia. In that process India suddenly found virtue in that policy since nearly 120 UN members, including India's own neighbours Bhutan, Bangladesh, Nepal, Maldives and Sri Lanka were still members of the Non-Aligned Group.

On 13 May 2022, India abstained on the UN Human Rights Council resolution on the deteriorating human rights situation in Ukraine following Russian aggression. Some observers, however, felt that, although India had abstained eleven times in the UN voting till 23 April 2022, it had indicated a subtle shift towards the Western position. *The Diplomat* said that India "may have already started taking steps to maintain distance from Russia in the future", in case Russia became China's junior partner after the war, as predicted by some experts.[30]

Similarly, India chose not to sign the "Ukraine declaration" on 16 June 2024 at the two-day summit at Burgenstock, Switzerland, along with South Africa, Saudi Arabia and United Arab Emirates. This was signed by eighty of the ninety countries present to end the war on the grounds that "only those options acceptable to both parties can lead to abiding peace."[31] Yet India realises that the Ukraine war had introduced a dangerous example in international relations to be settled through cross-border aggression. The worry was whether China would copy the same policy towards its "claimed territories" on the Indian border.

On 10 June 2022, while speaking at the 350th birthday celebrations of Peter the Great, Russian President Vladimir Putin said that he was "strengthening" the country as Peter the Great had done with Sweden in the eighteenth century, where "he did not take anything from them, he returned [them]." Similarly, China's Border Law passed on 23 October 2021, showing many places in Arunachal Pradesh as theirs, had cast the responsibility of protecting their border on the PLA effective from 1 January 2022.[32]

Even earlier, the Putin–Xi summit of 4 February 2022 had introduced an uncertain dilemma for India's foreign policy orientations. A widely-circulated assessment by former Australian Prime Minister Kevin Rudd, one of the best China watchers in the world, had said on 25 February 2022 that Putin had "signed on Xi's 'global agenda'." Similarly, Putin chose China for his first international visit in May 2024 after his re-election in March 2024 during which both leaders agreed to oppose "further escalation" in the Ukraine conflict. As CNN said: "Xi and Putin used their meetings and hefty statement to take aim at what they described as a global security system defined by US-backed military alliances—and pledged to work together to counter it."[33]

## The Quad and Biden's Indo-Pacific Economic Framework

In February 2022 the White House announced President Joe Biden's Indo-Pacific Economic Framework (IPEF) as the proposed vehicle for US economic engagement in the Indo-Pacific region. This was to tap the economic potential of that region where half the global population resided. Ahead of the Quad Summit in Tokyo in May 2022 Prime Minister Modi announced that India was joining the IPEF.

# CONCLUSIONS

The idea of the IPEF can be attributed to a similar grouping of countries in the Trans-Pacific Strategic Economic Partnership Agreement (TPSEP), originally signed by Brunei, Chile, New Zealand, and Singapore in 2005. In 2012 eight more countries joined: the United States, Australia, Canada, Japan, Malaysia, Mexico, Peru and Vietnam. It then became the Transpacific Partnership Agreement (TPP).

Madhyam, a think-tank based in New Delhi, summarised the IPEF's difficulties in convincing other nations in the Indo-Pacific region. They are the lack of US market access, lack of US Congressional approval—meaning that a new administration could scrap it, that all IPEF participating countries are already China's leading trading partners, that most of Asian growth is increasingly being driven by intra-Asian trade and the complicated "*à la carte*" approach in which countries would launch separate negotiations under the four pillars ("Connected economy, Resilient economy, Clean economy, Fair economy").[34]

The reaction of the regional powers to Biden's IPEF was positive, although they would have liked America to re-join the TPP, now CPTPP. They also want Indonesia, Vietnam, Thailand and India to join. There is, however, a feeling that there is not enough clarity on the proposed working of the IPEF and a fear that regional perspectives have not been addressed.

For example, the region is uncomfortable with Biden's emphasis on democracy, which many nations are not. As Huong Le Thu, senior fellow at the Australian Strategic Policy Institute, said:

> The US is painting itself into a rhetorical corner by talking about democratic principles and its role as the defender of a free and open world, smack in the middle of the ASEAN region (which it claims to see as "central"), which includes Myanmar, a country essentially experiencing civil war.... The rhetorical note that Biden is hitting with his "democracy summit" is a bitter delusion for the Myanmar people.

Also, they do not want to be compelled to take sides if US–China competition results in bifurcation, thus leaving limited room for a positive relationship with both powers.[35] Pacific countries are also wary that US inflation-fuelled recession fears from June 2022 might impact funds being made available for this ambitious project.

## IPEF and BRI

An analysis by *The Diplomat* on 22 April 2022 said that regional partners would see "few tangible benefits for them, particularly when compared to new alternatives like the Chinese-led Regional Comprehensive Economic Partnership (RCEP) and Belt and Road Initiative (BRI)" if US market access incentives are "off the table" as the Biden administration had been saying.[36]

On 19 May 2022 *The Economic Times* reported that India was keen to join the IPEF and was "seeking a big role". However, the "disincentive" was that the IPEF is based on a Presidential Executive Order and could be discarded by subsequent administrations (as Trump had done previously) as it is not a Senate-ratified treaty.[37]

The US Institute of Peace (USIP) held a seminar on India joining the IPEF on 7 March 2022.[38] There was a consensus that the primary aim was to "reaffirm on the centrality of the region to core U.S. interests, its forthright characterization of challenges posed by China" and its "particular attention on supporting India's continued rise and regional leadership."[39] However, three difficulties were foreseen. First, the US administration's plan to drive new resources to the region could be delayed by the Ukraine war. Second, the new proposals on the TPP could face serious domestic opposition from both conservatives and liberals. Both President Trump and prominent Senator Bernie Sanders were against it as hurting American workers.

The third reason why the IPEF could be controversial is the US expectation of more European interest in Asia by endorsing the 2021 EU Strategy for Cooperation in the Indo-Pacific and linking it to the Australia–United Kingdom–United States (AUKUS) format. While the EU has clearly said that it is not against China ("The EU's approach to the region is one of cooperation not confrontation"),[40] the mention of "enhanced naval deployments by EU Member States" would create problems with China and even with ASEAN countries, some of whom would not want to join any security alliance against China.

*The Global Times* had felt that India, which "still sees China as its main threat," is reluctant "to see Quad become an Indo-Pacific version of NATO, as it doesn't want to become a victim of confrontation between different blocs. New Delhi believes that it is in its best interest to maintain a balanced posture on the global stage."[41] The USIP report also feels that India's reluctance has been towards alliances which suggest mutual dependence and a "diminution of sovereignty through ironclad commitments."

On the other hand, the Chinese Belt and Road Initiative (BRI) or One Belt One Road (OBOR), which started in 2013, has the participation of 146 countries, according to official Chinese announcements. However, a Council on Foreign Relations (CFR) report on 24 March 2021, put the number as 139 adding that China is opaque about the exact contours of different levels of participation.[42]

Yet it says that BRI is now a "truly global endeavour": thirty-nine countries in sub-Saharan Africa, thirty-four in Europe and Central Asia, twenty-five in East Asia and the Pacific, eighteen in Latin America and the Caribbean, seventeen in the Middle East and North Africa, and six in South Asia. These 139 members of BRI, including China, account for 40 per cent of global GDP. Some 63 per cent of the world's population lives within the borders of BRI countries.

As the *Dhaka Tribune* had said, the BRI "is the biggest initiative of its kind taken by any single nation in recorded human history, and, if implemented properly, could change the geo-political landscape of Eurasia to China's favour."[43] Another aim is to introduce the Renminbi as a currency of international transactions as well as to strategically channel Chinese foreign reserves to develop the infrastructures of Asian countries.

BRI has brought considerable policy puzzles for India, which is the only one in its neighbourhood not to have joined it. Pakistan, Sri Lanka, Bangladesh, Nepal, Myanmar, and Afghanistan attended the May 2017 Belt and Road global conference, which was attended by

1,500 delegates from 130 countries including twenty-nine heads of state.

The participation of India's smaller neighbours had raised questions on India's capability to offer any long-term development aid to its neighbourhood with China swamping the area with its projects.[44] Would all these be compensated by India being a member of the Quad? Asia-Pacific experts anticipate gloomy prospects about the ability of these nations to commit enough capital to match China's BRI, even with Japan, Australia, and the UK, if included.

The Biden administration's action in stopping the trade pillar in November 2023 due to objections from Democratic members, especially Congressman Sherrod Brown, has disappointed members although agreements on the other pillars—supply chains, clean economy, and fair economy—have been signed.[45]

## The Quad: Will it contain China?

The Quad (Quadrilateral Security Dialogue) has strong Indian connections which nobody remembers now. As I had pointed out in a column on 11 March 2021, it was first proposed by the late Japanese Prime Minister Shinzo Abe to the Indian Parliament on 22 August 2007, with his "Confluence of Two Seas" speech.[46] The session was chaired by former Vice-President M.H. Ansari, Chairman of the Rajya Sabha.

Abe recalled the visit of his grandfather Nobusuke Kishi, the first Japanese Prime Minister to come to India, in 1957 and how he was treated with great dignity by Prime Minister Jawaharlal Nehru despite being the leader of a "defeated nation". Abe told parliament "with pride" that he had heard stories as a little boy from his grandfather about how Nehru "brought my grandfather to an outdoor 'civic reception' at which tens of thousands of people had gathered, introducing him to a crowd energetically saying, 'this is the Prime Minister of Japan, a country I hold in the greatest esteem'."[47]

Kishi was also the first Japanese prime minister to start the Official Development Assistance (ODA) scheme, despite being a poor country. "At that time, the country that had accepted Japan's ODA was none other than India. My grandfather never forgot that fact either."

In 2004 the idea of a naval group comprising India, the United States, Australia, and Japan was formed for urgent humanitarian assistance after the 2004 tsunami on the initiative of the then US President George W. Bush and Indian Prime Minister Manmohan Singh. In May 2007 senior officials of the four countries met in Manila on the side-lines of the ASEAN Regional Forum to discuss regional security. In the same year they held "Malabar" naval exercises in the Bay of Bengal. Soon after China issued a demarche to them as to whether an anti-Beijing alliance was in the making.[48]

Unfortunately, the Quad went into a stupor from 2008 for ten years when Australian Prime Minister Kevin Rudd withdrew from it to mend fences with China. Only some infrequent military exercises took place. However, China challenged the Quad when it was revived in the present form in 2017.

There is a feeling in East Asia that the amorphous structure of the Quad, which nowhere mentions the real purpose of its existence, is the reason for confusion. For example, the communique issued by India's Ministry of External Relations after the Quad ministers' meeting hosted by US Secretary of State Antony J. Blinken on 17 February 2021 mentioned almost every subject other than security, like political democracies, market economies, pluralistic societies, rules-based international order, territorial integrity and sovereignty, rule of law, transparency, freedom of navigation and peaceful resolution of disputes, ASEAN cohesion and centrality, the Covid pandemic and vaccination programmes. It nowhere mentioned China.

It was first mentioned in 2022. But it went too far. Ahead of the Quad in-person summit in Tokyo on 24 May, President Biden gave a stern warning to China that the "US military would intervene to defend Taiwan." Later an official spokesperson explained that "Biden simply meant that US would provide military equipment to Taiwan, not send troops to defend the island if China attacks, which would be constitute a landmark shift in policy." *Bloomberg* carried this news with a headline "Biden Misspeaks on Taiwan,

Says US Military Would Intervene."[49] *The New York Times* was more forthright:

> Even before President Biden travelled to Tokyo this week to strengthen a partnership with Australia, India and Japan, the alliance was struggling to present a united front, as India refrained from condemning Russia's invasion of Ukraine.
>
> Now, with remarks that President Biden made about Taiwan on Monday, the Indo-Pacific bloc is facing another, unexpected complication. On the eve of a summit of the four nations, Mr. Biden said he would defend the democratic island militarily if it were invaded by China, sending shock waves around the globe and placing the allies in a tricky position as they seek to avoid further antagonizing Beijing.[50]

However, even in November 2020, China had mentally prepared how to deal with a revived Quad. It had warned that President Biden would most probably convert the Quad from "four sleeping partners to turn bilateral military alliances between the US and other countries into a quadrilateral one" as an "Asia-Pacific multilateral Alliance." The idea would be encircling China "with NATO expanding to the East until it is right on the China's doorstep."

The *Global Times* on 9 November 2020 had even recommended military action to guard China's core interests like Taiwan and the South China Sea, urging Beijing not to make even the "slightest compromises." It wanted China to improve relations with South Korea, New Zealand, and ASEAN members to prevent the US from forging new military alliances. It also wanted China to build up relations with Japan and India as neither of them wanted Washington to interfere with their relations with China.

In fact, this is the reason why the littoral countries of the South China Sea have been reluctant to join any security pact with the US. As a Stimson Center analysis on the possibility of South Korea joining "Quad Plus" had said in 2021: "South Korean foreign policy has consistently played an intricate balancing act between the US and China; the Quad and Quad Plus's image as an instrument of the US Indo-Pacific strategy—or, more bluntly, as an anti-China coalition to contain Chinese power—may complicate this juggling act."[51]

There is still elevated hope in some Indian circles, as in Washington, DC, that Vietnam would actively help in trying to checkmate China. This is an erroneous assessment if we study the China–Vietnam normalisation process from 1991 culminating in their Border Treaty signed in December 1999 including the "16-golden-word motto" on deepening bilateral economic interdependence.

Since 2004, China has been Vietnam's biggest trade partner and the second-largest export market after America, according to a *Vietnam News* article of 25 April 2019. Even after Chinese Coast Guards sank a Vietnamese vessel off the Paracel Islands on 3 April 2020, Vietnam was seen trying their policy of "compartmentalising" its response to China and "not allow them to disrupt other parts of the bilateral relationship."

This will be clearer if we read the above with their 2019 defence white paper "Four Noes and One Depend" not aligning with one great power against another as Derek Grossman from RAND had pointed out in *The Diplomat* on 5 August 2020.

In a way the reluctance of the US and NATO countries to commit "boots on the ground" in Ukraine through legal impediments, even as that country was being rendered barren by Russia's savage bombing since 24 February 2022, might be the reason for the reluctance of Indo-Pacific nations to join any security alliance against China.

The Quad cannot be sustained as a front against China merely by the US, India, Australia, and Japan without the solid cooperation of Indo-Pacific littoral countries like Vietnam, Philippines, Malaysia, Indonesia, South Korea, etc. in what is conceived as "Quad Plus." As of now there is no such possibility. As a Council on Foreign Relations Paper (21 May 2021) had concluded:

> Yet, few policymakers in the Quad countries see an advantage in trying to contain Chinese influence militarily. Instead, the Quad leaders have emphasized cooperation across areas of shared interest to bolster confidence in the democracies' ability

to counter China's assertion of regional influence. As long as tensions with China remain, the Quad's agenda is likely to expand as the democracies of the Indo-Pacific seek to balance China's growing power.[52]

India has found that it alone must deal with an expanding China which is entrenching firmly on its northern border. As Prime Minister Modi was flying to attend the Tokyo Summit of the Quad (24 May 2022), a report emerged on 19 May that the Chinese were constructing a broad bridge on Indian territory on the Pangong Tso lake in eastern Ladakh which would connect both sides of the lake and significantly cut down the time taken for PLA troops and armoured vehicles to cross over deep into the Indian side.

Another reason why the Quad may not succeed in its underlying security aims is the presence of AUKUS (Australia–UK–USA Security Pact), announced on 15 September 2021. A European Council of Foreign Relations paper wryly said that through this "Australia, America and Britain have achieved tactical gains at the expense of strategic goals in the Indo-Pacific. In fact, given how deeply the deal has divided the West, the biggest long-term winner may well be China." AUKUS has neglected Europe, especially France, which has strategic interests in Indo-Pacific. The paper also alleged that Biden, hot on the heels of a chaotic US withdrawal from Afghanistan, wanted to show that the US was "serious, competent, and tough on foreign policy."

It also annoyed France that Australia cancelled its submarines purchases, preferring American nuclear submarines.[53] France had promised Australia Barracuda submarines, taking the lead from European powers towards a new strategy for the Indo-Pacific.[54] If AUKUS is the main focus, India will have to be satisfied only with the second tier of the Quad US Indo-Pacific strategy by concentrating only on vaccines, climate change, technology, etc.

An analysis in an Indian paper on 29 May 2022 said that India's role in Indo-Pacific information exchange may be hampered by not locating Indian naval liaison officers at key centres in the region as part of the Indo-Pacific Maritime Domain Awareness initiative (IPMDA). Over the previous two years, the Defence bureaucracy had not cleared the Indian Navy's proposals to post their representatives at key locations.[55]

On 27 May 2022, China defiantly announced naval exercises in the South China Sea, 25 kilometres off the coast of south China's Hainan province. China's Maritime Safety Administration announced that an area of roughly 100 square kilometres would be closed off to maritime traffic for five hours. This was interpreted to be a snub to US Secretary of State Antony Blinken who had, on 26 May, called for efforts to counterbalance China's "intent to reshape the international order."[56]

*The Indian Economy*

In the 1980s both India and China had nearly similar levels of income—in GDP or per capita GDP. To be exact, India's GDP at 2022 prices was US$ 300 billion, while China's was US$ 400 billion. "However, since then, India could not keep up with the pace at which China grew; and by 2019—before the COVID pandemic shocked the world at an unprecedented scale—the Indian economy has been left behind to a great extent."[57]

In 2022, India's GDP was nearly $1.5 trillion; China's GDP was $7 trillion (according to IMF estimates, by 2024 India's stood at $4.1 trillion, and China's at $18.5 trillion). If China grows even at 1.5 per cent and India grows at 7 per cent, the same output would be achieved. Thus, economists say that there is no point in comparing each other's growth. Also, the Chinese economy has consistently grown during the past thirty years, compared to India's. China's manufacturing productivity is 1.6 times that of India. [58]

Also, India depends heavily on foreign workers' remittances to generate foreign exchange. This is subject to overseas variabilities needing sensitive diplomacy to iron out the wrinkles. According to the World Bank, India topped in receiving overseas remittances worth $125 billion in 2023, pushing China into third place ($50 billion).[59] Foreign Direct Investment (FDI) in India was less than this with only $83.7 billion.[60] China's FDI was $179 billion in 2021, an increase of 20 per cent over the previous year.[61]

China's success was because it was able to attract a huge amount of FDI by its sheer size and growing domestic market. It was $40 billion in 2000, $100 billion in 2008 and $124 billion in 2011. In 2010 foreign invested enterprises were responsible for over half of China's exports and imports according to its Ministry of Commerce (MOFCOM). They also provided for 30 per cent of Chinese industrial output and generated 22 per cent of industrial profits while employing only 10 per cent of labour because of their high productivity.[62] UNCTAD estimated in 2020 that 10.4 per cent of its FDI came from the USA, followed by Japan, the UK and Germany.[63]

China's crude oil production rose 4.6 per cent to 14.13 million barrels/day in 2021 despite refineries cutting crude runs by 2.1 per cent in December to offset product inventory pressure, according to the National Bureau of Statistics. Platts Analytics forecast China's crude "throughput" in 2022 to grow by 454,000 b/d. This reflected a c. 614,000 b/d increase in the country's oil demand in 2022 and at least a 25 per cent reduction in oil product exports.[64]

On the other hand, India's oil demand rose from 4.51 million b/d to 4.76 million b/d in 2021. Imports make up 85 per cent of Indian oil needs.[65] Its domestic production fell to an all-time low in FY 2022.

Another factor affecting the Indian economy, especially the stock market, is the behaviour of Foreign Portfolio Investors (FPI). In May 2022, FPI created a big problem by selling off Rs. 440 billion ($5.3 billion), which was the biggest sell off since the March 2020 Covid lockdown. In 2002 FPIs brought in Rs. 36.8 billion ($400 million) which grew to Rs. 1.79 trillion. In March 2020 FPIs withdrew Rs. 1.18 trillion ($22 billion), showing a lack of confidence in Indian growth.

When FPIs sell and repatriate funds, the Indian rupee takes a hit. In June 2022 it was at 78 rupees to the dollar compared to 73 a year ago. That fall has continued into 2024, when it hit 83 rupees to the dollar. This has made oil imports very expensive.[66] In April 2022 the IMF re-evaluated India's predicted growth for 2023 to

8.2 per cent from 9 per cent earlier; the actual growth was down to 6.3 per cent.

According to an early estimate (April 2022),[67] China has the means to curb any near-term volatility that would affect trade, investment, or consumption. It says that Chinese macroeconomic policy has remained "moderately loose, as there is still a focus on reducing financial risks." Unlike India, inflation in China does not seem to be a big threat. It says that Beijing has allowed the yuan to remain strong: at around 6.3 to the dollar in 2022, though it has climbed to above 7 to the dollar since mid-2023. If necessary, it could pump a lot of cash into the economy and supercharge exports by pushing the yuan lower. The IMF also agreed that China would not have much difficulty having the economy grow 4.5–5.0 per cent in 2023;[68] indeed, it grew at 5.2 per cent.

Still, China was worried about the fall-out of Covid on its economy as indicated by Chinese Premier Li Keqiang's address to 100,000 officials around the country on 26 May 2022. CNN called it the "grimmest picture." It said that UBS lowered its full-year GDP growth forecast to 3 per cent, citing risks from Beijing's strict zero-Covid policy. China had said it expected growth of around 5.5 per cent that year. The world's second biggest economy reported growth of 8.1 per cent in 2021.[69] China's 2024 growth target of "around 5 per cent" has been described as "requiring a lot of luck at the very least."[70]

When the pandemic hit India in 2020, the Indian economy was already on a downward spiral as its growth rate was dropping to an eleven-year low of 3.1 per cent in the March quarter of FY 2020. Nationwide restriction of movement dropped it further to India's first recession in FY 2021 at minus 6.6 per cent.[71] India's economic growth during the last quarter of FY 2021–22 hit a bump due to the Omicron variant/third wave and other reasons. The anticipated growth was only 2.5 per cent as against 4.4 per cent.

During this period India's trade deficit with China widened to $72.9 billion with imports surging to $94.16 billion, 44 per cent more than the previous year and pre-pandemic year 2020. Shipments from China comprised 15.38 per cent of India's total imports of $611.89 billion.[72] During this period the US surpassed China as India's biggest trading partner. Bilateral trade stood at $119.42 billion in 2021–22 as against $80.51 billion in 2020–21.

Quoting IMF figures, the Bangladesh paper *Daily Star* claimed in October 2021 that it would surge ahead of India in terms of per capita GDP in the next five years. It claimed that this trend had started in 2020 due to its continuous 6 per cent annual growth with more remittances, exports and agriculture. Bangladesh managed to grow even during the pandemic when other economies faltered.[73]

How did this happen? Was it because of social unrest in India? An IMF study in 2021 on the relationship between social unrest and economic growth had said that on average, major unrest events are followed by a 1 percentage point reduction in GDP six quarters after the event. Unrest motivated by socioeconomic factors is associated with sharper GDP contractions than unrest associated with political motives. Yet events triggered by a combination of both factors correspond to the sharpest GDP contractions.[74]

Raghuram Rajan, the popular former governor of the Reserve Bank of India, now professor at the Chicago Booth School of Business, added a new dimension to the IMF study. He told the Times Network "India Conclave" on 14 May 2022 that the political principle of majoritarianism and legislative restrictions on honest criticism would impair economic growth by treating a segment of the population as second-class citizens. An anti-minority tag would lead to a loss of market for Indian products. Apart from this, foreign governments would also believe that the nation is unreliable, he said.[75]

He said that India could become a $10 trillion economy with 8 per cent national growth only if the states also join the drive as a national passion like South Korea, which had transformed its economy into that of a "developed country" in three decades.[76]

Former Prime Minister Manmohan Singh had voiced this in April 2022 in an op-ed entitled "This is India's moment of reckoning: The country can be the fulcrum of the new global order as a peaceful democracy with economic prosperity": "To be a large-scale producing nation, India needs millions of factories with hundreds of millions of people of all religions and castes to work together. Social harmony is the edifice of economic prosperity. Fanning mutual distrust, hate and anger among citizens, causing social disharmony is a shameful slide to perdition."[77]

In 2022 business contraction was seen in all areas due to external factors like the Ukraine war and internal issues connected with socio-economic factors. Shortage of components due to the Ukraine war and Covid curbs in China had impacted the production of automobiles and electronic products in India in the June 2022 quarter.[78] Indian state-run oil companies were unable to repatriate about 8 billion roubles ($120 million) as dividend due to restrictions put in place by Moscow.[79]

On 20 March 2024, Modi claimed that India's startup ecosystem has witnessed rapid growth, creating employment for hundreds of thousands of people.[80] However *Business Standard* (23 January 2024) said that startup funding in India fell over 62 per cent in 2023 to Rs 669 billion as compared to Rs 1.8 trillion in 2022, quoting market intelligence platform PrivateCircle Research. These were the lowest funding numbers since 2018 when the startups in India raised Rs 1 trillion.[81]

Surat, the world's largest centre for processing diamonds, is affected by US sanctions on Russia. It has 5,000 diamond processing units employing nearly one million workers who polish about 90 per cent of the diamonds sold worldwide. India's export of cut and polished diamonds in 2022 was worth over $24 billion. Russian state-owned Alrosa is the world's largest diamond mining company and it became the subject of US sanctions. 30 per cent of Alrosa's production of rough diamonds comes directly to Surat. Alrosa also exports to other countries which finally reach Surat.[82]

Similarly, there was a report on 15 June 2024 that Indian electronics manufacturers have suffered a US$ 15 billion loss besides losing 100,000 jobs due to Indian government policies regarding China. The electronic manufacturing industry has said it has lost out on US$ 10 billion of export opportunities besides US$ 2 billion in value addition loss. Nearly 4000–5000 visa applications of Chinese executives were awaiting government clearance "hindering the Indian electronics manufacturing industry's expansion plans."[83]

Ashoka Mody, who teaches at Princeton University and had worked for the World Bank has warned against "irrational exuberance" over Indian economy "driven by policy makers wedded to an unhinged hype about the country's performance and prospects." In an article "India's looming financial crisis" on 12 June 2024, he highlighted the dangers to the economy through a household debt boom due to various factors like massive credit card usage, "a stock market rising unmoored from weak corporate investment and anaemic consumer spending, an overvalued exchange rate, a tendency for Indian authorities to talk up dodgy data," which "presents a text book example of the key elements that signal a looming financial crisis."

He attributes this to the three decades of economic policy: "Unable to generate job-rich manufacturing growth, successive policy makers have pushed the financial services industry to raise headline GDP growth rates; in the last decade, the financial sector has contributed over a quarter of GDP growth."[84]

*India's nuclear industry*

The Ukraine war has generated uncertainties for India regarding its expansion of civil nuclear industry. Officially it is reported that the Indian nuclear power sector has shown the slowest growth rate amongst fuels. This is despite generous budgetary allocations. The slow pace is attributed to technological problems and opposition from local populations. Between 2002 and 2006 nuclear capacity grew by over 23 per cent and by over 9 per cent between 2006 and 2017. However, the capacity has not grown since 2017.[85] There are indications that India is strongly pursuing the stalled Jaitapur (Maharashtra) project of setting up six 1650 megawatt reactors with the French company EDF.

Presently only Russia has been supplying light water reactors to India (Kudankulam in Tamil Nadu since 1998). Units 1 and 2 are in operation. Although the Russian "Rosatom" is not on the US sanctions list, it is feared that four more reactors (units 3 to 6), which had reached physical progress of 58 per cent in 3–4 and 8.12 per cent in 5–6 by mid-2022, are likely to be affected as components and equipment from Ukraine and Russia might be delayed due to logistical and shipping difficulties because of the war.[86]

*China and India: a comparative study*

*Trade interconnectivity between China and India*

Trade with China during the calendar year 2021 rose to $125 billion, which was higher than pre-pandemic or pre-Ladakh figures despite the 5 May 2020 Galwan (Ladakh) clash which killed twenty Indian soldiers. Imports from China reached $97.5 billion, exports more than $20 billion. This was despite India placing several restrictions on Chinese attempts to participate in the Indian economy and banning several apps popular in India such as Tik Tok.[87]

During the fiscal year 2024, bilateral trade between India and China reached US$118.4 billion. Imports from China increased by 3.24 per cent to US$101.7 billion, while exports to China surged by 8.7 per cent to US$16.67 billion. The Indian Ministry of External Affairs (Economic Diplomacy division) said, quoting the Global Trade Research Initiative (GTRI), that China has reclaimed its position as India's top trading partner, edging past the United States after a two-year gap.[88] It said:

> India's economic relationship with China has garnered significant attention due to its heavy reliance on Chinese imports in crucial sectors such as telecommunications, pharmaceuticals, and advanced technology. The GTRI report underscored this dependence, revealing that India imported US$4.2 billion worth of telecom and smartphone parts from China, accounting for 44% of total imports in this category. Similarly, laptops and PC imports from China totalled US$ 3.8 billion, comprising 77.7% of India's imports in this sector.

It is also true that India sources from Chinese markets when other supply areas fail. For example, India railways sourced 39,000 rail (solid forged) wheels from China in May 2022 when supplies from other countries dried up due to Ukraine war. This was despite restrictions on supplies from China made stricter after the Galwan Valley clash.[89]

### Science and technology

The first thing that strikes anybody is the very poor standard of Indian research. Brookings India said on 29 November 2019 that India has 216.2 researchers per 1 million inhabitants against 1,200 in China and 4,300 in the US. India spends less than 1 per cent of its GDP on research and development, while South Korea spends 4.23 per cent, and China 2.11 per cent. It also said that in 1996 India and China were on par in spending (0.6 per cent GDP) but two decades later China's expenditure on research and development jumped more than four-fold.

India's poor research data was confirmed by the participants in the Indian Science Congress on 3 January 2023, adding that the report of the Comptroller & Auditor General released on 20 December 2022 had said that the number of publications in high-impact journals was very low.[90]

The Brookings report said that, while research publications had grown seven-fold in last two decades in India, it is still far behind countries like China and the US. While China produces 483,595 research publications annually, the number in India is 148,832. The quality of research is judged by "citations." India lags behind other countries in the "citation per document" criterion. The report said that China's rise as a super-power in scientific knowledge in less than two decades was creditable as it was one of the lowest-income countries in the world at the turn of the twenty-first century.

India's poor record of research is reflected in patent applications. India filed 14,961 patent applications in 2017, while China filed 1.24 million applications in the same year. The report said that, despite having one of the largest higher education sectors in the world with 51,000 institutions and universities, India churns out only poor-quality graduates with low employability mainly because of poor quality of teaching, weak governance, insufficient funding, and complex regulatory issues.[91]

# CONCLUSIONS

Even earlier, a thesis in 2013 by Rahul Panat of the Arizona State University[92] comparing research output between India and China in science and technology since 1975 had shown that Indian research output had fallen far behind that of China with a gap that has only increased in recent times. Panat says that historically all the successful economies "have had a strong backbone of university and industrial research, constantly producing new ideas that spur new industries and/or perfect the existing ones." Such high growth was seen in UK in the eighteenth and nineteenth centuries, in the US in the second half of twentieth century, and in Germany in the first half of the twentieth century.

He quotes several past "scientometric" studies by scholars on the China–India comparison. The output of both countries was comparable during 1993–97 but China overtook India from 1997 to 2001.

China enacted a policy of "project 211" in 1995 with a "Decision on Accelerating Scientific and Technological Progress", which was a major push from the government that infused funding into science and technology. Panat says that this was a complete reversal from the isolationist policies enacted during the Cultural Revolution (1967–77).

In 1998, Beijing launched "Project 985" for promoting the development and reputation of the Chinese higher education system and certain universities. It authorised national and local governments allocating large amounts of funding for building new research centres, improving facilities, attracting world-renowned faculty and visiting scholars, etc. Panat says that Project 985 could indeed be a significant factor in the inflection point observed in the Chinese research output in 2003.

On the other hand, India did not embark upon specific thrusts for science and technology research. Instead, it relied upon a general increase in research funding as the economy grew in size. Also, the Indian government seemed to have neglected the Indian state university system during the latter decades of the twentieth century. "Clearly, this laissez-faire approach adopted by India has not helped in boosting the research output to the levels seen in China." Panat concludes: "From the perspective of the research paper output, India has fallen behind significantly behind that of China with no sign of catching up."

An Ohio State University paper from 2022[93] says that China edged past the US in 2019 on one important measurement of national research success after decades of dominance by the United States. It was found that Chinese research ranked as high or higher than US work in the top 1 per cent of studies in 2019. The new finding was published by Caroline S. Wagner, Lin Zhang and Loet Leidesdorff in *Scientometrics*. They observed: "However, this finding contrasts with repeated reports of Western agencies that the quality of China's output in science is lagging other advanced nations, even as it has caught up in numbers of articles."[94]

In 2019, 1.67 per cent of scientific articles with Chinese authors were in the top 1 per cent of the most highly cited articles, compared to 1.62 per cent of articles with US authors. The US was slightly ahead in 2018. The National Science Board in their report for 2020 had said about Science and Engineering (S&E) status: "The 28 nations that make up the EU collectively have the highest output of S&E publications globally. China's S&E publication output ranks next, followed by the United States. The citation impact of China's publications is rising rapidly, although it is currently lower than that of the United States and the EU." [95]

The report also said that the EU, China, United States, India, Japan, and South Korea together produce more than 70 per cent of the worldwide refereed S&E publications. It said that China's S&E publications had risen nearly tenfold since 2000, and as a result, China's output in terms of absolute quantity now exceeds that of the United States. In 2018 the output was EU (24%), China (21%), US (17%), India (5%), Japan (4%), South Korea (3%) and "Rest of the World" (27%).[96]

Another reason for the fall in scientific research in India could be the inadequate standard of key researchers selected for important posts. For example, a scientist who was accused of plagiarising her PhD research thesis and two scientific papers was promoted on 27 May 2022 to head the important department of epidemiology and communicable diseases like Covid at the apex health research body the Indian Council of Medical Research.[97] Such controversial promotions to key academic institutions like the University Grants Commission and Jawaharlal Nehru University were also made on criteria other than academic excellence.[98]

Yet another reason could be the RSS and BJP's smug belief that all that is wanted by a modern Indian student is available in the country's ancient Vedic texts.[99]

The crisis in Indian universities was explained in detail by BJP Member of Parliament Feroze Varun Gandhi, grandson of Indira Gandhi, in an op-ed in *The Hindu* from May 2022. He said that expenditure on higher education has stagnated at 1.3–1.5 per cent of total government expenditure since 2012. Also, there was a mismatch between policies undertaken by the government. While the Ministry of Education wants to increase admissions by 25 per cent (to implement a 10 per cent quota for economically weaker sections on political grounds) the Ministry of Finance has sought a ban on new teaching posts. Student financial aid was cut to Rs. 20.78 billion ($250 million) in FY 2022–23 from Rs. 24.82 billion ($300 million) in 2021–22. Worse, the allocation for research and innovation was cut by 8 per cent to just Rs. 2.18 billion ($26 million).[100]

At times such bureaucratic hold-ups affect India's international prestige. On 20 June 2024 it was reported that India's pledged contribution of US$10 million to the Digital Health (GIDH) of the WHO, announced during the G-20 Indian presidency in New Delhi on 9–10 September 2023 and part of the New Delhi declaration, was not carried out as Department of Economic Affairs objected to it.[101]

*Electronics and consumer goods*

In 1990 India's GDP was $320 billion, while China's was $360 billion. In 2021 India's GDP was $2.9 trillion compared to China's $16.8 trillion. Economists say that India's biggest challenge is to shift its workforce to productive domains. Reconfiguring growth calls for sequencing and speed in reforms. The rise of China illustrates this. While China modernised agriculture and opened its economy during the Deng Xiaoping era, India had to wait till

1991 for "liberalisation," which came in the wake of a crisis. Even these reforms were in fits and starts due to partisan politics and centre–state wars.

The much-advertised human capital, i.e. India's growing demography, by itself does not necessarily deliver results as 42 per cent of India's workforce is deployed in agriculture and must subsist on a sixth of national income. According to the UN, India overtook China as the most populous country in April 2023.[102] In other words, India will have more people than China restricted to about one-third the geographical area and its GDP at around $4.6 trillion will be roughly a sixth of China's GDP at $24 trillion.[103]

A very good survey in *The Economic Times* from 2020[104] gives details on how China became an electronics consumer goods giant penetrating India's digital economy within such a short time. In 2019 India overtook the US to become the second largest smartphone market in the world after China. However, 72 per cent of the smartphones in India (158 million) were Chinese brands like Xiaomi, Vivo, Realme and Oppo. "It has been an astounding market share grab, considering most of these brands have not been in India for more than a few years."

Even in June 2022 Xiaomi, which had faced certain litigations in India, topped the smartphone market with 23 per cent (2021: 26 per cent) while Samsung, the second most preferred, stayed constant at 20 per cent in 2021 and 2022.[105] Other Chinese computer and electronic goods were Lenovo, Haier, Huawei, MG Motor, etc. Perhaps nowhere in the world are two countries with such geopolitical suspicions that also share such deep trade links with each other. A cynical reader who offered his comments on this report said:

> While we Indians are busy in wasting our time and energy for petty political agenda like CAA, NRC[106] etc, China is quietly and effectively pursuing its economic and strategic agenda to sabotage India's aspiration of becoming a global power by making its economy overdependent on China's economic and business interest. Time for Indians to wake up and do their best to pursue the "Make in India" campaign a daily way of life.[107]

# CONCLUSIONS

## Rural communications and the internet

China announced on 7 January 2022 that all its "administrative villages" had received broadband connectivity before the end of November 2021.[108] Both India and China have nearly 600,000 villages.

In India it was revealed on 4 April that the implementation of "Bharat Net", the NDA government's flagship rural internet connectivity programme, would miss its target of 2025 for completion. In 2012, when it was originally started by the previous Congress government, only 250,000 villages were meant to be connected. In 2014 Prime Minister Modi gave it a new brand name "Bharat Net" instead of the old "National Optical Fibre Network." He also linked it to the "Digital India Initiative" and announced in August 2021 that it would connect 600,000 villages. By February 2022 only 172,000 villages were connected;[109] that went up to only 194,000 by August 2023.[110]

## Pharmaceuticals: India's dependency on China

Nowhere else is the stark contrast more visible than in the Indian pharmaceutical industry, as pointed out by a CNBC analysis on 26 May 2022. True, Prime Minister Modi had said on 18 November 2021, while inaugurating a global pharmaceutical summit, that India was being called the "pharmacy of the world."[111] Also true, India is the world's third largest manufacturer of medicine by volume, with the cheapest manufacturing costs. However, India's $42 billion pharmaceutical industry depends on China for active pharmaceutical ingredients (API) to the extent of 68 per cent according to a government report. According to the Indian Trade Promotion Council this dependency is 85 per cent.

CNBC quotes another study that in "certain life-saving antibiotics", like penicillin, cephalosporins and azithromycin, this dependence on Chinese API is around 90 per cent. However, in 1991 this dependence was only 1 per cent. China's success was because it opened 3,000 "Drug Parks" in the 1990s with good infrastructure such as effluent treatment plants, subsidized power and water, reducing production costs and edging India out of the API market.

The Government of India took the initiative to locally produce APIs only in 2020 with a "Production Linked Initiative" (PLI) when tensions with China were high. India now depends on China for fifty-three APIs. With PLIs it is expected that thirty-five of these APIs would be produced in thirty-two plants. This would reduce India's dependence to about 35 per cent in about a decade. However, according to Amitendu Palit of the Institute of South Asian Studies at the National University of Singapore, it will take a long time for India to catch up with China. Till then India will have to import APIs from China.

A survey by *The Economic Times* on 27 February 2024, on the question "Will India Pharma Sector be able to come out of its China dependence" resulted only in a bland conclusion: "The overall dependency on the import of bulk drugs from China is likely to continue to be high."[112]

Another area where India depends upon China is medical equipment in imaging technology or machines to perform magnetic resonance imaging and other types of sophisticated scans. Presently India imports $1.5 billion worth of such equipment. According to knowledgeable circles it will take longer time for India to be freed from such imports due to "technological complexity" whereas APIs depends only on a "chemical ecosystem" which exists in India.

An analysis by *The Wall Street Journal* in August 2020 on America's heavy dependence on Chinese APIs said that some Chinese thinkers had even been more vocal about "advocating the use of medical supplies for political advantage." Would China weaponize this against India? "'If China wants to retaliate against the U.S. at this time, aside from a travel ban, it could also announce strategic restrictions on the export of medical products to the U.S.,' said an opinion essay by Huang Sheng, a financial commentator and nationalist book author, published in March on state-run Xinhua News Agency."[113]

*Semi-conductor chip making: India vs China*

*Money Control*, a leading Indian business magazine, said on 22 February 2022 that India's ambitious plan of becoming the global hub of the semi-conductor industry through its Rs. 760 billion Production Linked Incentive scheme ignored the complexity of making "chips."[114] It said that Indian electronic and semiconductor bodies were "pessimistic" as they felt that the amount invested was "paltry" compared to the challenges. India currently imports 100 per cent of its chips, despite an excellent semiconductor design capability. This situation is because it is the chip manufacturing at fabrication plants (or fabs) that is key. The report said that India did not have a complementing manufacturing and infrastructural setup: "Chip fabrication operates on an atomic level, with hundreds of processes that rely on highly specialized suppliers for silicon wafers, chemicals, and equipment, etching transistors on wafer thin chips designed by other companies."

Government in their enthusiasm ignored how many years it would take to set up such a system. Also, government did not consult industry before announcing the ambitious plan which has strategic applications of semiconductors and India's defence self-reliance goals. *Money Control* should be quoted on the complexity of the venture:

> Qualcomm, NVIDIA, or Apple's chips are manufactured in the Taiwan Semiconductor Manufacturing Company (TSMC)'s fabs. South Korea's Samsung and US' Texas Instruments are the only two other foundries but are predominantly chip designers. The TSMC is an exclusive foundry, fabricating 92 percent of the world's advanced chips in a highly complex process of etching millions of transistors on every square millimetre.

A Brookings paper from January 2021 says that China imports more than $300 billion worth of semi-conductors. Major American companies benefit from 25 per cent of their sales from the Chinese market. This mutual dependence has benefitted both countries. "Despite the harsh rhetoric on both sides of the Pacific, American semiconductor companies and their Chinese counterparts today are working together on hundreds, if not thousands, of product designs and joint technology development efforts."[115]

The US-based Semiconductor Industry Association (SIA) has quoted the example of China, which despite a massive investment of over $150 billion from 2014 through 2030 in semiconductors, could be only a fringe player with 7.6 per cent of global semiconductor sales and that too in "lower-end logic chips, and analog chips to consumer, communications, and industrial end markets." The SIA says that China lags behind in advanced logic foundry production, EDA tools, chip design IP, semiconductor manufacturing equipment, and semiconductor materials. It is way behind in high-end logic, advanced analog, and leading-edge memory products.

However, China currently possesses considerable strength in the highly interconnected and layered global semiconductor supply chain. Firstly, it is already a global leader in outsourced assembly, packaging, and testing (OSAT). Secondly, China's leading OSAT players held 38 per cent of the total OSAT market in 2020. They are ranked among the top ten OSAT companies in the world. Thirdly, more than 30 per cent of Chinese OSAT firms have set up their manufacturing facilities based outside of China and gone global. The SIA says:

> While China holds only 7.6% of the market for global chip sales, this number is growing fast, and China is making significant progress thanks to a burgeoning domestic market. Chinese fabless firms and IDM leaders have made notable progress in mid-tier mobile processors and basebands, embedded CPUs, network processors, sensors, and power device development. Chinese firms already hold an impressive 16% of the global fabless semiconductor market in 2020, ranking third after the U.S. and Taiwan. China is also rapidly closing the gap in AI chip design, due partly to fast growing demand from China's hyperscale cloud and consumer smart device market and lower barriers to entry in chip design. Chinese fabless firms are now taping out 7/5nm chip designs for everything from AI to 5G.[116]

Another reason for this situation was analysed by the *Deccan Herald*, a newspaper based in Bengaluru, the "Indian Silicon Valley." It attributes this to "regulatory cholesterol" by way of high tariff barriers, red tape and infrastructural issues besides 26,134 "imprisonment clauses" in Indian business laws. It says that a 2021 parliamentary standing committee report "Attracting investment in post Covid economy-challenges and opportunities for India" had said that those foreign manufacturing bases which shifted out of China during the pandemic preferred to go to Vietnam, Taiwan, or Thailand and not India.[117]

A report dated 23 April 2024 from Taipei quoted Taiwan Foreign Affairs Minister Joseph Wu that India should address "the challenges" of its "cumbersome" administrative structure, lack of experienced engineers, high tariffs on electronic imports and inadequate infrastructure "before chip companies from the island territory start to commit serious investments."[118]

## China–India military comparison

### India's higher defence management

Six months after the sudden death of the first Chief of Defence staff (CDS) General Bipin Rawat in a helicopter crash on 9 December 2021, it almost appeared that there was serious rethinking on the role of the CDS as was originally envisaged. That might have been the reason why it took until September 2022 to appoint his replacement, Lt General Anil Chauhan. This delay was criticised by General V.P. Malik, former Army Chief who had won victory for India in the 1999 Kargil War: "That's not understandable at all. It has sent the wrong message." He also described the government decision to consider Lt Generals for the selection pool for the role as "flawed."[119]

Firstly, the incongruity: in the present format CDS is designated as Secretary to the Department of Military Affairs (DMA). Yet he is supposed to be senior to the three service chiefs, who according to India's protocol list, is senior to the Defence Secretary. By designating the CDA as Secretary DMA, government has unwittingly downgraded his protocol rank. Secondly, he has no "operational" role although he will "administer" tri-service assets like cyber weapons, missile agencies, space command and so on.

Although he will be an adviser to the Nuclear Command Authority, he is not made a member of the National Security

Committee. Similarly, he is the principal adviser to the defence minister—so are the service chiefs, NSA and Defence Secretary.

Most of all, what is missing is the "jointness" in military operations which is essential for any military operations. That is entirely missing in the CDS system. It is felt that there can be no improvement unless India formulates a law like the US Goldwater–Nicholas Act of 1986 creating a fully empowered Joint Chiefs of Staff, which was passed by the US Congress after America's disastrous experience in the Vietnam War and its failed attempt to rescue the Iranian hostages.[120]

Earlier, a system much like India's was prevailing in US. The three service chiefs used to elect a head of the Joint Chiefs of Staff who was only a nominal head. There was no "jointness" as procurement of defence equipment during peacetime and even operational plans were planned in isolation. The glaring defects noticed during the 1983 invasion of Grenada in effecting coordination led to a Congressional investigation and the passing of Goldwater–Nicholas Act of 1986. The new scheme was utilised during the 1992 First Gulf War against Saddam Hussein when General Colin Powell was the Chairman, Joint Chiefs of Staff. A study by the US National Defense University in 2017 concluded:

> Jointness was not the decisive factor in the coalition's victory over Saddam Hussein's Iraqi forces in the Gulf War. There were several factors to the victory, including superior technology, leadership, international support, plentiful resources, and limited objectives. It is more accurate to say jointness was a positive contributing factor.... It was not until the continuous joint operations of the war on terror compelled the Services to work together on a regular basis that the concept of jointness started to become fully realized.[121]

## Agnipath: New recruitment process for Indian military

On 15 June 2022 a new method of army recruitment was announced to make the Indian military "lean and mean." No public consultation was held although army recruitment affects the majority of India's states. Only "in house" consultations were held.

# CONCLUSIONS

To give it a Hindu "Puranic" touch, it was named "*Agnipath*" and recruits were named as "*Agniveers*" as opposed to sepoys.

According to the scheme, "*Agniveers*" would form a distinct rank in the three services and wear a distinct insignia as part of their uniform. They would be recruited between the ages of 17.5 and 21 and serve only four years. These soldiers would not be entitled to pension benefits and gratuity which the present sepoys enjoy. Also, 75 per cent of these recruits would be demobilised after the completion of four years. In other words, an Agniveer will serve for just two years after combat training in school or on the ground. The remaining 25 per cent will be retained in the regular cadre, based on merit and organisational requirements.

After four years of service, the troops are likely to be given a severance package of over Rs. 1 million ($12,000) but will not be entitled to pensions. However, the ones retained will serve in the defence services for another fifteen years and will be entitled to pensions.

The new policy has drawn criticism from several retired military veterans. Former Army chief General V.P. Malik said that the four-year tenure was too short for a technically savvy force.[122] Critics have argued that a four-year tenure would hit the fighting spirit in the ranks and make them risk-averse. It would also affect the overall morale of the troops as only 25 per cent would continue with pension and other benefits while 75 per cent would retire at such a young age with anxiety for further job opportunities.[123]

Presently all Sepoys enjoy pension and health benefits, including those injured or maimed during operations. Now only 25 per cent will enjoy those benefits. There is no mention that those among the 75 per cent who get injured during operations would continue to get facilities in military hospitals or whether they must go to crowded civil hospitals with poor medical facilities.

Also, there is no guarantee that all these 75 per cent would be absorbed in paramilitary forces as they would have to qualify for another gruelling recruitment process. True, the Ministry of Home Affairs had said that they would reserve a certain percentage to those *Agniveers*. However, there is no assurance that all demobilised from the military after four years would be accommodated or whether their four-year seniority would be respected.

Experts feel that this discrimination among Agniveers would lead to uncertainty, mass discontent and even serious law and order problems in future. A retired Lt General of the Indian army who was Director General of Military Operations has said that the "75% of the soldiers will go back to the villages rejected, dejected, and frustrated" and "may militarise the society."[124] Manavendra Singh, head of the Rajasthan Soldier Welfare Board, has quoted a 2012 Stanford study to say that there is a correlation between organised violence and demobilised soldiers after the Second World War.[125]

The initial reaction to the new scheme was very violent. Thousands of recruits who were not enlisted for the last two years due to Covid, but had undergone parts of the recruitment process before the pandemic, were enraged. In Bihar, trains were set on fire, rail and road traffic disrupted, windows of buses smashed, and passers-by, including a BJP MLA, pelted with stones by angry youths demanding the withdrawal of the new short-term recruitment scheme. Seventeen districts in Bihar were affected.

Admiral Harikumar, Chief of Naval Staff, said that he did not anticipate such mass protests although they had worked on the new scheme "for almost a year and a half."[126] This is in keeping with the NDA government's practice of introducing drastic new "reforms" like demonetization, farm laws, etc, without consulting the stakeholders.

Violent protests spread to multiple states across the country. Rajasthan, Haryana, Himachal, West Bengal and Uttar Pradesh also reported violent protests.[127] In Rohtak (Haryana), one boy who had spent two years in training for army recruitment was found hanging when he took his own life as the new scheme "crushed his dream." Since 2015 more than 186,795 sepoys had been recruited from just eight states: Punjab, Haryana, Bihar, Uttar Pradesh, Maharashtra, Rajasthan, Himachal Pradesh, and Uttarakhand according to army sources. Almost 78 per cent of them were from villages.

The immediate reason for the violent reaction was the sudden feeling in these areas that those who had participated in about forty-seven rallies felt let down. All these were across the country and could not complete the recruitment process due to suspension of the programme due to the pandemic.

Alarmed at these unexpected developments, the government raised the upper age to twenty-three as a one-time exception. They also announced that recruitment of *Agniveers* would start shortly. But this does not seem to have satisfied the affected people.[128] It has remained a hot topic of contestation in the run-up to the 2024 general election, with recruitment of Nepalese Gurkhas suspended,[129] and Congress vowing to scrap the scheme if elected.[130]

During the 2024 elections, it was found that this poorly formulated scheme was one of the reasons for the humiliating defeat of the BJP in the Hindi heartland.[131] Consequently, measures are afoot to consult stakeholders on how this scheme can be tweaked.

### Force levels in India and China

The Stockholm International Peace Research Institute (SIPRI) said in April 2024 that world military spending reached $2,443 billion in 2023. The five largest spenders in 2023 were the United States, China, Russia, India and Saudi Arabia which together accounted for 61 per cent of expenditure. US military expenditure was $916 billion, China's $296 billion, Russia's $109, India's $83.6 billion, and Saudi Arabia's $75.8 billion.[132]

With China's military expenditure approximately more than three times that of India, the size of their forces can also be usefully compared through data made available via *Global Firepower*:

|  | INDIA | CHINA |
| --- | --- | --- |
| Active Manpower | 1,455,550 | 2,035,000 |
| Reserves | 1,155,000 | 510,000 |
| Paramilitary | 2,527,000 | 625,000 |
| **Aircraft total** | **2,296** | **3,304** |
| Fighters | 606 | 1,207 |

| | INDIA | CHINA |
|---|---|---|
| Helicopters | 869 | 913 |
| Attack Helicopters | 37 | 281 |
| Tanks | 4,614 | 5,000 |
| Armoured Vehicles | 151,248 | 174,300 |
| Artillery: Self-propelled | 140 | 3,850 |
| Artillery: Towed | 3,243 | 1,434 |
| **Naval fleet total** | **294** | **730** |
| Aircraft Carriers | 2 | 2 |
| Submarines | 18 | 61 |
| Destroyers | 12 | 49 |
| Frigates | 12 | 42 |
| Corvettes | 18 | 72 |
| Patrol Vessels | 137 | 150 |
| Airports | 346 | 507 |

(Source: *Global Firepower*)[133]

*Would a better equipped military always win the war?*

The Ukraine war has exploded the myth that even a weaker country, which has only one third the number of military personnel and fewer than 320 fighter aircraft compared to the enemy's more than 1.3 million army and 4,000 fighter planes, would surrender in less than 72 hours. Instead, it showed the world that it can inflict crushing damage to a more powerful enemy which, according to *Newsweek*, quoting British sources, had lost as many soldiers as in the entire Afghan War (1979–89) by May 2022.[134]

It is said that the last regular war fought by the PLA was against Vietnam in 1979. The rest were all skirmishes. Compared to that, India had fought a regular war with tremendous skill in Kargil during May–July 1999, solidly defeating Pakistan.

I had written a column about the China–Vietnam war on 26 August 2020 analysing the results.[135] Communist China invaded Communist Vietnam on 17 February 1979, much to the embarrassment of the late Atal Bihari Vajpayee, then India's

External Affairs minister. Vajpayee, who had just begun his China visit to try to mend strained relations, then decided to end his mission and return to India. On 18 February 1979, Prime Minister Morarji Desai expressed "profound shock and distress over the invasion" and called for the immediate withdrawal of the Chinese forces from Vietnam.

*The New York Times* had quoted Taiwanese officials in February 1979 saying that the American decision to normalize relations with China had encouraged Beijing to undertake this invasion to irritate the Soviet Union. A story quoted much later by Japanese sources said that Deng Xiaoping, during his "charm offensive" to the West had reportedly told US President Jimmy Carter in January 1979 that "The little child is getting naughty, it's time he gets spanked."

Initially Mao's China and Communist North Vietnam had very cordial relations. Like in North Korea, China dispatched 320,000 PLA troops to help North Vietnamese legend Ho Chi Minh to fight the French colonialists and later the Americans. In 1974 China captured the Paracel Islands in the South China Sea from the anti-Communist regime in Saigon in South Vietnam. In 1975 both North and South Vietnam were joined under the Communist rule.

However, this cordial relationship was disrupted when Vietnam joined the Soviet-dominated "Comecon" for economic cooperation in 1978 and signed a mutual treaty of friendship. China branded Vietnam as the "Cuba of the East" with hegemonic intentions of dominating Southeast Asia. In December 1978, Vietnam annoyed Beijing by launching a full-scale war on the Khmer Rouge regime in Kampuchea (Cambodia), seizing its capital Phnom Penh. It toppled the brutal Pol Pot who had killed nearly two million Cambodians through forced labour and executions.

Like in India in 1962, the Sino–Vietnamese war started with border skirmishes from 25 August 1978. The real invasion started in the early hours of 17 February 1979, with 400 tanks, 1,500 artillery guns and 300,000 troops who crossed over from three directions. The PLA used the same tactics as the 1950 Korean war with human waves of "ragtag soldiers and a scorched-earth policy to completely destroy everything in their paths" as Vietnamese academic Nguyen Minh Quang had observed. Also, like in India, the Chinese suddenly withdrew on 16 March 1979, declaring that the mission was accomplished.

In the final analysis the war was futile as Vietnamese forces continued to stay in Cambodia till 1989. The PLA suffered 28,000 deaths compared to Vietnam which lost 10,000 lives. The only victory China can boast of was the absence of active Soviet intervention to help Vietnam. Yet, there were credible reports that the Soviet Union had given Vietnam equipment and live intelligence on China through their Pacific fleet stationed off the Vietnamese coast. However, from 1986 onwards the Soviet Union started reversing its policy and giving preference to mending fences with China at the expense of Vietnam.

## India's military capacity building

In 2019 the Parliamentary Standing Committee criticised the Modi government for not allotting enough funds to meet a "Two Front War."[136] The allocation of Rs 5.93 trillion in the defence budget for 2023–24 was 13.18 per cent of total Central government expenditure and 1.97 per cent of GDP. The committee noted the defence ministry's submission that the global "ideal" estimate for defence expenditure as a percentage of GDP is 3 per cent.

It said that the government should fix a "definite benchmark" percentage of GDP for the defence budget as military expenditure by neighbouring countries and the evolving global security scenario warrant such an outlay for the country to prepare for dealing with future security challenges like drones and electronic warfare systems.[137]

## Strategic Partnership Project (SP)

The Times of India said in May 2022 that not a single project has taken off under the SP model to boost indigenous defence production through tie ups with foreign armament majors even after five years of the "Make in India" project. These were to manufacture a new generation of submarines, helicopters, fighters, and battle tanks through long-term joint ventures between Indian companies and "Original Equipment Manufacturers" (OEMs) with "deep and extensive transfer of technology." One of the reasons for the lack of interest is reported to be the pricing methodology adopted in the SP model of May 2017 which failed to consider the need for assured and repeated orders.[138]

On 3 May 2022, a day before Prime Minister Modi was to visit France, the French company Naval Group announced that it was unable to participate in New Delhi's P-75I project, under which six conventional submarines were to be domestically built for the Indian Navy with AIP technology. AIP (Air-Independent Propulsion) is for non-nuclear submarines. AIP is required as presently conventional submarines, to prolong battery life, have to expose themselves to draw in air for running generators that charge their battery banks.[139]

In June 2021 India's Defence Ministry had cleared the P-75I project. Later "Requests for Proposal" (RFPs) were issued to two shortlisted Indian companies—private company Larsen and Toubro, and state-run Mazagaon Docks Limited—to tie up with one of the five shortlisted foreign companies—ThyssenKrupp Marine Systems (Germany), Navantia (Spain). Naval Group (France), Daewoo (South Korea) and Rosoboronexport (Russia).[140]

Another report said that the Russian and Spanish companies might back out. The reason appears to be reluctance to transfer the technology. Even if either the German or South Korean agrees to sign, the earliest date for the first P-75I to be commissioned could be 2032.[141] As against this Admiral Arun Prakash, former Naval Chief, said on 16 May 2022 that by 2028, Pakistan might field up to eleven AIP-equipped boats in addition to eight Yan class Chinese submarines. He blamed "policy flipflops" and "sluggish decision making" for over a decade for this situation.[142]

### Nuclear weapons capability

An August 2020 Carnegie Endowment for International Peace study on the Chinese view of India's nuclear deterrence would indicate several trends which have not appeared in Indian media, even in focussed security studies.[143] The paper's analysis of Chinese attitude toward India's nuclear deterrence is worth quoting:

> Chinese experts do not think of India in strategic terms. They see India mainly as a regional rival. The sense of superior power over India among Chinese officials and experts is long-standing and deep. Convinced that China's governance system has and will continue to outperform that of India's, Chinese experts have little doubt that China will maintain and enhance its military and nuclear advantages over India.

The findings are based on interviewing unnamed Chinese experts. There is a touch of arrogance in all their views. First of all, China does not consider India as a "strategic" rival, but only as a "regional" power. It feels that China will remain ten years ahead of India in nuclear and military advantages. "India's 'small arsenal can deter, but there is a qualitative gap' with China." Thus, most of the Chinese missiles are directed against the US to catch up with its arsenal and not against India.

True, its DF-21 missiles deployed in northwest and southwest China could be nuclear armed and could hit India. China might also have positioned its nuclear-capable DF-26 missiles (which can carry either nuclear or conventional warheads) in the southwest. There are also reports of DF-26 missiles located in Xinjiang. These could be used against India. "Yet the strategic sentiment of most Chinese experts is that China's nuclear weapons are not directed at India."

The other feeling among Chinese experts is that India's nuclear weapons programme is driven primarily for its international prestige and not intended for an offensive military aim. That is the reason for China's "relaxed" attitude, as they feel that India's growing nuclear capabilities "don't add to deterrence versus China." This attitude persisted even after India had deployed a nuclear-armed submarine, tested an anti-satellite missile and even after the news that India was developing a multiple warhead-capable ballistic missile.

The conclusion of the study is even more bewildering. It feels that this Chinese lack of sensitivity to India's views on bilateral nuclear relations has resulted in a situation which could be called "decoupled deterrence." Unlike a "security spiral" of actions and reactions between two adversaries, in a "decoupled deterrence," only the weaker power takes steps to bolster its capability in response to its perception by a bigger power. At the same time the bigger power ignores this by responding to a different threat.

Hence, in this case, India might respond to Chinese threats but not vice-versa as China is fixated only on threats from the United States. This "disinterest" might provoke India to boost its strategic capability and nuclear arsenal as India's policy is "inward-looking," more so under Prime Minister Modi: "India has set its standard for credible nuclear deterrence, independent from the capabilities and postures of its rivals."

Two more findings of this study based on Chinese opinion are relevant. Nuclear weapons have a "stabilising effect" and both powers would keep conventional conflicts under control. The Chinese have a conventional thinking that "big powers with large territories are very unlikely to face existential threats, and, therefore, it is unnecessary to resort to nuclear weapons." They also believe that the Indian civilian-controlled system of "command and control" of nuclear weapons lowers the risk of escalation. Also, Indian politicians clearly understand the need to avoid a nuclear conflict.

Secondly the treacherous, mountainous terrain would prevent any conflict widening into a "large-scale, high tempo conventional war" when neither side possesses "clear, conventional superiority" over the other even when locally some features might help either party. As far as China is concerned, it would fill in any capability gap with advanced transportation infrastructure to mobilise more troops from its hinterland. Yet neither country "could quickly overwhelm the other in a conventional conflict which reduces the pressure to escalate to nuclear weapons."

### The Nuclear Suppliers Group: How much India depends on the Chinese "nod"

On 7 June 2022, India's foreign minister S. Jaishankar told foreign envoys stationed in New Delhi that India would like to join the Nuclear Suppliers Group (NSG), overcoming "political" impediments. As is well known, the NSG was formed in 1974 after India's first Pokhran test, when it was felt that India's nuclear device had been built using civilian technology supplied to the country under the American "atoms for peace" programme initiated by President Dwight D. Eisenhower in 1953.[144]

The aim of the NSG was to prevent civilian nuclear material, equipment, and technology from reaching countries that could use it for making nuclear weapons. There are now forty-eight members. NSG member states are expected to refuse to export nuclear or nuclear-related technology to countries that do not agree to implement numerous monitoring and verification measures.[145] Almost all the big countries, like the US, UK, France and Russia, have backed India's membership. Admission is through consensus. However, China has been blocking India's entry on the ground that India has not signed the Nuclear Non-Proliferation Treaty (NPT).

The real reason for China's "hold" might be different. As mentioned in the above Carnegie analysis, China was noticeably dismissive of any nuclear threat from India even during the 2020 border stand-off as it felt that India's indigenous military technology was "significantly behind China's and that China will continue widening the gulf between the two countries' conventional and nuclear capabilities." On the other hand, China feels that India as an NSG member would enhance US–India defence technology cooperation and allow Washington to influence the Indo-Pacific region. That seems to be the real reason.

### The China–India border problem

On the eve of the second anniversary of the 2020 Galwan clashes, which was the most serious incident since 1962, Lt General D.S. Hooda, former Northern Army Commander, said that an "uneasy" stalemate exists even after fifteen rounds of Corps Commander-level talks and several political-level meetings between both sides. Yet complete disengagement had not been achieved. For the immediate future he did not see any possibility of restoring the status quo ante.[146]

A report emerged on 26 June 2022 that China had upgraded its manpower and firepower on Line of Actual Control (LAC). In the western sector the accommodation capacity, which was earlier 20,000, has been upgraded to 120,000 billets. They have set up captive solar energy and small hydro-electric power projects along the LAC, all within 100 kms. They have also inducted ZTQ 15, third generation light tanks (replacing first generation) and upgraded their APCs by inducting the latest ZTL-II types. Similar upgradation of air defence systems was also reported.[147]

*The Guardian* (UK) reported on 30 May 2024 that China introduced a mechanical canine with an automatic rifle on its back during their "Golden Dragon" joint military drills with Cambodia. It said that it resembled the Boston Dynamics' "BigDog," developed as a mechanical quadruped as a potential mechanical pack animal for the US army.[148]

*Meanwhile, China recruits*

On 29 November 2021, Xinhua had reported Xi Jinping's announcement on military modernisation to win "future wars." The aim is to display a dazzling performance by 2027, the PLA centenary. The intention is also to upgrade the PLA into a modern military on par with the USA by 2050. To this end Xi announced the recruitment of 300,000 additional personnel for "frontline positions" and also a plan to upgrade military personnel's scientific, literacy and technological knowledge.

In 2012, Xi was responsible for reducing the PLA's strength from 230,000 to 200,000 by cutting out its flab: non-combat units, staff in veterans' homes and general political and logistical branches. The present modernisation programme would include upgrading the PLA's airborne troops from division level to brigades and adding the number of pilots to fly the new generation fighter jets like Chengdu J-20s, J-16s and J-10s. The PLA marine corps would increase from 20,000 to 100,000. Some of these would be stationed abroad.[149]

Is China ready with the world's first anti-hypersonic missile system? On 2 June 2022, China claimed that it had successfully developed artificial intelligence technology that can predict the trajectory of a hypersonic glide missile as it approaches a target at speeds exceeding five times that of sound. This claim, as reported by the *South China Morning Post*, was made by Zhang Junbiao, a computer scientist from the early warning intelligence department of the Air Force Early Warning Academy in Wuhan. It also said that even the US has not been able to develop this so far.[150]

## *Possibility of future clashes with China*

### 1. India's "Great Nicobar project"

A Rs. 72,000 "Infra Upgrade" at the Great Nicobar Island in southeastern Bay of Bengal, close to the Malacca Strait, the main channel which connects the Indian Ocean with the Pacific, has become controversial in India. The Congress, the main opposition party, describes it as a "grave threat" to the island's indigenous inhabitants and fragile ecosystem. The upgrade, described by the media to convert the island into "India's Hongkong", incorporates a container transhipment terminal, a greenfield international airport with a peak-hour capacity to handle 4,000 passengers, a township, and a gas- and solar-based power plant located on 16,610 hectares. The Congress also warns that it is in a "seismically volatile zone that saw permanent subsidence of about 15 ft during the 2004 Tsunami."[151] *The Eurasian Times* said on 28 February 2024 that the upgrade was "believed to be largely driven by China's escalating influence in the Indian Ocean, aims to capitalize on the island's strategic location for security and commerce."[152]

### 2. "Resolve Tibet Act" (2024)

The "Resolve Tibet Act", amending the "Tibet Policy Act" of 2002, was passed by the US House of Representatives on 12 June 2024. The Senate had already passed it in May. President Biden signed it on 12 July. The amendment gives enhanced powers to US State

Department officials to actively and directly counter disinformation about Tibet from the Chinese government, and to counter claims that Tibet has been part of China since "ancient times." It also empowers them to coordinate with other governments in multilateral efforts toward the goal of a negotiated agreement on Tibet. China, which considers this as interference into its domestic affairs, has asked President Biden not to approve the bill. As the first step towards a move, former US House Speaker Nancy Pelosi reached India on 18 June among the delegation of senior US Congress leaders led by Michael McCaul, chairman of the US House Foreign Affairs Committee, to meet the Dalai Lama.[153]

The Chinese embassy in New Delhi reacted sharply to this, claiming that Xizang (shorter version of Tibet Autonomous Region) has always been part of China since ancient times. It may be recalled that Nancy Pelosi's official visit to Taiwan in August 2022 as Speaker had created severe turbulence in China–Taiwan relations, enhancing Chinese belligerent military presence in the Taiwan Strait, which is continuing even now. In a similar manner, it is not inconceivable that China would protest to India against the presence of US lawmakers or foreign officials in furtherance to the "Resolve Tibet Act."

## China–India relations by 2047

Our story had started in 1988 with the late Rajiv Gandhi's visit to Beijing. The reason why the late prime minister took the initiative to visit China was not because he wanted to bow before the "Middle Kingdom" but because he felt, like his grandfather or for that matter like US President Richard Nixon, that China was too large a global power to be ignored. Rajiv Gandhi had handled the 1986–87 Sumdorong Chu standoff between both countries with great firmness. He could have handled similar incursions with equal firmness. He was not egged on by foreign powers to make this visit. Nor did he agree with his advisers that he should not visit.

Yet, in the modern context certain doubts remain for policy formulation.

*Is China a "revisionist" or "status quo" power?*

In 2014 Professor Walter Russel Mead analysed the post-Cold War situation in *Foreign Affairs* and said that an "Axis of *Weevils*" had emerged with Russia, China, and Iran who were pushing back against the political settlement of the Cold War. He had called them "Revisionist" powers against a Western-inspired, US dominated "Status Quo" world order which had wanted to promote "the liberal world order, not playing classical geopolitics."[154] I feel that this issue needs to be revisited now to examine how the relationship between China and India may transform by the middle of the twenty-first century.

US Secretary of Defence James Mattis had agreed with Mead's assessment on 18 January 2018, while unveiling the "Pentagon Defence Strategy." He called Russia and China "Revisionist Powers" and said that the focus of US military strategy was shifting away from terrorism toward what he called "great power competition." He had said that China was using predatory economics to intimidate neighbours and militarising the South China Sea.[155]

In February 2018 the Australian Strategic Policy Institute (ASPI) felt that the US was a "Status Quo" power "led by a revisionist President" (Donald Trump) while China "loves the current status quo, while liking how the tide of change flows its way."[156] The ASPI had then reminded its readers what Henry Kissinger had said in his book *World Order* (2014) that China and the US were "indispensable pillars of world order" who should achieve "an unprecedented blend of partnership and military balance in Asia's modern system."

Professor Rana Mitter, in his review of Kissinger's book, had acknowledged that it was the US, more than anybody else, which had ended China's isolation from the "family of nations" through President Richard Nixon and his Secretary of State Henry Kissinger in 1972.[157] This was the beginning of China's quest as a global economic power through its admission to the WTO which would not have been possible without US backing. That was the start of China's attempts to be a "Status Quo" power, abiding by the world order. I may add here that China has contributed to the status quo and regional stability by mediating and restoring diplomatic relations between Saudi Arabia and Iran in August 2023, which Western powers could not do.

However, as I pointed out earlier in this book, these analysts had ignored what Jawaharlal Nehru had told US Ambassador Chester Bowles in New Delhi in 1951 that "China was potentially aggressive and expansionist" and "the best hope was an attempt to divide Russia and China—or if this was not possible, at least to modify China's viewpoint through outside contacts and thus convince China it did not need to depend entirely on Russia."

This was recorded by Ambassador Howard B. Schaffer in his biography of Chester Bowles.[158] Schaffer also added that Bowles had sent this to the highest level in US government through diplomatic telegrams. Nehru's subsequent actions of helping China especially by securing its rightful place as a permanent member of the UN Security Council, even by forgoing an American invitation to India in 1950 to take that place, were in continuation of this policy.

Yet China punished Nehru over a misunderstanding that he had, under Nikita Khrushchev's instigation, invaded China as I discussed in Chapter 2. In 1971 and 1972 China considered India as the Soviet Union's surrogate as the transcripts of Zhou–Enlai–Kissinger and Zhou–Enlai–Nixon talks indicate. Zhou condemned Nehru for claiming "their" Aksai-Chin plateau from 1956 onwards under Nikita Khrushchev's instigation.

Also, as Bertil Lintner had said in his book *China's India War*, the real reason was "not a response to India's outpost in Dhola, but a part of China's strategy to establish its international political dominance." He said that Mao took advantage of President John F. Kennedy's preoccupation with the Cuban missile crisis to attack India. Also, China's intention was not to occupy India's lands but to do a "limited action aimed at punishing India, dethroning it from the leadership of the Non-Aligned Movement." It was also to ridicule India for seeking military help from the "Capitalist world" even as it pretended to lead the non-aligned nations.[159]

*Would China indulge in fresh border rows with India?*

In a similar manner it is not unimaginable that China under Xi Jinping would punish Modi for several reasons at an opportune time. The first and foremost reason is that Modi is ruling India, which is the only country which could thwart China's regional political, economic, and perhaps security ambitions over Nepal, Bhutan, Sri Lanka, Maldives, Myanmar, not to speak of Pakistan and Afghanistan. Secondly, India could tilt the scales to some extent in Tibet, its sensitive underbelly, which has now come into the global limelight with the 2024 Tibet Policy Bill passed by US Congress. Also, India in partnership with global powers could checkmate China through the Quad, where Modi was seen "front leading" the Group as the senior-most member during the May 2022 summit in Tokyo.[160]

A hint of China's resentment against India was indicated by Xi Jinping on 23 June 2022 at the annual BRICS Summit (Brazil, Russia, China, India, and South Africa) in Beijing. He said that the world "must abandon Cold War mentality" and "bloc confrontation." Xi's reference to the Cold War and blocs was meant for Modi to describe the Quad, which China says is an extension of NATO.[161]

Some analysts feel that China would not fight a border war with India because of the booming bilateral trade. This is not very convincing since it is India which depends on China for the supply of goods vital for its economy like pharmaceuticals, whereas China imports from India only ores, seafoods and cotton, which can be sourced from other countries. Even after the 2020 Galwan incidents, India kept on importing goods from China, even as it was taking steps to curb Chinese influence on its economy. Also, China knows well that the rest of the world would not physically intervene in India's favour even if it commits a serious border aggression as its predatory activities in the South China Sea and the template of Russian aggression on Ukraine have revealed.

At the same time, India cannot catch up with China in any strategic area without first achieving a domestic concord and internal peace by sincerely implementing Prime Minister Modi's original slogan *"Sabka Saath, Sabka Vikas"*—"Everyone together, everyone's advancement"—by treating all citizens, irrespective of their religious or political differences, as one family.

# EPILOGUE

Bangladesh Prime Minister Sheikh Hasina Wazed's sudden flight to India from Dhaka on 5 August 2024, after weeks of protests by students and her political opponents, has resulted in considerable policy uncertainties for the Indian government. Her political opponent, Nobel laureate Muhammad Yunus, has been sworn in as the head of a new caretaker government.

Hasina's tenure from 2009 to 2024 as the head of the Awami League government had seen stability in bilateral relations, especially on the security front, in comparison with earlier regimes, which were marked by deep antipathy towards India. Between 1977 and 2009, the intelligence service, Directorate General of Forces Intelligence (DGFI), was seen actively helping hardcore Islamists like Harkat-ul-Jihad al-Islami and other extremist groups to operate against India. DGFI, in alliance with Pakistan's Inter-Services Intelligence, had also aided India's northeast militants like the United Liberation Front of Asom, the Muslim Liberation Tigers and others to launch operations against India by giving them sanctuaries.[1] This had totally stopped during Prime Minister Hasina's long rule.

Hasina's government had also skilfully managed closer relations with China, including the BRI, although some analysts had said that this association had impacted India's interests. MERICS (Mercator Institute for China Studies), the official partner of the Munich Security Conference, said on 8 August 2022, quoting a 2014 Pew Research Center survey, that 77% of Bangladeshis had viewed

China positively, the highest positive rating for all countries while only 43% had preferred the US as an ally. India was seen as a potential threat.

Bangladesh's military and business leaders were the strongest advocates of deeper Bangladesh–China relations. Their military planners saw a convergence with China in strategic calculations as India "engulfs Bangladesh on three sides" and hostile Myanmar shares the only other land border. In 2015, China replaced India as Bangladesh's top trading partner, after India had held that position for forty years. China accounted for 34% of Bangladesh's total imports in 2019.[2]

On 15 August 2024, *The Washington Post* claimed that US and Indian leaders had indeed discussed the troubling situation in Bangladesh one year before Sheikh Hasina's flight to India. The paper said: "As India grapples with the shock of suddenly losing one of its closest allies, Indian foreign policy circles and media have been awash with speculation that Washington orchestrated the removal of Hasina, who has long had a chilly relationship with the United States. U.S. officials have staunchly denied the claim."[3]

*Vappala Balachandran, August 2024*

# NOTES

MISE-EN-SCÈNE

1.  Fu Xiaoqiang, "Today's China-India summit may herald 'Asian Century'", *The Nation*, 26 April 2018, https://www.nationthailand.com/perspective/30344085.

2.  Praveen Davar, "Rajiv Gandhi's 'Wall Breaking' China Visit", *National Herald*, 20 August 2020, https://www.nationalheraldindia.com/opinion/rajiv-gandhis-wall-breaking-china-visit.

3.  Stephen P. Cohen, "India Rising", *Brookings*, 1 June 2000, https://www.brookings.edu/articles/india-rising/.

4.  Arvind Vermani, "A Tripolar World: India, China and US", *Indian Council for Research on International Economic Relations*, 18 May 2005, https://www.icrier.org/pdf/TripolarWrld_IHC5.pdf.

5.  N. Dayasindhu, "Leaders like F C Kohli laid the foundation for India's IT boom", *The Indian Express*, 2 December 2020, https://indianexpress.com/article/opinion/columns/f-c-kohli-death-tata-consultancy-services-ceo-india-it-boom-7075903/.

6.  Aarish Ansari, "When India last hosted the Asian Games: 1982 a memorable and colourful turn of events", *Olympics.com*, 1 May 2022, https://olympics.com/en/news/asian-games-1982-india.

7.  CIOL Bureau, "KPP Nambiar, the unsung giant of India", *CIOL*, 15 September 2003, https://www.ciol.com/kpp-nambiar-unsung-giant-india/.

8.  Ashok Gulati, "Standing up to China will require not only matching its military might but also economic prowess", *Indian Express*, 3 August 2020, https://indianexpress.com/article/opinion/columns/india-chian-dispute-military-economic-power-6536498/.

9. Dilip Bobb, "Prime Minister Rajiv Gandhi's visit to China marks a new beginning in bilateral relations", *India Today*, 15 January 1989, https://www.indiatoday.in/magazine/cover-story/story/19890115-prime-minister-rajiv-gandhi-visit-to-china-marks-a-new-beginning-in-bilateral-relations-815628-1989-01-15.

10. National Intelligence Council, "Global Trends 2030: Alternative Worlds", US Government, 2012, https://www.dni.gov/files/documents/GlobalTrends_2030.pdf.

11. National Intelligence Council, "Global Trends 2040: A More Contested World", US Government, 2021, https://www.dni.gov/files/ODNI/documents/assessments/GlobalTrends_2040.pdf.

12. Express News Service, "Arun Shourie: Deeper than this govt… systems have decayed over time… (But) Mrs Gandhi had some shame", *Indian Express*, 3 November 2020, https://indianexpress.com/article/india/arun-shourie-interview-idea-exchange-indira-gandhi-modi-govt-6912813/.

13. "India can overtake China in 4 years, if we can correct mistakes: Swamy", *The New Indian Express*, 6 October 2019, https://www.newindianexpress.com/cities/kochi/2019/oct/06/india-can-overtake-china-in-4-years-if-we-can-correct-mistakes-swamy-2043810.html.

14. DNA Web Team, "Indian economy to grow at historic 12.5% in 2021, to surpass China: IMF", *DNA*, 7 April 2021, https://www.dnaindia.com/business/report-indian-economy-to-grow-at-historic-125-in-2021-to-surpass-china-imf-2885083.

15. ET Bureau, "If China again carries out a Galwan, they will get it in same coin as last time: CDS Bipin Rawat", *The Economic Times*, 12 November 2021, https://economictimes.indiatimes.com/news/defence/if-china-again-carries-out-a-galwan-they-will-get-it-in-same-coin-as-last-time-cds-bipin-rawat/articleshow/87657202.cms.

16. ANI, "Indian Army prepared for a two and a half front war: Army Chief General Bipin Rawat", *The Indian Express*, 8 June 2017, https://indianexpress.com/article/india/indian-army-prepared-for-a-two-and-a-half-front-war-army-chief-general-bipin-rawat-4694292/. Half war is, according to Gen. Rawat, terrorism.

17. Carrie Gracie, "Qin Shi Huang: The ruthless emperor who burned books", *BBC News*, 15 October 2012, https://www.bbc.com/news/magazine-19922863.

18. J.K. Fairbank and S.Y. Têng, "On the Ch'ing Tributary System", *Harvard Journal of Asiatic Studies* 6, 2 (1941): 135–246, p. 137.

19. Ananth Krishnan, "China's nationalist turn under Xi Jinping", *The Hindu*, 21 September 2020, https://www.thehindu.com/opinion/op-ed/chinas-nationalist-turn-under-xi-jinping/article32655108.ece.

20. Doug Bandow, "Xi Jinping Wants to Become the New Mao", *Cato Institute*, 26 May 2020, https://www.cato.org/commentary/xi-jinping-wants-become-new-mao.

21. Pranab Dhal Samanta, "Jaish-e-Mohammed, Lashkar-e-Taiba back with Taliban, set up 11 camps since takeover: UNSC Report", *The Economic Times*, 30 May 2022, https://economictimes.indiatimes.com/news/defence/jaish-e-mohammed-lashkar-e-taiba-back-with-taliban-set-up-11-camps-since-takeover-unsc-report/articleshow/91875669.cms.

22. Scroll Staff, "India asked Washington not to bring up China's border transgressions: Former US ambassador", *Scroll.in*, 2 March 2022, https://scroll.in/latest/1018580/india-asked-washington-not-to-mention-chinas-border-transgressions-former-us-ambassador-to-india.

23. Express Web Desk, "Congress digs out PM Modi's 2013 tweet on India-China: 'Why Indian soldiers were withdrawn from own land'", *The Indian Express*, 8 July 2020, https://indianexpress.com/article/india/congress-reminds-pm-modi-of-his-old-tweet-on-india-china-asks-why-indian-soldiers-were-withdrawn-from-their-own-land-6495877/.

24. "China overtakes US to become India's top trading partner in FY24", *The Economic Times*, 12 May 2024, https://economictimes.indiatimes.com/news/economy/foreign-trade/china-overtakes-us-to-become-indias-top-trading-partner-in-fy-2023-24/articleshow/110049223.cms.

25. TNN, "'China violated written pacts', Jaishankar blames Beijing for tension at LAC", *The Times of India*, 13 February 2022, https://timesofindia.indiatimes.com/india/beijing-violated-written-pacts-says-jaishankar/articleshow/89534947.cms.

26. "Quad Joint Leaders' Statement", 24 May 2022, https://www.whitehouse.gov/briefing-room/statements-releases/2022/05/24/quad-joint-leaders-statement/.

27. Manish Chand, "Without India and Modi, Quad could not fly: Former Abe adviser", *The Sunday Guardian*, 28 May 2022, https://www.sundayguardianlive.com/news/without-india-modi-quad-not-fly-former-abe-adviser.

## INTRODUCTION

1. "Prime Ministerial Visits to China", Ministry of External Affairs, Government of India, https://mea.gov.in/photo-features.htm?895/Prime+Ministerial+Visits+to+China.

2. Dilip Bobb, "Prime Minister Rajiv Gandhi's visit to China marks a new beginning in bilateral relations", *India Today*, 15 January 1989, https://

www.indiatoday.in/magazine/cover-story/story/19890115-prime-minister-rajiv-gandhi-visit-to-china-marks-a-new-beginning-in-bilateral-relations-815628-1989-01-15.

3.  Praveen Davar, "Rajiv Gandhi's 'Wall Breaking' China Visit", *National Herald*, 20 August 2020, https://www.nationalheraldindia.com/opinion/rajiv-gandhis-wall-breaking-china-visit. The book is out of print.

4.  *Security and Development Assistance: Hearings Before the Committee on Foreign Relations*, United States Senate, Ninety-ninth Congress, First Session, 1985, volume 4, p. 541.

5.  Arvind Vermani, "A Tripolar World: India, China and US", Indian Council for Research on International Economic Relations, 18 May 2005, https://www.icrier.org/pdf/TripolarWrld_IHC5.pdf.

6.  Bobb, "Prime Minister Rajiv Gandhi's visit".

7.  Although Deng appeared modest, he had actually hidden his covert global power quest so ably described by French journalist Roger Faligot, first in 2008 in French and in 2019 in English. Roger Faligot, *Les Services Secrets Chinois* (2008); English translation *Chinese Spies: From Chairman Mao to Xi Jinping*, London: Hurst & Company, 2019, which I had reviewed for *Outlook*: https://magazine.outlookindia.com/story/books-a-sea-lamprey-waits-for-them/301982.

8.  Chengxin Pan, "The Asian/Chinese Century from the Chinese Perspective", *Griffith Asia Quarterly* 1, 1 (2013): 30–52, https://research-repository.griffith.edu.au/bitstream/handle/10072/340294/260-701-1-PB.pdf.

9.  *Deng Xiaoping Wenxuan* (Selected Works of Deng Xiaoping), Vol. 3, Beijing: Renmin chubanshe (People's Publishing House), 1993, p. 281

10. Bobb, "Prime Minister Rajiv Gandhi's visit".

11. *Deng Xiaoping Wenxuan*, p. 281

12. N. Dayasindhu, "Leaders like F C Kohli laid the foundation for India's IT boom", *The Indian Express*, 2 December 2020, https://indianexpress.com/article/opinion/columns/f-c-kohli-death-tata-consultancy-services-ceo-india-it-boom-7075903/.

13. National Intelligence Council, "Mapping the Global Future", US Government, 2004, https://www.dni.gov/files/documents/Global%20Trends_Mapping%20the%20Global%20Future%202020%20Project.pdf.

14. IANS, "India, US need to jointly confront China's threats to security: Pompeo in New Delhi", *National Herald*, 27 October 2020, https://www.nationalheraldindia.com/national/india-us-need-to-jointly-confront-chinas-threats-to-security-pompeo-in-new-delhi.

15. Suhasini Haider, "LAC standoff | India will not accept less than bottom line in talks with China, says Jaishankar", *The Hindu*, 2 December 2020, https://

www.thehindu.com/news/national/s-jaishankar-interview-on-india-china-talks/article33233775.ece.

1.   A LONG HISTORY OF CONNECTIONS

1.   Michael Edwards, *A History of India*, The New English Library, 1961, pp. 58–60.

2.   Alain Daniélou, *A Brief History of India*, Simon and Schuster, 2003, p. 111.

3.   H.G. Wells, *The Outline of History*, Volume 1, Doubleday & Co., 1971, p. 484.

4.   Daniélou, *A Brief History of India*.

5.   Wells, *The Outline of History*, vol. 1, p. 339.

6.   Kelly Pang, "Buddhism in China—Ancient History to Beliefs Today", *China Highlights*, 21 November 2023, https://www.chinahighlights.com/travelguide/buddhism.htm.

7.   Barbara O'Brien, "History of Buddhism in China: The First Thousand Years", *Learn Religions*, 25 June 2019, https://www.learnreligions.com/buddhism-in-china-the-first-thousand-years-450147.

8.   *The Hutchinson Encyclopaedia*, Helicon, 1995, p. 228.

9.   Victor H. Mair, Sanping Chen, Frances Wood, *Chinese Lives: The People Who Made a Civilization*, Thames & Hudson, 2013.

10.  R.C. Majumdar, "Intercourse with the Outside World", in R.C. Majumdar (ed.), *The History and Culture of the Indian People, volume 3: The Classical Age*, Bombay: Bharatiya Vidya Bhavan, 1970 [1954], p. 610.

11.  Ibid., p. 611.

12.  Sadguru, "Who Was Bodhidharma and Why Did He Go to China?", https://isha.sadhguru.org/en/wisdom/article/bodhidharma.

13.  R.C. Majumdar, "Intercourse with the Outside World", p. 614.

14.  Ibid., p. 616.

15.  Ibid., p. 618.

16.  R.C. Majumdar, "Harsha-Vardhana and His Time", in R.C. Majumdar (ed.), *The History and Culture of the Indian People*, p. 120.

17.  Sujan Chinoy, "Tribute to a true Ambassador", *The Hindu*, 17 April 2010, https://www.thehindu.com/opinion/op-ed/Tribute-to-a-true-Ambassador/article16366997.ece.

18.  V.V. Paranjpe, "How to Understand China", Indira Gandhi National Centre for the Arts, n.d., http://ignca.gov.in/how-to-undersand-china-v-v-paranjpe/.

19.  Ibid.

20.  R.C. Majumdar, "Harsha-Vardhana and His Time", p. 120.

21.  Will Durant, *The Story of Civilization, vol. I: Our Oriental Heritage*, Simon & Schuster, 1954 [1935], p. 797.

22. R.C. Majumdar, "Harsha-Vardhana and His Time", p. 126.

23. John W. Garver, "China's Decision for War with India in 1962", in Alastair Iain Johnston and Robert S. Ross (eds), *New Directions in the Study of China's Foreign Policy*, Stanford University Press, 2006, pp. 86–130.

24. R.C. Majumdar, "Harsha-Vardhana and His Time", p. 130.

25. Nirupama Subramanian, "Explained: Going back 1300 years, the story of Mahabalipuram's China connection", *Indian Express*, 11 October 2019, https://indianexpress.com/article/explained/explained-going-back-1300-yrs-story-of-mahabalipurams-china-connection-6061391/.

26. Ibid.

27. H. Adabiya, "Kollam Port: An emporium of Chinese trade", *Advance Research Journal of Social Science* 9, 2 (2018): 254–7, http://researchjournal.co.in/upload/assignments/9_254-257.pdf.

28. Ibid.

29. Ullattil Manmadhan, "Zheng He: The Chinese at Calicut", *Peepul Tree*, 16 March 2021, https://www.livehistoryindia.com/story/cover-story/zheng-he/.

30. R.C. Majumdar, "Intercourse with the Outside World", p. 622.

31. "Bolor", *JatLand*, n.d., https://www.jatland.com/home/Bolor.

32. R.C. Majumdar, "Intercourse with the Outside World", p. 623.

33. Adabiya, "Kollam Port".

34. Manmadhan, "Zheng He: The Chinese at Calicut". "Junks" are Chinese ships with fully battened sails.

35. It is not clear how "Zamorin" (Anglicized word for "Samoothiri") originated. According to Kerala historian Sreedhara Menon, the reference to the king was first used by Ibn Battuta.

36. Giovanni Andornino, "The Nature and Linkages of China's Tributary System under the Ming and Qing Dynasties", Working Papers of the Global Economic History Network (GEHN) No. 21/06, London School of Economics and Political Science, 2006, https://www.lse.ac.uk/Economic-History/Assets/Documents/Research/GEHN/GEHNWP21-GA.pdf.

37. J.K. Fairbank and S.Y. Têng, "On the Ch'ing Tributary System", *Harvard Journal of Asiatic Studies* 6, 2 (1941): 135–246.

38. R.C. Majumdar, H.C. Raychaudhuri and Kalikinkar Datta, *An Advanced History of India*, Macmillan & Co., 1985 [1946], p. 309.

39. "The Travels of Ibn Battuta: A Virtual Tour", Office of Resources for International and Area Studies, UC Berkeley, https://orias.berkeley.edu/resources-teachers/travels-ibn-battuta.

40. "History of Opium Cultivation", Central Bureau of Narcotics, Government of India, http://www.cbn.nic.in/en/opium/overview/.

41.  Soutik Biswas, "How Britain's opium trade impoverished Indians", *BBC News*, 5 September 2019, https://www.bbc.com/news/world-asia-india-49404024.

42.  "Red Fear: Qing China and the Government of India", *The New Indian Express*, 14 November 2020, https://www.newindianexpress.com/magazine/2020/nov/15/red-fear-qing-china-and-the-government-of-india-2223007.html.

43.  Margaret Macmillan, *Paris 1919: Six months that changed the world*, New York: Random House, 2003, p. 49.

44.  The Editors of Encyclopaedia Britannica, "United Front", *Encyclopaedia Britannica*, 18 September 2018, https://www.britannica.com/topic/United-Front-Chinese-history-1937-1945.

45.  Vappala Balachandran, *A Life in Shadow: The Secret Story of A.C.N. Nambiar*, Roli Books, 2016, pp. 36–60.

46.  Zareen Fatima, "When Subhas Chandra Bose sent the 'Indian Medical Mission' to China against Japan", *Heritage Times*, 22 January 2021, https://heritagetimes.in/when-subhas-chandra-bose-sent-the-indian-medical-mission-to-china-against-japan/.

47.  Agnes Smedley, *Battle Hymn of China*, New York, Alfred A. Knopf, 1943, p. 230.

48.  R.L. Duffus, "The March of the Famous Eighth Route Army", *The New York Times*, 10 July 1938, https://www.nytimes.com/1938/07/10/archives/the-march-of-the-famous-eighth-route-army-in-china-agnes-smedley.html; a review of Agnes Smedley's book.

49.  TNN, "Mao Zedong letter to Dr Dwarkanath Kotnis kin restored by China, to be unveiled at Mumbai University", *The Times of India*, 8 January 2017, https://timesofindia.indiatimes.com/city/mumbai/mao-letter-to-kotnis-kin-restored-by-china-to-be-unveiled-at-univ/articleshow/56396479.cms.

50.  Ipsita Chakravarty, "The Chinese Mahatma: Tan Yun-Shan and a forgotten 'plea for Asia'", *Scroll.in*, 29 November 2020, https://scroll.in/article/977591/the-chinese-mahatma-tan-yun-shan-and-a-forgotten-plea-for-asia.

51.  Balachandran, *A Life in Shadow*, pp. 116–17

52.  Guido Samarani, "Shaping the Future of Asia: Chiang Kai-shek, Nehru and China-India Relations During the Second World War Period", Working papers in contemporary Asian studies; No. 11, Centre for East and South-East Asian Studies, Lund University, 2005 https://lucris.lub.lu.se/ws/portalfiles/portal/4571404/3128707.pdf.

53.  "Spanish Civil War", *Making Britain: Discover how South Asians shaped the nation, 1870–1950*, The Open University, n.d., https://www5.open.ac.uk/research-projects/making-britain/content/spanish-civil-war.

54.  Samarani, "Shaping the Future of Asia".

55. Ramachandra Guha, "Jawaharlal Nehru: A Study in Failure?", Harvard–Yenching Institute Working Paper Series, 2011, pp. 2–3, https://www.harvard-yenching.org/wp-content/uploads/legacy_files/featurefiles/Ramachandra%20Guha_Jawaharlal%20Nehru%20and%20China.pdf.

56. Samarani, "Shaping the Future of Asia".

57. V.P. Menon, *The Transfer of Power in India*, Orient Longman, 1957, p. 114.

58. Donovan Webster, *The Burma Road: The Epic Story of the China–Burma–India Theater in World War II*, New York, Farrar, Straus and Giroux, 2003, pp. 158–9.

59. Ibid., p. 164.

60. Barbara W. Tuchman, *Stilwell and the American Experience in China 1911–45*, Bantam Books, 1972, p. 477.

61. Samarani, "Shaping the Future of Asia".

62. Phillips Talbot, "As the British Empire Was Falling Apart, Gandhi Gave This Advice to the Rest of Asia", *The New Republic*, 28 April 1947, https://newrepublic.com/article/120516/1947-india-conference-marked-end-colonialism.

63. M.K. Gandhi, "Speech to the Inter-Asian Relations Conference", 2 April 1947, published in *Harijan*, 20 April 1947, https://www.mkgandhi.org/speeches/interasian.htm.

64. The Editors, "Chinese Civil War: Nationalist collapse and the establishment of the People's Republic of China (1949)", *Encyclopaedia Britannica*, n.d., https://www.britannica.com/event/Chinese-Civil-War/Nationalist-collapse-and-the-establishment-of-the-Peoples-Republic-of-China-1949.

65. Sankalp Gurjar, "Time to Resurrect the Asian Relations Conference", *The Diplomat*, 18 April 2017, https://thediplomat.com/2017/04/time-to-resurrect-the-asian-relations-conference/.

2. DIPLOMACY AND DIVERGENCE

1. "Top Ten Places to See Cherry Blossoms in China this Spring", *The China Guide*, 8 May 2020, https://www.thechinaguide.com/blog/top-ten-places-to-see-cherry-blossoms-in-china-this-spring.

2. "The Meaning of Cherry Blossoms in Japan: Life, Death and Renewal", *Not Without My Passport*, 2 April 2016, https://notwithoutmypassport.com/cherry-blossom-meaning-in-japan/.

3. V.V. Paranjpe, "How to Understand China", Indira Gandhi National Centre for the Arts, n.d., http://ignca.gov.in/how-to-undersand-china-v-v-paranjpe/.

4. Jawaharlal Nehru, "Note on Visit to China and Indo-China", 14 November 1954, Wilson Center Digital Archive, https://digitalarchive.wilsoncenter.org/document/jawaharlal-nehru-note-visit-china-and-indo-china.

5.　John W. Garver, "China's Decision for War with India in 1962", in Alastair Iain Johnston and Robert S. Ross (eds), *New Directions in the Study of China's Foreign Policy*, Stanford University Press, 2006, pp. 86–130, p. 115.

6.　Guido Samarani, "Shaping the Future of Asia: Chiang Kai-shek, Nehru and China-India Relations During the Second World War Period", Working papers in contemporary Asian studies; No. 11, Centre for East and South-East Asian Studies, Lund University, 2005.

7.　Vappala Balachandran, *A Life in Shadow: The Secret Story of A.C.N. Nambiar*, Roli Books, 2016, pp. 116–17.

8.　"Exchange of views between Generalissimo Chiang Kai-shek and President Roosevelt regarding situation in India", Office of the Historian, Foreign Service Institute, United States Department of State, https://history.state.gov/historicaldocuments/frus1942China/comp17.

9.　AAP–Reuter, "Asian Conference Recommends Transfer Complete Power to Indonesia", *The Morning Bulletin*, 24 January 1949, https://trove.nla.gov.au/newspaper/article/56892037.

10.　John F. Burns, "Biju Patnaik, 81: Daring Pilot-Patriot of India, *The New York Times*, 21 April 1997, https://www.nytimes.com/1997/04/21/world/biju-patnaik-81-daring-pilot-patriot-of-india.html.

11.　"NSC 98/1 January 22, 1951", quoted by Ambassador Howard B. Schaffer, *Chester Bowles: New Dealer in the Cold War*, Prentice-Hall of India, 1994, pp. 51–2.

12.　Andrew Glass, "Prime Minister Nehru visits Capitol Hill, October 13, 1949", *Politico*, 13 October 2015, https://www.politico.com/story/2015/10/prime-minister-nehru-visits-capitol-hill-october-13-1949-214690.

13.　Schaffer, *Chester Bowles*, p. 80.

14.　Ibid., pp. 80–84.

15.　Kevin Rudd, "How Ukraine fits into China's long game", *Australian Financial Review*, 25 February 2022, https://www.kevinrudd.com/media/how-ukraine-fits-into-chinas-long-game-australian-financial-review.

16.　"Bill of Rights in Action 17 3 b: Truman, MacArthur, and the Korean War", *Teach Democracy* (formerly Constitutional Rights Foundation), n.d., https://www.u.crf-usa.org/online-lessons/bill-of-rights-in-action/bria-17-3-b-4.

17.　Anton Harder, "Not at the Cost of China: New evidence regarding US proposals to Nehru for joining the United Nations Security council", Woodrow Wilson International Center for Scholars, Cold War International History Project Working Paper #76, March 2015, https://www.wilsoncenter.org/sites/default/files/media/documents/publication/cwihp_working_paper_76_not_at_the_cost_of_china.pdf.

18.　Wayne Thompson and Bernard C. Nalty, "Within Limits: The U.S. Airforce and the Korean War", Air Force History and Museums Program, 1996, https://

media.defense.gov/2010/Oct/06/2001329755/-1/-1/0/AFD-101006-032.pdf.

19. Embassy of India, Seoul, Republic of Korea, "India–RoK Defence Relations", updated 10 November 2022, https://www.indembassyseoul.gov.in/india-rok-defence-relations/.

20. Nona Brown, "CHINA STILL HOLDS MANY AMERICANS; India and Other Nations Join U.S. in Seeking Release of Peiping's Prisoners", *The New York Times*, 19 June 1955, https://timesmachine.nytimes.com/timesmachine/1955/06/19/82201474.pdf.

21. Jairam Ramesh, *A Chequered Brilliance: The Many Lives of V.K. Krishna Menon*, Penguin–Viking, 2019, p. 434.

22. Ibid., p. 441.

23. Ibid., p. 449.

24. Rosie Tan Segil, "The Limits of Jawaharlal Nehru's Internationalism and Sino–Indian Relations, 1949–1959", MA Dissertation, Salem State University, May 2015, available at https://digitalrepository.salemstate.edu/bitstream/handle/20.500.13013/540/The_Limits_of_Jawaharlal_Nehrus_Asian_Internationalism_and_Sino_.pdf.

25. K.R. Narayanan, "Revitalising Panchsheel", remarks published by the Ministry of External Affairs, Government of India, 20 July 2004, https://www.mea.gov.in/articles-in-indian-media.htm?dtl/15408/Revitalising+Panchsheel. K.R. Narayanan was President of India.

26. *Panchsheel*, External Publicity Division, Ministry of External Affairs, Government of India, n.d. [2004], http://www.mea.gov.in/Uploads/PublicationDocs/191_panchsheel.pdf.

27. Segil, "The Limits of Jawaharlal Nehru's Internationalism".

28. Ibid.

29. "Sino–Soviet Border Talks: Problems and Prospects", Central Intelligence Agency, US Government, 10 November 1969, available at https://nsarchive2.gwu.edu/NSAEBB/NSAEBB49/sino.sov.26.pdf.

30. Garver, "China's Decision for War with India in 1962", p. 95.

31. F. Yorick Blumenfeld, "Russia and Red China", CQ Press, 1960, https://library.cqpress.com/cqresearcher/document.php?id=cqresrre1960100500.

32. The White House, "Memorandum of Conversation, Feb 23, 1972 at the President's Guest House, Peking", https://history.state.gov/historicaldocuments/frus1969-76v17/ch4?start=31.

33. Austin Jersild, "Sharing the Bomb among Friends: The Dilemmas of Sino-Soviet Strategic Cooperation", CWIHP e-Dossier No. 43, Wilson Center, n.d., https://www.wilsoncenter.org/publication/sharing-the-bomb-among-friends-the-dilemmas-sino-soviet-strategic-cooperation.

34. Jersild, "Sharing the Bomb among Friends".

35. "From the Journal of Ambassador Pavel Yudin: Record of Conversation with Mao Zedong, 4 January 1954", Wilson Center, https://digitalarchive. wilsoncenter.org/document/journal-ambassador-pavel-yudin-record-conversation-mao-zedong-4-january-1954.

36. Garver, "China's Decision for War with India in 1962".

37. Seth Faison, "Jean Pasqualini Dies at 71; Told of China's Penal Horrors", *The New York Time*, 13 October 1997, https://www.nytimes.com/1997/10/13/world/jean-pasqualini-dies-at-71-told-of-china-s-penal-horrors.html.

38. Roger Faligot, *Chinese Spies: From Chairman Mao to Xi Jinping*, London, Hurst & Company, 2019, p. 64.

39. Christopher Andrew, *The Defence of the Realm: The Authorized History of MI-5*, Penguin Books, 2009, p. 443.

40. Alfred D. Wilhelm, Jr., *The Chinese at the Negotiating Table: Style and Characteristics*, Washington, DC, National Defense University Press, 1994.

41. L.L. Mehrotra, "India's Tibet Policy: An Appraisal and Options", Tibet Parliamentary and Policy Research Centre, New Delhi, 2000 [1997], https://tibet.net/wp-content/uploads/2017/05/Inidas-Tibet-Policy.pdf.

42. Ibid., pp. 8–9.

43. The White House, "Memorandum of Conversation, Feb 23, 1972 at the President's Guest House, Peking", https://history.state.gov/historicaldocuments/frus1969-76v17/ch4?start=31.

44. Harold C. Hinton, "Review of *The Chinese Calculus of Deterrence: India and Indochina*. By Allen S. Whiting", *American Political Science Review* 71, 3 (1977): 1269. doi:10.2307/1960250.

45. Garver, "China's Decision for War with India in 1962", p. 93

46. Ibid., pp. 96–7.

47. Steven A. Hoffmann, *India and the China Crisis*, University of California Press, 2018 [1990].

48. Andrew, *The Defence of the Realm*, pp. 444–5.

49. Garver, "China's Decision for War with India in 1962", p. 102.

50. Ibid., p. 116

51. Ibid., p. 123.

52. John W. Garver, *China's Quest: The History of the Foreign Relations of the People's Republic of China*, Oxford, Oxford University Press, 2016.

53. Rup Narayan Das, *India–China Relations: A New Paradigm*, New Delhi, Institute for Defence Studies and Analyses, 2013, p. 39.

54. "Nuclear Anxiety: Indian's [sic] Letter to Clinton on the Nuclear Testing", *The New York Times*, 13 May 1998, https://www.nytimes.com/1998/05/13/

world/nuclear-anxiety-indian-s-letter-to-clinton-on-the-nuclear-testing.
html.

55. For example, (Senior Colonel) Zou Yunhua, "Chinese Perspectives on the
South Asian Nuclear Tests", Working Paper, Center for International Security
and Cooperation Stanford University, 1999, https://www.files.ethz.ch/
isn/20015/Chinese_Perspectives_SAsian_Nuclear_Tests.pdf.

56. "China has not forgotten Vajpayee's missive to Clinton", *Zee News*, 19
November 2006, https://zeenews.india.com/news/nation/china-has-not-
forgotten-vajpayees-missive-to-clinton_336686.html.

57. John W. Garver, "The Restoration of Sino–Indian Comity following India's
Nuclear Tests", *The China Quarterly* 168 (2001): 865–89, https://library.fes.
de/libalt/journals/swetsfulltext/12919246.pdf

58. "Sino–U.S. Presidential Joint Statement on South Asia", 27 June 1998,
published in *Strategic Studies* 19/20, 19, 4/20, 1 (1998): 142–5, https://
www.jstor.org/stable/45182311.

59. Pravin Sawhney, "Ladakh Stand-off Has Exposed India's Failed Nuclear
Deterrence against China. Now What?", *The Wire*, 1 September 2021, https://
thewire.in/security/ladakh-stand-off-has-exposed-indias-failed-nuclear-
deterrence-against-china-now-what.

60. Garver, "The Restoration of Sino–Indian Comity".

61. Nilova Roy Chaudhury, "China lays claim to Arunachal", *Hindustan Times*, 19
November 2006, https://www.hindustantimes.com/india/china-lays-claim-
to-arunachal/story-QDVTkQ1kDNBBf9QMvsDdBM.html.

62. "Press Statement by Prime Minister during the visit of President Xi Jinping of
China to India", 18 September 2014, Ministry of External Affairs, Government
of India, https://www.mea.gov.in/Speeches-Statements.htm?dtl/24014/
Press+Statement+by+ Prime+Minister+during+the+visit+of+President+
Xi+Jinping+of+China+to+India+September+18+2014.

63. "Diary no. 3904 Informal Summit with China", answer to question in the
Lok Sabha, 11 August 2021, Ministry of External Affairs, Government of
India, https://mea.gov.in/lok-sabha.htm?dtl/34175/DIARY_NO3904_
INFORMAL_SUMMIT_WITH_CHINA.

64. Sushant Singh, "Big surge in Chinese transgressions, most of them in Ladakh",
*The Indian Express*, 22 May 2020, https://indianexpress.com/article/india/
aksai-chin-army-big-surge-in-chinese-transgressions-most-of-them-in-
ladakh-6421674/.

65. Shubhajit Roy, "18 Modi-Xi meetings, several pacts: killings breach consensus,
dent diplomacy", *The Indian Express*, 17 June 2020, https://indianexpress.com/
article/india/india-china-standoff-diplomacy-lac-incident-mea-6462195/.

66.  "India-China clash: 20 Indian troops killed in Ladakh fighting", *BBC News*, 16 June 2020, https://www.bbc.com/news/world-asia-53061476.

67.  Vijay Gokhale, "The Road from Galwan: The Future of India–China Relations", Carnegie India, 10 March 2021, https://carnegieindia.org/2021/03/10/road-from-galwan-future-of-india-china-relations-pub-84019.

68.  Martin Bernal, "Contradictions: Review of Franz Schurmann, *Ideology and Organization in Communist China*", *New York Review of Books*, 7 July 1966; reproduced and available at https://www.chinafile.com/library/nyrb-china-archive/contradictions.

69.  Wilhelm, *The Chinese at the Negotiating Table*.

70.  "The Sino–Soviet Dispute on Aid to North Vietnam (1965–1968)", Central Intelligence Agency, US Government, available at https://archive.org/details/ESAU-CIA/Annex_%20The%20Sino-Soviet%20Dispute%20on%20Aid%20to%20North%20Vietnam%20%281965-1968%29/.

71.  Press Trust of India, "India should look to convert world's 'hatred' for China into economic opportunity: Nitin Gadkari", *Hindustan Times*, 27 April 2020, https://www.hindustantimes.com/india-news/ india-should-look-to-convert-worlds-hatred-for-china-into-economic-opportunity-nitin-gadkari/story-dYbh3q AargLbBMlJ8XR8wK.html.

72.  Rajat Pandit, "Eye on China, Philippines to buy BrahMos in $375m deal", *The Times of India*, 15 January 2022, https://timesofindia.indiatimes.com/india/india-bags-order-from-philippines-for-brahmos-missiles-    amidst-chinas-belligerence-in-south-china-sea/articleshow/88904359.cms.

73.  "Duterte says Philippines won't take sides as US and China tussle", *Nikkei Asia*, 21 May 2021, https://asia.nikkei.com/Spotlight/The-Future-of-Asia/The-Future-of-Asia-2021/Duterte-says-Philippines-won-t-take-sides-as-US-and-China-tussle.

74.  Mimi Lau, "Vietnam says it will not side against China, as US' Kamala Harris visits", *South China Morning Post*, 25 August 2021, https://www.scmp.com/news/china/diplomacy/article/3146273/vietnam-says-it-will-not-side-against-china-us-kamala-harris.

75.  Ben Bland, "If the U.S. is Serious about China Competition, it Needs Indonesia", *The New York Times*, 12 December 2021, https://www.nytimes.com/2021/12/12/opinion/indonesia-us-jokowi-biden.html.

76.  PTI, "Article 370: China says opposed to Ladakh as Union Territory", *India Today*, 6 August 2019, https://www.indiatoday.in/india/story/china-reaction-jammu-kashmir-article-370-1577915-2019-08-06.

77.  "The Evolution of Soviet Policy in the Sino-Soviet Border Dispute", 28 April 1970, p. 1, https://www.cia.gov/library/readingroom/docs/esau-44.pdf.

78.  Sarmad Ishfaq, "India and America collude to disrupt the China-Pakistan economic corridor", *Open Democracy*, 3 June 2019, https://www.opendemocracy.net/en/india-and-america-colludes-disrupt-china-pakistan-economic-corridor/.

79.  Sumit Ganguly and Frank O'Donnell, "China Is Taking Advantage of India's Intelligence Failures", *Foreign Policy*, 27 August 2020, https://foreignpolicy.com/2020/08/27/india-china-galwan-intelligence-failure/.

80.  Zhao Yusha, "Quad alliance countering China doomed to fail due to member's 'all-for-self' attitudes", *Global Times*, 8 March 2021, https://www.globaltimes.cn/page/202103/1217756.shtml.

81.  Liy Caiyu and Zhao Yusha, "US attempt to unite Asian allies against China fails to live up to expectations: observers", *Global Times*, 21 March 2021, https://www.globaltimes.cn/page/202103/1219007.shtml.

82.  Gokhale, "The Road from Galwan".


3.   THE RASHTRIYA SWAYAMSEVAK SANGH

1.   "RSS does not impose its ideology on anyone: Mohan Bhagwat at RSS event", *The Indian Express*, 17 September 2018, https://indianexpress.com/article/india/rss-mohan-bhagwat-event-future-of-the-bharat-lecture-series-delhi-5361082/.

2.   Karan Thapar, "Has the RSS ground shifted?", *The Indian Express*, 21 September 2018, https://indianexpress.com/article/opinion/columns/mohan-bhagwat-rss-event-hindutva-congress-5367217/.

3.   On 28 September 2015 Mohammed Aklaq, aged 52, whose elder son Sartaj was serving the Indian Air Force, was lynched and killed in Dadri in UP by a mob accusing him of cow slaughter. Fearing more reprisals, the Indian Air Force Chief Arup Raha shifted the family to an Air Force secure area. It is amazing that, even by 28 September 2020, when this article in *The Quint* was originally published, the trial of his murderers had not started: Aishwarya S. Iyer, "Dadri Lynching Trial Begins: How Akhlaq's Kin Waited for 5 Years", *The Quint*, 26 March 2021, https://www.thequint.com/news/india/dadri-lynching-five-years-mohammad-akhlaq.

4.   "Vedas order killing of sinners: RSS mouthpiece Panchjanya over Dadri lynching", *India Today*, 18 October 2015, https://www.indiatoday.in/india/story/vedas-order-killing-of-sinners-rss-mouthpiece-panchjanya-over-dadri-lynching-268656-2015-10-18.

5.   "Islam came to India with invaders, this is history and should be told in that manner: RSS chief Mohan Bhagwat", *Times Now*, 7 September 2021,

https://www.timesnownews.com/india/article/islam-came-to-india-with-invaders-this-is-history-and-should-be-told-in-that-manner-rss-chief-mohan-bhagwat/808583.

6.   "RSS chief Mohan Bhagwat raises concerns about rising Muslim population, says temples being given to heretics", *The Times of India*, 15 October 2021, https://timesofindia.indiatimes.com/city/nagpur/bhagwat-raises-concerns-about-rising-muslim-population-says-temples-being-given-to-heretics/articleshow/87037046.cms.

7.   Makarand R. Paranjpe, "How RSS predicted China's true colours", *DailyO*, 1 July 2020, https://www.dailyo.in/politics/india-china-clash-rss-congress-nehru-1962-india-china-war-33222.

8.   R.C. Majumdar, H.C. Raychaudhuri and Kalikinkar Datta, *An Advanced History of India*, Macmillan & Co., 1985 [1946], p. 879.

9.   Ibid., p. 881

10.  Ibid., p. 914.

11.  M.G. Chitkara, *Rashtriya Swayamsevak Sangh: National Upsurge*, New Delhi, A.P.H. Publishing Corporation, 2004, p. 4.

12.  Annie Besant, *The Future of Indian Politics: A Contribution to the Understanding of Present-Day Problems*, London, Bombay, etc., Theosophical Publishing House, 1922, pp. 252, 301.

13.  Chitkara, *Rashtriya Swayamsevak Sangh*, p. 4.

14.  Marzia Casolari, "Hindutva's Foreign Tie-up in the 1930s: Archival Evidence", *Economic and Political Weekly*, 35, 4 (January 2000): 218–28, p. 218.

15.  Chitkara, *Rashtriya Swayamsevak Sangh*, p. 3.

16.  Ruhi Tewari and Pragya Kaushika, "We analysed 1,000 BJP leaders & found the party remains a Brahmin–Baniya club", *The Print*, 1 August 2018, https://theprint.in/politics/ambedkar-on-its-agenda-but-bjp-has-little-place-for-dalits-is-still-a-brahmin-baniya-party/91449/.

17.  Christophe Jaffrelot, *The Hindu nationalist movement and Indian politics, 1925 to the 1990s: strategies of identity-building, implantation and mobilisation*, London, Hurst & Co., 1996, p. 39. An "*akhara*" is a school, circle or gymnasium.

18.  Chitkara, *Rashtriya Swayamsevak Sangh*, pp. 99–101.

19.  Manoj Mitta, "India: Melting pot vs salad bowl", 7 March 2010, https://timesofindia.indiatimes.com/home/sunday-times/deep-focus/india-melting-pot-vs-salad-bowl/articleshow/5652863.cms.

20.  Chitkara, *Rashtriya Swayamsevak Sangh*, p. 135.

21.  "States Can Give Hindus Minority Status If They're In Minority There; Minority Welfare Schemes Not Unconstitutional: Centre Tells Supreme Court", *Live Law*, 27 March 2022, https://www.livelaw.in/top-stories/

hindus-minority-status-in-states-where-they-are-in-minority-centre-tells-supreme-court-195122.

22. "Mohan Bhagwat in Overdrive to Portray RSS as Inclusive, Evolving Organisation", *The Wire*, 19 September 2018, https://thewire.in/politics/mohan-bhagwat-views-rss-conclave.

23. "Bhagwat reiterates RSS concern at 'rising Muslim share' in population", *The Times of India*, 16 October 2021, https://timesofindia.indiatimes.com/india/bhagwat-reiterates-rss-concern-at-rising-muslim-share-in-population/articleshow/87051323.cms.

24. Chitkara, *Rashtriya Swayamsevak Sangh*, p. 239.

25. Ibid., p. 271.

26. Sagar, "How Mohan Bhagwat outlined a vision for a casteist, theocratic Hindu state on national TV", *The Caravan*, 15 November 2020, https://caravanmagazine.in/politics/how-mohan-bhagwat-outlined-a-vision-for-casteist-theocratic-hindu-state-on-national-tv.

27. Ragini Nayal, "RSS mindset of women exclusion is not 'Indian culture'", *Daily O*, 8 March 2016, https://www.dailyo.in/politics/international-womens-day-narendra-modi-rss-sangh-parivar-sexism-patriarchy-sati-manusmriti/story/1/9425.html.

28. "Night out for girls not in our culture, says Union culture minister Mahesh Sharma", *The Times of India*, 19 September 2015, https://timesofindia.indiatimes.com/india/night-out-for-girls-not-in-our-culture-says-union-culture-minister-mahesh-sharma/articleshow/49019712.cms.

29. Shivani Azad, "Shocked to see women in ripped jeans, what message are they sending to society: Uttarakhand CM Tirath Singh Rawat", *The Times of India*, 17 March 2021, https://timesofindia.indiatimes.com/city/dehradun/shocked-to-see-women-in-ripped-jeans-what-message-are-they-sending-to-society-ukhand-cm/articleshow/81537465.cms.

30. Chitkara, *Rashtriya Swayamsevak Sangh*, p. 269

31. Katey Hearth, "India's RSS wants Christians, Muslims out by December 31", *Mission Network News*, 6 January 2021, https://www.mnnonline.org/news/indias-rss-wants-christians-muslims-out-by-december-31/.

32. Chitkara, *Rashtriya Swayamsevak Sangh*, p. 255.

33. Manmohan Vaidya, "Our Revered Baba", *The Sunday Guardian*, 30 January 2021, https://www.sundayguardianlive.com/news/our-revered-baba.

34. Not to be confused with Swami Chinmayanand (Krishna Pal Singh) of Gonda (Uttar Pradesh), three time BJP MP, who was arrested in 2019 for allegedly raping a law student. He was also a Minister of State in Vajpayee's BJP coalition government during 1999–2004. See Chandan Kumar, "BJP's Chinmayanand, accused of rape by law student, arrested by UP Police",

NOTES

*Hindustan Times*, 2 July 2020, https://www.hindustantimes.com/india-news/bjp-s-chinmayanand-taken-to-lucknow-hospital-by-up-police-special-team/story-uG7ML38CNUlvbfBBYQhTrM.html.

35. Swami Chinmayananda, *Isavasya Upanisad*, Central Chinmaya Trust, Mumbai, December 2001, pp. 99–101.

36. A.C. Bhaktivedanta Swami Prabhupada, *Śrī Īśopanishad*, Bhaktivedanta Book Trust, 1969, available at https://prabhupadabooks.com/iso.

37. Kaushik Vaidya, "'No Company is Anti-National': Mohandas Pai on Panchjanya–Infosys Row". *NDTV Profit*, 6 September 2021, https://www.bloombergquint.com/business/no-company-is-anti-national-mohandas-pai-on-panchjanya-infosys-row.

38. "RSS distances itself from Panchjanya article criticising Infosys", *Business Today*, 5 September 2021, https://www.businesstoday.in/latest/trends/story/rss-distances-itself-from-panchjanya-article-criticising-infosys-305973-2021-09-05.

39. Nistula Hebbar, "'Panchjanya' a herald of 'Dharma Yudh': RSS leader Manmohan Vaidya", *The Hindu* 7 September 2021, https://www.thehindu.com/news/national/panchjanya-a-herald-for-dharma-yudh-rss-leader-manmohan-vaidya/article36331748.ece.

40. Sagar, "How Mohan Bhagwat outlined a vision for a casteist, theocratic Hindu state on national TV", *The Caravan*, 15 November 2020, https://caravanmagazine.in/politics/how-mohan-bhagwat-outlined-a-vision-for-casteist-theocratic-hindu-state-on-national-tv.

41. Harinder Baweja, "Furore over tax summons to Vishwa Hindu Parishad", *India Today*, 15 April 1990, https://www.indiatoday.in/magazine/indiascope/story/19900415-furore-over-tax-summons-to-vishwa-hindu-parishad-812477-1990-04-15.

42. Priti Gandhi, "Rashtriya Swayamsevak Sangh: How the world's largest NGO has changed the face of Indian democracy", *DNA*, 15 May 2014, https://www.dnaindia.com/analysis/standpoint-rashtriya-swayamsewak-sangh-how-the-world-s-largest-ngo-has-changed-the-face-of-indian-democracy-1988636.

43. Amarnath Tewary, "RSS can prepare an army within three days, says Mohan Bhagwat", *The Hindu*, 12 February 2018, https://www.thehindu.com/news/national/other-states/rss-can-prepare-an-army-within-3-days-mohan-bhagwat/article22727198.ece.

44. See the blog entitled "Coins and more", entry "535) Swami Chinmayananda…", 17 July 2017, https://exclusivecoins.blogspot.com/2017/07/535-swami-chinmayananda-08051916.html.

45. Parasnath, "Kurien was chummy with Guru Golwalkar!", *Indian Cooperative*, 27 November 2018, https://www.indiancooperative.com/from-states/kurien-was-chummy-with-guru-golwalkar/.

46. Rasheed Kidwai, "Forget WhatsApp Rumours, Here are the Facts about 1966 Anti-cow Slaughter Agitation", *News18*, 3 December 2018, https://www.news18.com/news/opinion/rajasthan-assembly-election-2018-forget-whatsapp-rumours-here-are-the-facts-about-1966-cow-slaughter-agitation-1958749.html.

47. "CIA classifies VHP, Bajrang Dal as militant religious outfits", *India Today*, 14 June 2018, https://www.indiatoday.in/india/story/cia-classifies-vhp-bajrang-dal-as-millitant-religious-outfits-1260635-2018-06-14.

48. "Bajarangis [sic] – Do not become Hindu Jihadis", *Hindutva.org*, August 2001; content archived from the original available at https://web.archive.org/web/20040612044145/http://hindutva.org/bajrang.html.

49. Sreshta Ladegaam, "Telugu man, member of VHP-USA, raises Indian flag during Capitol Hill attack", *The Siasat Daily*, 9 January 2021, https://www.siasat.com/telugu-man-member-of-vhp-usa-raises-indian-flag-during-capitol-hill-attack-2064152/.

50. Chitkara, *Rashtriya Swayamsevak Sangh*, p. 251.

51. Ibid., p. 252.

52. Ibid., p. 254.

53. I am grateful to Dr Usha Thakkar, Director of Mani Bhavan Gandhi Museum, Mumbai, and Ms Sandhya Mehta for their assistance.

54. *The Collected Works of Mahatma Gandhi*, vol. 89, Publications Division, Ministry of Information and Broadcasting, Government of India, 1958, p. 193.

55. Pyarelal, *Mahatma Gandhi: The Last Phase, vol. II*, Ahmedabad, Navajivan Publishing House, 1958, p. 440.

56. "Amit Shah calls Mahatma Gandhi 'chatur baniya', Congress demands apology", *Daijiworld*, 10 June 2017, https://www.daijiworld.com/news/newsDisplay?newsID=456114.

57. Translation by Guy L. Beck, *Sacred Sound: Experiencing Music in World Religions*, Waterloo, Wilfrid Laurier University Press, 2006, p. 137.

58. Granville Austin, *The Indian Constitution: Cornerstone of a Nation*, Oxford University Press, 1999, p. 13.

59. Chitkara, *Rashtriya Swayamsevak Sangh*, p. 251

60. "Tri-colour hoisted at RSS HQ after 52 years", *The Times of India*, 26 January 2002, https://timesofindia.indiatimes.com/city/pune/Tri-colour-hoisted-at-RSS-HQ-after-52-yrs/articleshow/1561733136.cms.

61. Shyamlal Yadav, "RSS and the idea of Akhand Bharat", *The Indian Express*, 4 January 2016, https://indianexpress.com/article/explained/rss-akhand-bharat/.

62. Prashant V. Singh, "'Akhand Bharat' row", *Zee News*, 28 December 2015, https://zeenews.india.com/news/india/akhand-bharat-row-meet-

al-jazeera-anchor-who-is-making-news-over-ram-madhavs-your-isis-remark_1839077.html.

63.  "India–Pak ceasefire agreement rekindles hope for peace among border residents", *Hindustan Times*, 26 February 2021, https://www.hindustantimes.com/india-news/indiapak-ceasefire-agreement-rekindles-hope-for-peace-among-border-residents-101614335305209.html.

64.  Sribala Vadlapatla, "Akhand Bharat possible, will be good for Pakistan, says RSS chief Mohan Bhagwat", *The Times of India*, 26 February 2021, https://timesofindia.indiatimes.com/city/hyderabad/akhand-bharat-possible-will-be-good-for-pakistan-says-bhagwat/articleshow/81216895.cms.

65.  Chitkara, *Rashtriya Swayamsevak Sangh*, p. 150

66.  Austin, *The Indian Constitution*, p. 40.

67.  Ibid., pp. 43–4.

68.  Ibid., pp. 36–40.

69.  Ibid., pp. 55–6.

70.  Chitkara, *Rashtriya Swayamsevak Sangh*, p. 150

71.  V.P. Menon, *The Story of the Integration of the Indian States*, Orient Longmans, 1961, p. 376.

72.  Lionel Carter (ed.), *Mountbatten's Report on the Last Viceroyalty: 22 March–15 August 1947*, New Delhi, Manohar, 2003.

73.  Ibid., p. 67.

74.  Ibid., p. 123.

75.  Ibid., p. 249.

76.  Ibid., p. 95.

77.  Ibid., p. 250.

78.  Ibid., p. 250.

79.  See *Collected Works of Mahatma Gandhi* vol. 96, materials from 5–6 August 1947.

80.  Priti Gandhi, "Rashtriya Swayamsevak Sangh: How the world's largest NGO has changed the face of Indian democracy", *DNA*, 15 May 2014, https://www.dnaindia.com/analysis/standpoint-rashtriya-swayamsewak-sangh-how-the-world-s-largest-ngo-has-changed-the-face-of-indian-democracy-1988636.

81.  Chitkara, *The Rashtriya Swayamsevak Sangh*, p. 263.

82.  Balraj Puri, *Kashmir Towards Insurgency*, Orient Longman, 1993, p. 5.

83.  M.S. Golwalkar, *We, or Our Nationhood Defined*, Nagpur, Bharat Publications, 1939; e-book (n.d.), to which page references apply, available at https://sanjeev.sabhlokcity.com/Misc/We-or-Our-Nationhood-Defined-Shri-M-S-Golwalkar.pdf.

84.  Ibid., p. 6.

85.  Ibid., from pp. 10–31.

86. Akshaya Mukul, "RSS officially disowns Golwalkar's book", *The Times of India*, 9 March 2006, https://timesofindia.indiatimes.com/india/RSS-officially-disowns-Golwalkars-book/articleshow/1443606.cms.

87. Akhilesh Singh, "Parts of Golwalkar's 'Bunch of Thought' [sic] not valid anymore: RSS chief Mohan Bhagwat", *The Times of India*, 19 September 2018, https://timesofindia.indiatimes.com/india/parts-of-golwalkars-bunch-of-thought-not-valid-anymore-rss-chief-mohan-bhagwat/articleshow/65877873.cms.

88. Rajeshwar Dayal, *A Life of our Times*, Orient Longman, p. 93 .

89. Ibid., p. 94.

90. Priti Gandhi, "Rashtriya Swayamsevak Sangh".

91. Chitkara, *Rashtriya Swayamsevak Sangh*, p. 255.

92. Bharat Bhushan, "Exclusive: RSS chief Golwalkar threatened to kill Gandhi—1947 CID report", *Catch News*, 10 February 2017, http://www.catchnews.com/politics-news/exclusive-rss-chief-golwalkar-threatened-to-kill-gandhi-1947-cid-report-1469535385.html.

93. A.G. Noorani, *The RSS: A Menace to India*, Left Word Books, 2019, appendix 7, pp. 488–99.

94. Sandra Marina Fernandes, "Churches under fire! A list of recent church attacks in the country", *One India*, 1 May 2015, https://www.oneindia.com/india/churches-under-fire-a-list-of-recent-church-attacks-in-the-country-1685114.html.

95. Harriet Sherwood, "Christians in India increasingly under attack, study shows", *The Guardian*, 11 January 2017, https://www.theguardian.com/world/2017/jan/11/christians-in-india-increasingly-under-attack-study-shows.

96. Iram Siddique, "Identifying missionaries who carry out illegal religious conversions: VHP", *The Indian Express*, 12 March 2021, https://indianexpress.com/article/india/identifying-missionaries-who-carry-out-illegal-religious-conversions-vhp-7224594/.

97. Dilip Mandal, "Don't listen to VHP and panic. Christianity is a failed project in India", *The Print*, 9 September 2020, https://theprint.in/opinion/vhp-rss-panic-christianity-religious-conversion-failed-project-india/498698/.

98. "Violent Cow Protection in India: Vigilante Groups Attack Minorities", *Human Rights Watch*, 18 February 2019, available at https://www.hrw.org/report/2019/02/19/violent-cow-protection-india/vigilante-groups-attack-minorities.

99. "Database for religion-based hate crimes launched in Delhi", *Business Standard*, 7 March 2018, https://www.business-standard.com/article/news-ians/database-for-religion-based-hate-crimes-launched-in-delhi-118030700923_1.html.

100. Alison Saldanha, "Incomes shrink as cow-related violence scuttles beef, leather exports: new report", *India Spend*, 19 February 2019, https://www.indiaspend.com/incomes-shrink-as-cow-related-violence-scuttles-beef-leather-exports-new-report/.

101. Fauzan Alavi, "Stray cattle issue, a reality check", *The Indian Express*, 29 June 2019, https://indianexpress.com/article/opinion/columns/stray-cattle-issue-a-reality-check-cow-slaughter-india-livestock-5805684/.

102. "In Yogi's UP, schools and hospitals turn into temporary cow shelters", *News18*, 27 December 2018, https://www.news18.com/news/india/in-yogis-up-schools-and-hospitals-turn-into-temporary-cow-shelters-1984995.html.

103. Abhishek De, "Five times when RSS Chief Mohan Bhagwat left BJP red-faced", *The Indian Express*, 18 September 2018, https://indianexpress.com/article/india/mohan-bhagwat-rss-event-congress-bjp-5363174/.

104. Liz Mathew, "Nadda on BJP-RSS ties: We have grown, more capable now… the BJP runs itself", *The Indian Express*, 22 May 2024, https://indianexpress.com/article/political-pulse/nadda-on-bjp-rss-ties-we-have-grown-more-capable-now-the-bjp-runs-itself-9336205/.

105. Chitkara, *The Rashtriya Swayamsevak Sangh*, p. 235.

106. "Mohan Bhagwat's appeal to India's youth to imbibe Gandhian principles indicates RSS success in distancing Congress from the Mahatma", *Firstpost*, 18 February 2020, https://www.firstpost.com/politics/mohan-bhagwats-appeal-to-indias-youth-to-imbibe-gandhian-principles-indicates-rss-success-in-distancing-congress-from-the-mahatma-8053891.html.

107. Chander Uday Singh, "Bombay BJP leader Ramdas Nayak files criminal case against Abdul Rahman Antulay", *India Today*, 31 August 1982, https://www.indiatoday.in/magazine/indiascope/story/19820831-bombay-bjp-leader-ramdas-nayak-files-criminal-case-against-abdul-rahman-antulay-772143-2013-10-07.

108. M.S. Nawaz, "PM Modi will be worshipped in future: Tirath Rawat", *The Times of India*, 15 March 2021, https://timesofindia.indiatimes.com/india/pm-modi-will-be-worshipped-in-future-tirath-rawat/articleshow/81501696.cms.

109. Rajmohan Gandhi, "Lessons from the Republican cult of Trump", *The Indian Express*, 6 March 2021, https://indianexpress.com/article/opinion/columns/narendra-modi-donald-trump-republican-lesson-7216140/.

110. Neelam Pandey and Moushumi Das Gupta, "RSS won't push Varanasi, Mathura mosque issues after Ayodhya verdict, says Mohan Bhagwat", *The Print*, 9 November 2019, https://theprint.in/india/rss-wont-push-varanasi-mathura-mosque-issues-after-ayodhya-verdict-says-mohan-bhagwat/318409/.

111.  Liz Mathew, "In words and between the lines, the messages in RSS chief Mohan Bhagwat's speech", *The Indian Express*, 3 June 2022, https://indianexpress.com/article/india/political-pulse/rss-chief-mohan-bhagwat-speech-gyanvapi-mosque-7951089/.

112.  Harish Khare, "Mohan Bhagwat rescues Prime Minister Narendra Modi", *The Wire*, 6 June 2022, https://thewire.in/communalism/mohan-bhagwat-rescues-prime-minister-narendra-modi.

4.     THE IDEA OF INDIA

1.    See A.C.N. Nambiar, "Oral history transcripts", Prime Ministers' Museum and Library (formerly Nehru Memorial Museum and Library), p. 50; see also Vappala Balachandran, *A Life in Shadow: The Secret Story of ACN Nambiar, a Forgotten Anti-Colonial Warrior*, Roli Books, 2016, p. 131.

2.    Einstein's letter is reproduced on the back cover of the 1981 edition of *Discovery*.

3.    A.M. Rosenthal, "India's Gift: The Discovery", *The New York Times*, 7 October 1984, https://www.nytimes.com/1984/10/07/magazine/india-s-gift-the-discovery-of-each-day.html.

4.    "Nehru, Jawaharlal", The Martin Luther King, Jr. Research and Education Institute, Stanford University, https://kinginstitute.stanford.edu/encyclopedia/nehru-jawaharlal.

5.    During his earlier imprisonment (October 1940–December 1941) he had started writing his autobiography.

6.    Jawaharlal Nehru, *The Discovery of India*, Oxford University Press, 1994, p. 178.

7.    Jawaharlal Nehru, *An Autobiography*, Oxford University Press, 1936.

8.    Ibid., p. 73.

9.    Mridula Mukherjee, "How Jawaharlal Nehru travelled through India, in his own words", *National Herald*, 14 November 2020, https://www.nationalheraldindia.com/india/how-jawaharlal-nehru-travelled-through-india-in-his-own-words.

10.   R.C. Majumdar, "Indian history, its nature, scope and method", in *The History and Culture of the Indian People: The Vedic Age*, Mumbai, Bharatiya Vidya Bhavan, 2017 [1951], p. 38.

11.   Nehru, *The Discovery of India*.

12.   Michael Edwards, *A History of India*, London, The New English Library, 1961, p. 21.

13.   A.L. Basham, *The Wonder that was India*, New Delhi, Rupa and Co., 1981

[1954], p. 25n; see also https://www.speakingtree.in/blog/meaning-and-origin-of-the-word-hindu.

14.  https://www.speakingtree.in/blog/we-are-neither-indian-nor-hindu.

15.  "Vajpayee a statesman who asked Gujarat CM Modi to follow 'rajdharma' in 2002 riots: Congress", *The New Indian Express*, 17 August 2018, https://www.newindianexpress.com/nation/2018/aug/17/vajpayee-a-statesman-who-asked-gujarat-cm-modi-to-follow-rajdharma-in-2002-riots-congress-1858771.html.

16.  Gandhi, *Young India*, 1 June 1921.

17.  Gandhi, *Young India*, 22 December 1927.

18.  Gandhi, *Young India*, 9 January 1930.

19.  Dhammapada 5, quoted by Michael Edwards, *A History of India: From the Earliest Times to the Present Day*, The New English Library/Thames and Hudson, 1961, p. 32.

20.  Vikas Nain, "Second Urbanization in the Chronology of Indian History", *International Journal of Academic Research and Development* 3 (2) (March 2018), pp. 538–42.

21.  It is also represented visually: see, for example, the painting available at https://www.pinterest.com/pin/444308319466464803/, "King Bimbisara offering his kingdom to the Buddha" taken from *The Life of Buddha in Pictures*, Penang, Dhammikarama Burmese Buddhist Temple, n.d., p. 29.

22.  Edwards, *A History of India*, p. 39, quoting from Arthasastra, 4.1.

23.  Ibid., p. 41.

24.  Edwards, *A History of India*, pp. 41–3

25.  Suraj Yengde, "Whatever we have today in Brahminism is a twisted history of Buddha's work", *Indian Express*, 7 February 2021, https://indianexpress.com/article/opinion/columns/india-buddhism-ashoka-nalanda-7177789/.

26.  Ibid.

27.  Edwards, *A History of India*, p. 55.

28.  Nehru, *Discovery of India*, p.120.

29.  Vincent Smith, quoted in Nehru, *The Discovery of India*.

30.  Edwards, *A History of India*, p. 56.

31.  "Asvaghosa, the philosopher-poet", *The Free Press Journal*, 31 May 2019, https://www.freepressjournal.in/latest-news/asvaghosa-the-philosopher-poet.

32.  Edwards, *A History of India*, p. 58.

33.  Anand, "The Empire of Kushana: Ancient History of India", *History Discussion*, n.d., https://www.historydiscussion.net/history-of-india/kushana/the-empire-of-kushana-ancient-history-of-india/5723.

34.  Carolyn M. Heitmeyer, "Identity and difference in a Muslim community in

Central Gujarat, India following the 2002 communal violence", PhD thesis, London School of Economics and Political Science, n.d. [2014], http://etheses.lse.ac.uk/2355/1/U615304.pdf.

35.   James M. Campbell, *History of Gujarát (Gazetteer of the Bombay Presidency, Vol 1, Part 1)*, Bombay, Government Central Press, 1896.

36.   Sribala Vadlapatla, "Akhand Bharat possible, will be good for Pakistan, says RSS chief Mohan Bhagwat", *The Times of India*, 26 February 2021, https://timesofindia.indiatimes.com/city/hyderabad/akhand-bharat-possible-will-be-good-for-pakistan-says-bhagwat/articleshow/81216895.cms.

37.   See Kapadia's discussion of Udayaraja's *Rājavinodamahākāvyam* on Sultan Mahmud Begada of Gujarat, Aparna Kapadia, "Text, Power and Kinship in Medieval Gujarat, c. 1398-1511", PhD thesis, SOAS University of London, 2010, pp. 160–99, available at https://eprints.soas.ac.uk/28731/1/10672899.pdf.

38.   Arvind Chauhan, "BJP should change Amit Shah's name because of its Persian origins", 11 November 2018, https://timesofindia.indiatimes.com/city/agra/bjp-should-change-amit-shahs-name-because-of-its-persian-origin/articleshow/66573980.cms.

39.   Edwards, *A History of India*, p. 68, quoting K. M. Panikkar, *Survey of Indian History*, p. 49.

40.   Muhammad Bin Naveed, "White Huns (Hephthalites)", *World History Encyclopedia*, 22 June 2015, https://www.ancient.eu/White_Huns_(Hephthalites)/.

41.   Ibid.

42.   Nehru, *The Discovery of India*, p. 120.

43.   Edwards, *A History of India*, pp. 71–9.

44.   Ibid., p. 76.

45.   Nehru, *Discovery of India*, p. 192.

46.   Ibid., p.122.

47.   Will Durant, *The Story of Civilization, vol. I: Our Oriental Heritage*, Simon & Schuster, 1954 [1935], pp. 414–15.

48.   S.N. Das Gupta, "Philosophy", in A.L. Basham (ed.), *A Cultural History of India*, Oxford University Press, 1975, p. 119.

49.   Swami Ranganathananda, *Eternal Values for a Changing Society, Vol II: Great Spiritual Teachers*, Bombay, Bharatiya Vidya Bhavan, 1987, pp. 92–3.

50.   Nehru, *Discovery of India*, p. 192.

51.   Swami Paramananda, *The Upanishads*, Boston, The Vedanta Centre, 1919, pp. 13–16 .

52.   Ibid., p. 16.

53.   Nehru, *Discovery of India*, p. 80.

54.   Edwards, *A History of India*, p. 30.

55. Swami Dharma Theertha, *History of Hindu Imperialism*, Madras, Dalit Educational Literature Centre, 1992 [1941].

56. Asokan Vengassery Krishnan, *Sree Narayana Guru: The Perfect Union of Buddha and Sankara*, Konark Publishers, 2018.

57. C. Ahamed Fayiz, "Caste and Judiciary: Looking for Dalit and Adivasi Judges in Supreme Court of India", *Round Table India*, 3 April 2019, https://www.roundtableindia.co.in/caste-and-judiciary-looking-for-dalit-and-adivasi-judges-in-supreme-court-of-india/.

58. Theertha, *History of Hindu Imperialism*, pp. 231–6.

59. A. Sreedhara Menon, *A Survey of Kerala History*, DC Books, 2007, pp. 306–9.

60. Swami Ranganathananda, *Science and Religion*, Calcutta, Advaita Ashram, 1982, pp. 15–16.

61. Menon, *A Survey*, p. 85.

62. Ibid., p. 87: "*Buddham saranam gacchami, dharman saranam gacchami, sangham saranam gacchami*" (I take refuge in Buddha, Dharma and Sangha).

63. Ibid., p. 92.

64. Rajeev K.R., "Hindus, Muslims unite for renovation of 400-year-old Durga temple in Kerala", *The Times of India*, 10 April 2024, https://timesofindia.indiatimes.com/city/kozhikode/hindus-muslims-unite-for-renovation-of-400-year-old-durga-temple-in-kerala/articleshow/109174308.cms.

65. Devdutt Pattanaik, "Sea of Spices: How trade gets intertwined with myths", *The Economic Times*, 26 December 2020, https://economictimes.indiatimes.com/news/politics-and-nation/how-mythology-too-contributes-to-development/articleshow/79957862.cms.

66. B.C. Deva, *Indian Music*, Indian Council for Cultural Relations, 1974, pp. 7–8, 94–5.

67. Kuldeep Kumar, "Syncretic Music: The Rich History of Muslims in Indian Music", *The Wire*, 17 March 2017, https://thewire.in/culture/music-muslims-fatwa-history.

68. Granville Austin, *The Indian Constitution: Cornerstone of a Nation*, Oxford, 1966, pp. 10–11.

69. Ibid., p. 3, n. 8.

70. Ibid., p. 24.

71. Ibid., pp. 30–31.

5.    THE UNITED PROGRESSIVE ALLIANCE: 2004–2014

1. Kanchan Vasdev and Liz Mathew, "Manmohan Singh targets Modi: Hugging, swings, eating biryani do not improve ties", *The Indian Express*, 18 February

2022, https://indianexpress.com/elections/polls-manmohan-singh-hits-out-bjp-maligning-punjab-punjabis-7778211/.

2.   Venkitesh Ramakrishnan, "Drowning in scams", *Frontline*, 15 May 2013, https://frontline.thehindu.com/cover-story/drowning-in-scams/article4710850.ece.

3.   Vappala Balachandran, *A Life in Shadow: The Secret Story of A.C.N. Nambiar, a Forgotten Anti-Colonial Warrior*, Roli Books, 2016, p. 32.

4.   "Amit Shah says Congress ideology should be replaced with that of BJP", *India Today*, 9 August 2014, https://www.indiatoday.in/india/north/story/bjp-amit-shah-president-bjp-council-meeting-203370-2014-08-09.

5.   "The Weimar constitution", *Britannica.com*, n.d., https://www.britannica.com/place/Germany/The-Weimar-constitution.

6.   G. Mohan Gopal, "Emergency had a reason", *The Indian Express*, 4 July 2015, https://indianexpress.com/article/opinion/columns/emergency-had-a-reason/.

7.   Margaret Macmillan, *Paris 1919: Six Months that Changed the World*, Random House, 2001, p. 480.

8.   Balachandran, *A Life in Shadow*, p. 70.

9.   Manoj C G, "Explained: How Left opposed India–US nuclear deal, leading to split with UPA govt", *The Indian Express*, 6 August 2021, https://indianexpress.com/article/explained/explained-how-left-opposed-india-us-nuclear-deal-leading-to-split-with-upa-govt-7440555/.

10.  "My Dear Chief Minister … Three Letters Nehru Wrote That Indians Today Need to Read", *The Wire*, 27 May 2017, https://thewire.in/government/three-letters-nehru-wrote-chief-ministers-indians-today-need-read.

11.  Episodes available at https://www.pmindia.gov.in/en/mann-ki-baat/.

12.  Government of India, Second Administrative Reforms Commission, "Twelfth Report: Citizen Centric Administration", February 2009, https://darpg.gov.in/sites/default/files/ccadmin12.pdf.

13.  "RTI pending cases have risen to 57,000: Shailesh Gandhi writes to Chief Information Commissioner", *Mumbai Mirror*, 16 March 2020, https://mumbaimirror.indiatimes.com/mumbai/other/rti-pending-cases-have-risen-to-57000-shailesh-gandhi-writes-to-chief-information-commissioner/articleshow/74655465.cms.

14.  "Over 32,000 RTI appeals pending with Central Information Commission: Govt", *Hindustan Times*, 16 December 2021, https://www.hindustantimes.com/india-news/over-32-000-rti-appeals-pending-with-central-information-commission-govt-101639657691173.html.

15.  Parikshit Shah, "Eight laws in 10 years of UPA government that changed India",

NOTES

*India.com*, 1 April 2014, available from the Internet Archive's Wayback Machine at https://web.archive.org/web/20150314232146/http://us.india.com/election-2014/parties/eight-laws-in-ten-years-of-upa-government-that-changed-india-31994.

16. Justice K.S. Puttaswamy vs Union of India on 26 September, 2018, in the Supreme Court of India; judgement available at https://indiankanoon.org/doc/127517806/.

17. B. Chandrasekaran, "RTE Access to Poor Students: Challenges Faced by the States", *Centre for Public Policy Research*, 2019, https://www.cppr.in/wp-content/uploads/2020/01/RTE-Access-to-Poor-Students_Challenges-Faced-by-the-States.pdf.

18. "India launches children's right to education", *BBC News*, 1 April 2010, http://news.bbc.co.uk/2/hi/8598167.stm.

19. Nilanjana Bhowmik, "10 Years Of Right To Education: A Progress Report", *Reader's Digest*, 26 August 2019, https://www.readersdigest.in/features/story-right-to-education-a-progress-report-125002.

20. Ankur Sarin, "Mandate for social inclusion in RTE", *LiveMint*, 15 June 2015, https://www.livemint.com/Opinion/nUts2tKLEynCe8yiBfZaBM/Mandate-for-social-inclusion-in-RTE.html.

21. Chandrasekaran, "RTE Access".

22. Ventikesh Ramakrishnan, "Naxal terror", *Frontline*, 21 September 2007, https://frontline.thehindu.com/cover-story/article30192801.ece.

23. "People's discontent and system failure", *Mainstream* 46, 25 (8 June 2008), https://www.mainstreamweekly.net/article749.html.

24. Walter Fernandes, "Singur and the Displacement Scenario", *Economic and Political Weekly* 42, 3 (20 January 2007), https://www.epw.in/journal/2007/03/commentary/singur-and-displacement-scenario.html.

25. "Government has lost plot on land bill, say Opposition members of parliamentary panel", *The Economic Times*, 27 February 2018, https://economictimes.indiatimes.com/news/politics-and-nation/government-has-lost-plot-on-land-bill-say-opposition-members-of-parliamentary-panel/articleshow/63099991.cms.

26. Ishani Sonak, "State govts acquire land by subverting rights and bending the law", *Down to Earth*, 12 December 2018, https://www.downtoearth.org.in/news/agriculture/-state-govts-acquire-land-by-subverting-rights-and-bending-the-law--62463.

27. Ibid.

28. "MGNREGA: Features, Problems, Achievements, and Way forward", *Sociology Group*, 17 March 2020, https://www.sociologygroup.com/mgnrega-features-problems-achievments/.

29. "MNREGA is a monument of UPA government's failures, we won't stop it: PM Modi", *News18*, 27 February 2015, https://www.news18.com/news/politics/modi-speech-9-969834.html.

30. "MGNREGA: Features, Problems, Achievements, and Way forward", *Sociology Group*.

31. "10 years on, Centre hails MGNREGA as 'national pride'", *Business Standard*, 2 February 2016, https://www.business-standard.com/article/economy-policy/10-years-on-centre-hails-mgnrega-as-national-pride-116020200037_1.html.

32. "₹3,358 crore in MGNREGA wages not paid", *The Hindu*, 2 February 2022, https://www.thehindu.com/news/national/3358-crore-mgnrega-wage-payments-pending-government-tells-rajya-sabha/article38366264.ece.

33. "Budget 2022: Demand for work higher than pre-Covid level but MGNREGS allocation not raised", *The Indian Express*, 1 February 2022, https://indianexpress.com/article/business/budget/budget-2022-demand-for-work-higher-than-pre-covid-level-but-mgnregs-allocation-not-raised-7751373.

34. "India isolated; voices of States muffled: Rahul Gandhi", *The Hindu*, 2 February 2022, https://www.thehindu.com/news/national/india-isolated-voices-of-states-muffled-rahul-gandhi/article38366707.ece.

35. Ahmed Ali, "Now, FIR on Rashmi Shukla in Mumbai for Sanjay Raut and Eknath Khadse phone taps", *The Times of India*, 5 March 2022, https://timesofindia.indiatimes.com/city/mumbai/now-fir-on-shukla-in-city-for-raut-and-khadse-phone-taps/articleshow/90003307.cms.

36. See collated coverage at http://www.rediff.com/news/dubey.htm.

37. Rohit K. Singh et al., "Eight killed in violence during protest against ministers in UP's Lakhimpur Kheri: Police", *Hindustan Times*, 3 October 2021, https://www.hindustantimes.com/india-news/eight-dead-in-up-s-lakhimpur-kheri-after-jeep-runs-over-protesting-farmers-101633273679900.html.

38. "UP cop calls Mayawati govt corrupt, dumped in mental asylum", *The Times of India*, 5 November 2011, https://timesofindia.indiatimes.com/india/up-cop-calls-mayawati-govt-corrupt-dumped-in-mental-asylum/articleshow/10616560.cms.

39. Maitreesh Ghatak, Parikshit Ghosh, and Ashok Kotwal, "Growth in the time of UPA: Myth and reality", *Economic and Political Weekly* 49, 16 (19 April 2014): 34–43, available at https://personal.lse.ac.uk/ghatak/upa-epw.pdf.

40. UNCTAD Secretariat, "The Least Developed Countries Report 2008", United Nations, 2008, available at https://unctad.org/press-material/despite-rapid-economic-growth-number-poor-still-rising-least-developed-countries.

41. https://interstatecouncil.gov.in/report-of-the-commission-on-centre-state-relations/

42. Sandeep Joshigargi Parsai, "Government forced to defer Communal Violence Bill", *The Hindu*, 5 February 2014, http://www.thehindu.com/news/national/government-forced-to-defer-communal-violence-bill/article5656766.ece.

43. "Joint Statement Between President George W. Bush and Prime Minister Manmohan Singh", The White House, 18 July 2005, https://georgewbush-whitehouse.archives.gov/news/releases/2005/07/20050718-6.html.

44. Deepshikha Ghosh, "Cash-for-vote scam: Amar Singh, three BJP leaders who waved cash in Parliament let off", NDTV, 22 November 2013, https://www.ndtv.com/india-news/cash-for-vote-scam-amar-singh-three-bjp-leaders-who-waved-cash-in-parliament-let-off-542036.

45. Ajaz Ashraf, "The BJP's ads during the 2008 Mumbai attacks expose its hypocrisy on questioning national security", *The Caravan*, 15 March 2019, https://caravanmagazine.in/politics/bjp-ads-2008-mumbai-attacks-expose-hypocrisy-questioning-national-security.

46. "Read reports on the 26/11 Mumbai attacks accessed from the Maharashtra legislature under the RTI act, while the Union Home Ministry denies access", Commonwealth Human Rights Initiative, n.d. [November 2018], https://www.humanrightsinitiative.org/blog/read-reports-on-the-2611-mumbai-attacks-accessed-from-the-maharashtra-legislature-under-the-rti-act-while-the-union-home-ministry-denies-access.

47. Geeta Pandey, "Delhi loses patience with Commonwealth Games", *BBC News*, 3 September 2010, https://www.bbc.com/news/world-south-asia-11101288.

48. Ibid.

49. "CVC finds irregularities in several CWG projects", *The Economic Times*, 28 July 2010, https://economictimes.indiatimes.com/cvc-finds-irregularities-in-several-cwg-projects/articleshow/6229429.cms.

50. Mihir Vasavda, "10 years on, CWG mess: 50 payment cases, Rs 40-crore aerostat idle", *The Indian Express*, 3 October 2020, https://indianexpress.com/article/sports/commonwealth-games-payment-dispute-sports-ministry-6674483/.

51. Surendra Singh, "Explained: Nuts and bolts of the controversial Antrix-Devas case", *The Times of India*, 18 January 2022, https://timesofindia.indiatimes.com/business/india-business/explained-nuts-and-bolts-of-the-controversial-antrix-devas-case/articleshow/88971725.cms.

52. "Antrix-Devas deal: Madhavan Nair met mastermind twice, says CBI", *The Hindu*, 13 August 2017, https://www.thehindu.com/news/national/

antrix-devas-deal-madhavan-nair-met-mastermind-twice-says-cbi/
article19486705.ece.

53.  Chethan Kumar, "I'm no politician, joined BJP because I liked PM Modi's
     vision: Ex-Isro chairman G Madhavan Nair", *The Times of India*, 28 October
     2018,    https://timesofindia.indiatimes.com/india/im-no-politician-joined-
     bjp-because-i-liked-pm-modis-vision-ex-isro-chairman-g-madhavan nair/
     articleshow/66401088.cms.

54.  Krishnadas Rajagopal, "Supreme Court upholds tribunal decision to wind up
     Devas", *The Hindu*, 17 January 2022, https://www.thehindu.com/news/
     national/supreme-court-upholds-tribunal-decision-to-wind-up-devas/
     article38281536.ece.

55.  Sreya Chatterjee, "Antrix-Devas deal is fraud of Congress, by Congress, for
     Congress, says finance minister Sitharaman", *India Today*, 18 January 2022,
     https://www.indiatoday.in/india/story/antrix-devas-deal-fraud-congress-
     finance-minister-nirmala-sitharaman-1901525-2022-01-18.

56.  Comptroller and Auditor General of India, "Performance Audit Report on the
     Issue of Licences and Allocation of 2G Spectrum", Government of India, 2010–
     11,   available   at   https://web.archive.org/web/20110721155418/http://
     cag.gov.in/html/reports/civil/2010-11_19PA/Telecommunication%20
     Report.pdf.

57.  "Indian media: '2G scam' probe", *BBC News*, 21 November 2014, https://
     www.bbc.com/news/world-asia-india-30140856.

58.  Priyanka Mittal and Aditi Singh, "2G spectrum scam: A timeline of events",
     *LiveMint*,   22   December   2017,   https://www.livemint.com/Politics/
     lhr4Lk37t2WooRRijoitxN/2G-spectrum-scam-verdict-A-timeline-of-
     events.html.

59.  Binoy Prabhakar, "Central Board of Direct Taxes raises questions on
     CAG's 2G scandal loss estimates", *The Economic Times*, 13 December 2011,
     https://economictimes.indiatimes.com/industry/telecom/central-
     board-of-direct-taxes-raises-questions-on-cags-2g-scandal-loss-estimates/
     articleshow/11087725.cms.

60.  Ibid.

61.  Dhananjay Mahapatra, "2G loss? Govt. gained over Rs 3,000cr: Trai", *The
     Times of India*, 7 September 2011, archived at https://web.archive.org/
     web/20111106234144/http://articles.timesofindia.indiatimes.com/2011-
     09-07/india/30122800_1_spectrum-trai-2g.

62.  Aneesha Mathur, "Padmanabha Swamy Temple case: SC upholds Travancore royal
     family's rights to administer historic temple", *India Today*, 13 July 2020, https://
     www.indiatoday.in/india/story/padmanabha-swamy-temple-sc-travancore-
     royal-family-administration-of-historic-kerala-1699951-2020-07-13.

63.  "Vinod Rai has been complete failure in implementing Lodha reforms: Amitabh Choudhary", *The Economic Times*, 3 August 2018, https://economictimes. indiatimes.com/news/sports/vinod-rai-has-been-complete-failure-in-implementing-lodha-reforms-amitabh-choudhary/articleshow/65259322.cms.

64.  "Ed vs . (1) A. Raja; on 21 December, 2017", Delhi District Court, available at https://indiankanoon.org/doc/37508020/.

65.  "2G scam verdict: All 18 accused including A Raja acquitted, Congress seeks ex-CAG Vinod Rai's apology", *Business Today*, 21 December 2017, https://www.businesstoday.in/industry/telecom/story/2g-scam-verdict-a-raja-kanimozhi-cag-vinod-rai-spectrum-87503-2017-12-21.

66.  Anand Mohan J, "Ex-CAG Vinod Rai tenders unconditional apology to Congress leader Sanjay Nirupam in defamation case", *The Indian Express*, 29 October 2021, https://indianexpress.com/article/cities/delhi/ex-cag-vinod-rai-tenders-unconditional-apology-to-congress-leader-sanjay-nirupam-in-defamation-case-7595422/.

67.  "'Does it now not appear that then CAG Vinod Rai was the Agent Provocateur?': Cong leader Salman Khurshid", *The Indian Express*, 5 November 2021, https://indianexpress.com/article/india/cag-vinod-rai-agent-provocateur-cong-leader-salman-khurshid-7608698/.

68.  Aasha Kapur Mehta and Trishna Satpathy, "Escaping Poverty: The Ralegan Siddhi Case", Chronic Poverty Research Centre/Indian Institute of Public Administration, Working Paper 38, n.d. [2008], https://www.chronicpoverty. org/uploads/publication_files/CPRC-IIPA_38.pdf.

69.  Prafulla Marpakwar, "Snap poll woke Rane up to sack Gholap", *Indian Express*, 28 April 1999, archived at https://web.archive.org/web/19991007070036/ http://www.expressindia.com/ie/daily/19990428/ipo28060.html.

70.  "VK Singh now battles with Baba Ramdev", *Zee News*, 12 August 2012, https://zeenews.india.com/news/nation/vk-singh-now-battles-with-baba-ramdev_793178.html.

71.  "Sharad Pawar quits corruption panel as support for Anna Hazare grows", *The Times of India*, 7 April 2011, archived at https://web.archive.org/ web/20121105155732/http://articles.timesofindia.indiatimes.com/2011-04-07/india/29391933_1_anna-hazare-corruption-panel-sharad-pawar.

72.  Sunanda Mehta, "Fast Forward, 1980 to 2011", *Indian Express*, 19 August 2011, https://indianexpress.com/article/news-archive/web/fast-forward-1980-to-2011/.

73.  "Bollywood continues to support Hazare": https://gulfnews.com/world/ asia/india/bollywood-continues-to-support-hazare-1.789310

74.  "Ordinance shielding convicted lawmakers: Rahul calls it 'nonsense'", *Hindustan Times*, 3 October 2013, https://www.hindustantimes.com/india/

ordinance-shielding-convicted-lawmakers-rahul-calls-it-nonsense/story-cn4NKNY8RM2qMGd8fSuYcK.html.

75. Sunetra Choudhury, "Was too aggressive, says Rahul Gandhi on tearing ordinance on corrupt netas", *Hindustan Times*, 10 May 2019, https://www.hindustantimes.com/india-news/was-too-aggressive-says-rahul-gandhi-on-tearing ordinance on corrupt-netas/story-fcIaD2aRCcMXDDoQNYftMP.html.

76. "Pranab, Sibal meet Baba Ramdev at Delhi airport", *Deccan Herald*, 1 June 2011, https://www.deccanherald.com/national/pranab-sibal-meet-baba-ramdev-at-delhi-airport-159696.html.

77. Manoj C G, "Meeting Baba Ramdev: I should not have done it, admits Pranab Mukherjee", *The Indian Express*, 25 October 2017, https://indianexpress.com/article/india/pranab-mukherjee-baba-ramdev-anna-hazare-agitation-congress-upa-ii-government-kapil-sibal-4892334/.

78. Vasdev and Mathew, "Manmohan Singh targets Modi".

79. "Modi calls PM 'Maun' Mohan Singh while campaigning in HP", ABP News, 29 October 2012, https://www.youtube.com/watch?v=MxNCsCGwhN0.

6.   THE NATIONAL DEMOCRATIC ALLIANCE: 2014–2024

1. Harish Khare, "The Modi Triumph: From 1984 to 2014 and back to 1984", *Scroll*, 2 January 2015, https://scroll.in/article/697923/the-modi-triumph-from-1984-to-2014-and-back-to-1984.

2. Suhas Palshikar, "What voters are saying through BJP's poll wins", *Indian Express*, 12 March 2022, https://indianexpress.com/article/opinion/columns/assembly-election-results-2022-uttar-pradesh-punjab-uttarakhand-goa-manipur-7813753/.

3. Seema Chishti, "Five State polls, their messages and implications", *The Hindu*, 11 March 2022, https://www.thehindu.com/opinion/lead/five-state-polls-their-messages-and-implications/article65212045.ece.

4. Madeeha Fatima, Naomi Barton and Alishan Jafri, "100+ Instances of Hate Speech, Religious Polarisation, Hindutva Supremacy in Adityanath's Poll Speeches", *The Wire*, 3 March 2022, https://thewire.in/communalism/100-instances-of-hate-speech-religious-polarisation-hindutva-supremacy-in-adityanaths-poll-speeches.

5. Alishan Jafri, "Despite BJP Win, Several Hardcore Hindutva Poster Boys Lost Their Seats in UP", *The Wire*, 11 March 2022, https://thewire.in/communalism/despite-bjp-win-several-hardcore-hindutva-poster-boys-lost-their-seats-in-up.

6.  "India's MLA count reveals BJP is not as ahead as you thought", *The Times of India*, 22 March 2022, https://timesofindia.indiatimes.com/india/indias-mla-count-reveals-bjp-is-not-as-ahead-as-you-thought/articleshow/90353921.cms.

7.  Liz Mathew, "Need governance too, not just halal, hijab: BJP brass signal to Bommai", *Indian Express*, 9 April 2022, https://indianexpress.com/article/india/need-governance-too-not-just-halal-hijab-bjp-brass-signal-to-bommai-7860652/.

8.  "BJP heading for 'India Shining' fiasco in 2024", *Times Now*, 20 May 2022, https://www.timesnownews.com/india/bjp-heading-for-india-shining-fiasco-in-2024-due-to-failing-economy-illegal-chinese-occupation-subramanian-swamy-article-91694410.

9.  Bhuvan Bagga, "What makes NDA's 'India Shining' campaign the 'worst' poll strategy in Indian history", *India Today*, 14 May 2013, https://www.indiatoday.in/india/story/nda-india-shining-worst-poll-strategy-162922-2013-05-14.

10. "People from different states should speak in Hindi, not English: Amit Shah", *Indian Express*, 9 April 2022, https://indianexpress.com/article/india/people-different-states-should-speak-hindi-not-english-shah-7858861/.

11. "Angry Tamil Nadu netas claim attack on national integrity", *The Times of India*, 9 April 2022, https://timesofindia.indiatimes.com/india/angry-tamil-nadu-netas-claim-attack-on-national-integrity/articleshow/90737865.cms.

12. "Tamil Nadu Governor RN Ravi's remarks on Sanatan Dharma draws flak from DMK", *The New Indian Express*, 13 June 2022, https://www.newindianexpress.com/states/tamil-nadu/2022/jun/13/tamil-nadu-governor-rn-ravis-remarks-on-sanatan-dharma-draws-flak-from-dmk-2464907.html.

13. "Assam CM emerges player in Maharashtra political crisis", *The Hindu*, 22 June 2022, https://www.thehindu.com/news/national/other-states/assam-cm-emerges-player-in-maharashtra-political-crisis/article65552640.ece.

14. Shivam Vij and Ben Arnoldy, "US, India dance awkwardly around the man who might be India's next leader", *The Christian Science Monitor*, 14 May 2013, https://www.csmonitor.com/World/Asia-South-Central/2013/0514/US-India-dance-awkwardly-around-the-man-who-might-be-India-s-next-leader.

15. "Narendra Modi's electoral milestone: 437 rallies, 3 lakh km", *The Times of India*, 30 April 2014, https://timesofindia.indiatimes.com/news/narendra-modis-electoral-milestone-437-rallies-3-lakh-km/articleshow/34400255.cms.

16. Manish Kumar, "4 get Death Sentence for 2013 Blasts in Patna ahead of PM Modi's Rally", *NDTV*, 1 November 2021, https://www.ndtv.com/india-news/4-get-death-sentence-for-2013-blasts-in-patna-ahead-of-pm-modis-rally-2596041.

17. Khare, "The Modi Triumph".

18. Harish Khare, "In India, a Hindu revolution", *The New York Times*, 7 January 1985, https://www.nytimes.com/1985/01/07/opinion/in-india-a-hindu-revolution.html.

19. Because of the Gujarat riots in 2002.

20. Khare, "The Modi triumph".

21. "France bets on the Left", *The New York Times*, 12 July 1981, https://www.nytimes.com/1981/07/12/magazine/france-bets-on-the-left.html.

22. Lopa Ghosh (ed.), "100 Days Review of NDA Government", Wada Na Todo, September 2014, https://gcap.global/wp-content/uploads/2018/07/Review-of-NDA-Government-2014.pdf.

23. "PM Narendra Modi scraps Planning Commission", *Hindustan Times*, 15 August 2014, https://www.hindustantimes.com/india/pm-narendra-modi-scraps-planning-commission/story-EJdGN4v0ETFV1SJZEeFy1J.html.

24. "United Opposition firm on PM's response", *The Hindu*, 16 November 2021, https://www.thehindu.com/news/national/Parliament-session-United-Opposition-firm-on-Narendra-Modi%E2%80%99s-response/article60321226.ece.

25. "Ghar wapsi to continue till conversions are banned: Adityanath", *The Hindu*, 24 February 2015, https://www.thehindu.com/news/national/other-states/ghar-wapsi-to-continue-till-conversions-are-banned-adityanath/article6929001.ece.

26. Ram Puniyani, "Is there a Difference Between Ghar Vapasi And Forcible Conversions?", *The Citizen*, 18 December 2014, https://www.thecitizen.in/index.php/en/newsdetail/index/4/1774/is-there-a-difference-between-ghar-vapasi--and-forcible-conversions.

27. Jeffrey Gettleman and Suhasini Raj, "Arrests, Beatings and Secret Prayers: Inside the Persecution of Indian Christians.", *The New York Times*, 22 December 2021, https://www.nytimes.com/2021/12/22/world/asia/india-christians-attacked.html.

28. "Pastor critical as carol singers attacked in India", *Premier Christian News*, 14 December 2014, https://premierchristian.news/us/news/article/pastor-critical-as-carol-singers-attacked-in-india.

29. "Madhya Pradesh: Hindutva groups vandalise Christian management school", *Maktoob Media*, 7 December 2021, https://maktoobmedia.com/2021/12/07/madhya-pradesh-hindutva-groups-vandalise-christian-management-school/.

30. "Beaten to death for being a dairy farmer", *BBC News*, 8 April 2017, https://www.bbc.com/news/world-asia-india-39511556.

31. "India 2018 International Religious Freedom Report", US State Department, 2018, https://www.state.gov/wp-content/uploads/2019/05/INDIA-2018-INTERNATIONAL-RELIGIOUS-FREEDOM-REPORT.pdf.

32. "2021 Report on International Religious Freedom: India", US State Department, 2021, https://www.state.gov/reports/2021-report-on-international-religious-freedom/india/.

33. "Modi Claims 'UPA Took No Action After 26/11', But Is That True?", *The Quint*, 1 March 2019, https://www.thequint.com/news/webqoof/pm-modi-kanyakumari-upa-no-action-after-2611-fact-check#read-more.

34. "Backtracking: India says no helicopters used in 'surgical strikes'", *The Express Tribune*, 30 September 2016, https://tribune.com.pk/story/1191350/backtracking-india-says-no-helicopters-used-surgical-strikes.

35. "'6 surgical strikes' in UPA tenure: Cong backs Manmohan Singh with dates", *Hindustan Times*, 2 May 2019, https://www.hindustantimes.com/india-news/6-surgical-strikes-in-upa-tenure-congress-leader-provides-dates/story-VhiGIV6WcSB1oEkBTRMXxH.html.

36. Ibid.

37. "Balakot air strike: Pakistan shows off disputed site on eve of India election", *BBC News*, 10 April 2019, https://www.bbc.com/news/world-asia-47882354.

38. "Sankalp Patra, Lok Sabha 2019" (Manifesto, General Election 2019), Bharatiya Janata Party, pp. 5–6, https://www.bjp.org/files/2019-10/BJP-Election-english-2019.pdf.

39. Ravichandran Bathran, "What Swachh Bharat Abhiyan ignores", *The Hindu*, 21 August 2018, https://www.thehindu.com/opinion/op-ed/what-swachh-bharat-abhiyan-ignores/article24738978.ece.

40. "India's Total Sanitation Campaign", Centre for Public Impact, 25 August 2017, https://www.centreforpublicimpact.org/case-study/total-sanitation-campaign-india.

41. See chapter 8 of the report by the Comptroller and Auditor General, available at https://cag.gov.in/uploads/download_audit_report/2015/Union_Performance_Nirmal_Bharat_Abhiyan_Report_28_2015_chap_8.pdf.

42. Lopa Ghosh (ed.), "100 Days Review of NDA Government".

43. Harikishan Sharma, "CAG report on Rajasthan: In ODF state, toilets missing in half of PMAY houses surveyed", *The Indian Express*, 31 August 2020, https://indianexpress.com/article/india/cag-report-on-rajasthan-in-odf-state-toilets-missing-in-half-of-pmay-houses-surveyed-6576714/.

44. Shivangi Aggarwal, "Is India really open-defecation-free? Here's what numbers say", *Down To Earth*, 13 July 2021, https://www.downtoearth.org.in/news/rural-water-and-sanitation/is-india-really-open-defecation-free-here-s-what-numbers-say-77918.

45. Bathran, "What Swachh Bharat Abhiyan ignores".

46. "Transforming denial into deliberation: The case of manual scavenging", Observer Research Foundation, 21 December 2021, https://www.orfonline. org/expert-speak/transforming-denial-into-deliberation-the-case-of-manual-scavenging/.

47. "Nearly One in Five Households in India Practise Open Defecation: NFHS-5 Data", *The Wire*, 9 May 2022, https://thewire.in/government/nearly-one-in-five-households-in-india-practise-open-defecation-nfhs-5-data.

48. "Fact check: Did Modi really promise Rs 15 lakh to every Indian?", *Yahoo News*, 24 January 2019, https://sg.news.yahoo.com/fact-check-modi-really-promise-rs-15-lakh-every-indian-111135514.html.

49. Mudit Kapoor, "Report card: Modi government's fight against black money", *India Today*, 3 August 2018, https://www.indiatoday.in/india/story/report-card-modi-government-s-fight-against-black-money-1303933-2018-08-03.

50. "Since Nov 8, over 80 people have died in ATM queues. Is it mere coincidence?", *Mumbai Mirror*, 27 December 2018, https://mumbaimirror.indiatimes.com/mumbai/cover-story/since-nov-8-over-80-people-have-died-in-atm-queues-is-it-mere-coincidence/articleshow/56398080.cms.

51. "Thanks to Demonetization and GST, India's GDP growth hit a 4-year low at 6.5 per cent", *India Today*, 6 January 2018, https://www.indiatoday.in/education-today/gk-current-affairs/story/demonetization-gst-sloweddown-gdp-growth-of-india-1123939-2018-01-06.

52. Michael Safi, "Demonetisation drive that cost India 1.5m jobs fails to uncover 'black money'", *The Guardian*, 30 August 2018, https://www.theguardian.com/world/2018/aug/30/india-demonetisation-drive-fails-uncover-black-money.

53. Arun Kumar, "Five years later, it's even more clear that demonetisation was a disaster for India", *Scroll*, 6 November 2021, https://scroll.in/article/1009871/five-years-later-its-even-more-clear-that-demonetisation-was-a-disaster-for-india.

54. Vikas Dhoot, "Is the economy still reeling from demonetisation?", *The Hindu*, 12 November 2021, https://www.thehindu.com/opinion/op-ed/is-the-economy-still-reeling-from-demonetisation/article37445099.ece.

55. Asad Rehman and Manish Sahu, "P Jain and P Jain: Tale of 2 perfume merchants raises some stink in UP", *The Indian Express*, 29 December 2021, https://indianexpress.com/article/cities/lucknow/p-jain-p-jain-tale-of-2-perfume-merchants-raises-some-stink-in-up-7695439/.

56. Kundan Pandey, "COVID-19 lockdown will damage more than demonetisation: Pronab Sen", *Down To Earth*, 1 April 2020, https://www.downtoearth.org.

in/interviews/governance/covid-19-lockdown-will-damage-more-than-demonetisation-pronab-sen-70143.

57.  Justice Ashok Bhushan, "Suo Moto Writ Petition (Civil) no. 6 of 2020: Judgment", Supreme Court of India, https://main.sci.gov.in/supremecourt/2020/11706/11706_2020_36_1501_28166_Judgement_29-Jun-2021.pdf.

58.  "Migrant woes 'greatest manmade tragedy' in India since Partition: Ramchandra Guha", *The Hindu*, 24 May 2020, https://www.thehindu.com/news/national/migrant-woes-greatest-manmade-tragedy-in-india-since-partition-ramchandra-guha/article61653329.ece.

59.  "India's Coronavirus Lockdown Leaves Vast Numbers Stranded and Hungry", *The New York Times*, 29 March 2020, https://www.nytimes.com/2020/03/29/world/asia/coronavirus-india-migrants.html.

60.  Soutik Biswas, "India Covid-19 migrants: 'Lockdown will make us beg for food again'", *BBC News*, 14 April 2021, https://www.bbc.com/news/world-asia-india-56711150.

61.  Umesh Kumar Ray, "From Gurgaon to Bihar, 15-Year-Old Girl Cycles 1,200 km With Injured Father", *The Wire*, 21 May 2020, https://thewire.in/rights/jyoti-kumari-bihar-gurgaon-cycle-covid-19-lockdown.

62.  Geeta Pandey, "Coronavirus in India: Desperate migrant workers trapped in lockdown" *BBC News*, 22 April 2020, https://www.bbc.com/news/world-asia-india-52360757.

63.  "UP CM giving advertisements when bodies of people floating in river during Covid 2nd wave: Kejriwal", *The Times of India*, 8 February 2022, https://timesofindia.indiatimes.com/india/up-cm-giving-advertisements-when-bodies-of-people-floating-in-river-during-covid-2nd-wave-kejriwal/articleshow/89418904.cms.

64.  Soutik Biswas, "Coronavirus: India faces oxygen scarcity as cases surge", *BBC News*, 15 September 2020, https://www.bbc.com/news/world-asia-india-54139112.

65.  Soutik Biswas, "Covid-19: How India failed to prevent a deadly second wave", *BBC News*, 19 April 2021, https://www.bbc.com/news/world-asia-india-56771766.

66.  Sandeep Unnithan, "India's covid collapse, part 7: Why did we face an acute oxygen shortage?", *India Today*, 10 May 2021, https://www.indiatoday.in/magazine/cover-story/story/20210517-india-s-covid-collapse-part-7-why-did-we-face-an-acute-oxygen-shortage-1800939-2021-05-10.

67.  Rahul Shrivastava, "Mumbai vs Delhi: Why the capital is facing an oxygen crisis?", *India Today*, 7 May 2021, https://www.indiatoday.in/coronavirus-outbreak/story/mumbai-delhi-oxygen-crisis-covid-cases-deaths-1799979-2021-05-07.

68.  Meghna Sen, "Examine 'Mumbai Model', learn from it: Supreme Court

to Centre on Delhi oxygen crisis", *Live Mint*, 5 May 2021, https://www.livemint.com/news/india/examine-mumbai-model-learn-from-it-supreme-court-tells-centre-on-oxygen-crisis-in-delhi-11620204087661.html.

69. "Health minister Harsh Vardhan resigns ahead of Cabinet reshuffle", *Hindustan Times*, 7 July 2021, https://www.hindustantimes.com/india-news/health-minister-harsh-vardhan-resigns-ahead-of-cabinet-reshuffle-101625650188177.html.

70. Milan Sharma and Sneha Mordani, "No deaths due to lack of oxygen reported during second Covid wave: Centre", *India Today*, 20 July 2021, https://www.indiatoday.in/coronavirus-outbreak/story/covid-second-wave-lack-shortage-liquid-medical-oxygen-lmo-deaths-health-ministry-response-parliament-1830549-2021-07-20.

71. "With Goa Toll, Hospital Oxygen Shortage Has Taken Lives of at Least 223 COVID Patients in India", *TheWire*, 12 May 2021, https://thewire.in/health/oxygen-shortage-deaths-india-covid-19.

72. Saurav Das, "Death Count In 24 UP Districts 43 Times More Than Official Covid-19 Toll", *Article 14*, 21 June 2021, https://article-14.com/post/untitled-60cf605395758.

73. "Covid-19: Over 100 bodies found floating in River Ganga in Ghazipur, Uttar Pradesh", *The Times of India*, 11 May 2021, https://timesofindia.indiatimes.com/videos/city/lucknow/covid-19-over-100-bodies-found-floating-in-river-ganga-in-ghazipur-uttar-pradesh/videoshow/82540887.cms.

74. Santosh Singh, Asad Rehman, "Nearly 100 bodies found floating in Ganga, spark panic in Bihar, Uttar Pradesh", *Indian Express*, 12 May 2021, https://indianexpress.com/article/india/nearly-100-bodies-found-floating-in-ganga-spark-panic-in-bihar-up-7311518/.

75. Geeta Pandey, "Covid-19: India's holiest river is swollen with bodies", *BBC News*, 19 May 2021, https://www.bbc.com/news/world-asia-india-57154564.

76. "750 Died During Farmers Protest, No Condolence From Centre: Farmer Leader", *NDTV*, 8 November 2021, https://www.ndtv.com/india-news/750-died-during-farmers-protest-no-condolence-from-centre-rakesh-tikait-2602504.

77. "How India's Farmers, Organized and Well Funded, Faced Down Modi", *The NewYorkTimes*, 20 November 2021, https://www.nytimes.com/2021/11/20/world/asia/india-modi-farmer-protests.html.

78. "India Covid-19: PM Modi 'did not consult' before lockdown", *BBC News*, 29 March 2021, https://www.bbc.com/news/world-asia-india-56561095.

79. "The Full List of 20 Countries and Bodies That Have Condemned the BJP Leaders' Remarks", *TheWire*, 7 June 2022, https://thewire.in/communalism/

NOTES

the-full-list-of-18-countries-and-bodies-that-have-condemned-the-bjp-leaders-remarks.

80. "Pakistan will be part of India after 2025, claims RSS leader Indresh Kumar: Report", *Scroll*, 17 March 2019, https://scroll.in/latest/916896/pakistan-will-be-part-of-india-after-2025-claims-rss-leader-indresh-kumar-report.

81. "Nepal lodges protest over Tripura CM's 'BJP will form govt' remark", *The Times of India*, 17 February 2021, https://timesofindia.indiatimes.com/india/nepal-lodges-protest-over-tripura-cms-bjp-will-form-govt-remark/articleshow/81024408.cms.

82. Syed Mohammed, "Bhagyalakshmi temple came into existence after merger of Hyderabad with India: ASI", *The Hindu*, 17 February 2021, https://www.thehindu.com/news/cities/Hyderabad/no-records-of-chilla-adjacent-to-charminar-says-asi/article33864233.ece.

83. Srinivas Mazumdaru, "Modi visits Myanmar as Rohingya crisis worsens", *DW*, 9 May 2017, https://www.dw.com/en/indias-narendra-modi-visits-myanmar-as-rohingya-crisis-worsens/a-40366559.

84. Dipanjan Roy Chaudhury, "Pakistan provides key support to boost Myanmar Air Force", *The Economic Times*, 4 June 2022, https://economictimes.indiatimes.com/news/defence/pakistan-provides-key-support-to-boost-myanmar-air-force/articleshow/91993510.cms.

85. P. Raman, "Modi's Raid Raj: 'Janampatri' Has Emerged as Key Instrument of Power Against the Opposition", *The Wire*, 25 March 2022, https://thewire.in/politics/modis-raid-raj-janampatri-has-emerged-as-key-instrument-of-power-against-the-opposition.

86. "Centre extends ED Director SK Mishra's tenure by one year", *Business Today*, 14 November 2020, https://www.businesstoday.in/latest/economy-politics/story/centre-extends-ed-director-sk-mishra-tenure-by-one-year-278694-2020-11-14.

87. Deeptiman Tiwary, "Centre brings Ordinances to extend tenure of ED, CBI directors up to 5 years", *The Indian Express*, 15 November 2021, https://indianexpress.com/article/india/centre-ordinances-tenure-ed-cbi-directors-extended-7622361/.

88. "CBI, ED, other agencies biggest allies of BJP-led central government: Shatrughan Sinha", *Deccan Herald*, 22 March 2022, https://www.deccanherald.com/national/national-politics/cbi-ed-other-agencies-biggest-allies-of-bjp-led-central-government-shatrughan-sinha-1093621.html.

89. "'CBI team found nothing, timing of search interesting': P Chidambaram", *India TV*, 17 May 2022, https://www.indiatvnews.com/news/india/chidambaram-reacts-on-cbi-raids-on-karti-chidambaram-residences-in-chennai-and-delhi-2022-05-17-777182.

90.  "P Chidambaram, Kapil Sibal Among 41 Elected Unopposed To Rajya Sabha", *NDTV*, 3 June 2022, https://www.ndtv.com/india-news/p-chidambaram-kapil-sibal-among-41-elected-unopposed-to-rajya-sabha-3036598.

91.  Vishal Kant, "Jharkhand's first family hit by graft charges", *Hindustan Times*, 2 May 2022, https://www.hindustantimes.com/india-news/sorens-first-political-family of jharkhand and its tryst with controversies-101651429152813. html.

92.  "JMM snubs Sonia, puts up Rajya Sabha nominee; doesn't even say its alliance candidate", *The Times of India*, 31 May 2022, https://timesofindia.indiatimes. com/india/jmm-snubs-sonia-puts-up-rajya-sabha-nominee-doesnt-even-say-its-alliance-candidate/articleshow/91900483.cms.

93.  Krishnadas Rajagopal, "Land grabbing case: Supreme Court stays Allahabad High Court's bail condition to Azam Khan", *The Hindu*, 27 May 2022, https://www.thehindu.com/news/national/other-states/land-grabbing-case-sc-stays-allahabad-hcs-bail-conditionto-azam-khan/article65467004.ece.

94.  Prafulla Marpakwar, "A year on: Congress, NCP question CBI on Sushant Singh Rajput case", *The Times of India*, 15 June 2021, https://timesofindia. indiatimes.com/city/mumbai/a-yr-on-cong-ncp-question-cbi-on-sushant-case/articleshow/83524917.cms.

95.  "On quiet visit to Mumbai, NCB boss preps for crackdown in Bollywood drugs case", *Hindustan Times*, 23 October 2020, https://www.hindustantimes.com/india-news/on-quiet-visit-to-mumbai-ncb-boss-preps-for-crackdown-in-bollywood-drugs-case/story-rOdh5KBdUifNgjZrjciAAP.html.

96.  "Collapse of NCB's case against Aryan Khan points to a failed witch hunt. Those who were complicit in it must pay", *The Indian Express*, 28 May 2022, https://indianexpress.com/article/opinion/editorials/hounding-of-aryan-khan-7940105/.

97.  "ED's list of political accused reads like a Opposition's who's who. Makes it harder for the agency to earn trust", *The Indian Express*, 3 June 2022, https://indianexpress.com/article/opinion/editorials/enforced-directorate-7949693/.

98.  Vappala Balachandran, "ED's powers and functions call for scrutiny", *The Tribune*, 24 December 2021, https://www.tribuneindia.com/news/comment/eds-powers-and-functions-call-for-scrutiny-353803.

99.  Vappala Balachandran, "NCB should meet international obligations", *The Tribune*, 6 December 2021, https://www.tribuneindia.com/news/comment/ncb-should-meet-international-obligations-346725.

100. "As ED Chief Gets One-Year Extension, Here's a List of Cases He's Probing Against Opposition Leaders", *The Wire*, 15 November 2020, https://thewire. in/government/enforcement-directorate-sanjay-mishra-extension.

101. While Mukul Roy returned to Trinamool Congress (TMC) following the landslide win of Mamata Banerjee in 2021, Sarma was the Chief Minister of Assam from May 2021.

102. Sujit Mahamulkar, "Shiv Sena MLA Pratap Sarnaik urges Uddhav Thackeray to join hands with BJP", *The Times of India*, 20 June 2021, https://timesofindia. indiatimes.com/city/mumbai/shiv-sena-mla-pratap-sarnaik-urges-uddhav-thackeray-to-join-hands-with-bjp/articleshow/83686242.cms.

103. Zeeshan Shaikh, "Rebel Sena leaders, MLAs in Eknath Shinde camp facing ED, IT heat: Sarnaik, Jadhav, Gawali", *The Indian Express*, 24 June 2022, https:// indianexpress.com/article/political-pulse/rebel-sena-leaders-mlas-in-shinde-camp-facing-ed-it-heat-sarnaik-jadhav-gawali-7986497/.

104. Sagar Rajput and Vallabh Ozarkar, "ED summons Shiv Sena MP Sanjay Raut, he calls it 'conspiracy'", *The Indian Express*, 28 June 2022, https://indianexpress. com/article/india/ed-summons-shiv-sena-mp-sanjay-raut-7993622/.

105. Aditi Raja et al., "MVA crisis | Behind Surat to Guwahati flight: fear of rebels returning to Shiv Sena next door", *The Indian Express*, 23 June 2022, https:// indianexpress.com/article/cities/mumbai/behind-surat-to-guwahati-flight-fear-of-rebels-returning-to-sena-next-door-7985464/.

106. Mrinal Pande, "Mrinal Pande writes: Maharashtra rebels in Guwahati—Horsetrading amid floods", *The Indian Express*, 24 June 2022, https:// indianexpress.com/article/opinion/columns/maharashtra-political-crisis-eknath-shinde-shiv-sena-7987038/.

107. "Yes, I was back after 2.5 years, but I caused 2 parties to split: Devendra Fadnavis", *The Indian Express*, 21 March 2024, https://indianexpress.com/ article/cities/mumbai/devendra-fadnavis-says-was-mocked-returned-after-breaking-two-parties-9219249/.

108. Anuj Srivas, "IT Dept and ED Raids Are at an All-Time High, but Convictions Remain Elusive", *The Wire*, 3 March 2020, https://thewire.in/political-economy/it-dept-and-ed-raids-are-at-an-all-time-high-but-convictions-remain-elusive.

109. Bharti Jain, "Of 548 held, just 12 in 7 cases convicted", *The Times of India*, 10 May 2022, https://timesofindia.indiatimes.com/india/of-548-held-just-12-in-7-cases-convicted/articleshow/91451710.cms.

110. Deeptiman Tiwary, "Since 2014, 25 Opposition leaders facing corruption probe crossed over to BJP, 23 of them got reprieve", *The Indian Express*, 4 April 2024, https://indianexpress.com/article/express-exclusive/since-2014-25-opposition-leaders-facing-corruption-probe-crossed-over-to-bjp-23-of-them-got-reprieve-9247737/.

111. Kumar Sambhav et al., "Inside Facebook and BJP's world of ghost advertisers", *Al*

*Jazeera*, 15 March 2022, https://www.aljazeera.com/economy/2022/3/15/inside-facebook-and-bjps-world-of-ghost-advertisers.

112. "Court must settle challenge to the electoral bonds scheme quickly. The sanctity of elections is at stake", *The Indian Express*, 11 April 2022, https://indianexpress.com/article/opinion/editorials/court-must-settle-challenge-to-the-electoral-bonds-scheme-quickly-7863042/.

113. Krishnadas Rajagopal, "Supreme Court declares electoral bonds scheme unconstitutional", *The Hindu*, 15 February 2024, https://www.thehindu.com/news/national/electoral-bonds-scheme-unconstitutional-sbi-should-reveal-the-details-of-donors-rules-sc/article67848211.ece.

114. "Yale University scholars 'warn' Congress: There has been 0.8% rise in BJP vote share following every riot", *Counterview*, 19 November 2014, https://www.counterview.net/2014/11/yale-university-scholars-warn-congress.html.

115. Liz Mathew, "PM Modi on The Kashmir Files: Entire ecosystem worked to hide truth, now rattled by a film", *The Indian Express*, 16 March 2022, https://indianexpress.com/article/india/pm-narendra-modi-on-kashmir-files-row-7820791/.

116. Meryl Sebastian, "Kashmir Files: Vivek Agnihotri's film exposes India's new fault lines", *BBC News*, 15 March 2022, https://www.bbc.com/news/world-asia-india-60732939.

117. Raju Vernekar, "IAF Ravi Khanna's Family Objects to 'Kashmir Files' Movie", *Transcontinental Times*, 12 March 2022, https://www.transcontinentaltimes.com/2022/03/12/iaf-ravi-khannas-family-objects-to-kashmir-files-movie/.

118. Aditya AK, "[Hijab Ban verdict] Why the Karnataka High Court held that wearing hijab is not an essential religious practice of Islam", *Bar and Bench*, 15 March 2022, https://www.barandbench.com/news/litigation/hijab-ban-verdict-why-karnataka-high-court-held-that-wearing-hijab-not-essential-religious-practice-islam.

119. Iram Siddique, "10 houses burnt, many hurt in Madhya Pradesh city; curfew imposed", *The Indian Express*, 11 April 2022, https://indianexpress.com/article/cities/bhopal/10-houses-burnt-many-hurt-in-mp-city-curfew-imposed-7863135/.

120. "Delhi Riots | 'No Regrets, Will Do It Again If Required': Kapil Mishra On His Speech", *Outlook*, 22 February 2021, https://www.outlookindia.com/national/india-news-no-regrets-will-do-it-again-if-required-kapil-mishra-on-his-controversial-speech-before-delhi-riots-news-375078.

121. Samrat Sharma, "India's meat map: 7 out of 10 people relish non-vegetarian items, East & South lead the way", *India Today*, 18 November 2021, https://

www.indiatoday.in/diu/story/india-meat-map-people-relish-non-vegetarian-items-east-south-lead-way-1878313-2021-11-18.

122. Vineet Khare, "Yati Narsinghanand Saraswati: Who is the arrested Hindu priest?", *BBC News*, 20 January 2022, https://www.bbc.com/news/world-asia-india-59952851.

123. "Yati Narsinghanand, Others Booked for Hate Speech at Delhi's Hindu Mahapanchayat", *The Quint*, 4 April 2022, https://www.thequint.com/news/india/yati-narsinghanand-others-booked-for-hate-speech-at-delhis-hindu-mahapanchayat#read-more.

124. Kaushik Raj and Alishan Jafri, "Mahant Bajrang Muni Udasin, Who Repeatedly Called for Rape of Muslim Women, Is a Serial Offender", *The Wire*, 9 April 2022, https://thewire.in/communalism/mahant-bajrang-muni-udasin-hate-speech.

125. Sparsh Upadhyay, "'Had Union Minister Not Made Alleged Utterances Threatening Farmers, Lakhimpur Kheri Violence Might Not Have Happened': Allahabad HC Denies Bail To 4 Accused", *LiveLaw*, 9 May 2022, https://www.livelaw.in/top-stories/allahabad-hc-lakhimpur-kheri-ajay-mishra-violence-ashish-misha-bail-198621.

126. "'Shivling' or water fountain: Row after UP Gyanvapi mosque survey", *Hindustan Times*, 17 May 2022, https://www.hindustantimes.com/india-news/shivling-or-water-fountain-row-erupts-after-gyanvapi-video-survey-5-points-101652747851891.html.

127. Dheeshma Puzhakkal, "Fact Check: Fountain pic used to discredit alleged Shivling discovery at Gyanvapi Masjid is actually from Kolkata mosque", *India Today*, 17 May 2022, https://www.indiatoday.in/fact-check/story/fountain-pic-used-to-discredit-alleged-shivling-discovery-at-gyanvapi-masjid-from-kolkata-mosque-1950686-2022-05-17.

128. "Manipur violence: From alleged China's links to President rule's appeal, here are 10 updates", *LiveMint*, 30 July 2023, https://www.livemint.com/news/india/manipur-violence-governor-president-rule-bjp-opposition-india-alliance-kuki-meitei-cm-n-biren-singh-narendra-modi-govt-11690687271579.html.

129. "Chinese army trained Manipur militants", *India Today*, 4 November 2009, https://www.indiatoday.in/latest-headlines/story/chinese-army-trained-manipur-militants-60175-2009-11-04.

130. "Incidents and Statements involving People's Liberation Army", South Asia Terrorism Portal, Institute for Conflict Management, n.d., https://www.satp.org/satporgtp/countries/india/states/manipur/terrorist_outfits/Pla.htm.

131. Sravasti Dasgupta, "'Manipur United in Affection for Rahul Gandhi': K.C. Venugopal on Day 2 of Congress Yatra", *The Wire*, 16 January 2024, https://thewire.in/politics/manipur-united-in-affection-for-rahul-gandhi-k-c-venugopal-on-day-2-of-congress-yatra.

132. Sheikh Saaliq, "India Prime Minister Narendra Modi uses the G20 summit to advertise his global reach and court voters at home", *PBS*, 6 September 2023, https://www.pbs.org/newshour/politics/india-prime-minister-narendra-modi-uses-the-g20-summit-to-advertise-his-global-reach-and-court-voters-at-home.

133. "PM Modi on 'The Kerala Story' controversy: 'Film based on terror conspiracy, shows ugly truth'", *LiveMint*, 5 May 2023, https://www.livemint.com/news/the-kerala-story-based-on-terror-conspiracy-congress-shielding-it-pm-modi-in-karnataka-11683278170318.html.

134. "Income Tax department freezes bank accounts of Congress; Ajay Maken says, 'no money to pay bills or salary…'", *LiveMint*, 16 February 2024, https://www.livemint.com/politics/news/income-tax-dept-freezes-4-main-bank-accounts-of-congress-on-flimsy-grounds-claims-party-treasurer-ajay-maken-11708063699771.html.

135. Meryl Sebastian, "Arvind Kejriwal: India court grants bail to Delhi leader", *BBC*, 10 May 2024, https://www.bbc.com/news/world-asia-india-68767574.

136. "Arvind Kejriwal vs. Directorate of Enforcement", Supreme Court of India, https://webapi.sci.gov.in/supremecourt/2024/16350/16350_2024_2_50_53083_Judgement_10-May-2024.pdf.

137. Rhea Mogul, "India's election campaign turns negative as Modi and ruling party embrace Islamophobic rhetoric", *CNN*, 8 May 2024, https://edition.cnn.com/2024/05/28/india/india-narendra-modi-hate-speech-analysis-intl-hnk/index.html.

138. "The Guardian view on Modi's election disappointment: the winner is democracy in India", *The Guardian*, 5 June 2024, https://www.theguardian.com/commentisfree/article/2024/jun/05/the-guardian-view-on-modis-election-disappointment-the-winner-is-democracy-in-india.

139. Kumar Abhishek, "What went wrong for BJP in Ayodhya? Decoding the political shocker", *India Today*, 6 June 2024, https://www.indiatoday.in/india/story/bjp-ayodhya-ram-mandir-faizabad-lok-sabha-election-loss-samajwadi-party-caste-equation-2549769-2024-06-06.

140. "Lok Sabha elections results: Nine of 13 turncoats being probed by Central agencies lost polls", *Indian Express*, 8 June 2024, https://indianexpress.com/article/explained/explained-politics/nine-of-13-being-probed-by-central-agencies-jumped-party-lost-polls-9374823/.

141. "YouTubers earn eyeballs, give oppn a leg up", *The Times of India*, 5 June 2024,

https://timesofindia.indiatimes.com/city/delhi/youtubers-play-significant-role-in-ls-2024-elections-reshaping-media-landscape/articleshow/110714607.cms.

142. Mayank Kumar, "Social media, citizen journalism flag bearers of social justice, says Akhilesh", *The Hindu*, 9 June 2024, https://www.thehindu.com/news/national/social-media-citizen-journalism-flag-bearers-of-social-justice-says-akhilesh/article68270749.ece.

143. "Supreme Court stays Union govt's notification on fact-checking unit", *The News Minute*, 21 March 2024, https://www.thenewsminute.com/news/supreme-court-stays-union-govts-notification-on-fact-checking-unit.


CONCLUSIONS

1.    "PM Modi takes oath for 3rd time: Politics behind the Cabinet picks", *The Times of India*, 10 June 2024, https://timesofindia.indiatimes.com/india/pm-modi-takes-oath-for-3rd-time-politics-behind-the-cabinet-picks/articleshow/110857733.cms.

2.    "Kharge attends swearing-in, rest of opposition boycotts", *The Times of India*, 10 June 2024, https://timesofindia.indiatimes.com/india/kharge-attends-swearing-in-rest-of-opposition-boycotts/articleshow/110854495.cms.

3.    Deeptiman Tiwary and Nikhila Henry, "Day after Meghwal says UCC still on table, ally JD(U) says only through consensus", *The Indian Express*, 13 June 2024, https://indianexpress.com/article/india/day-after-meghwal-says-ucc-still-on-table-ally-jdu-says-only-through-consensus-9389007/.

4.    Rishi Iyengar, "Modi's Taiwan Ties Have Rattled China", *Foreign Policy*, 11 June 2024, https://foreignpolicy.com/2024/06/11/modi-lai-india-taiwan-china-relations.

5.    "Chinese Premier Congratulates Modi, But Unlike 2019, No Word From Xi", *The Wire*, 12 June 2024, https://thewire.in/diplomacy/chinese-premier-congratulates-modi-but-unlike-2019-no-word-from-xi.

6.    Sunil Bhat and Jitendra Bahadur Singh, "Pak-backed Lashkar front claims responsibility for J&K bus terror attack", *India Today*, 10 June 2024, https://www.indiatoday.in/india/story/reasi-bus-attack-terrorist-open-fire-pilgrims-fall-gorge-jammu-and-kashmir-nia-probe-search-operation-2551146-2024-06-10.

7.    "Doda terror attacks: J&K Police releases 4 terrorists' sketch; 7 security personnel injured", *Hindustan Times*, 13 June 2024, https://www.hindustantimes.com/india-news/doda-terror-attacks-j-k-police-releases-4-terrorists-sketch-7-security-personnel-injured-101718239618934.html.

8.    K.N. Pandita, "Pakistan Adopts 4 New Strategies To Bleed Jammu & Kashmir;

Report Hints At China's 'Hidden Hand' In Conflict", *Eurasian Times*, 18 June 2024, https://www.eurasiantimes.com/pakistan-adopts-4-new-strategies-to-bleed/.

9. Prawesh Lama, "Advance security convoy of Manipur CM ambushed", *Hindustan Times*, 11 June 2024, https://www.hindustantimes.com/india-news/advance-security-convoy-of-manipur-cm-ambushed-101718048412816.html

10. Deeptiman Tiwary, "Mohan Bhagwat: 'True sevak is never arrogant… in polls, decorum was not kept'", *The Indian Express*, 11 June 2024, https://indianexpress.com/article/political-pulse/mohan-bhagwat-elections-decorum-sevakl-campaign-9384552/.

11. Deeptiman Tiwary, "Election results reality check for overconfident BJP workers: RSS leader in 'Organiser'", *The Indian Express*, 11 June 2024, https://indianexpress.com/article/political-pulse/lok-sabha-election-results-bjp-rss-9384697.

12. "April Industrial output growth declines to 5%", *The New Indian Express*, 13 June 2024, https://www.newindianexpress.com/business/2024/Jun/13/april-industrial-output-growth-declines-to-5.

13. "India to lead world in fuel demand growth: IEA", *The Economic Times*, 12 June 2024, https://economictimes.indiatimes.com/industry/energy/oil-gas/india-to-lead-world-in-fuel-demand-growth-iea/articleshow/110938209.cms.

14. "Priority Areas For Jaishankar In Modi 3.0 Government: Border Stability With China, Cross-Border Terror Solution With Pakistan", *DD News*, 11 June 2024, https://ddnews.gov.in/en/priority-areas-for-jaishankar-in-modi-3-0-government-border-stability-with-china-cross-border-terror-solution-with-pakistan/.

15. Sana Hashmi, "Beijing is looking at Lok Sabha polls and blames Modi for fanning anti-China mood", *The Print*, 15 May 2024, https://theprint.in/opinion/eye-on-china/beijing-2024-lok-sabha-polls-blames-modi-anti-china-mood/2086390/.

16. James C. Thomson, "The Rouge Elephant and Us", *The New York Times*, 7 June 1992, https://www.nytimes.com/1992/06/07/books/the-rouge-elephant-and-us.html.

17. Vappala Balachandran, "When America favoured Chinese communists", *The Tribune*, 7 August 2021, https://www.tribuneindia.com/news/comment/when-america-favoured-chinese-communists-294098.

18.. Harry Harding, *A fragile relationship: The United States and China since 1972*, The Brookings Institution, Washington DC, 1992.

19. Thomson, "The Rouge Elephant".

20. Ambassador Howard B. Schaffer, *Chester Bowles: New Dealer in the Cold War*,

Prentice-Hall of India private Ltd, New Delhi, 1994, p. 81. Bowles sent this as diplomatic despatch to the State Department: "New Delhi despatch 149, July 17, 1952", National Archives, Diplomatic Branch.

21. Harding, *A Fragile Relationship*, p. 329.

22. Le Nguyen and Khanh An, "Hanoi Faces Balancing Act With China as Vietnam–US Ties Tighten", *VOA*, 26 September 2023, https://www.voanews.com/a/hanoi-faces-balancing-act-with-china-as-vietnam-us-ties-tighten/7284987.html.

23. Sheila Chiang, "U.S. loses its spot to China as Southeast Asia's most favored ally, survey shows", *CNBC*, 3 April 2024, https://www.cnbc.com/2024/04/03/us-loses-its-spot-to-china-as-southeast-asias-most-favored-ally-survey-finds.html.

24. Rana Mitter and Elsbeth Johnson, "What the West Gets Wrong About China: Three fundamental misconceptions", *Harvard Business Review*, May–June 2021, https://hbr.org/2021/05/what-the-west-gets-wrong-about-china.

25. Thomson, "The Rouge Elephant".

26. Lisa Curtis, "India's last best chance", *Foreign Affairs*, 31 May 2022, https://www.foreignaffairs.com/articles/india/2022-05-31/indias-last-best-chance.

27. "China keeping border row alive: Army Chief General Manoj Pande", *The Tribune*, 10 May 2022, https://www.tribuneindia.com/news/nation/china-keeping-border-row-alive-army-chief-393340.

28. Ameya Pratap Singh, "'What's in a Name?' The Non-Aligned Movement in Modi's Foreign Policy", *Statecraft*, 7 May 2020, https://www.statecraft.co.in/article/what-s-in-a-name-the-non-aligned-movement-in-modi-s-foreign-policy.

29. Pragya Kaushika, "'Nehru Responsible for Partition, Rejecting UCC': Rambahadur Rai's Book To Be Unveiled by PM Modi Today", *News18*, 18 June 2022, https://www.news18.com/news/india/nehru-responsible-for-partition-rejecting-ucc-rambahadur-rais-book-to-be-unveiled-by-pm-modi-today-5396185.html.

30. Niranjan Marjani, "India's Subtle Shifts Toward the West and Away From Russia", *The Diplomat*, 23 April 2022, https://thediplomat.com/2022/04/indias-subtle-shifts-toward-the-west-and-away-from-russia/.

31. Shubhajit Roy, "Swiss peace summit: Flagging need for Russia to be in, India opts out of Ukraine declaration", *The Indian Express*, 17 June 2024, https://indianexpress.com/article/india/swiss-peace-summit-flagging-need-for-russia-to-be-in-india-opts-out-of-ukraine-declaration-9396505/.

32. "China implements new border law, India likely to face more challenges", *Business Standard*, 1 January 2022, https://www.business-standard.com/

article/international/china-implements-new-border-law-india-likely-to-face-more-challenges-122010100169_1.html.

33. Simone McCarthy, "In Beijing, Xi and Putin left no question of their close alignment in a divided world", *CNN*, 17 May 2024, https://edition.cnn.com/2024/05/17/china/xi-putin-china-visit-takeaways-intl-hnk/index.html.

34. Kavaljit Singh, "The What, How and Why of the Indo-Pacific Economic Framework", *TheWire*, 27 May 2022, https://thewire.in/economy/the-what-how-and-why-of-the-indo-pacific-economic-framework.

35. Huong Le Thu, "Biden's Indo-Pacific Strategy: Traps to Avoid in Southeast Asia", *Global Asia* 16, 4 (December 2021), https://www.globalasia.org/v16no4/cover/bidens-indo-pacific-strategy-traps-to-avoid-in-southeast-asia_huong-le-thu.

36. Matthew P. Goodman and Aidan Arasasingham, "Regional Partners Seek Clarity on Biden's Indo-Pacific Economic Framework", *The Diplomat*, 15 April 2022, https://thediplomat.com/2022/04/regional-partners-seek-clarity-on-bidens-indo-pacific-economic-framework/.

37. Dipanjan Roy Chaudhury, "Joe Biden set to launch Indo-Pacific economic plan; seeks big role for India", *The Economic Times*, 19 May 2022, https://economictimes.indiatimes.com/news/india/joe-biden-set-to-launch-indo-pacific-economic-plan-seeks-big-role-for-india/articleshow/91648675.cms.

38. Carla Freeman et al., "A closer look at Biden's Indo-Pacific strategy", United States Institute for Peace, 7 March 2022, https://www.usip.org/publications/2022/03/closer-look-bidens-indo-pacific-strategy.

39. Ibid.

40. "Questions and Answers: EU Strategy for Cooperation in the Indo-Pacific", European Commission, 16 September 2021, https://ec.europa.eu/commission/presscorner/detail/en/qanda_21_4709.

41. Lan Jianxue, "No place for Europe-style conflict in Indo-Pacific", *Global Times*, 22 March 2022, https://www.globaltimes.cn/page/202203/1256562.shtml.

42. David Sacks, "Countries in China's Belt and Road Initiative: Who's In And Who's Out", Council on Foreign Relations, 24 March 2021, https://www.cfr.org/blog/countries-chinas-belt-and-road-initiative-whos-and-whos-out.

43. Rubiat Saimum, "What One Belt One Road means for Bangladesh", *Dhaka Tribune*, 31 October 2017, https://archive.dhakatribune.com/opinion/op-ed/2017/10/31/one-belt-one-road-means-bangladesh.

44. Younis Dar, "Will India Join Joe Biden's 'Infrastructure Plan' To Counter Xi Jinping's Ambitious BRI?", *The EurAsian Times*, 31 March 2021, https://

eurasiantimes.com/will-india-join-bidens-infrastructure-plan-to-counter-xi-jinpings-ambitious-bri/.

45. "Joe Biden halts plan for Indo-Pacific trade deal after opposition from Democrats", *The Financial Times*, https://www.ft.com/content/d124ee69-dc6e-4a84-b18a-26a39235ab11.

46. Vappala Balachandran, "Will The Quad Summit Dare Mention China?", *Outlook*, 11 March 2021, https://www.outlookindia.com/national/opinion-will-the-quad-summit-dare-mention-china-news-376849.

47. "'Confluence of the Two Seas': Speech by H.E. Mr Shinzo Abe, Prime Minister of Japan at the Parliament of the Republic of India", Ministry of Foreign Affairs of Japan, 22 August 2007, https://www.mofa.go.jp/region/asia-paci/pmv0708/speech-2.html.

48. Rabi Sankar Bosu, "Why the Quad Will Not Succeed to Subjugate China", *China Focus*, 6 May 2021, http://www.cnfocus.com/why-the-quad-will-not-succeed-to-subjugate-china/.

49. Jennifer Jacobs, "Biden Misspeaks on Taiwan, Says US Military Would Intervene", *Bloomberg*, 23 May 2022, https://www.bloomberg.com/news/articles/2022-05-23/biden-says-us-military-will-defend-taiwan-from-any-china-attack.

50. Zolan Khanno-Youngs, "Biden's Words on Taiwan Leave Allies in an Awkward Spot", *The New York Times*, 25 May 2022, https://www.nytimes.com/2022/05/24/world/asia/biden-taiwan-china-australia.html.

51. Jason Li, "South Korea's Formal Membership in the Quad Plus: A Bridge Too Far?", Stimson Center, 4 October 2021, https://www.stimson.org/2021/south-koreas-formal-membership-in-the-quad-plus-a-bridge-too-far/.

52. Sheila A. Smith, "The Quad in the Indo-Pacific: What to Know", Council on Foreign Relations, 27 May 2021, https://www.cfr.org/in-brief/quad-indo-pacific-what-know.

53. Sakshi Tiwari, "US Submarine, British Engine—Australian Official Reveals 'Key Info' About AUKUS Nuke Subs For Canberra", *The EurAsian Times*, 14 June 2022, https://eurasiantimes.com/us-submarine-british-engine-australian-revels-key-info-about-aukus/.

54. Amy Remeikis, "'We felt fooled': France still furious after Australia scraps $90bn submarine deal", *The Guardian*, 20 September 2021, https://www.theguardian.com/world/2021/sep/20/we-felt-fooled-france-still-furious-after-australia-scraps-90bn-submarine-deal.

55. Dinakar Peri, "Twin hurdles hinder India's maritime role", *The Hindu*, 29 May 2022, https://www.thehindu.com/news/national/indo-pacific-information-exchange-twin-hurdles-hinder-indias-maritime-role/article65470051.ece.

56. "China plots fresh military exercises in South China Sea", *The Guardian*, 27 May 2022, https://guardian.ng/news/china-plots-fresh-military-exercises-in-south-china-sea/.

57. "India and China: Three Decades of Great Divergence", https://www.worldscientific.com/doi/pdf/10.1142/9789811248795_0001.

58. "GDP: India vs. China: Is There Even a Comparison?", *Management Study Guide*, n.d., https://www.managementstudyguide.com/india-vs-china.htm.

59. https://www.worldbank.org/en/news/press-release/2023/12/18/remittance-flows-grow-2023-slower-pace-migration-development-brief#:~:text=The%20United%20States%20continued%20to,and%20Egypt%20(%2424%20billion).

60. "India gets the highest annual FDI inflow of USD 83.57 billion in FY21-22", Press Information Bureau, Government of India, 20 May 2022, https://pib.gov.in/PressReleasePage.aspx?PRID=1826946.

61. "Annual inflow of foreign direct investment (FDI) to China from 2012 to 2022", *Statista*, 13 July 2023, https://www.statista.com/statistics/1016973/china-foreign-direct-investment-inflows/.

62. "Foreign Direct Investment – the China story", The World Bank, 16 July 2010, https://www.worldbank.org/en/news/feature/2010/07/16/foreign-direct-investment-china-story.

63. "Estimated distribution of inward foreign direct investment (FDI) stock in China in 2020, by leading ultimate investor", *Statista*, 2 January 2024, https://www.statista.com/statistics/1288819/china-inward-fdi-stock-distribution-by-ultimate-investor/.

64. "Inside Fujairah: A gateway for energy and commodities in the Middle East", S&P Global, May 2022, https://www.spglobal.com/commodityinsights/en/market-insights/special-reports/oil/inside-fujairah.

65. "India's oil demand likely to jump 8% to 5.15 mn barrels per day in 2022", *Business Standard*, 17 March 2022, https://www.business-standard.com/article/economy-policy/india-s-oil-demand-likely-to-jump-8-to-5-15-mn-barrels-per-day-in-2022-122031700708_1.html.

66. K. Bharat Kumar, "Explained | Why are FPIs dumping Indian stocks?", *The Hindu*, 5 June 2022, https://www.thehindu.com/business/markets/explained-why-are-fpis-dumping-indian-stocks/article65493881.ece.

67. Scott Kennedy, "China's Economy and Ukraine: All Downside Risks", Center for Strategic and International Studies, 3 March 2022, https://www.csis.org/analysis/chinas-economy-and-ukraine-all-downside-risks.

68. Aryan Prakash, "IMF revises India's growth projection to 8.2%, China to 4.4%", *Hindustan Times*, 19 April 2022, https://www.hindustantimes.

com/business/imf-revises-india-s-growth-projection-to-8-2-china-to-44-101650378891637.html.

69.  Jessie Yeung, "100,000 Chinese officials attend emergency meeting to revive Covid-hit economy", *CNN*, 26 May 2022, https://edition.cnn.com/2022/05/26/business/china-state-council-economic-meeting-intl-hnk/index.html.

70.  Peter Hannam, "China may be facing too many economic obstacles to hit its ambitious growth target for 2024", *The Guardian*, 14 March 2024, https://www.theguardian.com/business/2024/mar/14/china-may-be-facing-too-many-economic-obstacles-to-hit-its-ambitious-growth-target-for-2024.

71.  Asit Ranjan Mishra, "Two years after Covid, Indian economy hopping from one crisis to another", *Business Standard*, 23 March 2022, https://www.business-standard.com/article/economy-policy/two-years-after-covid-indian-economy-hopping-from-one-crisis-to-another-122032301440_1.html.

72.  Kirtika Suneja, "FY22 trade gap with China swells to $72.9 billion", *The Economic Times*, 30 May 2022, https://economictimes.indiatimes.com/news/economy/foreign-trade/fy22-trade-gap-with-china-swells-to-72-9-billion/articleshow/91875990.cms.

73.  Rejaul Karim Byron and Sohel Parvez, "Bangladesh keeps outrunning India in per capita GDP race", *The Daily Star*, 14 October 2021, https://www.thedailystar.net/business/economy/industries/news/bangladesh-keeps-outrunning-india-capita-gdp-race-2197991.

74.  Philip Barrett and Sophia Chen, "The Economics of Social Unrest", International Monetary Fund, August 2021, https://www.imf.org/external/pubs/ft/fandd/2021/08/economics-of-social-unrest-imf-barrett-chen.htm.

75.  Sameer Khan, "Majoritarianism poses threat to economy: Raghuram Rajan", *The Siasat Daily*, 15 May 2022, https://www.siasat.com/majoritarianism-poses-threat-to-economy-raghuram-rajan-2327338/.

76.  Raghuram Rajan and Rohit Lamba, "An 8% national growth agenda: India's guiding light should be becoming a $10 trillion economy by 2035, with states also setting high goals", *The Times of India*, 7 June 2022, https://timesofindia.indiatimes.com/blogs/toi-edit-page/an-8-national-growth-agenda-indias-guiding-light-should-be-becoming-a-10-trillion-economy-by-2035-with-states-also-setting-high-goals/.

77.  Manmohan Singh, "This is India's moment of reckoning", *The Hindu*, 22 April 2022, https://www.thehindu.com/opinion/lead/this-is-indias-moment-of-reckoning/article65342705.ece.

78.  Writankar Mukherjee and Ketan Thakkar, "Parts supply still the weakest link in India's production chain", *The Economic Times*, 3 May 2022, https://

economictimes.indiatimes.com/industry/cons-products/electronics/parts-supply-still-the-weakest-link-in-indias-production-chain/articleshow/91274142.cms.

79. Rituraj Baruah, "Dividends for Indian oilcos stuck in Russia", *Live Mint*, 27 May 2022, https://www.livemint.com/news/india/dividends-worth-8-billion-rubles-of-indian-oil-psus-stuck-in-russia-11653668033704.html.

80. https://ddnews.gov.in/en/indias-youth-shift-from-job-seekers-to-job-providers-pm-modi-at-startup-mahakumbh/

81. https://www.business-standard.com/companies/start-ups/startup-funding-in-india-fell-62-to-six-year-low-in-2023-privatecircle-124012300099_1.html

82. Sutanuka Ghosal, "No Russian rocks! US companies want cast in stone guarantee", *The Economic Times*, 25 May 2022, https://economictimes.indiatimes.com/industry/cons-products/fashion-/-cosmetics-/-jewellery/no-russian-rocks-us-companies-want-cast-in-stone-guarantee/articleshow/91797142.cms.

83. "India-China tensions: Himalayan headache for electronics makers", *The Economic Times*, https://economictimes.indiatimes.com/industry/cons-products/electronics/industry-executives-a-worried-lot-why-india-china-tensions-are-equal-to-a-big-headache-for-electronics-makers/articleshow/111006153.cms.

84. Ashoka Modi, "India's looming financial crisis", *The Hindu*, 12 June 2024, https://www.thehindu.com/opinion/lead/indias-looming-financial-crisis/article68278359.ece.

85. Akhilesh Sati, Lydia Powell and Vinod Kumar Tomar, "Nuclear energy in India: Small may not be beautiful", Observer Research Foundation, 3 February 2022, https://www.orfonline.org/expert-speak/nuclear-energy-in-india/.

86. Mihir Mishra and Anil Sasi, "Supply of six nuclear reactors: Question mark on Russia inputs, India evaluates French push at Jaitapur", *The Indian Express*, 13 June 2022, https://indianexpress.com/article/india/supply-of-six-nuclear-reactors-question-mark-on-russia-inputs-india-evaluates-french-push-at-jaitapur-7966435/.

87. Nirupama Subramanian, "Explained: Two years after Galwan clash, where India–China relations stand today", *The Indian Express*, 18 June 2022, https://indianexpress.com/article/explained/explained-2-years-after-galwan-clash-where-india-china-relations-stand-today-7974230/.

88. "China overtakes US as India's top trading partner in FY24: GTRI", Ministry of External Affairs, Government of India, 13 May 2024, https://indbiz.gov.in/china-overtakes-us-as-indias-top-trading-partner-in-fy24-gtri/.

89. "Railways Awards Contract For 39,000 Train Wheels To Chinese Firm As Russia-Ukraine War Hits Deliveries From Other Countries: Report",

*Swarajya*, 17 May 2022, https://swarajyamag.com/infrastructure/railways-awards-contract-for-39000-train-wheels-to-chinese-firm-as-russia-ukraine-war-hits-deliveries-from-other-countries-report.

90. Rohini Krishnamurthy, "Indian Science Congress: India not producing quality research material, government adviser says", *Down To Earth*, 3 January 2023, https://www.downtoearth.org.in/news/science-technology/indian-science-congress-india-not-producing-quality-research-material-government-adviser-says-86922.

91. Prashant K. Nanda, "India has far fewer researchers than China, US, says think tank", *Live Mint*, 27 November 2019, https://www.livemint.com/education/news/india-has-six-times-less-researchers-than-china-33-times-less-than-south-korea-11574865096710.html.

92. Rahul Panat, "On the data and analysis of the research output of India and China: India has significantly fallen behind China", *Scientometrics* 100 (2014): 471–81, https://s3.wp.wsu.edu/uploads/sites/238/2014/10/India-China-Paper.pdf.

93. "Analysis suggests China has passed U.S. on one research measure", Ohio State University News, 8 March 2022, https://news.osu.edu/analysis-suggests-china-has-passed-us-on-one-research-measure/.

94. Wagner, C.S., Zhang, L. & Leydesdorff, L., "A discussion of measuring the top-1% most-highly cited publications: quality and impact of Chinese papers", *Scientometrics* 127 (2022): 1825–39, https://link.springer.com/article/10.1007/s11192-022-04291-z.

95. Beethika Khan, Carol Robbins, and Abigail Okrent, "The State of U.S. Science and Engineering 2020", National Science Foundation, 15 January 2020, https://ncses.nsf.gov/pubs/nsb20201/global-science-and-technology-capabilities.

96. Ibid.

97. "ICMR Scientist Facing Plagiarism Charge Promoted to Head of Epidemiology Dept", *TheWire*, 1 June 2022, https://thewire.in/government/icmr-scientist-facing-plagiarism-charge-promoted-to-head-of-epidemiology-dept.

98. Ajoy Ashirwad Mahaprashasta, "Allegations of Political Bias in Faculty Hiring the Latest Battleline in JNU", *TheWire*, 18 January 2018, https://thewire.in/education/allegations-political-bias-faculty-hiring-latest-battleline-jnu.

99. Pankaj Jagannath Jayswal, "Vedic knowledge compatible with modern science", *The Times of India (Readers' Blog)*, 15 October 2021, https://timesofindia.indiatimes.com/readersblog/youth2020/vedic-knowledge-compatible-with-modern-science-38284/.

100. Feroze Varun Gandhi, "The multiple crises in Indian universities", *The Hindu*, 9

May 2022, https://www.thehindu.com/opinion/op-ed/the-multiple-crises-in-indian-universities/article65394633.ece.

101. Harikishan Sharma, "Finance says no to Health request for $10-million fund to meet G20 pledge", *The Indian Express*, 20 June 2024, https://indianexpress. com/article/india/finance-says-no-to-health-request-for-10-million-fund-to-meet-g20-pledge-9403130/.

102. Sara Hertog, Patrick Gerland and John Wilmoth, "India Overtakes China as the World's Most Populous Country", United Nations Department of Economic and Social Affairs, 15 June 2023, https://www.un-ilibrary.org/content/papers/10.18356/27081990-153.

103. Shankkar Aiyar, "Hope 2022: India's rise in $100 trillion global GDP", *The New Indian Express*, 2 January 2022, https://www.newindianexpress.com/opinions/columns/shankkar-aiyar/2022/jan/02/hope-2022-indias-rise-in-100-trn-global-gdp-2402051.html.

104. Shelley Singh, "China's mobile and digital dominance runs deep into Indian economy", *The Economic Times*, 16 February 2020, https://economictimes. indiatimes.com/tech/hardware/chinas-mobile-and-digital-dominance-run-deep-into-indian-economy/articleshow/74154017.cms.

105. Subhrojit Mallick, "Xiaomi may top Q2 smartphone charts here, but rivals closing in", *The Economic Times*, 8 June 2022, https://economictimes. indiatimes.com/markets/stocks/news/xiaomi-may-top-q2-smartphone-charts-here-but-rivals-closing-in/articleshow/92070040.cms.

106. CAA is the Citizenship Amendment Act (2019), the most controversial amendment brought by the NDA government which is viewed anti-Muslim. NRC is the National Register of Citizens, another controversial step undertaken under Supreme Court direction to exclude Muslim migrants. Both these measures continue to draw country-wide protests.

107. Ibid.

108. James Barton, "China claims rural broadband milestone", *Developing Telecoms*, 7 January 2022, https://developingtelecoms.com/telecom-technology/wireless-networks/12640-china-claims-rural-broadband-milestone.html.

109. Aashish Aryan, "BharatNet likely to miss deadline as shifting goalposts slow roll out", *The Indian Express*, 4 April 2022, https://indianexpress.com/article/business/bharatnet-likely-to-miss-deadline-as-shifting-goalposts-slow-roll-out-7851531/.

110. Vasudha Venugopal, "Big Change In BharatNet Project For Last-Mile Broadband Connectivity: Sources", *NDTV*, 6 August 2023, https://www.ndtv.com/india-news/bharatnet-latest-news-big-change-in-bharatnet-project-for-last-mile-broadband-connectivity-sources-4273690.

111. "India is now being called 'pharmacy of the world', says PM Modi", *Business*

*Standard*, 18 November 2021, https://www.business-standard.com/article/current-affairs/india-is-now-being-called-pharmacy-of-the-world-says-pm-modi-121111801288_1.html.

112. Surabhi Sarda, "Will India's pharma sector be able to come out of its China dependence?", *The Economic Times*, 27 February 2024, https://economictimes.indiatimes.com/industry/healthcare/biotech/pharmaceuticals/will-indias-pharma-sector-be-able-to-come-out-of-its-china-dependence/articleshow/108048363.cms.

113. Chuin-Wei Yap, "Pandemic Lays Bare U.S. Reliance on China for Drugs", *The Wall Street Journal*, 5 August 2020, https://www.wsj.com/articles/how-the-u-s-ceded-control-of-drug-supplies-to-china-11596634936.

114. Parth Satam, "Semiconductors | With China struggling, India has a long way to go", *Money Control*, 17 February 2022, https://www.moneycontrol.com/news/opinion/semiconductors-with-china-struggling-india-has-a-long-way-to-go-8114011.html.

115. Christopher A. Thomas, "Lagging but motivated: The state of China's semiconductor industry", Brookings, 7 January 2021, https://www.brookings.edu/techstream/lagging-but-motivated-the-state-of-chinas-semiconductor-industry/.

116. "Taking Stock of China's Semiconductor Industry", SIA Blog, 13 July 2021, https://www.semiconductors.org/taking-stock-of-chinas-semiconductor-industry/.

117. Skariachan et al, "Why MNCs are quitting India".

118. "Amid India's chip push, Taiwan flags talent gaps, high import tariff", *The Indian Express*, https://indianexpress.com/article/technology/tech-news-technology/amid-indias-chip-push-taiwan-flags-talent-gaps-high-import-tariff-9285256/.

119. Mayank Singh, "Agnipath: Four-year tenure not good enough, says Former Chief of Army Staff General VP Malik", *The New Indian Express*, 21 June 2022, https://www.newindianexpress.com/nation/2022/jun/21/agnipath-four-year-tenure-not-good-enough-says-former-chief-of-army-staff-general-vp-malik-2467907.html.

120. Lt General Harwant Singh, "Second Coming of the Chief of Defence Staff", *The Citizen*, 16 June 2022, https://www.thecitizen.in/opinion/second-coming-of-the-chief-of-defence-staff-280991.

121. Christopher G. Marquis, Denton Dye, and Ross S. Kinkead, "The Advent of Jointness During the Gulf War: A 25-Year Retrospective", *Joint Force Quarterly* 85 (2017): 76–83, https://ndupress.ndu.edu/Media/News/Article/1130670/the-advent-of-jointness-during-the-gulf-war-a-25-year-retrospective/.

122. Singh, "Agnipath: Four-year tenure not good enough".

123. Arun Prakash, "Agnipath, between the lines", *The Indian Express*, 21 June 2022, https://indianexpress.com/article/opinion/columns/agnipath-scheme-armed-forces-protests-7979936/.

124. Anirban Bhaumik, "Agnipath will sound the death knell for armed forces: Lt Gen (retd) Vinod Bhatia", *Deccan Herald*, 21 June 2022, https://www.deccanherald.com/opinion/panorama/agnipath-will-sound-the-death-knell-for-armed-forces-lt-gen-retd-vinod-bhatia-1119921.html.

125. Saumitra Jha and Steven Wilkinson, "Does Combat Experience Foster Organizational Skill? Evidence from Ethnic Cleansing during the Partition of South Asia", *American Political Science Review* 106, 4 (November 2012): 883–907, https://web.stanford.edu/~saumitra/papers/JhaWilkinsonAPSR2012.pdf.

126. "Did not anticipate protests against Agnipath scheme, says Navy chief", *Scroll*, 18 June 2022, https://scroll.in/latest/1026419/did-not-anticipate-protests-against-agnipath-scheme-says-navy-chief.

127. Manish Kumar, "Violence Over 'Agnipath' Spreads, Opposition Ramps Up Pressure", *NDTV*, 16 June 2022, https://www.ndtv.com/india-news/agnipath-scheme-violent-protests-in-bihar-tear-gas-fired-3071554.

128. "As protests rage, Services ready to start Agnipath recruitment", *The Indian Express*, 18 June 2022, https://indianexpress.com/article/india/amid-protests-against-agnipath-scheme-armed-forces-announce-notification-dates-for-recruitment-process-7975924/.

129. Sanjeev Satgainya, "Agnipath scheme could mean the end of Nepalese Gurkhas in Indian Army", *The Hindu*, 10 January 2024, https://www.thehindu.com/news/international/agnipath-scheme-could-mean-the-end-of-nepalese-gurkhas-in-indian-army/article67723243.ece.

130. "Will scrap 'Agnipath', revert to old recruitment scheme if voted to power: Congress", *The Economic Times*, 26 February 2024, https://economictimes.indiatimes.com/news/elections/lok-sabha/india/will-scrap-agnipath-revert-to-old-recruitment-scheme-if-voted-to-power-congress/articleshow/108004511.cms.

131. https://economictimes.indiatimes.com/news/elections/lok-sabha/rajasthan/lok-sabha-polls-how-jat-unity-took-down-bjp-in-rajasthan-haryana/articleshow/110713402.cms?from=mdr.

132. SIPRI Fact Sheet- TRENDS IN WORLD MILITARY EXPENDITURE, 2023 https://www.sipri.org/sites/default/files/2024-04/2404_fs_milex_2023.pdf.

133. "Comparison of India and China Military Strengths (2024)", *Global Firepower*, https://www.globalfirepower.com/countries-comparison-detail.php?country1=india&country2=china.

134. "Russia's Death Toll in Ukraine Already the Same as 10 Years in Afghanistan",

*Newsweek*, 23 May 2022, https://www.newsweek.com/Russia-death-toll-ukraine-already-same-10-years-afghanistan-1708991.

135. Vappala Balachandran, "Will Vietnam Join A Common Front Against China?", *Outlook*, 27 August 2020, https://www.outlookindia.com/national/opinion-will-vietnam-join-a-common-front-against-china-news-359391.

136. Shaurya Karanbir Gurung, "Parliamentary standing committee criticises government for inadequate allocation of funds to Army", *The Economic Times*, 8 January 2019, https://economictimes.indiatimes.com/news/defence/parliamentary-standing-committee-criticises-govt-for-inadequate-allocation-of-funds-to-army/articleshow/67427334.cms.

137. "House panel recommends benchmark percentage of GDP for defence allocation", *Business Standard*, 20 December 2023, https://www.business-standard.com/industry/news/house-panel-recommends-benchmark-percentage-of-gdp-for-defence-allocation-123122001218_1.html.

138. Rajat Pandit, "5 years on, 'strategic partnership' defence projects yet to take off", *The Times of India*, 4 May 2022, https://timesofindia.indiatimes.com/india/5-years-on-strategic-partnership-defence-projects-yet-to-take-off/articleshow/91296132.cms.

139. Arun Prakash, "For a stronger navy, India needs to fast-track the submarine project", *The Indian Express*, 16 May 2022, https://indianexpress.com/article/opinion/columns/induction-of-submarines-project-75-i-indian-navy-7919079/.

140. "Day Ahead Of PM Modi's Visit, France Backs Out Of Key Submarine Project", *NDTV*, 3 May 2022, https://www.ndtv.com/india-news/day-ahead-of-pm-narendra-modis-visit-france-backs-out-of-key-submarine-project-2941800.

141. Krishn Kaushik, "Explained: Submarine tech that India wants", *The Indian Express*, 4 May 2022, https://indianexpress.com/article/explained/submarine-tech-that-india-wants-aip-technology-7900043/.

142. Ibid.

143. Toby Dalton and Tong Zhao, "At a Crossroads? China-India Nuclear Relations After the Border Clash", CEIP, 19 August 2020, https://carnegieendowment.org/2020/08/19/at-crossroads-china-india-nuclear-relations-after-border-clash-pub-82489.

144. "Atoms for Peace speech", *Encyclopaedia Britannica*, 1 December 2023, https://www.britannica.com/event/Atoms-for-Peace-speech.

145. "Nuclear Suppliers Group", *Encyclopaedia Britannica*, 20 March 2023, https://www.britannica.com/topic/Nuclear-Suppliers-Group.

146. Ananth Krishnan, "The LAC crisis has been a wake-up call in how we deal with China, says former Northern Command chief", *The Hindu*, 8 May 2022,

https://www.thehindu.com/opinion/interview/the-lac-crisis-has-been-a-wake-up-call-in-how-we-deal-with-china-says-former-northern-command-chief-lt-gen-ds-hooda/article65394688.ece.

147. Dinakar Peri, "China upgraded firepower on LAC: official source", *The Hindu*, 27 June 2022, https://www.thehindu.com/news/national/china-upgraded-firepower-on-lac/article65567560.ece.

148. Alex Hern, "Meet the Chinese army's latest weapon: the gun-toting dog", *The Guardian*, 30 May 2024, https://www.theguardian.com/science/article/2024/may/30/chinese-armys-latest-weapon-gun-toting-dog.

149. "Xi Jinping asks Chinese military to step up recruitment of new talent to gain ascendancy in future wars", *The Times of India*, 29 November 2021, https://timesofindia.indiatimes.com/world/china/xi-jinping-asks-chinese-military-to-step-up-recruitment-of-new-talent-to-gain-ascendancy-in-future-wars/articleshow/87981953.cms.

150. Sakshi Tiwari, "World's 1st Anti-Hypersonic System? China Says It Is Ready With An AI-Powered Defense Against Mach 5+ Missiles", *The EurAsian Times*, 2 June 2022, https://eurasiantimes.com/worlds-1st-anti-hypersonic-system-china-says-its-is-ready/.

151. Nikhil Ghanekar, "Strategic imperative and environment concern in Great Nicobar project", *The Indian Express*, 19 June 2024, https://indianexpress.com/article/explained/great-nicobar-project-concern-9400418.

152. Ashish Dangwal, "India's To Be 'Hong Kong' Gets Massive Economic & Military Makeover; Looks To Check Chinese Ambitions In IOR", *The Eurasian Times*, 28 February 2024, https://www.eurasiantimes.com/ransforming-great-nicobar-islands-into-indias/.

153. "US lawmakers to meet the Dalai Lama; China urges Biden not to sign Tibet Bill", *The Indian Express*, 19 June 2024, https://indianexpress.com/article/india/us-lawmakers-to-meet-the-dalai-lama-china-urges-biden-not-to-sign-tibet-bill-9400868/.

154. Walter Russell Mead, "The Return of Geopolitics: The Revenge of the Revisionist Powers", *Foreign Affairs*, 17 April 2014, https://www.foreignaffairs.com/articles/china/2014-04-17/return-geopolitics.

155. Mike Eckel, "Pentagon Chief Calls Russia, China 'Revisionist Powers'", *Radio Free Europe/Radio Liberty*, 19 January 2018, https://www.rferl.org/a/pentagon-mattis-calls-russia-china-revisionist-powers/28985632.html.

156. Graeme Dobell, "The US and China: status quo powers in revisionist times", *The Strategist*, 5 February 2018, https://www.aspistrategist.org.au/us-china-status-quo-powers-revisionist-times/.

157. Rana Mitter, "World Order by Henry Kissinger – review", *The Guardian*, 1

October 2014, https://www.theguardian.com/books/2014/oct/01/world-order-by-henry-kissinger-review-account.

158. Howard B. Schaffer, *Chester Bowles: New Deal in the Cold War*, Georgetown University/Prentice-Hall India, 1994, pp. 80–3.

159. Bertil Lintner, "The Sino-Indian War Was 'A Masterstroke That Placed China as the Leader of the Third World'", *The Caravan*, 22 October 2017, https://caravanmagazine.in/vantage/sino-indian-war-masterstroke-placed-china-leader-third-world.

160. "PM Modi leading from front", *ABP* Live, https://news.abplive.com/web-stories/pm-modi-leading-from-front-at-quad-2022-meet-in-japan-s-tokyo-1533527.

161. Shubhajit Roy, "Modi listening, Xi: Cold War mentality, bloc confrontation must be abandoned", *The Indian Express*, 24 June 2022, https://indianexpress.com/article/india/modi-listening-xi-cold-war-mentality-bloc-confrontation-must-be-abandoned-7987468/.

EPILOGUE

1.    "Imperiled Frontiers: Security Scenario in Northeast India", Institute of Peace and Conflict Studies, 27 September 2007, https://www.ipcs.org/comm_select.php?articleNo=2379.

2.    "China-Bangladesh relations: A three way balance between China, India and the US", Mercator Institute for China Studies, 18 August 2022, https://merics.org/en/china-bangladesh-relations-three-way-balance-between-china-india-and-us.

3.    "India pressed U.S. to go easy on Bangladeshi leader before her ouster, officials say", *The Washington Post*, 15 August 2024, https://www.washingtonpost.com/world/2024/08/15/india-bangladesh-sheikh-hasina/.

# SELECT BIBLIOGRAPHY

Adabiya, H., "Kollam Port: An emporium of Chinese trade", *Advance Research Journal of Social Science* 9, 2 (2018): 254–7, http://researchjournal.co.in/upload/assignments/9_254-257.pdf

Abe, Shinzo "'Confluence of the Two Seas': Speech by Prime Minister of Japan at the Parliament of the Republic of India", Ministry of Foreign Affairs of Japan, 22 August 2007, https://www.mofa.go.jp/region/asia-paci/pmv0708/speech-2.html

Anand, "The Empire of Kushana: Ancient History of India", *History Discussion*, n.d., https://www.historydiscussion.net/history-of-india/kushana/the-empire-of-kushana-ancient-history-of-india/5723

Andornino, Giovanni, "The Nature and Linkages of China's Tributary System under the Ming and Qing Dynasties", Working Papers of the Global Economic History Network (GEHN) No. 21/06, London School of Economics and Political Science, 2006, https://www.lse.ac.uk/Economic-History/Assets/Documents/Research/GEHN/GEHNWP21-GA.pdf

Andrew, Christopher, *The Defence of the Realm: The Authorized History of MI-5*, Penguin Books, 2009, p. 443.

Austin, Granville, *The Indian Constitution: Cornerstone of a Nation*, Oxford University Press, 1999, p. 13.

Balachandran, Vappala, *A Life in Shadow: The Secret Story of A.C.N. Nambiar*, Roli Books,
2016, pp. 36–60.

Basham, A.L., *The Wonder that was India*, New Delhi, Rupa and Co., 1981 [1954], p. 25n.

# SELECT BIBLIOGRAPHY

Beck, Guy L., *Sacred Sound: Experiencing Music in World Religions*, Waterloo, Wilfrid Laurier University Press, 2006, p. 137.

Besant, Annie, *The Future of Indian Politics: A Contribution to the Understanding of Present-Day Problems*, London, Bombay etc., Theosophical Publishing House, 1922, pp. 252, 301.

Bhowmik, Nilanjana, "10 Years Of Right To Education: A Progress Report", *Reader's Digest*, 26 August 2019, https://www.readersdigest.in/features/story-right-to-education-a-progress-report-125002

Campbell, James M., *History of Gujarát (Gazetteer of the Bombay Presidency, Vol 1, Part 1)*, Bombay, Government Central Press, 1896.

Carter, Lionel, (ed.), *Mountbatten's Report on the Last Viceroyalty: 22 March–15 August 1947*, New Delhi, Manohar, 2003.

Chinmayananda, Swami, *Isavasya Upanisad*, Central Chinmaya Trust, Mumbai, December 2001.

Chitkara, M.G., *Rashtriya Swayamsevak Sangh: National Upsurge*, New Delhi, A.P.H. Publishing Corporation, 2004, p. 4.

Dalton, Toby, and Tong Zhao, "At a Crossroads? China-India Nuclear Relations After the Border Clash", CEIP, 19 August 2020, https://carnegieendowment.org/2020/08/19/at-crossroads-china-india-nuclear-relations-after-border-clash-pub-82489

Daniélou, Alain, *A Brief History of India*, Simon and Schuster, 2003, p. 111.

Dayal, Rajeshwar, *A Life of our Times*, Orient Longman, 1998, p. 93.

*Deng Xiaoping Wenxuan* (Selected Works of Deng Xiaoping), Vol. 3, Beijing: Renmin Chubanshe (People's Publishing House), 1993, p..281.

Deva, B.C., *Indian Music*, Indian Council for Cultural Relations, 1974, pp. 7–8, 94–5.

Dharma Theertha, Swami, *History of Hindu Imperialism*, Madras, Dalit Educational Literature Centre, 1992 [1941].

Durant, Will, *The Story of Civilization, vol. I: Our Oriental Heritage*, Simon & Schuster, 1954 [1935], p. 797.

Edwards, Michael, *A History of India*, The New English Library, London, 1961, p. 21; pp. 58–60.

Fairbank J.K. and S.Y. Têng, "On the Ch'ing Tributary System", *Harvard Journal of Asiatic Studies* 6, 2 (1941): 135–246, p. 137.

Faligot, Roger, *Chinese Spies: From Chairman Mao to Xi Jinping*, London, Hurst, 2019, p. 64.

Freeman, Carla, et al., "A closer look at Biden's Indo-Pacific strategy", United States Institute for Peace, 7 March 2022, https://www.

usip.org/publications/2022/03/closer-look-bidens-indo-pacific-strategy

Gandhi, M.K., "Speech to the Inter-Asian Relations Conference", 2 April 1947, published in *Harijan*, 20 April 1947, https://www.mkgandhi.org/speeches/interasian.htm

Gandhi, Mahatma, *The Collected Works of Mahatma Gandhi,* vol. 89, Publications Division, Ministry of Information and Broadcasting, Government of India, 1958, p. 193.

Garver, John W., "The Restoration of Sino–Indian Comity following India's Nuclear Tests", *The China Quarterly* 168 (2001): 865–89.

——, "China's Decision for War with India in 1962", in Alastair Iain Johnston and Robert S. Ross (eds), *New Directions in the Study of China's Foreign Policy*, Stanford University Press, 2006, pp. 86–130.

Ghatak, Maitreesh, Parikshit Ghosh, and Ashok Kotwal, "Growth in the time of UPA: Myth and reality", *Economic and Political Weekly* 49, 16 (19 April 2014): 34–43, available at https://personal.lse.ac.uk/ghatak/upa-epw.pdf

Ghosh, Lopa (ed.), "100 Days Review of NDA Government", Wada Na Todo, September 2014, https://gcap.global/wp-content/uploads/2018/07/Review-of-NDA-Government-2014.pdf

Golwalkar, M.S., *We, or Our Nationhood Defined*, Nagpur, Bharat Publications, 1939; e-book (n.d.), to which page references apply, available at https://sanjeev.sabhlokcity.com/Misc/We-or-Our-Nationhood-Defined-Shri-M-S-Golwalkar.pdf

Guha, Ramachandra, "Jawaharlal Nehru: A Study in Failure?", Harvard–Yenching Institute Working Paper Series, 2011, pp. 2–3, https://www.harvard-yenching.org/wp-content/uploads/legacy_files/featurefiles/Ramachandra%20Guha_Jawaharlal%20Nehru%20and%20China.pdf

Harder, Anton, "Not at the Cost of China: New evidence regarding US proposals to Nehru for joining the United Nations Security council", Woodrow Wilson International Center for Scholars, Cold War International History Project Working Paper #76, March 2015, https://www.wilsoncenter.org/sites/default/files/media/documents/publication/cwihp_working_paper_76_not_at_the_cost_of_china.pdf

Harding, Harry, *A fragile relationship: The United States and China since 1972*, The Brookings Institution, Washington DC, 1992.

Heitmeyer, Carolyn M., "Identity and difference in a Muslim community in Central Gujarat, India following the 2002 communal violence",

PhD thesis, London School of Economics and Political Science, n.d. [2014], http://etheses.lse.ac.uk/2355/1/U615304.pdf

Hinton, Harold C., "Review of *The Chinese Calculus of Deterrence: India and Indochina*. By Allen S. Whiting", *American Political Science Review* 71, 3 (1977): 1269. doi:10.2307/1960250.

Hoffmann, Steven A., *India and the China Crisis*, University of California Press, 2018 [1990]
https://library.fes.de/libalt/journals/swetsfulltext/12919246.pdf

*The Hutchinson Encyclopaedia*, Helicon, 1995, p. 228.

Jaffrelot, Christophe, *The Hindu nationalist movement and Indian politics, 1925 to the 1990s: strategies of identity-building, implantation and mobilisation*, London, Hurst & Co., 1996, p. 39.

Jersild, Austin, "Sharing the Bomb among Friends: The Dilemmas of Sino-Soviet Strategic Cooperation", CWIHP e-Dossier No. 43, Wilson Center, n.d., https://www.wilsoncenter.org/publication/sharing-the-bomb-among-friends-the-dilemmas-sino-soviet-strategic-cooperation

Kapadia, Aparna, "Text, Power and Kinship in Medieval Gujarat, c. 1398-1511", PhD thesis, SOAS University of London, 2010, pp. 160–99, available at https://eprints.soas.ac.uk/28731/1/10672899.pdf

Kennedy, Scott, "China's Economy and Ukraine: All Downside Risks", Center for Strategic and International Studies, 3 March 2022, https://www.csis.org/analysis/chinas-economy-and-ukraine-all-downside-risks

Krishnan, Asokan Vengassery, *Sree Narayana Guru: The Perfect Union of Buddha and Sankara*, Konark Publishers, 2018.

Macmillan, Margaret, *Paris 1919: Six months that changed the world*, New York: Random House, 2003, p. 49.

Mair, Victor H., Chen, Sanping and Frances Wood, *Chinese Lives: The People Who Made a Civilization*, Thames & Hudson, 2013.

Majumdar, R.C., "Intercourse with the Outside World", in R.C. Majumdar (ed.), *The History and Culture of the Indian People, volume 3: The Classical Age*, Bombay: Bharatiya Vidya Bhavan, 1970 [1954], p. 610.

——, "Indian history, its nature, scope and method", in *The History and Culture of the Indian People: The Vedic Age*, Mumbai, Bharatiya Vidya Bhavan, 2017 [1951], p. 38

Majumdar, R.C., H.C. Raychaudhuri and Kalikinkar Datta, *An Advanced History of India*, Macmillan & Co., 1985 [1946], p. 309.

Manmadhan, Ullattil, "Zheng He: The Chinese at Calicut", *Peepul Tree*,

16 March 2021, https://www.livehistoryindia.com/story/cover-story/zheng-he/

Marquis, Christopher G., Denton Dye, and Ross S. Kinkead, "The Advent of Jointness During the Gulf War: A 25-Year Retrospective", *Joint Force Quarterly* 85 (2017): 76–83, https://ndupress.ndu.edu/Media/News/Article/1130670/the-advent-of-jointness-during-the-gulf-war-a-25-year-retrospective/

Mehrotra, L.L., "India's Tibet Policy: An Appraisal and Options", Tibet Parliamentary and Policy Research Centre, New Delhi, 2000 [1997], https://tibet.net/wp-content/uploads/2017/05/Inidas-Tibet-Policy.pdf

Menon, A. Sreedhara, *A Survey of Kerala History*, DC Books, 2007, pp. 306–9

Menon, V.P., *The Transfer of Power in India*, Orient Longman, 1957, p. 114.

——, *The Story of the Integration of the Indian States*, Orient Longmans, 1961, p. 376.

Mitter, Rana and Elsbeth Johnson, "What the West Gets Wrong About China: Three fundamental misconceptions", *Harvard Business Review*, May–June 2021, https://hbr.org/2021/05/what-the-west-gets-wrong-about-china

Nambiar, A.C.N., "Oral history transcripts", Prime Ministers' Museum and Library (formerly Nehru Memorial Museum and Library), p. 50.

Narayan Das, Rup, *India–China Relations: A New Paradigm*, New Delhi, Institute for Defence Studies and Analyses, 2013, p. 39.

Naveed, Muhammad Bin, "White Huns (Hephthalites)", *World History Encyclopedia*, 22 June 2015, https://www.ancient.eu/White_Huns_(Hephthalites)/

Nehru, Jawaharlal, *An Autobiography*, Oxford University Press, 1936.

——, "Note on Visit to China and Indo-China", 14 November 1954, Wilson Center Digital Archive, https://digitalarchive.wilsoncenter.org/document/jawaharlal-nehru-note-visit-china-and-indo-china

——, *The Discovery of India*, Oxford University Press, 1994, p. 178.

Panat, Rahul, "On the data and analysis of the research output of India and China: India has significantly fallen behind China", *Scientometrics* 100 (2014): 471–81, https://s3.wp.wsu.edu/uploads/sites/238/2014/10/India-China-Paper.pdf

Paramananda, Swami, *The Upanishads*, Boston, The Vedanta Centre, 1919, pp. 13–16.

Paranjpe, V.V., "How to Understand China", Indira Gandhi National

Centre for the Arts, n.d., http://ignca.gov.in/how-to-undersand-china-v-v-paranjpe/

Prabhupada, A.C. Bhaktivedanta Swami, *Srī Īśopanishad*, Bhaktivedanta Book Trust, 1969, available at https://prabhupadabooks.com/iso.

Pyarelal, *Mahatma Gandhi: The Last Phase, vol. II*, Ahmedabad, Navajivan Publishing House, 1958, p. 440.

Ramesh, Jairam, *A Chequered Brilliance: The Many Lives of V.K. Krishna Menon*, Penguin–Viking, 2019, p. 434.

Ranganathananda, Swami, *Science and Religion*, Calcutta, Advaita Ashram, 1982, pp. 15–16.

——, *Eternal Values for a Changing Society, Vol II: Great Spiritual Teachers*, Bombay, Bharatiya Vidya Bhavan, 1987, pp. 92–3.

Sadhukhan, Amit, "India and China: Three Decades Divergence", *Great Transition in Indian Society*, (2022): 1–16, https://www.worldscientific.com/doi/pdf/10.1142/9789811248795_0001

Samarani, Guido, "Shaping the Future of Asia: Chiang Kai-shek, Nehru and China-India Relations During the Second World War Period", Working papers in contemporary Asian studies; No. 11, Centre for East and South-East Asian Studies, Lund University, 2005 https://lucris.lub.lu.se/ws/portalfiles/portal/4571404/3128707.pdf.

Sati, Akhilesh, Lydia Powell and Vinod Kumar Tomar, "Nuclear energy in India: Small may not be beautiful", Observer Research Foundation, 3 February 2022, https://www.orfonline.org/expert-speak/nuclear-energy-in-india/

Schaffer, Ambassador Howard B., *Chester Bowles: New Dealer in the Cold War*, Prentice-Hall of India, 1994, pp. 51–2.

Smedley, Agnes, *Battle Hymn of China*, New York, Alfred A. Knopf, 1943, p. 230

Talbot, Phillips, "As the British Empire Was Falling Apart, Gandhi Gave This Advice to the Rest of Asia", *The New Republic*, 28 April 1947, https://newrepublic.com/article/120516/1947-india-conference-marked-end-colonialism

Tan Segil, Rosie, "The Limits of Jawaharlal Nehru's Internationalism and Sino–Indian Relations, 1949–1959", MA Dissertation, Salem State University, May 2015, available at https://digitalrepository.salemstate.edu/bitstream/handle/20.500.13013/540/The_Limits_of_Jawaharlal_Nehrus_Asian_Internationalism_and_Sino_.pdf

Thomas, Christopher A., "Lagging but motivated: The state of China's semiconductor industry", Brookings, 7 January 2021, https://www.

brookings.edu/techstream/lagging-but-motivated-the-state-of-chinas-semiconductor-industry/

United States Senate Ninety-ninth Congress, First Session, *Security and Development Assistance: Hearings Before the Committee on Foreign Relations*, 1985, volume 4, p. 541.

Virmani, Arvind, "A Tripolar World: India, China and US", Indian Council for Research on International Economic Relations, 18 May 2005, https://www.icrier.org/pdf/TripolarWrld_IHC5.pdf

Webster, Donovan, *The Burma Road: The Epic Story of the China–Burma–India Theater in World War II*, New York, Farrar, Straus and Giroux, 2003, pp. 158–9.

Wells, H.G., *The Outline of History*, Volume 1, Doubleday & Co., 1971, p. 484.

Wilhelm, Jr., Alfred D., *The Chinese at the Negotiating Table: Style and Characteristics*, Washington DC, National Defense University Press, 1994.

## Online reports/articles/documents

"2021 Report on International Religious Freedom: India", US State Department, 2021, https://www.state.gov/reports/2021-report-on-international-religious-freedom/india/.

"Atoms for Peace speech", *Encyclopaedia Britannica*, 1 December 2023, https://www.britannica.com/event/Atoms-for-Peace-speech

"Bill of Rights in Action 17 3 b: Truman, MacArthur, and the Korean War", *Teach Democracy* (formerly Constitutional Rights Foundation), n.d., https://www.u.crf-usa.org/online-lessons/bill-of-rights-in-action/bria-17-3-b-4

"Chinese Civil War: Nationalist collapse and the establishment of the People's Republic of China (1949)", *Encyclopaedia Britannica*, n.d., https://www.britannica.com/event/Chinese-Civil-War/Nationalist-collapse-and-the-establishment-of-the-Peoples-Republic-of-China-1949

"Comparison of India and China Military Strengths (2024)", *Global Firepower*, https://www.globalfirepower.com/countries-comparison-detail.php?country1=india&country2=china

Comptroller and Auditor General of India, "Performance Audit Report on the Issue of Licences and Allocation of 2G Spectrum", Government of India, 2010–11, available at https://web.archive.

org/web/20110721155418/http://cag.gov.in/html/reports/
civil/2010-11_19PA/Telecommunication%20Report.pdf

"Exchange of views between Generalissimo Chiang Kai-shek and President Roosevelt regarding situation in India", Office of the Historian, Foreign Service Institute, United States Department of State, https://history. state.gov/historicaldocuments/frus1942 China/ comp17

"Foreign Direct Investment – the China story", The World Bank, 16 July 2010, https://www.worldbank.org/en/news/feature/2010/ 07/16/foreign-direct-investment-china-story

Government of India, Second Administrative Reforms Commission, "Twelfth Report: Citizen Centric Administration", February 2009, https://darpg.gov.in/sites/default/files/ccadmin12.pdf

"History of Opium Cultivation", Central Bureau of Narcotics, Government of India, http://www.cbn.nic.in/en/opium/overview/

"India 2018 International Religious Freedom Report", US State Department, 2018, https://www.state.gov/wp-content/ uploads/2019/05/INDIA-2018-INTERNATIONAL-RELIGIOUS-FREEDOM-REPORT.pdf

"Joint Statement Between President George W. Bush and Prime Minister Manmohan Singh", The White House, 18 July 2005, https://georgewbush-whitehouse.archives.gov/news/ releases/2005/07/20050718-6.html

National Intelligence Council, "Global Trends 2030: Alternative Worlds", US Government, 2012, https://www.dni.gov/files/documents/ GlobalTrends_2030.pdf

——, "Global Trends 2040: A More Contested World", US Government, 2021, https://www.dni.gov/files/ODNI/documents/assessments/ GlobalTrends_2040.pdf

"Nehru, Jawaharlal", The Martin Luther King, Jr. Research and Education Institute, Stanford University, https://kinginstitute.stanford.edu/ encyclopedia/nehru-jawaharlal

"Nuclear Suppliers Group", *Encyclopaedia Britannica*, 20 March 2023, https://www.britannica.com/topic/Nuclear-Suppliers-Group

"Questions and Answers: EU Strategy for Cooperation in the Indo-Pacific", European Commission, 16 September 2021, https:// ec.europa.eu/commission/presscorner/detail/en/qanda_21_4709

"Sino–Soviet Border Talks: Problems and Prospects", Central Intelligence Agency, US Government, 10 November 1969, available at https:// nsarchive2.gwu.edu/NSAEBB/NSAEBB49/sino.sov.26.pdf

# SELECT BIBLIOGRAPHY

SIPRI Fact Sheet- TRENDS IN WORLD MILITARY EXPENDITURE, 2023 https://www.sipri.org/sites/default/files/2024-04/2404_fs_milex_2023.pdf

"Spanish Civil War", *Making Britain: Discover how South Asians shaped the nation, 1870–1950*, The Open University, n.d., https://www5.open.ac.uk/research-projects/making-britain/content/spanish-civil-war

"Spanish Civil War", *Making Britain: Discover how South Asians shaped the nation, 1870–1950*, The Open University, n.d., https://www5.open.ac.uk/research-projects/making-britain/content/spanish-civil-war

"Taking Stock of China's Semiconductor Industry", SIA Blog, 13 July 2021, https://www.semiconductors.org/taking-stock-of-chinas-semiconductor-industry/

"The Meaning of Cherry Blossoms in Japan: Life, Death and Renewal", *NotWithout My Passport*, 2 April 2016, https://notwithoutmypassport.com/cherry-blossom-meaning-in-japan/

"The Travels of Ibn Battuta: A Virtual Tour", Office of Resources for International and Area Studies, UC Berkeley, https://orias.berkeley.edu/resources-teachers/travels-ibn-battuta

"Top Ten Places to See Cherry Blossoms in China this Spring", *The China Guide*, 8 May 2020, https://www.thechinaguide.com/blog/top-ten-places-to-see-cherry-blossoms-in-china-this-spring

"Transforming denial into deliberation: The case of manual scavenging", Observer Research Foundation, 21 December 2021, https://www.orfonline.org/expert-speak/transforming-denial-into-deliberation-the-case-of-manual-scavenging/

The White House, "Memorandum of Conversation, Feb 23, 1972 at the President's Guest House, Peking", https://history.state.gov/historicaldocuments/frus1969-76v17/ch4?start=31

UNCTAD Secretariat, "The Least Developed Countries Report 2008", United Nations, 2008, available at https://unctad.org/press-material/despite-rapid-economic-growth-number-poor-still-rising-least-developed-countries

"United Front", *Encyclopaedia Britannica*, 18 September 2018, https://www.britannica.com/topic/United-Front-Chinese-history-1937-1945

# INDEX

# INDEX

# INDEX

# INDEX

# INDEX

# INDEX

# INDEX

# INDEX

# INDEX

# INDEX

# INDEX

# INDEX

# INDEX

# INDEX

# INDEX

# INDEX

# INDEX

# INDEX

# INDEX

# INDEX

# INDEX

# INDEX

# INDEX